GREAT TALES

From the History of South Texas

GREAT TALES

From the History of South Texas

MURPHY GIVENS

Published by Nueces Press, Corpus Christi, Texas.

Cover design by Jeff Chilcoat

Library of Congress Control Number   2012951258

Givens, Murphy

Great Tales from the History of South Texas / Murphy Givens.

ISBN   978-0-9832565-3-3

www.nuecespress.com

We dedicate this book to local historians throughout South Texas who do so much to keep the memory of the past alive.

PUBLISHER'S FOREWORD

After the publication of "Corpus Christi — A History," Murphy Givens and I felt there were people and incidents in the book that deserved more thorough treatment. The result is "Great Tales," which frames the stories of South Texas history around the heroes, heroines and villains, the personalities that make history come alive.

Murphy Givens has written expanded accounts of important chapters in the history of South Texas from a wider perspective than the more narrowly focused volume on Corpus Christi history. While this book strives to entertain and inform, in equal measure, it is not intended to compete with more scholarly works on the subjects, which are readily available for those who hunger for greater depth and detail. These accounts are based on a wide reading of the best available sources, which are cited by chapter at the end of the book.

As publisher and sometime editor and business manager, my role has been that of a sounding board, offering comments, asking questions, watching for the occasional error and preparing the manuscript for publication. In the end, it was a collaborative effort that follows the models we established with the publication of "1919: A Storm," "A Soldier's Life," and "Corpus Christi — A History."

As a child I was a fan of the Lone Ranger, Roy Rogers, Hopalong Cassidy and Gene Autry, early TV shows set in the legendary Old West. Little did I realize then that so much of the Old West had its genesis in South Texas, which produced the original cowboys and the prototype cattle barons, the Texas Rangers, battles with hostile Indians and bad hombres of the Wild Horse Desert. Where the Old West began — a vast diamond-shaped area from San Antonio to Corpus Christi to the Rio Grande — is also the area where much of Texas history unfolded, beginning with Cabeza de Vaca. This is the geographic area covered by "Great Tales."

Special thanks are offered to the Corpus Christi Public Library for use of the Local History Archives, where much of the basic research was done. A debt of gratitude is also owed to Dr. Norman Delaney for reviewing the manuscript and offering constructive comments before publication. Thanks also to Jeff Chilcoat who provided critical help in designing the cover for publication. In the event of any errors, omissions, misstatements of fact or general incompetence, we assume all responsibility, that is, if we can't find someone else to blame.

Jim Moloney

BOOKS FROM NUECES PRESS

1919 – The Storm – A Narrative and Photographic History

Corpus Christi – A History

A Soldier's Life

www.nuecespress.com

TABLE OF CONTENTS

CHAPTER 1

CABEZA DE VACA:
SLAVE AND MEDICINE MAN
IN SOUTH TEXAS
1528 — 1536

They are the size of eggs, red and black, and taste very good.
—Cabeza de Vaca on prickly pear fruit

One of the greatest adventure tales ever told happened on the Gulf Coast, from Florida to South Texas, nearly 500 years ago. It is the incredible story of Alvar Núñez Cabeza de Vaca. He spent six years as a slave, trader, and medicine man among the fierce Karankawa Indians of South Texas. In literature, the story of Robinson Crusoe is the classic tale of a shipwrecked man's struggle to survive against tremendous odds in a remote place far from civilization. That is also the story of Cabeza de Vaca, whose tale is true.

Alvar Núñez Cabeza de Vaca was born about 1490 near Cadiz, Spain, in the village of Jerez de la Frontera. His father was Francisco de Vera and his mother was Teresa Cabeza de Vaca, an unusual name that literally means cow's head. An ancestor was given the name in recognition for helping Spanish forces defeat the Moors in 1212 by marking a hidden mountain passage with the skulls of cows.

Alvar Núñez Cabeza de Vaca was proud of his name and illustrious ancestor. He joined the military and in February, 1527, he was appointed royal treasurer of a Spanish fleet of five ships and 400 men being sent to explore the new world from Florida to the Rio de las Palmas, a vast area defined on maps as Terra Incognita. At the end of it all, their mission was carried out in a tragic way.

The captain general of the fleet was Pánfilo de Nárvaez, described as a one-eyed man of limited ability. The fleet sailed from Spain in June 1527 and, after stops along the way and encountering a storm at sea, the fleet made landfall on the west coast of Florida on April 15, 1528. They anchored in a bay later known as Old Tampa Bay. It being Good Friday, Nárvaez named it *Bahía de la Cruz*.

On Easter Sunday, Nárvaez and men explored the land, looking for evidence of gold. They found the corpses of dead Spaniards wrapped in deerskin and packed in Castilian merchandise crates. They were the victims of an earlier Spanish shipwreck. In an Indian village, they discovered a gold trinket, a rattle, which excited their greed.

Nárvaez sent the ships ahead to look for the Spanish settlement of Pánuco. The remaining 300 men under Nárvaez marched overland, looking for the origin of that gold trinket. They had no knowledge of where they were, or what might be in front of them, or what they might encounter, or what the layout of the land was like, or what their destination might be. Once they were separated, the land party never saw the ships again. The fleet searched for the land party for a year, sailing back and forth along the coast, then finally sailed for Mexico.

The men in the land expedition were stranded in an unknown land. They were surrounded by hostile Indians, whom they made even more hostile by haughty and cruel actions. At one village, Nárvaez cut off the nose of an Indian chief who offended him. The Spanish marched north, crossed the Withlacoochee and Suwannee rivers, and were attacked by Indians, whom they abused, in one way or another, in every encounter. Day by day, the explorers grew weak from lack of food and they suffered fever and chills in the malarial swamps of Florida. First the horses then the men began to die.

After months of hardships and Indian attacks, they built crude rafts to reach Pánuco, the Spanish settlement far down on the coast of Mexico. They fashioned bellows from deerskin and melted spurs and stirrups to make tools. They felled trees, made sails from underclothes, and wove ropes from the tails of horses. When they slaughtered the last of the horses for food, they used the skin of the legs to make water bags.

In 20 days, after they had eaten the last of the horses, they had built five rafts about 30 feet long. They departed from the Bay of Horses and set course across the Gulf toward the setting sun, hoping to reach Pánuco, near today's Tampico. Each boat carried about 50 men. That was all the weight they could carry. The barges were still so overloaded the sea reached within a hand's length of the gunwales.

They discovered that the water bags made from the skin of the horses' legs had rotted and spoiled the water. They were out of water and several men died from drinking seawater. Others were killed by Indians when they tried to land to find food and water, first at what we know as Pensacola and then at Mobile Bay. Sailing west toward the setting sun, the swift current of the Mississippi River, where it enters the Gulf in a broad brown stream, drove

2

them away from land and out to sea. The barges were hit by a storm and separated.

The men were near death when the storm carried Cabeza de Vaca's barge onto a barrier island off the Texas coast, somewhere between St. Joseph's and Galveston Islands. Where Cabeza de Vaca's barge washed ashore has been argued about ever since. It is hard to put this in today's context, since Cabeza de Vaca's island is part of a vanished world. The date is more certain. It was Nov. 6, 1528. Wherever it was on the Texas coast, Cabeza de Vaca called this island Malhado, the Isle of Misfortune.

Dozens of Nárvaez shipwreck survivors landed on the island, which was inhabited by Karankawa Indians. Many Spaniards were near death and others died of starvation and exposure and some were slain by the Karankawas. Another raft of Nrávaez castaways came ashore on another part of the island. The Spaniards, weak and barely alive, were tormented by Karankawa boys who pulled their beards and scratched them with long sharp fingernails until the blood ran. The Spaniards were treated as slaves.

During the winter, with food scarce, the Indians forced five of the Spaniards to leave. The starving men sliced up and ate their dead companions, which outraged the Indians.[1] The shipwreck survivors passed a cruel winter on Malhado. They ate roots collected from under water near the shore, which tasted like nuts. In the spring, when the roots began to sprout, they were inedible.[2] By spring, most of the 80 castaways on Malhado had died. Only 15 were still alive.

The Indians moved to the mainland to eat blackberries and gorge on oysters taken from the inner bays. This happened somewhere along the coast probably closer to Corpus Christi than Galveston. Cabeza de Vaca escaped from the island Indians and lived with mainland Indians. He found the mainland Indians less cruel than the Karankawas on Malhado.

Though he was a slave, he was allowed to become a trader and was free to move about. As he explained it, "The Indians would beg me to go from one quarter to another for things of which they had need; for in consequence of incessant hostilities, they cannot traverse the country, nor make many exchanges. With my merchandise and trade I went into the interior as far as I pleased, and traveled along the coast 40 or 50 leagues." He carried shell knives and shell ornaments from the coast to trade with inland Indians for hides, red ochre, canes and flints for arrow heads. He learned the language. Six years passed.

---

[1] Historians have argued that the Karankawas became cannibals after learning the practice from the Spanish visitors. They were probably cannibals already and their reaction to the Spanish cannibalism was misinterpreted.

[2] These may have been the tuber-like roots of the water chinquapin or American lotus, but it is unclear what the root was or whether it still exists.

When the coastal tribes met at a pecan grove (perhaps near Victoria) to feast on pecans, Cabeza de Vaca found three other shipwreck survivors. They agreed to try to escape in the summer when the tribes would gather to eat the prickly pear cactus tunas (probably around Alice). Cabeza de Vaca called this event the feast of the tunas. He described the fruit of the prickly pear — "They are the size of eggs, red and black, and taste very good."

"When the time came," Cabeza de Vaca wrote, "and we went to eat tunas, there were a great many mosquitoes of three kinds, all very bad and troublesome, which during most of the summer persecuted us. In order to protect ourselves we built, all around our camps, big fires of damp and rotten wood, that gave no flame but much smoke, and this was the cause of further trouble to us, for the whole night we did nothing but weep from the smoke that went to our eyes, and the heat from the fire was insufferable. When sometimes we were able to sleep, the Indians aroused us again with blows to go and kindle the fires."

At the feast of the tunas Cabeza de Vaca and three surviving Spaniards escaped from their Indian captors and began the long trek home. It was in the fall of 1534. They walked across South Texas, traveling north by northwest. They wanted to stay clear of the fierce coastal Indians. As they walked inland, they became known as healers and were followed by friendly Indian tribes. They were treated better as they moved away from the coast. At one village, they ate mesquite beans mixed with earth, which they found sweet and wholesome. At another village, they found all the Indians were blind.

During their travels, they ate two dogs. They were naked and exposure to the harsh rays of the sun caused them to shed their skins like snakes. At one village, the Indians told Cabeza de Vaca about a mysterious demon they called "Bad Thing." The Indians described this demon as small, with a beard, and it came out of a crack in the earth. It would pick a victim and with a knife cut a gash in its side, take out the victim's entrails, cut off a piece and throw it on the fire. Bad Thing would make three diagonal slash marks on the victim's arms, then place his hands on the cuts and they would heal at once. Cabeza de Vaca scoffed. Seeing his disbelief, the Indians brought forth several victims. They all had scars in the places described.

* * *

Cabeza de Vaca and three companions — Dorantes, Castillo and Estevanico — made it to Mexico City. They walked across half the continent to the Gulf of California. They traveled from Florida to Texas on a raft, lived with fierce Texas coastal Indians six years as slaves, crossed South Texas on foot to El Paso, walked across northern Mexico to the Gulf of California, then

4

made their way south to Mexico City, a journey of 5,000 miles. For the first time, Spanish Mexico knew that a great, unexplored land existed to the north.

They had been sent to explore the new world and that they did. Of course it was not a new world but an old world seen with new eyes. Paul Horgan in "Great River" wrote of Cabeza de Vaca and companions that, "They were delivered from their prison of space. The wilderness of their tremendous passage ceased to be an abstraction as soon as they found succor amongst those who could hear what they had to tell, Spaniard to Spaniard."

The four men who survived the travails of six years were, in Cabeza de Vaca's words, "Alonso del Castillo Maldonado, a native of Salamanca and son of Doctor Castillo and Doña Aldonza Maldonado. The second is Andrés Dorantes, son of Pablo Dorantes, born at Béjar, but a resident of Gibraléon. The third is Alvar Núñez Cabeza de Vaca, son of Francisco de Vera and grandson of Pedro de Vera, who conquered the Canarian Islands. His mother was called Doña Teresa Cabeza de Vaca, and she was a native of Jerez de la Frontera. The fourth was Estévanico, an Arab negro from Azamor."

There was a fifth survivor of the Nárvaez expedition. Juan Ortiz was held captive by Indians in Florida until he was rescued by Hernando de Soto. He died soon afterwards.

In Mexico City, Cabeza de Vaca, Dorantes, Castillo and Estevanico had to endure the discomforts of civilization. They could hardly stand to wear clothes. During their trek from South Texas, they shed their skin and the under skin was so sensitive they could not bear the touch of even the finest silk. They could not wear boots, only soft Indian moccasins. They could not sleep on soft beds, preferring to sleep under buffalo robes on the hard floor. They had become more Indian than Spaniard and had to relearn how to wear clothes and boots and sleep in beds.

The adventures of Alvar Núñez Cabeza de Vaca were far from over. After his return to Spain, he was appointed governor, captain-general and *adelantado* of the province of Rio de la Plata. He reached Brazil in March 1541. Cabeza de Vaca tried to enforce policies of justice and mercy in regard to the native population, but the Spanish continued their practice of enslaving and abusing native Indians. Greedy officials rebelled against Cabeza de Vaca's benign rule and brought false charges against him. He was arrested and sent under guard back to Spain. There he was banished to Africa for eight years, but the sentence was never enforced. He died in 1557.

Of the others, Andrés Dorantes married a wealthy widow who owned extensive properties. They had 11 children and Dorantes finished his life in wealth and comfort. One of his sons was appointed the king's treasurer at Veracruz. Alonso del Castillo Maldonado also married a widow with property and they had 11 daughters. They lived in Mexico City. The last of the four was the slave Estévanico. The viceroy in Mexico City, Don Antonio de Mendoza, sent Estévanico with several friars to blaze a trail for Coronado's search for the fabled Seven Cities of Cibola. Estévanico, with his experience learned with Cabeza de Vaca, took charge of the expedition. He was killed by Indians at a Zuni village in what is today northwestern New Mexico. His run of good luck ran out.

* * *

Cabeza de Vaca's *Los Naufrágios* (The Castaways) was written after he returned to civilization. As a narrative of endurance, of the struggle to survive against tremendous odds in an unexplored wilderness, *Los Naufrágios* is unmatched in history. Cabeza de Vaca and companions were the first Europeans to describe the land and people of North America. They were the first white men to see the buffalo and the armadillo (little armored ones), the first Europeans to see and live to tell about the strange land called Texas. The history of Texas, at least the written portion of it, began with Cabeza de Vaca.

CHAPTER 2

THE TREASURE FLEET
AND MASSACRE ON PADRE ISLAND
1554

Woe be those who are going to Spain. Neither we nor the fleet will ever arrive. Most of us will perish.

—Fr. Juan Ferrer to fellow passengers

On April 9, 1554, two decades after Alvar Núñez Cabeza de Vaca's sojourn in Texas, four ships were making ready to sail from the port of Veracruz — San Juan de Ulúa. They were homeward bound for Seville with a stop to meet the rest of the armada at Havana.

As the ships took on cargo and passengers, a Dominican priest named Juan Ferrer shared his forebodings of disaster ahead. "Woe be those who are going to Spain," Ferrer warned fellow passengers, "Neither we nor the fleet will ever arrive. Most of us will perish."

He was right.

Four great galleons — *Santa Maria de Yciar, San Estebán, Espíritu Santo,* and *San Andrés* — were loaded with gold, cochineal, and silver from the vast silver mines, worked by Indian slaves, at Zacatecas. It was a treasure fleet — *Plata Flota,* the silver fleet.

The priest's forebodings of disaster were forgotten as the ships found smooth sailing across the Gulf. They arrived at Havana to join other ships in the armada, a precaution against pirates.

After the ships sailed for Spain they were caught in an early tropical storm, which forced them back across the Gulf and wrecked the *Santa Maria de Yciar, San Estebán, Espíritu Santo* on an island. The battered San Andrés returned to Havana; another ship from the armada made it back to San Juan de Ulúa to tell the grim news of the loss of the *Plata Flota.*

The storm carried the ships *Santa Maria de Yciar, San Estebán and Espíritu Santo* aground on the white islands — *Las Islas Blanca.* Some 300 crewmen, soldiers, priests and passengers, including women and children, struggled ashore by swimming or clinging to pieces of floating wreckage.

They stayed by the wrecks for six days. Some of the men swam back to the San Estebán, whose masts were above water, and brought back ham, hardtack, and a jam in a wooden box called a *cajeta*. They retrieved five quivers of arrows and two crossbows made of well-tempered steel.

The survivors decided to try to walk to a Spanish settlement to the south rather than wait for the expected arrival of a salvage fleet. They thought they were only three or four days away from the Pánuco River near Tampico.

In reality, they were hundreds of miles away — about 40 days walking instead of three. On the seventh day, they woke to find the dunes crowded with tall painted men, who brought fish and fire. As they ate, the Indians — Karankawas — attacked. Two soldiers with the crossbows killed three Indians and wounded many more. The Karankawas retreated after killing a single Spaniard.

The survivors escaped into the dunes, protected by the two crossbows. They began to march down the island toward the Pánuco River. Thinking it was close, they didn't carry much food.

After walking five days down the island, they ate shellfish found on the beach and licked the early morning dew from island grasses. They didn't know, as the Karankawas knew and residents of the island would discover later, that they could have dug a hole two to three feet in the sand to find drinking water, a little brackish, but drinkable.

At every opportunity, the Indians, who followed from a distance, continued to attack. Many of the Spaniards were killed as they fled under a blazing sun with the relentless Karankawas in pursuit.

The sands were burning hot. Most were without shoes. Children cried as they struggled to keep up, but their mothers were too weak to carry them. The Karankawas captured two stragglers, made them undress, then let them go. This led the Spanish to think that perhaps it was their clothes the Indians wanted.

Men, women and children undressed and left their clothes heaped on the sand. One man who refused to give up his red jacket became a special target for the Indians. They killed him, tore his jacket into pieces, and distributed bits of cloth like prize ribbons given out at a county fair.

For safety, the women and children were sent ahead, since the attacks had always come from the rear. The Indians, moving as swift as deer, raced around to the front and attacked the defenseless women and children. Children with arrow wounds cried to their mothers who were helpless to shield and protect them. Terror wiped out what little strength they had left. The women and children were all slain before the party reached the lower end of the island at Brazos Pass.

Nearly 200 men were still alive, though barely. They were weary and miserable, with no food or water, and their strength was ebbing. They made

8

rafts out of driftwood to cross Brazos Pass. A priest tired of lugging his belongings threw them into the waters of the pass. By mistake he threw the wrong bundle overboard, the one with their only weapons, the two precious crossbows.

The Indians moved in close, killing at will. By the time the Spanish reached the Rio Grande, almost all of the men had been slain.

One man, Francisco Vásquez, hid and retraced the route of march. He returned to the site of the shipwreck.

Another man, a Dominican lay brother, Marcos de Mena, received seven arrow wounds, including one in his right eye, but he managed, in delirium, to make his way to Tampico.

Of the 300 in that terrible journey of death, these two — Francisco Vásquez and Marcos de Mena — were the only survivors. Their accounts have given us the details of this tragedy.

When the news reached Mexico City, salvage expeditions were launched. When the salvage fleet arrived, divers were put to work bringing up the silver and gold bullion from the San Esteban, which was easily found with its masts above the water.

They found the *Santa Maria de Yciar* and *Espíritu Santo* by dragging a chain between two small vessels. Most of the treasure was recovered, carefully weighed and catalogued in Veracruz before it was sent on to Seville.

* * *

Four centuries later, a hurricane uncovered the resting place of one of the ancient *Plata Flota* ships. The wreck was found north of the Mansfield cut on Padre Island. In 1967, a salvage operation by Platoro, Ltd., recovered items from the wrecked galleon. They found silver and gold coins, a small gold crucifix, cannonballs, astrolabes, even cockroach fossils. The state sued the salvage firm. The case took 17 years to settle before the treasure was obtained by the state.

Excavations in 1972 and 1973 by the Texas Antiquities Committee confirmed that three shipwreck sites — within 2½ miles of each other, 2.8 miles north of the Mansfield Cut — were those of the *Santa Maria de Yciar, San Esteban*, and *Espíritu Santo*, ships of the silver fleet lost in that tragic year of 1554. The collection from the *San Esteban* is housed in the Corpus Christi Museum of Science and History. The remains of the *Santa María de Yciar* were destroyed in the 1950s when the Port Mansfield channel was dredged.

CHAPTER 3

LA SALLE
AND THE FRENCH EXPEDITION IN TEXAS
1685 — 1766

There thou liest, great Bashaw! There thou liest!
—The surgeon Liotet exulting over La Salle's body

S panish Mexico, New Spain, knew little about the land called Tejas, a word derived from "Techas! Techas!" which the Indians used to greet Spaniards, meaning "allies" or "friends."

What New Spain did know was that the land to its north and east was unexplored wilderness, far from civilization.[3] What New Spain knew about the barbarous north was based on dreadful and tragic first-hand accounts.

One first-hand account came from Alvar Núñez Cabeza de Vaca, the shipwrecked survivor of the Pánfilo de Nárvaez expedition of 1528. Information also came from Francisco Vásquez de Coronado, Hernando de Soto and greedy conquistadors who mounted expeditions in search of the Seven Cities of Gold they heard about from Cabeza de Vaca. Another bit of knowledge came from two tormented survivors of ships wrecked on *Las Islas Blancas,* what we know today as Padre Island.

Tejas was shrouded in myth. It was claimed by Spain, though it had little use for this barbarous and dangerous land and was content to leave the wild north to its wild tribes.

That changed in 1685 when the great French explorer, René Robert Cavelier, Sieur de la Salle, landed on the Texas coast. Whatever interest Spain had in Tejas was stoked by the threat of a rival European power with designs on the hemisphere.

La Salle had been a fur-trader in Canada. He explored the Mississippi River, reaching the mouth of the river and claimed all the land that it drained

---

[3] In our time, geographic prejudice holds that civilization to barbarism runs from north to south and from east to west. Back then, in New Spain, it was reversed, running from south to north and from west to east.

11

for France, which was ready to expand that claim to the west. What became French Louisiana was a result of La Salle's exploration. He returned to France a national hero and convinced the king of the need to establish a French colony at the mouth of the Mississippi River to consolidate the French hold on, and its claim to, North America.

La Salle, with plans to establish a permanent French colony, left France with four ships filled with soldiers, settlers and their families, all unprepared for what lay ahead. By mistake — or by intent, as some believe — La Salle veered off course and made landfall not at the mouth of the Mississippi but far to the west on Matagorda Bay. Much of what we know of early South Texas history began at this time and place.

In every particular, the French expedition was ill-fated, unlucky, unprepared and undisciplined. Its members were not equipped to deal with the South Texas wilderness. They found death and misfortune at every turn. One of the four vessels, the *St. Francois*, was captured en route by the Spanish. The captain of the *L'Aimable*, a 300-ton supply ship, missed the entrance to Matagorda Bay at Pass Cavallo, a treacherous pass, and ran his ship aground on a sandbar. It broke up in a storm. The captain of the ship *Le Joli*, a jealous rival of La Salle, disobeyed orders and returned to France.

La Salle had one ship left, *La Belle*. His men salvaged the timbers from the wreckage of the *L'Amiable* and built a log structure, which some have claimed was named Fort St. Louis, in honor of the king of France, while others say it never had a name, just a description. However, we will call it Fort St. Louis. Next to the main two-story building was an adjoining lean-to which served as the chapel and there were five or six mud-chinked houses covered with buffalo hides.

The French flag flew over this crude settlement upstream from the mouth of Garcitas Creek, in today's Victoria County, on Lavaca Bay, an inner arm of Matagorda Bay.[4] The colony might have given France a springboard into Spanish Tejas, a base from which French ships could pursue outward-bound Spanish treasure galleons and given France a claim to the region by right of possession.

La Salle took *La Belle* to explore the coast. He visited bays and rivers and sailed as far south as the Rio Grande, which he called the River of Palms. Then *La Belle* sank in Lavaca Bay[5] and La Salle's small colony was truly stranded, with no means to return home.

---

[4] The site was confirmed in 1996 when eight French cannons were recovered.

[5] La Salle's *La Belle*, which sank in Matagorda Bay in 1686, was discovered and excavated by the Texas Historical Commission in 1995. Of the million or so artifacts recovered, many are on display at the Corpus Christi Museum of Science and History.

To make matters worse for the French colonists, La Salle, in an incredibly stupid move, antagonized neighboring Karankawas by stealing their canoes and kidnapping a young Karankawa girl, who died after she was captured. The Karankawas may have proved hostile in any event, but La Salle's treatment did not serve to make them friendly when the French settlers most needed their help.

After the loss of *La Belle,* La Salle decided to take some men and march overland in search of the other Fort St. Louis way up on the Illinois River. From there they could make it to French Canada and get help for the colony on the Texas coast.

On Christmas 1686 at Fort St. Louis, La Salle's lieutenant Henri Joutel tells us that, "Monsieur de la Salle being recovered from his Indisposition, preparations were again made for his Journey. But we first kept the Christmas Holy-Days. The Midnight mass was sung, and on Twelve-Day, we cried 'The King drinks,' though we had only Water. When that was over we began to think of setting out."

In January 1687 La Salle did set out. He took 17 men and left the fort to march to the north. They had five horses to carry supplies. They carried knives and hatchets and trade gifts for the Indians they would encounter on the way. The hardships they had already endured showed. La Salle's men were dressed in tattered and torn remains of uniforms, patched with deerskin and sailcloth.

The group setting out included La Salle's brother, the Abbé Jean Cavelier, La Salle's nephew, Crevel de Moranget, La Salle's lieutenant Joutel, Friar Anastase Douay, malcontented soldier, Pierre Duhaut, a surgeon known only as Liotot, a servant of Duhaut named Jean L'Archevêque, and an English seaman called Jim or James (the French called him "Hiems"). There was a Shawnee Indian La Salle brought with him from his earlier explorations named Nika, who had traveled with La Salle to France and back to America.

On their way to the land of the Hasinai (a Caddo tribe, also called Asenai and Cenis) they killed and ate buffalo. They used untreated buffalo hide to make crude shoes and were able to trade some of their gifts with Indians for deerskin to make better fitting moccasins.

As they neared a Hasinai village in East Texas, according to Father Douay's account, "One of our Indians went on to announce our coming. The chiefs and youths, whom we met a league from the village, received us with the calumet (a ceremonial smoking pipe) which they gave us to smoke. Some led our horses by the bridle. Others, as it were, carried us in triumph, taking us for spirits and people of another world. All the village being assembled, the women, as is their wont, washed our head and feet with warm water, and then placed us on a platform covered with a very neat white mat. Then followed banquets, calumet-dances and other public rejoicings, day and night."

At a hunting camp six miles away from La Salle's main camp, several men grew mutinous. They were nursing old grievances against La Salle and his relatives. The surgeon Liotet hated Moranget, La Salle's nephew, whom he had treated and brought back to health after he was wounded by an Indian arrow. Moranget repaid him by abuse. Pierre Duhaut hated La Salle, whom he blamed for the death of his younger brother on an earlier expedition. "English Jim" (James or Heims) joined the conspirators though he was one of La Salle's favorites. At the hunting camp in the night, the surgeon Liotet, wielding an axe, split the skulls of Moranget, the Shawnee Nika, and the servant Saget.

Six miles away, at the main camp, La Salle grew uneasy when the hunting party did not return. Joutel writes — "That evening, while we were talking about what could have happened to the absent men, he seemed to have a presentiment of what was to take place. He asked me if I had heard of any machinations against him, or if I had noticed any bad design on the part of Duhaut and the rest. I answered that I had heard nothing, except that they sometimes complained of being found fault with so often. And that was all I knew. Besides which, as they were persuaded that I was in his interest, they would not have told me of any bad design they might have. We were very uneasy the rest of the morning."

La Salle left to find the missing hunting party, taking the friar Anastasius Douay and a local Hasinai Indian guide with him. As La Salle approached the hunting camp, Jean L'Archevêque, Duhaut's servant, appeared some distance away. Behind him, hiding in tall grass, was Duhaut, who fired from ambush. The shot struck La Salle in the forehead, killing him instantly.

The surgeon Liotet danced and crowed over the crumpled body, shouting, "There thou liest, great Bashaw! There thou liest!" They stripped the body and dragged it into the bushes and left it for the animals of the forest.[6] It was March 1687.

The conspirators behind La Salle's murder had a falling out among themselves. "English Jim" shot and killed Duhaut. Another killed the surgeon Liotet. The rest of the party split up, with seven proceeding on to find the original Fort St. Louis on the Illinois. Among these were Joutel, La Salle's brother, Jean Cavelier, and a nephew, Colin Cavelier, and the friar Anastasius

---

[6] Where was La Salle killed? Based on the journal of Joutel, the consensus has long been that he was slain on the Navasota River near the present town of Navasota. A statue there claims the historical distinction. Others have argued that La Salle was killed near Larrison Creek in Cherokee County and others say it was on a tributary of the Trinity River between Huntsville and Madisonville.

Douay. Joutel, Cavelier, and Douay eventually made it back to France and wrote accounts of La Salle's ill-fated expedition.

Six others remained with the Hasinai Indians. Two French deserters were already living with the Indians. The group that stayed behind included Jean L'Archevêque, Duhaut's servant, Jacques Grollet, a man named Ruter or Rutre, James or Jim, and two boys, Pierre Talon and Pierre Meunier, whom La Salle was planning to leave with the Hasinai Indians to learn their language. James and Ruter were killed as a result of dissension among themselves, leaving only four: L'Archevêque, Grollet, and the two boys, Talon and Meunier.

At Fort St. Louis on Garcitas Creek, 100 of the inhabitants died in a smallpox epidemic. At Christmas time 1688, Karankawas attacked the survivors in the fort; only 20 to 25 were still alive at the time of the attack. The Karankawas may have been seeking to avenge the earlier mistreatment by La Salle and his colonists — the theft of canoes and the kidnapping of the girl — or the smallpox epidemic had spread to the Indians and the Karankawas blamed the French for the outbreak. Something similar happened with Cabeza de Vaca on Malhado. An epidemic on the island decimated the Indians, who blamed the Spaniards for the outbreak.

After the massacre at Fort St. Louis, Karankawa women protected five children who had survived. They carried them away on their backs. Pierre Talon's sister, three younger brothers, and Eustace Bréman, the son of the expedition's paymaster, were saved from the general slaughter.

New Spain reacted quickly after rumors were heard about La Salle and the French incursion. Five separate Spanish naval expeditions were dispatched to search the bays and inlets along the coast to find and destroy the French colony. They had no luck. They found the wreckage of one of LaSalle's ships, but misunderstood the information and did not find the fort. Four land expeditions were mounted, which inaugurated New Spain's first official explorations of the land called Tejas.

On March 23, 1689, Alonso de León, governor of Coahuila, set out from Monclova on a major expedition to find the French. He had with him a 50-year-old Frenchman, Jean Géry, who had been living with Indians near the Rio Grande. Géry had arrived with La Salle five years earlier and knew the location of the settlement.

De León's party crossed the Rio Grande near today's Guerrero, 30 miles below Eagle Pass, where he picked up an old Indian trail. The clink of armor must have been a new sound on that ancient Indian passage. De León's party — with 80 soldiers on horseback, several hundred servants and officials, and a long train of supply wagons — was a projection of Spanish power in this almost empty landscape.

15

De León crossed a river with no name on April 4, 1689. He called it Río de las Nueces for pecan trees growing on its banks. De León's chosen names for three major rivers in Texas have survived for 300 years — the Nueces, Guadalupe and Trinity.

De León's men used axes to cut through thickets, but in most places they followed old, well-trodden Indian paths. Using today's place names, De León's route slanted northeasterly. They traveled from Guerrero on the Rio Grande to above Crystal City to Frio Town, then moved southeasterly to Pearsall, east to Jourdanton and to a point between Floresville and Karnes City, east to Cuero, and southeasterly along Garcitas Creek.

In April 1689, as De León drew near the site of Fort St. Louis on Garcitas Creek, he found French Bibles and French artifacts in Indian villages. On April 22, De León's party came upon a few scattered houses and the fort built of salvaged ship timbers.

De León's account said — "Three leagues down the creek (the Garcitas) from the point where they reached it in coming from the crossing of the Guadalupe, we found it. Having halted with the force about an arquebus-shot away, we went to see it and found all the houses sacked. All the chests, bottle cases, and all the rest of the settlers' furniture broken; apparently more than 200 books torn apart and the rotting leaves scattered throughout the patio, all in French. We found three dead bodies scattered over the plains. One of these from the dress that still clung to it appeared to be a woman. We took the bodies up and chanted Mass and buried them. We looked for other dead bodies, but could not find them, whence we supposed they had been thrown into the creek and had been eaten by the alligators of which there were many. The principal house of this settlement is in the form of a fort, made of ship timbers. The other five houses were of stakes, covered with mud inside and out, their roofs covered with buffalo hides."

De León recovered two Frenchmen living with the Indians, Jacques Grollet and Jean L'Archevêque, the man who had lured La Salle into the ambush that killed him. The men were naked, covered with tattoos, and carried an antelope skin. They were questioned and eventually taken to Spain. Grollet returned to New Spain, married a wealthy widow, and settled at Bernalillo in New Mexico. L'Archevêque, going by the name of Juan de Archibeque, became a successful trader before he was killed by Indians on a Spanish expedition to the North Platte or on the Arkansas in 1720.

De León on a return trip in 1690 and burned what was left of Fort St. Louis. On this trip, he explored the area around *La Bahia del Espiritu Santo*, which we know today as Matagorda Bay. At Pass Cavallo, his horses had trouble walking in the soft sand. Other survivors of the La Salle expedition were recovered. The two boys who were with La Salle when he was killed, whom he planned to leave with the Hasinai and learn their language, were found.

16

Pierre Talon was fourteen, living with Indians on the Colorado River, and Pierre Meunier was twenty. Pierre Talon pleaded with De León to rescue his three brothers and sister, who were living with Karankawas.

They were all recovered, some by force. The Karankawas demanded a horse for each captive, but wanted two for the girl. De León refused to pay for the release of the children. In a fight that followed four Indians were killed and De León was hit by two arrows, which were deflected by his armor.

Marie Magdelaine Talon was 16 when she was found; only she could communicate with her three younger brothers, who had forgotten how to speak French. These were Jean Baptiste, Lucien, and Robert. Their faces were tattooed with black stripes in the Karankawa fashion, perhaps to show they had been adopted by the tribe.

The Talon children were taken to Mexico City to become servants in the house of the viceroy. Several made it to France and then back to America. Depositions of the Talon survivors gave details of La Salle's murder and the massacre at Fort St. Louis. Jean Baptiste witnessed his mother's slaying.

In 1692, a new expedition was planned. De León, in bad health, was not chosen to lead this one; he died a few months later. It was led by Domingo Terán de los Ríos, a Spanish officer in Peru who had been appointed governor of Tejas. Terán's orders were to establish missions in East Texas and investigate rumors of foreign settlements. He was instructed to give names to places and rivers. He named every place he visited, choosing the names casually, in passing, with no real relationship to a land that was already old, with its own ancient names that the newcomers did not know and would never know.

Terán saw mesquite, oak and pecan trees along the Río de las Nueces and saw large herds of buffalo. His party — including a priest and 50 soldiers — camped near an Indian village named Yanaquana. Terán noted in his diary — "This I called San Antonio de Padua, because we had reached it on his day."

Terán traveled on to a log mission that had been established by De León, the first in East Texas, called San Francisco de los Tejas, on San Pedro Creek, in present-day Houston County. This was at the place called Los Adaes, near Natchitoches, La. Terán's route was called the Camino Real — the King's Highway. It was more of a faint trace or trail than a highway, but it was the route that connected New Spain to the missions to come on the Texas frontier.

* * *

New Spain was still worried about the French interest in Texas when another Frenchman arrived. Louis Juchereau de St. Denis was sent to open a trade route between the French outpost at Mobile and New Spain. With St.

17

Denis were Pierre and Jean Baptiste Talon. Their tattoos and knowledge of the language helped St. Denis with the Indians.

Most of the expedition turned back, but St. Denis and the Talons arrived at the mission and presidio of San Juan Bautista on the Rio Grande on July 19, 1714. While there, St. Denis married the daughter of Capt. Domingo Ramón, commander of the presidio.

St. Denis, sent on to Mexico City, was imprisoned for making an illegal entry into Spanish territory. After he talked his way out of jail in 1716, he was asked to guide a Spanish expedition to East Texas, with his father-in-law, Capt. Ramón, in charge. Their orders were to pacify the Hasinai Indians and establish missions and forts in East Texas.

St. Denis went back to Louisiana, bought a supply of goods and returned to New Spain, figuring to get rich. Instead, he was thrown into prison again on trumped-up charges and barely got away with his life. Angry about his treatment, he sold guns to Indians in Texas and tried to start an uprising. He returned to Mobile, where he became a wealthy man. He died in 1744.

* * *

After reacting to French incursions by the explorer La Salle in 1685 and St. Denis in 1714, New Spain lost interest in the land called Tejas until three decades later.

A plan was devised for the colonization of Tejas, with interest shifting from East to South Texas. A man from Santander in the Basque region of Spain, Col. José de Escandón, was commissioned in 1746 to colonize *Seno Mejicano,* a coastal strip 200 miles deep stretching from the San Antonio River to Tampico. This covered much of South Texas and Tamaulipas. Escandón called it *Colonia del Nuevo Santander* after his home in Spain.

Escandón's strategy involved sending several probes into the region at the same time. One was an expedition led by the captain of the presidio of Nuestra Señora de Loreto, established in 1722 near the remains of old Fort St Louis. Capt. Joaquín Basterra y Orobio was ordered to march south, keeping close to the coast, until he reached the mouth of the Rio Grande.

Basterra and 50 soldiers set out on Jan. 29, 1747. He described Corpus Christi Bay and called it San Miguel Arcangel. His report included the first detailed description of Corpus Christi Bay and the mouth of the Nueces River. Until Basterra's report, it was thought the Río de las Nueces emptied into the Rio Grande.

Two years later, Escandón tried to establish a colony at the mouth of the Nueces, which he called Villa de Vedoya. It was supposed to be settled by 50 families recruited in Mexico, but they got as far as the Rio Grande. After a year of hardship, they drifted away. Escandón's other efforts were more successful. He became the greatest of New Spain's colonizers, establishing six permanent towns on the Rio Grande, including Camargo and Reynosa, in 1749, Dolores and Revilla, in 1750, Mier in 1753, and Laredo in 1755.

One aspect of Escandón's colonizing was the establishment of ranches in South Texas. Sometime before 1766, the first ranch in today's Nueces County was built on Santa Petronila Creek. The ranch, named after the creek, was founded by Blas María de la Garza Falcón, captain of Camargo. He stocked his ranch with cattle, sheep and goats.

About this time, the king's inspector general, Marquis de Rubí, was ordered to inspect the frontiers. Rubí spent three years visiting missions and garrisons to prepare his report. When he crossed the Rio Grande, he found a village of 60 huts; this was Escandón's settlement called Laredo. After his inspection tour, Rubí recommended abandoning missions in Texas, except for those at San Antonio and La Bahia, and recommended moving the capital of Tejas from the mission/presidio at Los Adaes, in today's Louisiana, to San Antonio.

Rumors of another foreign incursion — this time by the British — led New Spain to mount another seek-and-destroy expedition. This one was mounted in 1766 under the command of Diego Ortiz Parrilla. He followed De León's old trail and established a camp at Blas María de la Garza Falcón's Santa Petronilla ranch. He sent one party to explore Padre Island looking for the English. His men dug in the sand to get drinking water. Parilla called the bay Corpus Christi Bay.

* * *

In 1769, nearly a century after La Salle's incursion, French Canadians — Acadians — traveling by ship to join their fellow refugees in Louisiana were shipwrecked during a storm on Matagorda or St. Joseph's Island. The captain at La Bahia presidio found the shipwrecked French Canadians — men, women and children — and marched them back to the presidio at La Bahia.

There they waited for permission from Mexico City to join other French Canadians in Louisiana. It took years before the captain at La Bahia was ordered to march them overland to Louisiana. Few were still alive at the journey's end.

In the next century, during the 10-year struggle that led to Mexico's independence in 1821, Spain pulled its soldiers from presidios in Texas, ordering them back into the interior of Mexico. This left missions and ranches open to attack and the attacks came from Comanche, Lipan-Apache and Karankawa tribes.

Remote ranches in South Texas were burned and the rancheros fled to Escandón's settlements on the Rio Grande for safety. During this time, the region between the Nueces and Rio Grande rivers became depopulated and

19

would remain depopulated until a new breed of colonizers arrived, with the Irish and the Anglo-Americans, an influx that would lead to another revolt. The Anglos arrived and took over, said one Mexican official, like hungry crows in a cornfield.

CHAPTER 4

KARANKAWA SUNSET
1528 — 1911

*They live on fish and alligators, with a man for fête days when they can catch
one.*

—*Noah Smithwick of Karankawa Indians*

Roy Bedichek called the Texas Coast "Karankaway Country." He
wrote a book by that name in which he related the story of a
Karankawa warrior — with a reputation as a barbarous cannibal —
mesmerized by watching the evening sun go down.

The Karankawas roamed the coast from Galveston Island to Corpus Christi
Bay, drifting in and out of their favorite haunts, following the seasonal
availability of food. The men were tall, well over 6 feet, and carried bows of
red cedar as tall as they were. They could use those bows with great skill and
accuracy. The women wore deerskin skirts and made pottery decorated with
asphaltum, the deposits of oil seepage that wash ashore on Gulf beaches.

They smeared their bodies with alligator grease. The men's hair was
braided, with rattlesnake rattles tied at the end, which made a dry rustling
sound when they walked. They poled slim, light dugouts on lagoons and bays
and ate great quantities of shellfish. Their old campsites were middens of
accumulated oyster shells discarded over the centuries.[7] One of the
Karankawa's favorite meats was skunk, according to Fray Gaspar José de
Solís. Their guttural language consisted of whistles and sighs and grunts and
was like nothing ever heard. In conversing, they avoided eye contact. By
most accounts, they practiced ritual cannibalism.

When Cabeza de Vaca was shipwrecked on the coast in 1528, the curious
Karankawas reached out to touch his face. Cabeza took this as a gesture of
shared human identity. They were satisfying themselves that he was not some
strange animal washed up from the sea. They kept him as a slave for years

---

[7] What are we leaving behind in our own middens? Plastic bottles impervious to time and
worms that will last a thousand years?

21

before he and three companions escaped and walked back to "civilization" in Mexico. The landing of the shipwrecked survivors of the Nárvaez Expedition on a Texas coastal island in 1528 introduced the Karankawa and sub-tribes — Cocos, Cujanes, Copanos — to Spanish awareness.

Two decades after Cabeza de Vaca's sojourn, 300 survivors of a shipwrecked Spanish fleet washed up half-dead on the sands of Padre Island. It was summer, when Karankawas normally camped on the island. The Indians brought food to the shipwreck survivors, but the Spanish noted that, for friends, they carried many arrows. They soon put them to use, slaying the Spanish as they tried to flee down the island. All but two of 300 were slain.

In 1684, Sieur de la Salle and his French colonists built a settlement, which we know as Fort St. Louis, on Garcitas Creek upstream from Matagorda Bay. After La Salle's men stole their dugouts and kidnapped an Indian girl, the Karankawas attacked the French settlement, killing all the colonists but five children, whom they took away. A Spanish expedition recovered four of five French children; one girl was killed. One of the children, Jean Baptiste Talon, told how he went hungry for three days rather than eat the flesh of the "Ayennis" (Hasinai) whom the Karankawas had killed and prepared for a feast. He also told how the Karankawas cried in great distress when the French youngsters were taken away.

Despite the disastrous results of the La Salle expedition more than three decades before, the French were not ready to give up their designs on Texas. French ship captain Jean Béranger explored the coast in 1720. He was chosen to find a site for a new French settlement somewhere on the coast.

Béranger anchored off the Aransas Pass channel and sent men ashore on Harbor Island to fill barrels with fresh water. When they saw Karankawas, knowing their reputation as cannibals, they were so frightened they ran away, leaving the barrels behind. The Indians carried them off.

Béranger thought they wanted the iron hoops and offered the Indians trade goods. Béranger and his men gathered acorns from the small stunted oak trees on Harbor Island, they found and collected tar resin (asphaltum) on St. Joseph's, which was used to repair leaks in ships, and Béranger killed a rattlesnake he found "coiled like a cable on some oyster shells." He watched Karankawas whip the water to attract fish, then shoot them with their arrows.

Béranger came back the following year to claim Matagorda Bay for France. Once again, he sent sailors ashore to fill casks with fresh water. They were still afraid of the Karankawas, who showed them a pile of human bones, as a clear warning. As the French sailors knowingly interpreted it, the Indians were indicating that they would like to eat them, too. After that, Béranger's men refused to go ashore.

The Spanish understood they needed a permanent presence on the coast. In April 1722, the Spanish established Mission *Nuestra Señora del Espiritu*

Santo de Zuñiga at the site of La Salle's old Fort St. Louis. The mission was established to civilize and Christianize the Indians in the vicinity, mostly the Karankawas of various tribes. To protect the mission, a fort, the *Presidio of Nuestra Señora de Loreto,* was built.

A year later trouble erupted. A Karankawa Indian living at the mission went into the hut of a soldier and asked for a piece of meat, his promised share of newly slaughtered beef. While waiting for his cut of meat, the Indian shook his blanket, which scattered dirt and dust over the area where the soldier's wife was grinding corn. The angry woman ordered her husband to send the Indian away. The Indian refused to go until he had received his piece of meat.

A fight erupted and it spread until it took in the whole Indian population around the mission and presidio. Soldiers and horses were killed and the Indians fled to the woods. Spanish soldiers captured some Karankawa women and imprisoned them in a small hut. Several were hanged. Others managed to escape. Captain Domingo Ramón, in charge of the presidio, died of a stab wound to the breast.

Because of the Karankawa uprising, the La Bahía mission and presidio were moved ten leagues inland to the west on the Guadalupe River. They continued to have trouble with the Indians. A Karankawa chief called *El Mocho,* who had a missing ear, encouraged the Indians to leave the mission. (Spanish names for a few Karankawa chiefs have survived, such as Frazada Pinto, Spotted Blanket; El Surdo, Lefty; Chief Boruca, Chatterbox; Chief Cojo, Peg Leg; Manteca Mucho, Too Much Fat.)

The missionaries were urged to do all they could to pacify and convert the Indians — to treat them with kindness, give them presents, and supply their material and spiritual needs. But the Cujanes, Copanes, Karankawa and other tribes quarreled between themselves, rejected attempts to "civilize" them, and remained relentless enemies of the Spanish. They would return to the missions to take presents and accept food, then drift away when it pleased them. They would raid stock, eating horses and cattle, and they would kill, scalp and torture any unlucky Spaniard they captured.

The Spanish were never able to subdue or pacify the Karankawas and their various sub-tribes, or the other hostile Indians in South Texas.

In 1749, the mission was moved again, this time to Goliad. The new mission was established five miles upstream on the banks of the San Antonio River in 1754, the *Nuestra Señora del Rosario.* Within four or five years, some 400 to 500 Karankawas, Cujanes and Copanes lived around the mission. They helped to erect the buildings and worked the fields.

In an inspection tour in 1767, the Marqués de Rubí found the number of Indians living at the *Nuestra Señora del Rosario* to be uncertain. They frequently deserted the mission to return to the coast. When they did so, presidio forces were sent to make them return. Severe punishment was meted out for those who escaped. The Indians had no experience or understanding of Spanish attempts to restrict their freedom.

That year, 1767, Fray Gaspar José de Solís made an inspection tour of Texas missions and his diary recorded information about mission property. Rosario had 40 horses, 30 mules, 200 milk cows, 700 sheep and goats, and 5,000 head of cattle. Like Rubí, Solís reported that the Indians would escape, preferring to live free in their old ways rather than as righteous Christians and captive wards of the missions. Their old ways, if Solís is right, involved cannibalism for ritualistic purposes, rather than treating humans as another source of meat.[8]

Details in the account by Solís bear the impress of truth. The Karankawas, he wrote, "set a nailed stake in the ground in the place where they are to dance the *mitote*. They light a big fire, tying the victim who is to be danced about to that stake. All assemble together and when the harsh instrument, the *caymán*, begins to play they begin to dance and to leap, making many gestures and very fierce grimaces with funereal and discordant cries, dancing with well-sharpened knives in their hands. As they jump around they approach the victim and cut a piece of flesh off his body, going to the fire and half roasting it in sight of the victim, they eat it with great relish, and so they go on cutting off pieces and quartering him until they take off all the flesh and he dies. They take off his hair with the scalp and put it on a pole in order to bring it to the dance as a trophy. They do not throw the bones away but distribute them and each one whose turn it is to get one walks away sucking it until he is thus finished. They do the same thing with the priests and Spaniards if they catch one. Others they hang up by the feet and put fire underneath them and go on roasting them and eat them up. For others they make long poles of the thickness of an inch of resinous pine, of which there is a great deal, and set fire to him and half roast him and eat him up. For others they do not use a knife to cut them to pieces, but tear them to pieces with their teeth and eat them raw."[9]

Padre Joseph Escovar found Karankawas to be "barbarous and lazy." The priest lamented that despite every effort they made to save their souls, the Karankawas persisted in their savage, irreligious ways. Within 20 years, the Indians drifted away and the Rosario mission was all but abandoned, the land and cattle divided among rancheros brave enough to live in South Texas.

In the year 1818, Jean Laffite's pirates on Galveston Island kidnapped a Karankawa girl. In retaliation, the Indians captured and ate (ritualistically or

---

[8] People facing the prospect of being eaten might not appreciate the distinction.

[9] It has been pointed out that Solís didn't see this himself. He got it secondhand. Still, the details he provides are too vivid, apparently too factual, to be imagined.

not) two of Lafitte's men. This led to a battle in which 30 Indians were killed. After that, they left Galveston Island to the pirates.

Not long after this, one of the de Leons of Victoria grew tired of the Indians slaughtering and eating his cattle. They didn't get the concept of private property or ownership. This de Leon decided to poison the whole tribe by buying arsenic. The storekeeper, not wanting to be an accessory to mass murder, gave him cream of tartar instead. The man had his wife cook a pot of hominy, with the poison added, and gave it to the Indians. He was amazed and discouraged the next day when they came back asking for more.

In the 1820s, Stephen F. Austin's colonists signed a treaty with the Karankawas. The killings on both sides continued. Austin wrote that the cannibals were universal enemies to man and that the approach of civilization "will be the signal for their extermination." Mexico's Gen. Manuel de Mier y Terán, on an inspection tour of Texas, wrote in admiration that Austin's colonists knew how to deal with Karankawas. "If the Indians kill a settler, a large party of settlers set out to hunt down and kill 10 of the tribe, of any age or sex."

Noah Smithwick, a blacksmith in the Austin colony, wrote of the Karankawas — "They were the most savage-looking human beings I ever saw. Many of the bucks were six feet in height, with bows and arrows in proportion. Their ugly faces were rendered hideous by the alligator grease and dirt with which they are besmeared from head to foot as a defense against mosquitoes." They lived, said Smithwick, on fish and alligators "with a man for fête days when they could catch one."

A man named J. H. Kuykendall said that in 1834 people in Victoria persuaded a band of Tonkawas to wipe out some troublesome Karankawas in the neighborhood. The Tonkawas visited the Karankawa camp and took a small boy with them. The small boy was able, by stealth, to cut all the bowstrings of the Karankawa warriors. After this, the Tonkawas attacked, killing 20 Karankawa braves, all but two or three of that tribe. This wasn't the last time they tried to wipe out the Karankawas.

Kuykendall said the de Leons were still troubled by Karankawas killing and eating their cattle. Since the "arsenic" didn't work, Martin de Leon organized his men to attack the Karankawa camp. He mounted a four-pounder cannon on a jackass and planned to annihilate the tribe. His men ran the Karankawas to cover, he brought his cannon to bear and touched it off. But, wrote Smithwick, he did not take the precaution of bracing up the jackass and the recoil of the cannon turned the jackass into a flying somersault, landing him on top of the gun with his feet in the air. The Karankawas fled.

In 1844, a few ragged Karankawan survivors were killed in a battle south of Corpus Christi. Victor M. Rose had one account of the disappearance of one band of Karankawas. He wrote that "the Karankawas fled in their canoes down the Guadalupe River and escaped the party that was in pursuit. The Indians proceeded along the coast to the mouth of the Rio Grande and about 1846 took up their residence on Padre Island, then inhabited by an old wrecker called 'Uncle Telly.' This tribe, having been pressed on by the whites, pursued and hunted down by the Mexicans, defeated and cut to pieces by Comanches and Lipans, gained a scanty subsistence by gathering oysters along the sea shores and fishing in the bays — persecuted, oppressed, downtrodden and insulted, until driven to desperation by their sufferings, they finally resolved to put an end to their name and race forever. Murdering their women and children, the warriors sought this uninhabited island where they could wait patiently for that death which was to forever destroy all trace of their tribe."

Whether the details of this story are true or not, the general results — the extinction of the Karankawas — are true. Kuykendall reported that the last of the Karankawas, reduced to a dozen miserable families or so, were living in abject poverty in Tamaulipas, Mexico in the late 1840s and 1850s, doomed to extinction in a foreign land.

They were not absolutely the last. A Karankawa sister and brother — Mary and Tom Amaroo — were taken in by the Welder-Power family. Tom Amaroo served in the Confederate army and was killed in action. Mary Amaroo married a man named Pathoff, who was also killed in the war. Mary Amaroo Pathoff (also spelled Pothoff), the last full-blooded Karankawa, died in 1911. She is buried in the Welder plot in St. Joseph Cemetery in Beeville.

Beyond their graves and middens and general knowledge of their existence, nothing of the Karankawas remains. With no written record of their own, with history being written by their enemies, the Karankawa story from their point of view will never be told. All the Karankawa tales and legends and beliefs and myths, their names for places that are familiar to us, we will never know, no one will ever know.

We know only that their world collapsed and their race or tribe disappeared from the earth. Were they savage man-eaters as their enemies depicted? Probably, perhaps, who knows? But they were also a people trying to survive as they knew how, based on their own customs and cultural knowledge, in a world changing beyond their understanding or ability to cope. Who cannot sympathize with that?

They were a fierce tribe, yet Roy Bedichek gives us a more appealing image of the Karankawas.

"Early explorers report a curious habit of the Karankawa warrior," Bedichek wrote. "At times he was fascinated by the sight of the sun submerging itself in the sea. The wonder of sunset over water was too much for the mind of this simple savage. He became still as a statue, oblivious to his surroundings, gazing spellbound at the point on the horizon where the

26

waters closed over and quenched this great ball of fire. Finally, in the deepening dusk, he stirs. The fire has gone out. The sea is gray again. The rattles awaken as he moves away toward his camp behind the dunes."

CHAPTER 5

NOAH SMITHWICK
AND THE EVOLUTION OF A STATE
1836

Dick, I cried, are you hurt? Yes, Smith, he replied, I am killed; lay me down.
We buried him under a big pecan tree.
  —Noah Smithwick of Dick Andrews, the first Texas Revolution casualty

Noah Smithwick was nineteen when he left Kentucky for South Texas. He didn't want to farm — "I had a strong aversion to tearing up God's green earth" — and he disliked school so he had trained to become a blacksmith. In 1827, he took a flatboat to New Orleans and from there boarded a coastal schooner bound for Texas. When they crossed the bar and sailed into Matagorda Bay, no one was there to greet them but Karankawa Indians — "the most savage-looking human beings I ever saw." The captain warned them off by pointing his swivel cannon at them.

Two Americans arrived from upriver and Smithwick stayed with them. They gave him a supper of dried venison sopped in honey. He learned that wild game, usually venison, dipped in honey was standard fare on the Texas frontier. He left next day for Green DeWitt's colony, 10 miles up the Lavaca River. It was July and the heat was intense. He found a dozen families living in log cabins in uneasy proximity to alligators and Karankawas, both known to make a meal out of the unwary. He decided that Texas was not the wonderful and exciting land he had heard about in Kentucky.

Smithwick stayed with Green DeWitt. The fare was the eternal venison and wild honey. Few people had money and flour was expensive, so biscuits were a rare luxury. From Green DeWitt's he went on to Martin de Leon's town, Victoria, traveling with a man named Gibbs. From Victoria they rode on to Gonzales. It rained every day on the way and Gibbs couldn't swim. Smithwick made rafts to float him across swollen rivers. They killed deer and broiled the meat on a stick, with no honey to go with it.

Things looked better at the mouth of the Brazos. Corn was in roasting ear and people were feasting. When the corn began to harden, they would grate it by making graters from old tinware punched full of jagged holes. Smithwick came down with fever and was tormented by gnats.

"I would have given the whole territory of Texas to feel myself once more at home in a comfortable bed, with my mother's loving face beside me," he said. After he recovered, he went to Josiah Bell's settlement (West Columbia) where he had heard they needed a blacksmith. Soon afterwards, the Mexican garrison at San Antonio sought a blacksmith and Stephen F. Austin got the job for Smithwick.

Smithwick did not care for San Antonio. There were few Americans there and "more Mexicans than fiddlers in hell." He found the tools at the blacksmith shop were a century old and unlike the ones he was accustomed to using. He gave up his commission, which displeased Austin — "Young man," Austin told him, "you have thrown away an independent fortune." Smithwick moved on and set up a blacksmith shop at Bell's Landing.

He was invited to visit Thomas B. Bell on the San Bernard River. He found him "in a little pole cabin in the midst of a small clearing, upon which was planted a crop of corn. His wife, every inch a lady, welcomed me with as much cordiality as if she were mistress of a mansion. The whole family was dressed in buckskin and when supper was announced, we sat on stools around a clapboard table, upon which were arranged wooden platters. Beside each platter lay a fork made of a joint of cane. The repast was of the simplest, but served with as much grace as if it had been a feast."

Smithwick sold his blacksmith shop and with three partners invested in 1,000 pounds of leaf tobacco to smuggle into Mexico. On the trip, they ran out of food and his partners killed and ate a wild horse — "the very thought of eating which sickened me." But after three days with no food, Smithwick became so hungry he cooked and ate a big horse steak. "The boys said I was 'broke in.' " At Presidio del Norte, the tobacco smugglers saw boats on the Rio Grande made of cow hides stretched over a framework of poles.

Smithwick returned to San Felipe de Austin, a settlement of log buildings. Austin's house was a log cabin with a dog run in the middle. Besides Austin's house, there was a store owned by the Ingram brothers, the law office of Hosea League and David G. Burnet, a saloon, *The Cotton Plant* newspaper office, and Gail Borden's blacksmith shop. Smithwick opened his own blacksmith shop next door to Borden's.

One day James Bowie stopped by. He had his original Bowie knife fashioned by John Sowell at Gonzales. It was 10 inches long and two inches broad. It was set in an ivory handle mounted with silver. Bowie was proud of the knife and didn't want to use it for ordinary tasks. He wanted Smithwick to make him a duplicate, an everyday knife.

30

"When it became known," said Smithwick, "that I was making a genuine Bowie knife, there was a great demand for them, so I cut a pattern and started a factory, my knives bringing all the way from $5 to $20, depending on the finish."

In 1831, Smithwick ran afoul of the law. He slipped a file to a prisoner in leg irons, whom Smithwick was convinced was being treated unjustly. After the authorities discovered that the man escaped with Smithwick's assistance, he was banished from San Felipe. As he rode away, an angry Smithwick told them that being banished "was about the best thing they had ever done for me."

Smithwick went to Louisiana. He worked with a counterfeiter who made gold Mexican eagle dollars out of copper, which could be passed until the plating wore off. He returned in 1835 to find South Texas in turmoil, the place full of people with a long list of grievances and short tempers. "Couriers were flying, committees of safety forming, volunteers enrolling."

Smithwick hurried to Gonzales where they expected an attack by Mexican forces. Of the volunteers who were arriving, Smithwick said, "some were for independence, some for the constitution of 1824, and some for anything, just so it was a row."

Words, Smithwick wrote, couldn't describe this Texas army. "Men wore every shade of buckskin, with different kinds of shoes, boots, and moccasins, assorted headgear of sombreros and coonskin caps. It was a fantastic array. But the one great purpose animating every heart clothed us in a uniform more perfect in our eyes than was ever donned by regulars on dress parade."

The question arose about whether Smithwick could serve in the army since he had been banished not only from San Felipe but presumably all of Texas. In his defense, Smithwick said he was banished "in a Star Chamber proceeding in which I was not allowed to participate." Officials said they would take no action against Smithwick, that every gun would be needed in the coming fight and Smithwick, skilled in the blacksmith and gun trade, was especially valuable.

The object of the expected attack was an old cannon at Gonzales. Smithwick said it was practically useless. It had been spiked and the spike removed, leaving a touch-hole as big as a man's thumb. But Mexican authorities demanded the return of the cannon and sent 100 dragoons to reclaim it.

The Texans raised a white cotton sheet with the symbol of the old cannon painted in black and above it a crude lone star and below it the words "Come and Take It."

On Oct. 2, 1835, Texas volunteers mounted the cannon on an oxcart and fired the first shot of the revolution. The Mexicans retreated. Smithwick said

31

the battle of Gonzales "was our Lexington, the first battle in the struggle for independence."

A week after the "battle," Smithwick and the other volunteers marched toward San Antonio. The old cannon on the oxcart was pulled by two longhorn steers and they still had the "Come and Take It" flag. Halfway to San Antonio, the cart broke down and the cannon was unceremoniously dumped into a creek.

At Cibolo Creek, the volunteers heard that a large Mexican force was approaching. This resulted in an exhibition of nerves by one man and bravado by another. One fellow, nervous about the news, said, "Boys, if that's a big force, they'll whip us." This angered a big Dutchman, who said, "Shet up, damn you. Don't say they'll *weep* us; you think that and you're *weeped* already."

At Mission Concepción, on a bend of the San Antonio River, two miles from the city, Mexican soldiers advanced behind two field cannon. The Texans took cover in a pecan grove. Mexican grapeshot, said Smithwick, "thrashed through the pecan trees overhead, raining a shower of ripe nuts down on us. I saw men picking them up and eating them with as little concern as if they were shaken down by a norther."

The Texans fired back with telling effect. As Smithwick described it, "Our long rifles — and I thought I had never heard rifles crack so keen, after the dull roar of the cannon — mowed down the Mexicans at a rate that well might have made braver hearts than those encased in their shriveled little bodies recoil."

During the battle, Smithwick saw Dick Andrews of Lavaca go down, "lying as he had fallen, great drops of sweat gathering on his white, drawn face, and the lifeblood gushing from a hole in his left side. I ran to him and attempted to raise him. 'Dick,' I cried, 'are you hurt?' 'Yes, Smith,' he replied, 'I am killed; lay me down.' I laid him down and put something under his head."

Dick Andrews was the first Texas casualty of the Revolution. Smithwick said they buried him under a big pecan tree. In their defeat, the Mexican forces suffered 14 killed and 39 wounded.

While the Texans tried to deal with Santa Anna's army, Comanches were attacking settlers on the frontier. Smithwick joined a force of 60 Rangers in John Tumlinson's command. They were sent to protect settlers above Bastrop. They rescued a three-year-old boy who had been captured by a band of Comanches, who had killed the boy's family. Smithwick shot one Indian during the fight, the only one killed, and the Rangers awarded him the scalp. He did not want it, but allowed the loathsome and macabre trophy to be tied to his saddle.

Smithwick and other scouts served as a rear guard as Sam Houston retreated with the army east after the fall of the Alamo and the slaughter of prisoners at Goliad. This was the beginning of the great panic called the Runaway Scrape, with settlers fleeing east ahead of Santa Anna's advancing army.

Smithwick saw houses standing open, beds unmade, breakfast things left on the table. "There were cribs full of corn, yards full of chickens that ran after us for food. Forlorn dogs roamed around deserted houses, their doleful howls adding to the general sense of desolation."

To his dismay, Smithwick was delayed by swollen streams and he arrived at San Jacinto too late to take part in the battle. He found the battlefield strewn with "rifles broken off at the breech, the stocks smeared with blood and brains . . . dead Mexican soldiers lay in piles."

Texans had used the stocks of their guns to beat to death those trying to surrender, revenge taken on the battlefield for the slaughter of prisoners at the Alamo and Goliad. "Old Jimmie Curtice," wrote Smithwick, "had a son-in-law, named Wash Cottle, who was slain at the Alamo, whom he swore to avenge. San Jacinto gave him the opportunity. The boys said he clubbed his rifle and sailed in, accompanying each blow with 'Alamo! Alamo! You killed Wash Cottle!' "

After San Jacinto, the Texas army leisurely followed the retreating Mexican army as it made its way back to Mexico. A mile or so above Victoria, the Texans camped and made tents out of cowhide.

* * *

After he was mustered out with the general demobilization of Houston's army, Smithwick opened another blacksmith shop, then tried farming on Webber's Prairie, and lived for a time near Marble Falls.

He was selected as a commissioner of peace in 1837 and stayed with a band of Comanches. They called him "Juaqua" and he found life with the Comanches not bad, except for Comanche gastromony — "especially their method of preparing tripe, which they broiled without taking the trouble to wash it."

During his stay with Comanches, Smithwick related that a young Comanche would arise in the mornings and wake the rest of the village with a song. He described it as "a spontaneous outpouring more akin to that of feathered songsters than a religious rite; the song itself resembling the way of the birds in that it was wordless save for the syllables, *ha ah ha*, which furnished the vehicle on which the carol rode forth to the world; the performance ending in a keen yell." This final yell would bring them all out of their teepees and they would join in the yelling until the chief emerged and delivered his morning talk.

Smithwick found Comanche warriors the bravest of the brave. He said he never knew a Comanche warrior to submit to capture. They would fight to the death. More than once, he saw a wounded Comanche warrior lie flat on his back and fight until he was dead. During Smithwick's time with the Comanches, as a commissioner of peace, there was little trouble between Texans and Indians on the frontier.

After his return to "civilization," Smithwick tells how Texans shaped the law to fit the circumstances.

A German storekeeper in Austin, named Michael Ziller, was robbed by a man from his native land. As Smithwick relates, in Ziller's words: "I go way and leave him to keep my store. When I come back all my money and some my goods gone. I go to Judge Johnson and tell him I want one paper for catch ze damned scoundrel. Ze judge make out ze paper and I say, 'Where is ze constabler?' He say, 'I make you ze constabler, Captain Ziller.' I take ze paper and go after ze damned tief. I catch him at Walnut Creek. I get all my goods and zen I tie him to a tree and give him one damned good whipping. I turn him loose and go home. I go see Judge Johnson. He say, 'W'at you do mit him?' 'I tie him to a tree and give him one damned good whipping,' I say. 'O well,' he say, 'you make one good constabler, Captain Ziller.' "

After Texas seceded from the Union, Smithwick sold his one slave at half price, packed up his family and belongings and left for California. On the way, he visited the deposed Sam Houston on Houston's last night in the governor's mansion. Smithwick wrote, "I went to see General Houston and we had a long talk. 'General,' said I, 'if you again unfurl the Lone Star flag from the Capitol, I will bring you 100 men to help maintain it there.' "

* * *

Noah Smithwick finished dictating his memoirs to a daughter when he was 92. He recounted the details of long ago from memory. He was alert and clear-minded to the end. Smithwick's account of the early years of Texas, as T. R. Fehrenbach noted, "is rich in firsthand experience and observed detail." J. Frank Dobie said Smithwick added wit and perspective to honesty and his "Evolution of a State" is the meatiest and most readable of all Texian autobiographies. While Smithwick never returned to Texas, he was there at the beginning, one of the men who made it happen, a keen observer and brave participant in the evolution of a state.

CHAPTER 6

'WILDCAT' MORRELL
AND THE BATTLE AT SALADO CREEK
1842

I drew a pencil from my pocket and wrote down the names of the dead, so that I might make a correct report to the bereaved.
          —Z. N. Morrell after the battle at Salado Creek

In April 1838, a party of surveyors and land agents camped at the site where Corpus Christi would be built. Among the land agents was Baptist preacher Z. N. "Wildcat" Morrell.

Morrell called himself a cane-brake preacher. He moved his family from Mississippi to Texas at the time of the battle of San Jacinto. He started a farm at the Falls of the Brazos, settled by the Robertson Colony. Rangers stood guard while Morrell and neighboring farmers plowed fields and planted corn. They were always threatened by Indian attack. Whenever he could, at any opportunity, Morrell would preach a sermon, usually in a log cabin with a dirt floor.

After several Indian attacks, Morrell moved his family to Washington-on-the-Brazos. He opened a store and on Sundays he held prayer meetings in an old house. Saloon-goers had their fun by holding an opposition prayer meeting with mock hymn-singing filled with naughty choruses followed by the taunting question, "Brother, are you saved?" The saloon-goers would huddle outside Morrell's meeting place and hold a chicken by its neck to make it squawk. Morrell finally had enough and smashed one of them over the head with a heavy cane. The mocking stopped.

One Sunday, Morrell in his sermon took the position that "damn" was not always a swear word, that it could be used for simple emphasis without taking the Lord's name in vain. Shortly thereafter a young lady told him, "Preacher, that was a damned good sermon you preached Sunday."

Morrell invested in land certificates given to furloughed soldiers by the Republic of Texas because it had no money to pay them. Land certificates could be bought for next to nothing; holders of the certificates could claim

35

unclaimed land in the public domain. In April 1838, Morrell and three land agents took a trip to the Corpus Christi area to survey unclaimed lands. At Goliad, they saw the breastworks from 1836, two years after Fannin and his men were "butchered in cold blood." Morrell said there were only two or three Mexican families and about as many Irish in Goliad. Riding on to San Patricio, they saw antelope and a large number of rattlesnakes. Unlike Indians, Morrell wrote, the snakes never attacked unless threatened and they always gave fair warning.

Morrell's party found the village of San Patricio deserted. It was abandoned during the Revolution. They met up with a party of eight surveyors and rode on to Corpus Christi Bay. "We saw no indication of any former settlement at this place," wrote Morrell, "but were informed by an Irishman accompanying the surveyors that this was the point at which the colony of San Patricio had procured its supplies."

The surveying work was started, with the beginning corner established on the shore of the bay. As the surveyors worked, Morrell and another land agent, Matthew Burnett, rode southwest to get a view of the country. They passed the Salt Lake and saw mustang horses and wild game of every kind. They found fresh water and good grass for their horses and camped.

The next morning, they went to kill one of the wild cattle to replenish their meat supply. As they rode toward a bunch of cattle, and got close enough to take a shot, they saw an Indian. Burnett raised his gun to shoot, but Morrell stopped him.

"We were in no danger, could not plead self-defense, and in the commission of a deliberate murder I feared the judgment of God," Morrell wrote. They got close enough to talk. Morrell told the Indian, a Karankawa boy, in Spanish that they were friends. The Indian pointed to his camp, trying to get the two men to follow him there.

They decided it would not be prudent to follow him to the Indian camp. Morrell was suddenly worried about the rest of their party, 40 miles away, and they rode as fast as they could ride to get back to the camp. At daylight on the third day, they rode into camp and found the surveying party surrounded by 40 Karankawa warriors from the tribe of the young boy.

The Indians had disarmed the surveyors and taken their horses. The Karankawa boy pointed out Morrell and Burnett as the two men who befriended him.

"He recognized us, ran up smiling, as glad as if he had met relatives. Peace was made. Horses, guns, blankets, and everything was given up, and a treaty was made. I thank God that my motto ever was, even among Indians, not to kill except in self-defense." Morrell agreed to take a letter to Sam Houston asking him to recognize the treaty they made.

36

Morrell owned two tracts of land on the west side of the Nueces River, surveyed in 1838, land now occupied by the city of Corpus Christi. He apparently traded the two tracts for a homestead site on the Guadalupe River above Victoria.

Two years after the surveying trip, in 1840, Rev. Morrell fought in the battle of Plum Creek. This was after a large Comanche war party sacked and burned the little town of Linnville on Matagorda Bay. When the battle was over, Morrell heard a woman screaming from the bushes. She was Juliet Watts, whose husband Hugh Watts had been killed by the Indians at Linnville. She was trying to pull out an arrow from her breast. Morrell put down a blanket for her to rest on, using his saddle for a pillow.[10]

Two years after the battle at Plum Creek, in a series of probing attacks from Mexico, Mexican Gen. Adrian Woll, with 1,200 men, seized San Antonio on Sept. 11, 1842. Volunteers were mustered to repel the invaders.

Rev. Morrell arrived with Gen. Matthew "Old Paint" Caldwell's command. Caldwell asked for volunteers on fast horses to ride ahead and find Ranger Capt. Jack Hays. Morrell was one of 13 who volunteered.

Before he left Seguin, Morrell obtained 10 ears of corn and parched it in a campfire, ground the corn and mixed it with sugar. He called this "cold flour." On the way to meet Hays, Morrell saw plenty of game, but they were under orders not to use their guns for fear of alerting Gen. Woll to their location. They were hungry and Morrell had reason to recall one of his first meals in Texas, on the Little Brazos, that included bear bacon, turnip greens, and fresh buffalo beef.

Once the rendezvous with Hays was made, Morrell said, they had had nothing to eat but a few spoonfuls of cold flour mixed with water. The men were about to mutiny.

"Capt. Hays insisted I make them a speech," Morrell wrote. "I remembered an old saying, 'Never try to influence a man against his inclination when he is hungry.' But as I was under orders, I determined to try. To have approached these men with a long face and taxed their patience with a long speech on patriotism would have been sheer nonsense. So I mounted my horse and rode out in front, with as cheerful a face as I could command, and spoke: 'Boys, when I left Colonel Caldwell's camp, I felt like I was 40 years old. When I had starved one day, I felt like I was 35. After that, on two spoonfuls a day, I felt like I was 25; and this morning, when our cold flour and coffee were both out, I felt like I was only 21 years old, and ready for action.' "

---

[10] Juliet Watts survived. She married a man named Stanton and after that ended in divorce she married Dr. J. R. Fretwell. She ran the Stanton Hotel in Port Lavaca until her death in 1878.

When Gen. Woll's forces captured San Antonio, Capt. Jack Hays and his Rangers were away on a scouting expedition. Other Rangers in San Antonio were caught by surprise and taken captive. A Ranger named William Mason escaped by brandishing his pistol as he ran through the ranks of Mexican cavalry and got clean away. Woll's men captured many prominent citizens, for district court had been called and judge, jury, lawyers and witnesses were taken captive. In a proclamation to his soldiers, Woll said, "The second campaign against Texas has begun."

Hays made it back to find San Antonio occupied by Mexican soldiers. He rode around the city, reporting from Seguin to the secretary of war, "I have examined the camp and numbers, I think, correctly. I staid (sic) around town all day of the 11th and have left spies behind and if I can I will try and watch their approach to this river. All information will be reported (at) every opportunity."

When "Old Paint" Caldwell arrived from Gonzales with 200 volunteers, by consensus he took charge, as the senior officer present; he held the rank of general in the Texas Army. Jack Hays commanded the scouts. Caldwell, a crafty old Indian-fighter, knew better than to try to storm San Antonio against Woll's superior forces. He and Hays held a council of war and decided that Hays, who was more familiar with the terrain, was to choose a likely place for a battle and try to lure Woll there.

Hays chose a brushy area on the Salado Creek, seven miles northeast of San Antonio, which had an embankment that could serve as a natural breastwork. The Texans would assemble there and Hays would try to get Woll to attack them.

Jack Hays and a few picked men, including Rev. Morrell, rode into San Antonio to within a half-mile of the Alamo where Hays and six men galloped ahead. The last time Mexican soldiers had surrounded the Alamo resulted in a bloodbath during the Revolution six years before. Now, Hays, in full view of the Mexican soldiers, "cut capers" and shouted insults about the Mexicans' manhood, daring them to come out and fight.

It worked almost too well. Four or five companies of Mexican cavalry, about 400 men, took the bait and gave chase, with Hays and his men turning in their saddles and firing back at them as they raced away toward the chosen battlefield at Salado Creek.

The chase was in earnest with the Mexican soldiers firing at them as they drew near. Hays and men threw away hats, blankets and coats to lighten the load on their tired horses. "We reached camp," Morrell wrote, "and when formed into line every man was present, unhurt."

Between two and three in the afternoon of Sept. 18, 1842, Woll arrived with his infantry, cavalry and artillery. Morrell reckoned Woll had 1,600 men, including 40 Cherokees and about 100 San Antonio citizens of Mexican descent who had thrown in their lot with the invader.[11] Other accounts put the numbers of Woll's forces at 1,200. Caldwell had the Gonzales volunteers and Hays' Rangers. His forces were between 200 and 225, with no cavalry, unless you count Hays' Rangers, and no artillery.

At Salado Creek, the Mexican soldiers formed in line of battle opposite "Old Paint" Caldwell's Texans. The battle was fought on Sept. 18, 1842.

Gen. Woll relied on his artillery to try to drive Caldwell's men away from their position behind an embankment in a grove of pecan trees near the creek. Morrell said when the grapeshot of the Mexican guns hit the tops of the pecan trees it made a ripping noise like ripping up calico.

Woll stood with his artillery at the top of a hill and seeing that the guns were not going to do the job, with the Texans well-protected behind their embankment, he ordered an infantry charge.

"The Mexicans now advanced upon us," Morrell wrote, "under a splendid puff of music, the ornaments, guns, pikes and swords glistening in plain view."

Woll's infantry ran toward the Texans screaming and firing their guns. They were within 30 feet of the Texan lines when the rifles of the Texans began to fire and take a deadly toll, leaving hardly a man standing. Not all were hit, though, as some began to rise and run to the rear. In the battle, Woll lost 60 killed and many wounded. The Texans lost one man killed and three wounded. Hays' selection of a battlefield worked to perfection.

The week before, when Woll's men captured San Antonio, they plundered Hays' Ranger headquarters and someone confiscated a new pair of pants that belonged to Bigfoot Wallace, called "Foot" for short. Before the battle at Salado Creek, Wallace vowed to find and shoot an oversized Mexican wearing pants big enough to fit him. During the battle, he saw such a man, shot him, and secured his pants. He said he figured the Mexicans owed him a pair.

After the battle was over, the Texans were puzzled when they heard the sound of cannon and rifle fire coming from well behind Woll's position. They soon realized that Woll's forces were engaged with reinforcements who were rushing to join them.

As Gen. Woll began to withdraw from the battlefield, his troops came upon Capt. Nicholas Dawson, bringing 53 men to join Caldwell's men. Dawson's men were caught in the open and surrounded by the Mexican forces. Dawson

---

[11] One of those was Juan Seguin, a hero of the Texas Revolution who was twice elected mayor of San Antonio. He resigned as mayor in April 1842 and returned to Mexico. Seguin later said Gen. Santa Anna gave him the choice of going to prison or serving in the Mexican Army. He returned to Texas with Woll's forces in September, 1842.

raised a white flag and tried to surrender, but they were cut to pieces by the concentrated fire of Woll's artillery. Only 15 of Dawson's 53 men survived.

It was an anxious night for Morrell. He knew that his son Allen H. Morrell was with Dawson's forces and he worried about whether his son was dead or captured by Woll's men. As the sun rose and the day lightened, he and three other men made their way to the scene of the slaughter, which Morrell called the Mesquite Battleground. As his companions stood guard, in case Woll left spies behind, Morrell turned over the torn bloodied bodies in the search for his son. Morrell thought it painful beyond words.

"Thirty-five dead bodies of friends lay scattered and terribly mangled among the little cluster of bushes on the broad prairie," Morrell wrote. "I recognized the body of nearly every one. Here were 12 men, heads of families, their wives now widows and their children orphans; and here, too, lay dead the bodies of promising sons of my neighbors. The body of my son could not be found.

"The place was so horrible that two of the men with me rode away. One remained on guard while I continued my examination. A number of bodies were turned over before I could recognize them. One or two of my neighbors' sons were so badly mangled I could not recognize them at all. Supposing that one of these might be my son, I examined their feet for a scar that he had carried from childhood. By this time I was satisfied that he had escaped or was among the prisoners. I drew a pencil from my pocket and wrote down the names of the dead, so that I might make a correct report to the bereaved."

Gen. Woll retreated toward the Rio Grande, taking plunder from the stores of San Antonio and a number of citizens from that city who joined his forces and fought at Salado Creek. He also had 53 prisoners taken from San Antonio. These included the judge, jurors, lawyers and witnesses who were attending the District Court for Bexar County.[12]

Woll's retreating army was followed closely by Hays' Rangers, almost within shouting distance of Woll's rear guard. A few miles behind Hays was Caldwell's mixed force. They crossed the Medina River (two miles from today's town of Castroville) then traveled to a high ridge overlooking the Hondo River. The pursuit by the Texans was disorganized and scattered and they had no real plan of action.

Hays came upon Woll's rear guard, a battery with some infantry support, on the Hondo River. When Caldwell arrived, Hays urged an immediate attack to take the battery, but Caldwell demurred, arguing that they had seen what the fire of concentrated grapeshot did to Dawson's men. He also feared,

---

[12] One of the captives was George C. Hatch, uncle of James Bowie, who was imprisoned at Perote Castle with the other Bexar captives. He later settled at the present town of Ingleside. He was killed by bandits on the north side of the Reef Road at Corpus Christi.

based on some information, that Gen. Pedro Ampudia had brought 1,500 men as reinforcements to join Woll. The information was incorrect.

Hays convinced Caldwell to give him 50 volunteers to join his Rangers to charge and take the battery. Morrell, a participant in the skirmish, said, "At length, the shrill, clear voice of our captain sounded down the line — 'Charge!' Away went the company up a gradual ascent in quick time. In a moment the cannon roared, but according to Mexican custom overshot us. The Texan yell followed the cannon's thunder, and so excited the Mexican infantry, placed in position to pour fire down on our lines, that they overshot us; and by the time the artillery hurled its canister the second time, shotguns and pistols were freely used by the Texans. Every man at the cannon was killed, as the company passed it."

The plan was that once Hays' men captured the cannon, Caldwell would follow in support with a general attack on Woll's forces. Hays held the gun battery for 10 minutes, but no support came up. Some believed it was a missed opportunity to inflict more damage on Woll's demoralized forces. In his official report, Caldwell explained that owing to the boggy, wet ground, and his tired horses, he failed to support Hays' charge. After that, the decision was made to give up the pursuit since Woll had superior forces.

After the massacre of Dawson's men and Woll's unimpeded return to Mexico, it made the victory of Salado Creek something of a hollow victory. Z. N. Morrell was bitter that Woll was allowed to escape, taking his hostages with him. He thought it was a disgraceful affair. "The poor boys (Woll's captives, including Morrell's son) were carried to prison and chains, and we saw not their faces again for two years." Morrell's son was locked up at Perote Castle with other captives. He was released in 1844.

Rev. Z. N. "Wildcat" Morrell founded one of the first Baptist churches in Texas. He was a pioneer Indian fighter who could quote Scripture while loading his rifle. He never missed an opportunity to preach a sermon or join in the defense of settlers on the frontier. He wanted to make the spiritual wilderness of Texas "blossom as the rose." He wrote of his experiences in early Texas in his book, "Flowers and Fruits in the Wilderness."

Perote Castle

CHAPTER 7

BIGFOOT WALLACE,
THE BATTLE OF MIER
AND THE BEAN DRAWING
1842 — 1848

That ditch is for us.

—Henry Whaling to Bigfoot Wallace.

Following the battle of Salado Creek, Republic of Texas President, Sam Houston, authorized an expeditionary force to punish Mexico after Mexican Gen. Adrian Woll captured San Antonio and carried off Texas hostages.

Houston authorized Gen. Alex Somervell to launch reprisals by carrying the war into Mexico. Somervell's collection of unpaid volunteers — called the Southwestern Army of Texas — included Texas leaders Thomas Jefferson Green and William S. Fisher. Jack Hays, the Ranger captain, was part of that force; he was in command of a battalion of scouts. With him were Rangers Ben McCulloch, Sam Walker and Bigfoot Wallace, who was still wearing the britches he took from a dead Mexican soldier after the battle of Salado Creek.

Hays led the way for Somervell's expeditionary forces, which numbered 750 men. Houston called them light troops, meaning irregulars, but many were adventurers not used to military discipline. Since Houston was short of money, arms, men, everything needed to make war, Somervell's men would have to live off the land; their pay would come from whatever they could carry off. Houston could not afford a war; this was a quick raid.

Somervell's forces arrived at Laredo on Dec. 8, 1842 and camped downstream from town. Mexican soldiers at Laredo evacuated across the Rio Grande. Next day, Somevell's men plundered Laredo, which they considered a Mexican town, ignoring Houston's orders to conduct civilized warfare. As stragglers made it back to camp, Somervell ordered them arrested and their plunder returned to Laredo.

Somervell said those who wished to go home could do so and about 200 left for home. Somervell took the rest of his forces across the river and captured the town of Guerrero, where they demanded 100 horses and when these were not available demanded $5,000 in lieu of the horses. The alcalde (mayor) brought $700, all, he said, that could be raised. When Somervell ordered the men to cross into Texas and return home, some refused to obey. Five captains, with their men, decided to proceed downriver to obtain horses and provisions to see them home. About 200 men left with Somervell while 310 remained behind.

Jack Hays made the same offer to his Rangers that Somervell made to his men. They were free to go on, Hays said, but he warned them that the descent into Mexico could hold an unpleasant surprise. Though he was not one to back away from a fight, he had information from his network of border spies that a large Mexican force was being rushed to deal with the Texans. Don't go, he said. Bigfoot Wallace and Sam Walker, among others, did not heed the warning.

As Somervell[13] led the remnant of his command to the junction of the Frio and Nueces for mustering out, back on the Rio Grande those men and their leaders who wanted to press on elected to proceed under the command of an old border fighter, William S. Fisher. As it turned out, this was a mistake. If the Texans thought they could march into Mexico, take their revenge and portable plunder, especially horses, and march out again, the reality proved otherwise.

On Dec. 21, 1842, Fisher's men crossed over to Mier, the largest town next to Matamoros on the lower Rio Grande. They rode into town and demanded food for themselves and forage for their horses. The alcalde promised the food and forage would be delivered to the Texans' camp next day. They waited four days, until Christmas Day, for the demands to be met. They captured a Mexican who told them that Gen. Pedro Ampudia had arrived with 1,000 soldiers.

The Texans rode into town at sunset. They were expected. A bullet whizzed past the ear of Bigfoot Wallace, killing the man behind him. Mexican soldiers rushed out of houses lining the streets. The Texans, fighting at close quarters, used Bowie knives and rifle butts against Mexican soldiers. They made sallies against Ampudia's cavalry and artillery. The fighting was ferocious, more like a street brawl than a military engagement.

After it was over, the streets of Mier were littered with bodies of those who had been shot or stabbed or their heads bashed in by rifle butts. Some 600

---

[13] Alexander Somervell, one of three founders of the town of Saluria on Matagorda Island, was carrying a large amount of money from Lavaca to Saluria by boat on Jan. 25, 1854. His body was found in the boat and the money was gone.

Mexican soldiers were killed and 100 Texans, enough to fill a graveyard. Under a flag of truce sent over from the Mexican side, the Texans sued for peace, at the bidding of William S. Fisher, who was sick, and against the strong advice of Thomas Jefferson Green, who wanted to keep fighting. Fight first, said Green, and negotiate later. He was so upset he broke his sword rather than give it up.

At the time they surrendered, they had the fight virtually won, they learned later. General Ampudia and other Mexican leaders had their horses saddled and waiting and were ready to flee if the Texans did not accept the truce. "We fought Ampudia, and had him whipped, and he sent a flag of truce and Colonel Fisher very foolishly listened to him," said George Washington Trahern.[14] "We fought him two days and two nights, and he was ready to retreat, they were all ready to retreat. And Fisher let this flag of truce come in, instead of shooting at it."

Bigfoot Wallace thought that as many as 800 Mexicans were killed and said the battle was harder-fought than the battle at San Jacinto. From where the surrender took place, he saw row upon row of dead Mexican soldiers, with a priest moving among them making the sign of the cross. The bodies of 100 Texans killed in the fight were dragged through the streets, followed by a cheering crowd.

The battle at Mier left more casualties than any engagement between Mexico since San Jacinto. For Texans, Mier would leave such a bad taste they could hardly keep from spitting at the mention of the name.

* * *

After the surrender at Mier, 200 Texas prisoners were marched, under heavy guard, down the river toward Matamoros. It was the last day of 1842 and very cold. The captives built fires at night and when the fires burned down they slept in the warm ashes.

The towns they passed through along the river — Camargo, Reynosa, Guadalupe — became scenes of noisy and triumphant fanfare for their Mexican escorts. Their approach was announced with bugles, trumpets, and the pealing of church bells, as if it were a day for one of the saints. The captives were herded through the main plazas of the towns, surrounded by prancing horses of the cavalry guards and taunted by jeering mobs. The Texans knew enough Spanish to yell insults at their hosts.

The main body of the captives reached Matamoros on Jan. 9, 1843. One evening, they were penned up in a cattle corral and the Texans, as if they

---

[14] Trahern's family came to Texas from Mississippi and settled at Port Lavaca. He was 17 years old when he joined the Somervell expedition.

were in a play, some comic interlude, pawed the ground and snorted like mad bulls. When they were later put in a sheep pen, they bleated like lost lambs.

After a week, they left for Monterrey, guarded by a troop of cavalry, 600 infantry and one piece of artillery. They were fed very little and the stitching came out of their boots, then the boots fell apart, and they passed through the towns barefoot, ragged and starving.

Their putative leaders — William Fisher and Thomas Jefferson Green — were sent ahead by horseback and were treated much better, though Green wrote letters of complaint when they were not allowed bedding at one of their nightly stops. But Green praised his host at Monterrey. "Our table was supplied from the best French restaurant in the city; and our kind host, old Colonel Bermudez, was all the time apologizing for not having things good enough for us."

As the main body marched from Monterrey to Saltillo, beginning on Feb. 2, one plan to escape was made, but it was thwarted when one of the Texans turned informer and gave the game away. Bigfoot Wallace doesn't name the Texan. They reached their prison quarters at Hacienda Salado, 100 miles west of Saltillo, on Feb. 10. Fisher and Green had arrived the day before. At Hacienda Salado, they found six Texas captives already there, three from the Santa Fe Expedition in 1841 and three taken in San Antonio during Woll's raid. A plan to escape was refined under the leadership of Ewen Cameron, the big Scotsman.

Next morning at daybreak, Capt. Cameron gave the signal by raising his hat. The Texans attacked their guards, overpowering them in fierce fighting and taking their weapons. The whole compound was in motion. Some guards fired hastily, dropped their guns and fled.

There was a cheer as the Texans realized the courtyard was theirs and the Mexican guards surrendered. An inventory of their casualties showed five Texans dead and as many seriously wounded in the melee.

They borrowed a couple of hundred horses, mostly from their cavalry escort, and Bigfoot Wallace captured a large pacing mule that belonged to a Mexican captain named Arroyo.

Fisher and Green were not with them; they had been taken some distance away from Hacienda Salado before the breakout. Ewen Cameron was in charge. The escapees left by the main road to Saltillo, heading toward the Rio Grande. All 193 Texans were mounted.

They rode 60 miles, fed their horses, slept two hours, then left the main road to ride around Saltillo. They decided, after a dispute between two captains, to leave the road and strike out over the mountains, but soon learned they made a terrible mistake. It was barren, arid, desolate country, without water or food, and they became lost. They spent six days trying to get through.

46

Men were dying of thirst and starvation. Horses were killed and eaten. Bigfoot killed the big pacing mule and devoured mule steaks. He said they drank the red blood with gusto "as if they were drinking to one another's health in the saloons of San Antonio."

They were lost in the mountains, suffering from thirst, and losing stragglers. They were too weak to carry their guns. The horses were eaten or abandoned. Some of the men, delirious, wandered off to die alone; their bodies would never be found. It was as if the land of Mexico was closing in around them, trapping them, preventing their escape.

Bigfoot dried some of the mule meat, which he carried in a haversack. He would chew on bits from time to time until his tongue became too dry and swollen to swallow.

Bigfoot, with Ewen Cameron and two others, broke away from the main body. They thought by the looks of the land that water was near and, by a supreme effort of survival, used the last of their strength to reach it. They had a vision of splashing in a lake. They were captured by Mexican cavalry 150 yards from a pool of water.

When they were given water, Bigfoot grabbed the gourd and refused to give it up. He said it was the best he ever tasted. He drank all the water in the gourd, despite the guard's warning that it would kill him, then fell on the ground and promptly went to sleep. He hadn't slept for five or six days. When morning came, he opened his haversack and found the last of the mule meat. A guard asked what he was eating.

"Mule meat," he said.

"Whose mule was it?" the guard asked.

"My mule," said Wallace.

"It was not," said the Mexican. "He belonged to Captain Arroyo."

George Washington Trahern said he hadn't had a drink of water for six days. "An old Mexican picked me up — I was a little boy, 18 years old — and carried me behind him to water". In that stage a man would walk along and draw in wind like he was sucking water, and look like death.

"I got up the second morning," said Trahern, "and looked at a young fellow by the name of Lewis; we used to call him 'Legs.'[15] I says, 'What is the matter with you?' He says 'Nothing. I was going to ask you.' He says, 'You look like death.' Said I, 'You are the same.' I was all sunken and flesh all sunk off, and could take a thorn and run it in my leg and not draw a drop of blood."

---

[15] Legs Lewis would later join Richard King in founding the King Ranch. He was killed by a jealous husband in Corpus Christi.

Almost all the escapees were recaptured, except for five who died, four who made their way back to Texas, and four who simply disappeared, dead somewhere in the mountains.

After a few days spent rounding up stragglers, the prisoners were marched back to Hacienda Salado where Bigfoot Wallace and Henry Whaling noticed that the Mexicans were digging a big ditch. Whaling said, "That ditch is for us."

After wandering the hills without water, after eating their horses and drinking their own urine, after nearly dying from exhaustion, the escaped Mier prisoners looked like walking corpses.

Back at Hacienda Salado, the place they had escaped from, they learned that Gen. Antonio López de Santa Anna had ordered them to be shot as punishment for the escape.

While Santa Anna had been treated with every courtesy when he was a captive of the Texans, after San Jacinto, he would still rather shoot Texans than eat breakfast.

Despite his preference, Santa Anna was prevailed upon to modify the order and rather than kill all the prisoners kill one of 10, a decimation, as close to mercy as Santa Anna was capable. The men to be executed would be chosen by lot.

"We were in this big bull pen, we called it, a big adobe establishment made for horses," said Trahern. The prisoners were chained and guarded, allowing no chance to rush the guards. Since 176 prisoners were at Hacienda Salado when the order was given, 176 beans — 17 black and 159 white — were put in a clay jar. Each man had to draw a bean when his name was called.

Bigfoot Wallace noticed the white beans were placed in the jar and the black beans put on top, not mixed up. He thought they were trying to ensure that Ewen Cameron, who led the escape, got a black bean, since he had to draw first.

Someone whispered "dig deep, Captain" and Cameron pulled out a white bean.

After Cameron had drawn, Trahern said, the guard holding the jar of beans shook them to mix them up. William F. Wilson, chained to Cameron, drew a white bean. William Eastland, cousin of Nicholas Dawson, massacred at Salado Creek, was the first to draw a black bean. Legs Lewis drew a white bean.

Waiting to draw a bean to see who would live and who would die was worse than charging a blazing cannon, said Bigfoot Wallace. The black beans, Wallace noticed, were larger. His hand shook and he could barely get it in the jar. He felt around until he had two beans; he dropped one and held up a white bean.

One story said Wallace offered to swap his white bean with a young man with a black one. Not true, he said; he meant to stay alive as long as he could. "When I put my hand in and found two beans, one big and one small, I pulled out the small one because I thought the black beans looked bigger. I had only one life to give for William Wallace."

A gambler from Austin drew a black bean and muttered, "Just my luck." The guards taunted the condemned men, telling them better luck next time.

Henry Whaling got a black bean, then demanded food. "I do not want to starve and be shot too." They gave him double rations of mutton stew and beans.

The condemned men were led away. An infantry company called the Red Caps would be their executioners. The prisoners, blindfolded, asked to be shot from the front, but each man had a soldier standing behind him and each was shot in the back at point-blank range. Henry Whaling was shot several times before he died.

One corpse being piled up was not a corpse. James L. Shepard (also spelled Shepherd) was shot and stunned; he feigned death. When the soldiers left, he escaped into the mountains and made it back to Saltillo, 45 miles away, though all the flesh on one side of his head was gone and his arm was broken. He was captured after 10 days and executed.

The survivors, hollow-eyed and hollow-bellied, were put on the road to Mexico City. Some died on the way.

"Foot" Wallace was still wearing the Mexican pants he acquired in the battle at Salado Creek, though little more than the waistband was left and he wore a long shirt that reached his ankles. His shackles were too tight and his arms turned black. A woman at San Luis Potosí told a guard to take off his shackles; the guard refused, saying only the governor could make such an order; she said she was the governor's wife. The shackles were removed.

A few miles from Mexico City, orders came down from Santa Anna, with callous cruelty, that Ewen Cameron was to be executed, even though he had drawn a white bean. As the prisoners were marched away, they heard gunfire and knew Cameron was dead.

The prisoners arrived at Mexico City on May 1, 1843 and were kept there until October. They were put to work building roads, carrying sand in sacks, and the prisoners cut small holes in the sacks to let the sand dribble out as they walked to lighten the load.

In October, they were moved to the dungeon at Perote Castle, 300 miles from Mexico City, between Puebla and Veracruz, an ancient stone fortress surrounded by an alligator-filled moat.

Some prisoners from the Santa Fe Expedition and from Woll's San Antonio raid were already there. Earlier that year, 16 Texans escaped from Perote through a hole dug under the walls; eight were recaptured.

In the damp dungeon at Perote Castle, Bigfoot said the men were so desperately hungry they supplemented their diet by catching and eating rats. The men were hitched to carts like oxen and made to haul rocks down from the mountains.

Some prisoners died and a few were released through the good offices of British and American ambassadors. Bigfoot Wallace and three other men were freed on Aug. 5, 1844. The following month, on Sept. 16, 1844, those who remained in the prison were freed. It was said Santa Anna had promised his wife, on her deathbed, he would free them, and for once in his life, said Bigfoot, he kept his promise.

Four years later, during the Mexican War, Bigfoot Wallace surprised himself when he failed to blow the head off a Mexican soldier bearing a white flag. Bigfoot called it the greatest act of restraint in his life. "I didn't see the flag. I just saw his face. He was the man who held up the clay jar of beans at Hacienda Salado."

At the end of the Mexican War, the remains of the Texans executed in the black-bean drawing were exhumed and returned to Texas and reburied, with the remains of Capt. Dawson and his men, on a steep bluff overlooking LaGrange, known today as Monument Hill.

Jack Hays

CHAPTER 8

JACK HAYS,
RANGER ON THE TEXAS FRONTIER
1836 — 1848

Yellow Dog, son of a dog-mother, the Comanche liver is white!
*   —Jack Hays taunting Chief Yellow Wolf*

It was a stroke of luck that Texas found a bold and effective Ranger captain in the last years of the Republic with John Coffee "Jack" Hays, a boyish-looking man who came from the same part of Tennessee as Sam Houston.

Hays' time as a Ranger lasted from 1836 until 1848, but he seemed to be in almost every fight in the three-sided conflict between Texans, Indians and Mexicans. He was the model of leadership that all future Ranger captains were measured against, though no other captain of Rangers reached the measure of "Jack" Hays.

Physically, he was small. He was five feet eight inches tall and weighed about 150 pounds. There was no hint of self-importance about him. He was almost shy, always courteous, and didn't speak often but when he did, things happened. He was uncommonly brave. Perhaps it was more than bravery; the historian Walter Prescott Webb defined it as a complete absence of fear.

Hays never ran from the hostile Indians he encountered, and he was never defeated by them. He knew how to improvise on a battlefield in the turmoil of a fight, which was borne out in his famous battles at Bandera Pass, Uvalde Canyon, Enchanted Rock, Salado Creek, and the Pinta Trail Crossing. Jack Hays' first law of fighting was to never back down, for he understood that the sheer determination of a few could whip much larger forces.

Hays seemed to possess a certainty of how things would come out in battle — a feat of precognition, as if he could see the future — and that supreme confidence was an inspiration to his men.

How did this quiet and fairly small Jack Hays come to be the most deadly Ranger of them all?

He was born at Little Cedar Lick, Tenn., near Nashville, on Jan. 28, 1817. When he was 15, his father and mother died and he was sent to live with an uncle in Yazoo, Miss. The uncle wanted Jack to become a clerk and work in a store, but Hays wanted to pursue a military career.

He left his uncle's home and headed for Texas, arriving after the battle of San Jacinto. He joined the Texas Army.

In June 1836, Hays was part of a detail of soldiers sent to bury the scattered remains of some 400 of Fannin's men who were slaughtered by Mexican forces at Goliad after they surrendered.

Afterwards, Hays joined a company of Rangers commanded by "Deaf" Smith. He was with Smith's company when they were sent in March 1837 to assert Texas' claim to Laredo, considered by its inhabitants as a Mexican town. Smith and his 20 Rangers were attacked by soldiers from Laredo. Hays said the gunfire of the Rangers "threw them into confusion" with the result that 10 men from Laredo were killed.

After the Laredo expedition, Hays was promoted to sergeant and he led patrols in search of bandits, horse thieves and hostile Indians. In one encounter, Hays shot a bandit from his horse and chased down three outlaws, who were summarily hanged.

Hays was with Capt. Henry Karnes on a foray in 1839 on the Pedernales River. Hays and two scouts found the Comanche camp and the Rangers attacked. Twelve Indians were killed, one of them was believed to be Chief Isomania, also called Asa Minor. But days after the battle the Comanche chief was found alive and taken to his village. Years later, the chief would tell how he had been dead for three days and came back to life.

In 1840 Hays was promoted to command of a Ranger company headquartered in San Antonio. In choosing recruits, Hays wanted men of courage, of good character, and who owned a horse worth at least $100. Their lives depended on their horses.

In 1841, Hays with 40 Rangers rode up the Medina River toward Bandera Pass, separating the Medina and Guadalupe valleys. The Comanches saw the Rangers first and prepared an ambush, with warriors hiding among the rocks. When Hays' men were halfway through the pass, the Indians opened fire, taking the Rangers by surprise.

There was much confusion as the Rangers tried to regain control of their frightened mounts; they couldn't aim their guns and control their horses at the same time. Hays shouted, "Steady, boys. Get down and tie those horses."

In hand-to-hand fighting, one Ranger charged an Indian with his five-shot Colt pistol. As he was about to fire, the barrel fell off and he was left holding the handle. The Ranger and Comanche each had half a weapon. The Indian was too close to string his bow, so he stabbed the Ranger with an arrow. The

Comanche chief attacked Kit Ackland and Ackland killed him with a Bowie knife.

After the fight, the Indians moved toward the north end of the pass, where they buried their chief. The Rangers went to the south end where graves were dug and the wounded bandaged. Five Rangers were killed and six badly wounded. The battle at Bandera Pass was one of Hays' toughest fights with Comanches.

That June, Hays took 30 Rangers up the Sabinal River toward Uvalde Canyon. Near the canyon, circling buzzards denoted an Indian camp. The Indians were roasting venison.

Hays led an attack on the camp and the Comanches ran into a thicket. Hays had his men surround the thicket and he took a Ranger with him to drive out the Indians. The men outside heard shooting and Hays came out of the brush carrying a wounded Ranger. Hays went back into the thicket and, after several shots, Hays' men went in search of their captain. They found him with eight dead Comanches.

Between fights and scouting expeditions, the Rangers enjoyed time off around San Antonio. In early June, a ball was held to honor President Mirabeau Lamar. Hays and Rangers Mike Chevalier and John Howard attended, but they had only one dress coat.

Mary Maverick wrote that the Rangers took turns wearing that coat on the dance floor. "The two not dancing would stand at the hall door watching the happy one who was enjoying his turn and they reminded him when it was time for him to step out of that coat."

A fight in the fall of 1841 at the Enchanted Rock may be true or may be legend. In the case of Jack Hays, the two are often mixed, but based on Hays' known character, the story is entirely believable.

Hays was scouting alone, away from where the Rangers had pitched camp on Crabapple Creek near the Enchanted Rock. This ancient rock dominates the Llano Valley, near today's Fredericksburg. When Hays discovered Comanches behind him, he raced to the Enchanted Rock, slapped his horse on the rump, and scrambled to the top. He didn't have time to appreciate the view. As the Comanches ran up after the man they called "Devil Yack," he picked them off one by one from the summit. Hays saw a cloud of dust as the Rangers, alerted by his riderless horse which came into camp, raced to his rescue. The Indians took off, leaving 15 warriors dead on the Enchanted Rock, all killed by Hays.

The following year, Hays was instrumental in defeating and turning back Mexican Gen. Adrian Woll after he captured San Antonio in September 1842, known as the Woll Raid. Hays was not in charge of the Texans; Gen. Matthew "Old Paint" Caldwell was in command. But Hays, with a few chosen Rangers, drew Woll's forces out of San Antonio to a place picked by Hays for the battle, at Salado Creek.

In January, 1844, Sam Houston told Captain Hays that the Texas Navy, in the process of being dismantled, had a supply of Colt revolvers. Hays got them for his Rangers and they soon came in handy in a fight on the Pinta Trail crossing on June 8, 1844. This battle has also been called the battle of Walker's Creek and the battle on the Pedernales, but Rangers called it the fight on the Pinta Trail. It was one of the hardest fights Hays had since he was ambushed by Comanches at Bandera Pass.

Hays and 14 Rangers were scouting on the Pedernales, 80 miles from San Antonio. They were camped near the Pinta Trail, an old Indian route, when they discovered Indians following them. When the Rangers advanced, the Indians feigned alarm, making for the cover of a nearby wood.

Hays had been in too many fights to be taken in by this ruse, so he made no move to chase them. Fifteen warriors came out of the sheltering wood. Hays recognized Chief Yellow Wolf. The Indians yelled insults in Spanish, calling the Rangers cowards, and Hays yelled back his own taunting insult — "Yellow Dog, son of a dog-mother, the Comanche liver is white!" The chief was so incensed he nearly fell off his horse.

Hays saw a larger force of Indians under the cover of trees on the ridge. The Comanches made for the top of the hill and waited for the Rangers to attack. Hays noticed a ravine that could not be seen from the hilltop. He led the Rangers into the ravine, rode around the base of the hill and right up behind the Indians, who were watching for Hays to come up the front of the hill. They were taken by surprise when they were attacked from behind.

The Indians, yelling and whooping, rushed to lance-throwing distance and the Rangers fired their newly acquired Colts. Two dozen warriors dropped from their ponies.

As Yellow Wolf harangued his warriors, encouraging them to make another charge, Hays asked Richard "Ad" Gillespie to "make sure work of that chief." Gillespie got off his horse, took aim, and his rifle made a dull crack. Chief Yellow Wolf fell dead. The Comanches rode off a short way, then fled the battlefield.

Thirty Indians lay dead. Of the Rangers, two were killed and five wounded. In his report, Hays said, "Whenever pressed severely, the Indians were making the most desperate charges and efforts to defeat me. Had it not been for the five-shooting pistols, I doubt what the consequences would have been."

There has been much dispute about which battle Hays and his men first used Colt firearms. Some accounts place it in a fight near Corpus Christi two years earlier and others at a battle in the Nueces Canyon. Individual Rangers, including Hays himself, obtained Colt firearms as early as 1839. One man used a Colt rifle at the battle of Plum Creek in 1840 and Ranger Andrew Erskine was firing a Colt pistol at Bandera Pass in 1841 when the barrel fell off. But the Pinta Trail battle in 1844 was the first time an entire Ranger company was armed with Colt revolvers.

Before the emergence of the Colt revolvers, hostile Texas Indians could let fly half a dozen or more arrows and ride 300 yards in the time it took a Ranger to reload a .48 caliber flintlock rifle, which couldn't be done on a horse.

Noah Smithwick said Indians could discharge a dozen arrows while a man was loading a gun "and if they could manage to draw our fire all at once they had us at their mercy unless we had a safe retreat." But with the deadly accuracy of Colts, Rangers were mobile warriors who could fight like Indians from horseback, on equal terms.

Each age discovers marvels and becomes dependent upon them. So it was on the frontier of Texas with Colt repeaters. After the battles on the Pedernales, Samuel Colt's factory in Hartford could scarcely keep up with orders from Texas for his five-shot revolvers and later the famous six-shooter. Colt's weapon made a revolution on the frontier. An old Texas saying went, "God made some men big and some men small, but Sam Colt made them equal."

* * *

In the summer of 1845, as the Republic of Texas prepared to the join United States, the prospect of war with Mexico loomed. Mexico had repeatedly warned that any attempt to annex Texas would mean war. If the new state of Texas was in danger, it would have to be defended.

Hays raised a regiment of Rangers, which trained at Corpus Christi with U.S. troops in 1845 and early 1846. Many of Hays' Rangers, seasoned to the hazards of war, enlisted.

In Mexico during the war, an officer in the U. S. Army pointed to a man at the head of the First Regiment of Texas Volunteers and asked who that "little fellow" might be. He was surprised when someone said it was Jack Hays, the world-famous Ranger and Indian fighter.

If the war had lasted longer, Rip Ford wrote, Hays would have been in line to be promoted from colonel to brigadier general in the U.S. Army for his actions at Monterrey and Mexico City. He showed the same talent and skill in fighting Mexican soldiers as he did fighting Comanche braves. The boy who ran away from his uncle's home in Mississippi because he didn't want to be a clerk, but wanted a military career instead, achieved his goal, though it was a roundabout way.

Hays married Susan Calvert of Seguin in 1847. They went to California in the gold rush of 1849. He speculated in gold mining, became the first elected sheriff of San Francisco, and helped found the city of Oakland, but he was always best-known for his exploits on the Texas frontier when Comanches called him "Devil Yack." Jack Hays died in California in 1883 at age 66. It did not escape notice that he died on San Jacinto Day.

CHAPTER 9

DEATH OF AN INDIAN CHIEF:
FLACCO THE YOUNGER
1842

His heart no longer leaps at the sight of the buffalo.
                    —*Sam Houston to Flacco the Elder*

Near San Antonio, on the way from Laredo, a party of four men with a large herd of horses camped for the night. The leader of the group was a Lipan-Apache chief named Flacco. With him were two Texans and an elderly Lipan-Apache, a deaf-mute, known as a superb hand with horses.

They were driving a caballada of 40 horses that belonged to Chief Flacco.

In the late hours of the night, Flacco and the deaf-mute were murdered in their sleep. The two Texans rode away with the horses. That was in December 1842.

Flacco was the younger of two Lipan chiefs, father and son, both named Flacco.

Flacco the Elder was a friend of Sam Houston; he had been made a colonel in the Texas Army for services to the Republic of Texas. He could write his name and would sign his signature with a flourish as "Flacco Colonel."

Flacco the Younger led Lipan scouts for Jack Hays' company of Rangers. He taught Hays how to trail and about Comanche battle tactics. He and Hays were close. The younger Flacco, it was said, constantly watched Hays and nothing the Ranger captain did escaped his notice.

In Jack Hays' fights with Comanches from 1840 through 1842, Flacco was there with his Lipans as scouts and warriors. Several times Flacco saved Hays' life or Hays saved Flacco's.

On one foray in search of hostile Comanches, Rangers invited Flacco to share a meal. "No," he said, "warriors never eat much on warpath.

Captain Hays is great chief, but Rangers eat much too much on warpath. Too much eat, too much eat."

In a battle on the Llano River in 1841, Hays' Rangers attacked 200 Comanches and during the fight, Hays' horse spooked and ran straight at the Indian lines. Thinking that Hays was charging, Flacco went after him and both men raced through the Comanche lines, with arrows flying in their direction, and came out the other side untouched. Flacco said Captain Jack was "bravo too much." The Lipan chief added, "Me and Red Wing (his horse) not afraid to go to hell together. Captain Jack not afraid to go to hell by himself."

In 1842, at a soiree in LaGrange, Chief Flacco was an invited guest. He dressed for the occasion, wearing breechclout and leggings of white buckskin and a string of beads, amulets and silver wrist bands. He was in the company of Capt. Mark Lewis.

A young lady at the party played the piano for the chief's amusement and afterwards, someone remarked that she was a particular favorite of Capt. Lewis.

"Oh, no," she said, "I am not tall enough for the captain."

Chief Flacco scrutinized the young lady, who was somewhat short and overweight, and said, "You tall too, but Great Spirit put him hand on head and mash you down."

In 1842, Chief Flacco joined Jack Hays as part of the punitive Somervell expedition into Mexico that led to the disastrous Mier raid. When Somervell turned back, he gave permission for those of his men who needed fresh mounts to confiscate horses from a ranch near Laredo, a ranch known to supply horses to bandits.

Flacco rounded up a caballada of 40 horses, a valuable herd, and was on his way to San Antonio when he and his deaf-mute companion were murdered and the horses stolen.

There was no real mystery about who killed Flacco, but Sam Houston, in his second term as president of the Republic, was anxious to prevent an outbreak of hostilities with Lipan-Apaches, should they learn that their idolized young chief had been killed by two white horse thieves.

Houston spread the word that the young chief was killed by a Mexican bandit named Agaton. Houston asked Noah Smithwick, who lived near Flacco the Elder, to tell him that Mexican bandits had killed his son and stole his horses. Smithwick said it was a ruse to prevent the Lipans from going on the warpath.

A newspaper in Houston added misinformation with the report that the bandit Agaton had been sighted on the Nueces River and that some traders said he was responsible for murdering Flacco. Hays' and his Rangers were sent to capture or kill Agaton.

The real killers were the two men helping drive Flacco's horses from Laredo, identified as two men named James Ravis and Tom Thernon. They were seen in Seguin with the horses shortly after Flacco's murder. They were not pursued, arrested or charged because to arrest them and put them on trial would not fit the concocted story that the Mexican bandit Agaton was the killer.

Flacco the Elder distributed his son's possessions to friends. He sent one of his son's prized horses to Sam Houston, but before it was delivered pranksters at LaGrange, political opponents of Houston, disfigured the horse by cutting off its mane and tail.

Houston sent the Lipan-Apaches a poem he wrote about the young Flacco. Perhaps no single piece of Houston's writings has been reprinted as often as the words he penned in condolence to Flacco the Elder on the death of his son Flacco the Younger:

My heart is sad!
A cloud rests upon your nation.
Grief has sounded in your camp;
The voice of Flacco is silent.

His words are not heard in council;
The chief is no more.
His life has fled to the Great Spirit,
His eyes are closed;
His heart no longer leaps
At the sight of the buffalo.

The voices of your camp
Are no longer heard to cry
"Flacco has returned from the chase."

Grass will not grow
On the path between us.
Let your wise men give counsel of peace,
Let your young men walk in the white path.
The gray-headed men of your nation
Will teach wisdom.

—Thy brother, Sam Houston.

After the death of their son, Flacco and his wife began to fast, a Lipan custom. When they visited Noah Smithwick, they had starved themselves until, said Smithwick, they looked like shriveled-up, desiccated mummies. Smithwick convinced them to end their fast and share a meal cooked by his wife.

The name of Flacco the Younger is remembered in large measure due to his connection with Jack Hays and Sam Houston. He is remembered because of his devoted friendship with Hays in his many battles against Comanches and because of Houston's poignant elegy on his death, who captured the Indian spirit when he wrote of Flacco that — "His heart no longer leaps at the sight of the buffalo.

Zachary Taylor

CHAPTER 10

PRELUDE TO WAR:
ZACHARY TAYLOR LANDS IN SOUTH TEXAS
1845

*Corpus Christi is healthy, easily supplied, and well situated to hold in
observance the course of the Rio Grande from Matamoros to Laredo, being
about 150 miles from several points on the river.*
       —Gen. Zachary Taylor's report to Washington

After James K. Polk was elected president, the United States rushed to annex Texas, with Congress approving annexation on March 1, 1845 and the Ninth Congress of the Republic of Texas quickly giving its consent.

Mexico had warned that any attempt to annex Texas, which it considered a rebellious province, would lead to war, even though Texas had won its independence nine years before at San Jacinto.

To protect Texas from any hostile reaction from Mexico, U.S. military forces were being pulled from forts all over the country, unit by unit, and concentrated in Louisiana at Fort Jesup near Natchitoches.

As Texas joined the Union, one question was whether Texas' southern boundary was the Nueces River — as Mexico claimed when it was not claiming all of Texas — or the Rio Grande. Officials of the Republic of Texas cited Henry Kinney's trading post at Corpus Christi as proof that Texas controlled the region between the rivers. This provided the basis for the U.S. claim that the southernmost boundary of Texas was the Rio Grande.

In June 1845, a month before Texas ratified annexation, Gen. Zachary Taylor was ordered to move his growing army from Louisiana to Texas, but he was to avoid any overt acts of aggression. When annexation resolutions were accepted by Congress, Taylor was told to move his whole command to the extreme western border of Texas.

Capt. W. W. S. Bliss, Taylor's chief of staff and soon to be his son-in-law, jocularly known in the Taylor family as "Perfect" Bliss, read the orders to Ethan Allen Hitchcock, one of Taylor's commanders. Hitchcock wrote in his

65

diary, "I scarcely slept a wink, thinking of the needful preparations. Violence leads to violence, and if this movement of ours does not lead to bloodshed, I am much mistaken."

As the formalities of annexation proceeded, Corpus Christi's Henry Kinney wrote letters to Andrew Jackson Donelson, the U.S. charge d'affaires in Austin, pointing out that Corpus Christi would make a good location for the army. Donelson passed this on to Taylor, adding that "Corpus Christi is said to be as healthy as Pensacola." It was in the disputed territory, but not so far in as to be provocative, and it was about the same distance — 150 miles — to any potential trouble spot on the Rio Grande, from Laredo to Matamoros.

Taylor prepared to move his army. The seven companies of the Second Dragoons were to travel by horseback from Fort Jesup to San Antonio. The rest of the army was to be transported from New Orleans by steamship to the western Gulf Coast of Texas.

Units of the 3rd Infantry began to leave Fort Jesup on river steamboats. Taylor stayed behind to see the Dragoons off, under the command of Col. David Twiggs. The fierce-tempered Twiggs, with an aureole of bristling white hair, was a favorite with his troops, even though he would "curse them right down to their boots."

After the Dragoons left Jesup, Taylor traveled in a steamboat to New Orleans. He shared a stateroom with a fellow traveler, who said the general talked about planting and crops "and appeared to be as ignorant of our army as if he had never seen it." Taylor — a thickset man with stubby legs — gained his reputation as a fighting man in the Black Hawk and Seminole Indian wars. He was more comfortable with farmers, planters and frontiersmen than gentlemen officers and West Pointers.

On July 22, 1845, the advance units of Taylor's army embarked in the middle of the night by the Lower Cotton Press in New Orleans. The first aboard the steamer *Alabama* were companies of the 3rd Infantry under the command of Lt. Col. Hitchcock. "The moon was just rising as we marched out," wrote Capt. W. S. Henry, "gilding the house-tops, and caused our bayonets to glisten in the mellow light."

After eight companies of the 3rd Infantry were embarked, the *Alabama* left port at 3 a.m. on July 23 and headed into the Gulf "to plant the flag of the United States in Texas," Hitchcock wrote in his diary. "Gen. Taylor is on board, in command of the army (to be) of occupation."

Three days later, the *Alabama* arrived at the Aransas Pass channel and anchored off the southern end of St Joseph's Island, across the pass from Mustang Island. The soldiers watched the shoreline with close attention. Hitchcock sent 1st Lt. D. T. Chandler, quartermaster of the 3rd Infantry, ashore to plant the U.S. flag over a sand dune on St. Joseph's. Officially, it was the first American flag to fly over Texas soil.

Men of the 3rd Infantry were ferried ashore. Hitchcock went in with the last of his men. "We have found good water," he wrote, "and had fish and oysters for breakfast. There are two or three families living on shore."

Some of the younger soldiers played in the surf like children. "The beach on St. Joseph's," wrote Lt. John James Peck, "excels even far-famed Rockaway for its bathing."

In letters to Washington, Taylor wrote that eight companies of the 3rd Infantry were temporarily camped on St. Joseph's. He was trying to decide between Corpus Christi or Live Oak Point as the place to concentrate his forces. Taylor went to Live Oak Point, where he dined at the home of empresario Col. James Power.

Taylor sent a scouting party to Corpus Christi before deciding that this site had certain advantages. One was a large flat tableland behind a high bluff where large bodies of troops could be drilled. Taylor wrote Washington that "Corpus Christi is healthy, easily supplied, and well situated to hold in observance the course of the Rio Grande from Matamoros to Laredo, being about 150 miles from several points on the river."

Disadvantages he didn't mention included a shortage of fresh water, a lack of trees for firewood, and the fact that Corpus Christi was at the back of a shallow bay which would make it difficult to transport supplies.

The lighter *Undine* drew four feet, but there were only three feet and a half of water over the mudflats blocking Corpus Christi Bay. Hitchcock advised Taylor to keep the army on St. Joseph's until a southwest wind would increase the depth of water over the shoals. But Taylor wanted no delay in getting the army settled at its place of encampment.

In Hitchcock's papers, it is clear that he and the general did not agree on hardly anything. Hitchcock, a West Pointer, had little respect for Taylor and, in return, the old Indian fighter thought little of West Pointers. One of the few West Pointers that Taylor trusted was his aide "Perfect" Bliss.

Most of Taylor's top commanders — Col. William Whistler of the Fourth Infantry, Lt. Col. James S. McIntosh, "Old Tosh," Brig. Gen. David E. Twiggs, Brig. Gen. William J. Worth, and Lt. Col. William G. Belknap, Worth's second in command — were not West Point graduates.[16] Hitchcock, West Pointer and martinet, was dismissive of Taylor's other colonels. He noted that "Whistler cannot give the simplest command and McIntosh is unable to maneuver a brigade." It would be the young officers of the army who would make a difference in the coming war, and they were all West Point-trained.

---

[16] The fort and the town of Belknap were named for Col. Belknap. The fort and the town of Fort Worth were named for Gen. William J. Worth.

As Taylor prepared to move the army from St. Joseph's to the mainland, he ignored Hitchcock's advice to wait for favorable winds. He ordered companies K and G of the 3rd Infantry to sail across the bay on the lighter *Undine* and set up camp at Corpus Christi. As Hitchcock had warned, the vessel ran aground in the shallow mudflats and remained stuck for two days. Lt. Napoleon Jackson Tecumseh Dana wrote his wife that the men got into waist-deep water to try to tow the vessel off. While they were stuck, Dana took his gun, jumped overboard, and went hunting. He shot two birds for his supper.

Local fishing boats were hired to ferry the soldiers to Corpus Christi. They had to move the men from the *Undine* to the smaller vessels, which were bobbing like corks in a peevish sea, and the soldiers were tossed and knocked about in the fishing boats. Dana wrote his wife that the prevailing wind on Corpus Christi Bay made it "the roughest piece of water for its size I have ever seen."

On July 31, 1845, fishing vessels with men from companies K and G of the 3rd Infantry anchored 400 yards off shore. They landed at sundown, in gathering darkness, in small boats. There was a tremendous sea running. "I tell you the waves were bigger than ever you saw," Dana wrote. "Where we were it was out of the question to land any of the baggage in the night. We were on a sand beach, with no tents and I had no blanket." Dana ate a supper of hard ship's biscuits and slept on a borrowed buffalo rug under a canopy of stars.

Next morning the surf was still cutting up high, but the soldiers, with much difficulty, were able to land supplies. They put up tents, looked for water, and killed rattlesnakes buzzing in the salt grass of what would later be called North Beach. Lt. Napoleon Jackson Tecumseh Dana in a letter to his wife wrote, "Yesterday morning Whiting (his brother-in-law, Daniel P. Whiting) found a huge rattlesnake coiled up at the foot of his bed and Lt. Smith had one crawl over his bare legs; he laid still until His Snakeship crawled off."

They were camped on the lower edge of the shoreline, with a rising bluff behind them to the south and west. Lt. John James Peck wrote that, "This is a pretty spot with a fine bay." Military order began to emerge with tents, squared, stretching in perfect order across the mud slough toward the small village.

"I am now here," Col. Hitchcock wrote in his diary, "with two companies of the 3rd Infantry — K and G — the first troops occupying the soil of Texas. Corpus Christi is a very small village at the head of the bay. Our arrival is hailed with satisfaction."

The soldiers were not impressed by the village. One wrote that as far as he could tell the place was half-Mexico and half-criminal. Corpus Christi was a small settlement with a few hundred people and a scattering of buildings. Lt.

Richard Wilson called it "the most murderous, thieving, gambling, God-forsaken hole in the Lone Star State, or out of it." Many of them considered it part of Mexico. Lt. Grant called it a "Mexican hamlet" and another lieutenant wrote his wife that "we are over the line in Mexico, and ready for anything."

Taylor's Army of Observation at Corpus Christi included half the total strength of the army in 1845-1846, about 4,000 men, making it the largest concentration of American troops since the war of 1812. There were four batteries of artillery, five regiments of infantry, and one regiment of dragoons. They would spend the coming months in training before the army marched to the Rio Grande, closer to the actual theater of war.

Within days of the army's arrival, some officers were invited to dine at the home of merchant Frederick Belden and his wife Mauricia Arocha Belden. Capt. W. S. Henry said they were given a dish called "themales" (tamales) "made of corn meal, chopped meat, and cayenne pepper wrapped in a piece of corn husk, and boiled. I know of nothing more palatable."

On Aug. 15, 1845, two weeks after the first troops landed on North Beach, Taylor and staff arrived. Taylor issued his first order from Corpus Christi. The heading shows he was no longer calling it the Army of Observation but the Army of Occupation. Taylor in letters to Washington called the encampment Fort Marcy, naming it after his boss and friend, Secretary of War William Marcy. Although Taylor called it a fort in reality it was a camp with improvised dirt embankments in some places.

Col. Hitchcock, commander of the 3rd Infantry, had embankments thrown up as a line of defense, not knowing what to expect. Since no artillery had arrived, he borrowed two old cannons from Kinney, the founder of Corpus Christi. The old cannon, W. S. Henry reckoned, "were more dangerous to ourselves than to any enemy."

The lighter *Undine* had been trying to ferry soldiers from St. Joseph's to the encampment at Corpus Christi, but drew too much water to cross over the mudflats between Corpus Christi and the Aransas Pass channel. The *Undine* was replaced by a small steamboat hired in Galveston, the *Dayton*.

Other units arrived and the army settled into the routine of soldiering, with drills, marching, and target practice. Lt. Abner Doubleday wrote that "the Mexican Army being largely composed of cavalry, and a collision being more than probable, our infantry were constantly drilled in forming square to resist cavalry."

Sgt. George K. Donnelly wrote a friend, "We have been firing ball cartridges at targets. And in almost every instance, at a hundred paces, the targets fall shattered to the ground."

Officers on a three-day hunting trip to the Nueces River bottoms killed deer, geese, and a seven-foot panther that sprang at a lieutenant. The panther missed and when he tried again, the lieutenant shot him in the head.

"No one but the most irreclaimable cynic," wrote W. S. Henry, "could have ridden over this beautiful country in the vicinity of the Nueces without being enchanted with its beauty."

The soldiers dug a water well at what would later be called Artesian Park. The water had an unpleasant, acrid taste and smell. For drinking and for cooking, they hauled water in wooden casks from the Nueces River.[17]

Basic military training for setting up a campsite, dating back to the Roman legions, seems to have been ignored. It called for choosing a campsite on high ground, with good drainage, with sanitation trenches on lower ground, and the camp within easy reach of wood and water. The encampment at Corpus Christi, Fort Marcy, violated all the military rules.

Lt. Dana, in a letter to his wife, said they were kept busy clearing ground, digging wells, and that there was still a great amount of work to be done. "I have not changed my shirt for five days," he wrote. "I have not shaved for a week. You never saw such a hairy looking set of fellows in your life." He doubted they would ever look clean again.

In the third week of August 1845, Henry Kinney returned from Austin escorted by two Lipan-Apache Indians. One night the Lipan chief was shot in the head and chest. Dana said the wounds he sustained were enough to kill half a dozen men. Suspicion fell on a man named Louis Cook, who had lost an eye to an Indian arrow in a raid on Corpus Christi the year before. When Cook was questioned about the shooting he denied it and there was no evidence to charge him.

As the army trained, traders arrived from Mexico to buy goods from the merchants in Corpus Christi who specialized in the Mexican trade. The Mexican traders brought horses, mules, blankets, and crude silver bars. "They bring their money in silver bars, molded in sand, each embracing $50 to $60 of pure silver," wrote Hitchcock. The Mexican blankets they brought were said to be of unsurpassed beauty. The traders sold their goods and bought leaf tobacco and cotton domestics to sell in Mexico.

Gen. Taylor questioned Kinney's spy, Chipito Sandoval, for news of army movements in Mexico. Chipito was described as a man with dark piercing eyes, a man "devotedly attached to Col. Kinney."

On Aug. 24, 1845, a violent thunderstorm struck. Henry said the storm "would take your breath away, and make you sit bolt upright in your chair, feet on the rung, as if your life depended on it." During the storm, a baby was born to a woman laundress and W. S. Henry thought it should have been named "Thunder."

---

[17] Norwick Gussett, a sergeant in Grant's company, was a wagon-master who hauled water from the Nueces River to the encampment. After the war, Gussett returned to the Corpus Christi area and became one of the town's wealthiest wool merchants in the 1870s.

A lightning bolt hit a tent center pole and killed a slave owned by Lt. Braxton Bragg. The man killed was sitting with his head leaning against the tent pole. The air in the tent smelled like sulfur.

On Aug. 27th, Twiggs' Dragoons arrived at Corpus Christi and began to set up camp. Twiggs left two companies as an outpost at the all but deserted Irish settlement of San Patricio upriver from Corpus Christi.

On the following day, the steamship *Alabama* arrived off Aransas Pass with three companies of the 7th Infantry, which had been left behind at New Orleans Barracks when the 3rd Army left on July 23. As troops and supplies were offloaded to a lighter, Lt. Ulysses S. Grant fell head-first into the bay. Men lining the rail were laughing as he was hauled back on deck, like a wet parcel.

Two weeks later, on Sept. 12, the boilers on the steamship *Dayton*, leased by the Army, exploded off McGloin's Bluff, near today's Ingleside. The wounded and dead were brought to Corpus Christi. The toll from the *Dayton* explosion was 17 wounded and 10 killed. Col. Hitchcock picked a burial site on a hill overlooking Nueces and Corpus Christi bays.[18] W. S. Henry wrote that the burial ceremony on Sept. 13th was impressive, with the Fourth Regiment Band playing Handel's "Dead March in Saul."

"The sun had just set; the clouds, piled up in pyramids, were tinged with golden light; flashes of lightning were seen in the north; the pale moon, in the east, was smiling sweetly," wrote Henry. "The service of the dead was read by the light of a lamp. Three volleys were fired over their graves. The escort wheeled into column and, to a lively air from fife and drum, we left the soldiers to their long sleep. May the God of Battles receive and cherish them."

As the army continued to concentrate with the steady arrival of fresh units, the encampment stretched from North Beach almost to the town of Corpus Christi two miles away. The army was composed of about 3,900 men — "quite a dangerous crowd to fall in with," wrote Henry. Among the men were Texas Rangers under John Coffee Hays.

While Hays was respected by the army officers for his reputation as a fearless Indian fighter, the regular officers didn't think much of the Rangers. Lt. Dana wrote his wife that "the best of them looked like they could steal sheep." For their part, the Rangers knew how to provoke the soldiers, saying that they had been summoned, in the event of any hostile moves from Mexico, to protect the army.

During the pleasant days of October, some of the men slept outside their tents on beds of straw. Soldiers found that wild mustangs were cheap and Lt. Grant, a fine rider who loved horses, bought four mustang ponies. A free

---

[18] This was the beginning of Corpus Christi's oldest cemetery, Old Bayview.

black man named Valere, a hired servant who cooked and cleaned for Grant, was taking his horses to water and let them get away. Capt. Bliss, Taylor's adjutant, joked, "I heard that Grant lost five or six dollars' worth of horses the other day."

The men spent a lot of time buying and selling or racing horses. Henry wrote that almost every day for a month some kind of race was held. He described one race, for 300 yards, between two mustang ponies. "One pony bolted, and, not at all alarmed by the crowd, cleared two or three piles of rubbish, knocked one man down, threw his rider, ran about 50 yards, stopped, turned around, and snorted — as much as to say, 'Beat that if you can.' "

Wet weather began in late October. The men stared out their tent flaps at the incessantly falling rain. Lt. Dana wrote, "All is damp and wet and everything feels nasty."

On Dec. 3, the camp was hit by a norther and next morning every tent had a covering of ice. "The cracking of the canvas sounded like anything but music." The temperature dropped to 23 degrees and the cold stunned fish and turtles in the bays. Cartloads of fish and green sea turtles were gathered along the reef. Soldiers surrounded the camp with chaparral brush to help screen the bitterly cold wind.

Diarrhea and dysentery, which had plagued the army since its arrival, increased during the winter months. An average of 10 percent of the officers and 13 percent of the men were on sick rolls. The weather was awful, the water brackish, the men sick from dysentery or just plain ill-tempered. They were worn out by sickness, hardship, and exposure.

Even though the army was having a hard winter, Taylor wrote Secretary of War William Marcy that they could get by without having to build huts for winter quarters, that tents would suffice. The army's cemetery on the bluff, picked out by Hitchcock after the *Dayton* explosion, was needed again as men began to die from dysentery and other causes linked to bad water, poor sanitation, and the cold rainy weather.

New Year's Day 1846 marked the appearance of the *Corpus Christi Gazette*, published by pioneer Texas printer Samuel Bangs, who came over from Galveston. The editor of the paper was an influential member of the Mexican community, Jose de Alba. The newspaper cost 10 cents a copy. That first issue listed the units and officers in Taylor's army.

The first edition of the *Gazette* reported that a play called "The Wife" would open at the Army Theater, which had been constructed by army officers led by Capt. John B. Magruder of the 1st Artillery. Grant, because of his "girlish good looks," was coerced into playing Desdemona in "Othello." The officer cast to play the Moor couldn't look at Grant in a dress without breaking into laughter, so they sent to New Orleans for a professional actress. Gertrude Hart arrived to play the part.

On Feb. 16, 1846, Texas officially joined the Union. An "Annexation Ball" was held at the Union Theater, with music provided by the five army bands. Among the tunes played was one created for the occasion called the "Taylor Quick Step." The town's leading citizens and army officers attended the ball.

February was spent with intense activity in preparation for the army's departure. It was an open secret that any day Taylor would order the army to move to the Rio Grande. One question was why move the army since no threat to Texas had materialized along the border. At Corpus Christi, Taylor's army was still in a strategic position to protect Texas in the event of any hostile reaction to the annexation from Mexico. Some officers, including Grant and Hitchcock, believed the army had been sent not to protect Texas, but to provoke Mexico into starting a war. If the army had been placed at Corpus Christi as bait, it had not worked. If it was too far away to incite any aggressive reaction, then the army would have to be moved closer to Mexico. That was Grant's opinion — "We were sent to provoke a fight," Grant wrote, "but it was essential that Mexico should commence it."

The camp was all hurry and suppressed excitement as Gen. Taylor began to prepare to move his army to the border. For weeks he had the quartermasters scouring the area buying horses, mules, oxen, and wagons to carry the army's supplies and equipment.

Taylor sent two patrols to look for a suitable route of march. One party, under the command of Lt. George Gordon Meade, traveled down the middle of Padre Island. They found the bones of shipwreck victims, attached to ship hatch covers, and a large number of half-wild cattle that had belonged to Padre Nicolás Balli. Another scouting party followed the old Matamoros Road. They described the route as good for most of the distance with adequate water and grass. Because of a shortage of forage for horses and draft animals and the difficulty of marching through the dunes of Padre Island, Taylor chose the inland route.

Gen. Taylor issued the army's marching orders, which were printed in the *Gazette*: "The Army of Occupation is about to take up a position on the left bank of the Rio Grande. As the army marches south, the commanding general wishes it distinctly understood that no person not properly attached to it will be permitted to accompany the troops." Despite Taylor's orders, however, camp followers managed to do what camp followers always do, they followed the army. The gamblers and saloon-keepers and prostitutes, literally hundreds of them, managed to make their way south, either with the army or just behind the army.

While the soldiers knew they might be jumping from the frying pan into a hot fire, they were ready to leave, happy to be going somewhere, in a state of excitement and impatience.

"We are delighted at the prospects of the march," W. S. Henry wrote, "having become restless and anxious for a change; we anticipate no little fun, and all sorts of adventure, upon the route."

Sgt. Charles Masland of the 3rd Infantry wrote his brother: "Packing up was the order of the day. Here and there might be seen groups of Mexicans bargaining with our men for wearing apparel, and giving cash for what they might have had for nothing in a few days, for we could not carry half our 'plunder.' "

Impatient to get on with the war, the army was ready to march. U.S. Grant would later say that a better army, man for man, probably never faced an enemy.

In the coming war in Mexico, Zachary Taylor's top commanders were superannuated seniors who squabbled among themselves over brevet rank and everything else. That the war would ultimately be won was due in no small part to young West Point-trained officers who were stationed at Corpus Christi, and with Wool's Brigade at San Antonio, from the late summer of 1845 until March 1846.[19]

The seven months spent at Corpus Christi helped meld disparate units into a real army, but lack of good water, bad sanitation, prevalent sickness, inadequate tents that were often water-logged and offered little protection against the fierce northers, made them more than ready to leave. And they were eager for a fight. Their fighting abilities would soon be tested at places they had never heard of — Palo Alto and Resaca de la Palma, as well as famous battles to come in Mexico.

On Sunday morning, March 8, 1846, Taylor's army, unit by unit, decamped and began its long march to the Rio Grande. Elements of the 3rd Infantry, which had been the first to arrive, were the last to leave. Capt. W. S. Henry looked back at the site where the army had camped for the past seven months. "The fields of white canvas were no longer visible and the campground looked like desolation itself, but the bright waters of the bay looked as sweet as ever."

Taylor's army on its way south followed the old Camino Real, also known as the Matamoros Road, the same route the Mexican Army used after its defeat at San Jacinto. The 174-mile journey took 20 days of hard marching. Capt. W. S. Henry related details and stopping places of that march.

"March 11th (1846). The 3rd Brigade left their old stomping ground (Corpus Christi). We were the first to arrive, the last to leave. The day was

---

[19] Many of these young officers became famous generals in the Civil War, including George B. Thomas, the Rock of Chickamauga, James Longstreet, Braxton Bragg, Kirby Smith, George Meade, John Reynolds, Earl Van Dorn, George McClellan, John Bankhead Magruder and Ulysses S. Grant.

oppressively hot. After a march of 16 miles, we encamped on the Nueces. March 12th. A cold dreary morning. Route over a monotonous level prairie, called in Texas, from its peculiar appearance, Hogwallow Prairie. Our course was nearly west. Owing to the roads being so heavy, we marched only eight miles.

"March 13th. Our course today was southwest, crossed the Agua Dulce, a small stream about three miles from our last camp. Marched 11 miles and encamped at Los Pintas, some very extensive water holes.

"March 14th. Our course today has been nearly south. The morning was very cold, and we had quite a heavy frost. The road was very hard and some of the men became rather tender-footed. We reached San Gertrude about 4 p.m. and encamped. The water was quite brackish.

"Sunday, 15th. The road was very hard, and looked simply, by the passage of the advance brigades, like a well-beaten turnpike. "Taylor's Trail" will never be obliterated. We reached our camp, Santa Clara Motts, having marched 13 miles by 12 noon, under a scorching sun.

"March 16th. The dust was completely suffocating. Marched 13 miles and encamped at El Pista.

"March 17th. We entered a region of the country where the live-oak flourished. To the eye the whole country was beautiful; nothing can exceed in beauty the islands and clumps of oak stretching out in every diversity of form over a gently undulating country; but when you come to the feet it is a very different matter. It is deep, deep sand, of the heaviest description. We have entered upon that part of the country laid down as desert, midway between the Nueces and the Rio Grande. The men suffered a great deal from the heat and dust. Our road lives along the trail over which Gen. Filisola retreated after the battle of San Jacinto. The terrible suffering of his men is beyond description.

"March 18th. Did not march until 8 o'clock. By starting so late, the dew was off the sand, which rose in thick clouds to envelope, blind and choke us. We had 14 miles to march to get water, and were forced to halt repeatedly, and the men sat down, with parched mouths, upon the hot sand, with the tropical sun beating on them. The sand was like hot ashes and when you stepped upon it you sank up to the ankle. Many gave out, and lay down by the roadside perfectly exhausted, looking as if they did not care for life."

Officers and men had their lips and noses nearly raw from the sun and winds, wrote Samuel G. French, and could not put a cup of coffee to their lips until it was cold. "I wore an immense sombrero. On the route I was often told: 'When Gen. Taylor comes up you will be put in arrest for wearing that hat.' When the general commanding overtook us, I went over to call on him and found him in front of his tent sitting on a camp stool eating breakfast. His table was the lid of a mess chest. His nose was white from the peeling off of the skin, and his lips raw. As I came up he saluted me with, 'Good morning, lieutenant. Sensible man to wear a hat.' So I was commended instead of being censured for making myself comfortable."

Daniel P. Whiting

CHAPTER 11

DANIEL WHITING,
SARAH BOURJETT
AND THE BOMBARDMENT OF FORT BROWN
1846

You son of a bitch, there ain't Mexicans enough in Mexico to whip old Taylor. You spread that rumor and I'll beat you to death.
                              —Sarah Bourjett, the Great Western

On Sunday morning, March 8, 1846, the first units of the Zachary Taylor-led army left Corpus Christi, where it had been concentrated for seven months, for the Rio Grande 130 miles away. As they marched out of the small settlement on Corpus Christi Bay, army drummers beat out their old marching-away tune, "The Girl I Left Behind Me." The army left, brigade by brigade, on successive days.

Capt. Daniel P. Whiting, a veteran of the Seminole Wars in Florida and garrison duty in Indian Territory, like many of the officers in Taylor's command, marched at the head of his company in the 7th Regiment. Sarah Bourjett, who became well-known as "The Great Western," drove a mule-cart carrying her food supplies in the rear of Whiting's company.

Whiting wrote in his diary that he was broken down by the time they reached a camping place at Twelve Mile Motts, 12 miles up the river from Corpus Christi. He was less tired the next day but still regretted he was a captain of foot and not riding a horse. They marched 16 miles the second day and camped at Agua Dulce, then reached Santa Gertrudis Creek, where the King Ranch headquarters would later be built, on the third day.

Whiting got used to the rigors of the march and by the fourth day, "I arrived at camp quite efficient and elastic and afterwards, and throughout the war, I continued my pedestrianism, never mounted, without fatigue or weariness, and many a stout man succumbed where I never faltered."

On the ninth day of the march they halted for a blow in the middle of a prairie. As they rested, wild cattle were seen in the distance and several riders

79

gave chase. A soldier servant to a captain, an Irishman riding a pony, chased a longhorn bull, which ran toward the soldiers resting on the ground. The bull was running along the column when the servant fired. He missed the bull, but the ball struck near the resting soldiers. They later heard in camp the wife of the servant berating her husband — "A fine marksman you are. Shoot at a bull and miss a regiment."

They arrived at the Arroyo Colorado 30 miles north of the Rio Grande on March 20, 1846. When Mexican troops appeared on the opposite bank, Whiting's brigade formed ranks in battle order, with a battery in position, before they entered the ford. The Americans waded across, in water up to their armpits, and gained the opposite shore, 500 yards away. They met no resistance, the Mexican troops falling back toward Matamoros.

Whiting's company, with the rest of Taylor's army, reached the Rio Grande on March 25. They raised the American flag next to the river, opposite Matamoros "to the indignation of the good people of that city."

The American soldiers went to work building a set of field works, as laid out by the engineers, opposite Matamoros. When finished, the dirt banked fort had six bastions, with walls nine feet high, a parapet of 15 feet, and the whole surrounded by a ditch 15 feet deep. They called it Fort Texas.

While they were building the fort, Seth B. Thornton, a captain of dragoons with a reputation for being headstrong and reckless, led a squadron of 63 dragoons into a trap at a Mexican rancho 16 miles up the river. They were surrounded and attacked by a larger force of Mexican troops. Sixteen dragoons were killed in the fight and 47 captured. Gen. Taylor wrote Washington — "Hostilities may now be considered as commenced."

Taylor began to worry about Point Isabel, his base of supplies, near the mouth of the Rio Grande, 26 miles away. The supplies that were brought by wagon from Corpus Christi were running out and it was not safe to send a wagon train to Point Isabel, with Mexican army units hovering in the vicinity, without a strong covering force.

Taylor divided his forces, taking 2,000 men and hundreds of wagons to Point Isabel to get supplies and leaving behind 500 men of the 7th Infantry, under the command of Major Jacob Brown. The garrison forces included Whiting's company.

Whiting wrote in his memoirs that the new field work was finished on the first of May, except for a portion of the rear face and sally port. The 7th moved in and camped in the interior. When the rest of the army left with Taylor for Point Isabel, they left their baggage and women behind at the fort.

Just after Reveille on May 3, 1846, as Whiting was washing his face a round shot passed over the fort from the Mexican side, making a peculiar rushing sound, followed by another and still another in rapid succession. Whiting ran out and found his men running to get into position for an attack.

They were excited but "attended to their duties with great coolness and discipline."

As the bombardment began, Whiting wrote, the American flag was still located near the bank in front, but had not been raised. His sub, Earl Van Dorn, a native of Mississippi, volunteered to raise it, but Major Brown said it would be too dangerous. Van Dorn replied that "it ought to be elevated, as it will not answer to be fighting without our banner."

"Do it then," said Brown.

Van Dorn and several volunteers hoisted the flag while "every gun in the Mexican batteries bore upon the spot, the balls thickly furrowing the ground about it, but the party retired within the fort again after coolly accomplishing their object, without loss or injury."

Twenty-six miles away, as Taylor's soldiers were loading supplies at Point Isabel, they heard the cannon fire that signaled the beginning of the bombardment of Fort Texas by Mexican batteries across the river. Some officers with Taylor wanted to drop everything and rush to the defense of the fort. They listened to the distant guns.

"What Gen. Taylor's feelings were during this suspense I do not know," U.S. Grant wrote in his memoirs, "but as for myself, a young second lieutenant who had never heard a hostile gun before, I felt sorry that I enlisted."

Fort Texas was under bombardment from the Mexican batteries across the river. At the angle of the fort nearest the enemy, the bastion was furnished with a battery of four 24-pounders under the command of Capt. Allen Loud, whose guns began to fire back.

From the other side, Mexican guns were firing from the main battery, at the lower end of the city, and from a sand-bag redoubt opposite the ferry landing, where there was a single gun of large caliber.

"We could see its black muzzle with the naked eye from our parapet," Whiting wrote in his memoirs. "From the redoubt, at point blank distance, active discharge was commenced at the same time with the lower battery." When Capt. Loud directed one of his 24s at its gaping embrasure, one discharge was sufficient to put it out of action. Gun carriage and Mexican gunners flew into the air. The redoubt, a shattered wreck, was cleared of its occupants, who were seen running away. The main battery continued to fire. Capt. Loud occasionally fired back, but he ceased firing when he had used half his ammunition with no appreciable effect.

As Whiting's company was forming, a bomb plunged into the ground a few feet in front, the fuse burning. "I ordered my men to throw themselves flat on the ground, giving them the example myself at the same time. No sooner had we done so than the shell exploded, tearing up the ground for several yards, but all the fragments flying upward cleared the fort without further injury.

The next minute grapeshot struck a sergeant near me on the head; he was never aware of the fatal cause. Except this instance and that of Maj. Brown, our commander, who was afterwards killed, no deaths occurred, though many were wounded by fragments."

Casualties were low in the bombardment, wrote Whiting, "from the want of care or skill by the enemy in graduating their fuses. These should have ignited the bombs just before reaching the ground, whereas the explosion did not take place until after they had buried themselves, and even then, being of copper, only flew into two or three pieces." Whiting knew they would have been far more lethal, splintering into many fragments, if they had been made of iron.

After the guns inside the fort ceased fire, to save the scarce supply of shells, the Mexican forces extended their mortar batteries to an opposite point. The shells and cannonballs struck from so many directions that "it exercised our ingenuity in dodging them. The increasing accuracy and rapidity with which the bombs were showered upon us rendered necessary some defensive resort." During the night, the men were put to work erecting bomb-proofs — covered ways for protection — with whatever material they could find to block the jagged, flying pieces of shrapnel.

"One party piled the baggage, a large pile, which had been left by the absent troops, such as trunks, rolls of bedding, tents, into a mass above supporting articles that left space beneath in which to retire, while others placed double rows of our barrels of provisions, crossing them with sticks from the woodpile and heaping upon them a sufficient thickness of earth. Into these nests all withdrew themselves, except the sentries at the bastions during the day time."

They huddled under their bomb-proofs during the daylight hours. Whiting said their moral endurance was strongly tested by the suspension of activity and exertion, expecting an attack at any minute, while the enemy gunners were fast improving in accuracy and skill.

Chicken coops in the fort were knocked open and the chickens ran loose around the tents. One was killed by a flying fragment and Whiting's servant, an Irishman named Mac, prepared it for Whiting's dinner. "Frequently after, without waiting for an 'accident,' Mac served a fowl for our repast, accounting to no one for the delicacy, but often remarking, in soliloquy, whenever a shell burst in the fort, 'There goes another chicken.' "

Whiting said he usually wore a slouched black hat that at a distance looked not unlike the chapeau of a field officer. He was standing near a bastion when several shots struck nearby. Someone cried out, "Captain, look out, they are shooting at you! It must be your hat." The Mexican forces, said Whiting, had several sharp-shooting guns of small caliber. "Just then a ball about the size of a grapeshot struck the bastion about two inches from my head and rolled to

82

my feet. I squatted on the ground. Putting the hat on a stick, I repeatedly raised it above the line and as often as I did so, whiz!, came one of the balls. This convinced me that I should be cautious how I showed my hat, especially when my head was in it."

After Taylor left for Point Isabel, Mexican forces under Gen. Mariano Arista crossed the river and took a position to block his return. Their pickets and scouting parties could be seen by the soldiers in Fort Texas. About midnight May 4, a dispatch rider from Gen. Taylor slipped through the Mexican lines and reached the fort, bringing the message that Taylor would spare no effort to come to the fort's rescue.

On May 6, the commander of the fort, Major Jacob Brown, was making his round of inspection when he was struck in the leg by a shell. He was carried into one of the bomb-proof shelters. He died two days later and was buried in silence, below the rampart near the flagstaff.

On the same day, they received a demand to surrender from Gen. Pedro Ampudia, in command at Matamoros. This was declined. Anticipating an attack the following night, the men in Fort Texas slept at their posts. Whiting noted that the night passed quietly, "except for the whirring of a few bullets and the solitary blast of a trumpeter above us on our side of the river as he lay upon his belly in the grass."

The bombardment continued the next day. On May 7, supply wagons were loaded at Point Isabel and Taylor started to return to relieve the besieged Fort Texas. Grant wrote that they traveled over a treeless prairie until they reached a wooded area known as Palo Alto, tall trees, in the early afternoon of May 8.

As they approached Palo Alto, they could see a Mexican army of about 6,000 men, three times their strength, drawn up in line of battle in front of the stand of timber. Grant said their bayonets and spearheads glistened in the sun.

At Fort Texas, they heard a distant cannonading. They could see rising columns of smoke and knew that it meant that Taylor's forces were close at hand and engaged with the Mexican army. After a few hours, all became quiet and the men in the fort scanned the horizon and listened for the sound of guns.

At Palo Alto, Taylor sat on his horse — he often rode side-saddle — and without apparent concern formed a line of battle. He had two batteries of 18-pounder guns placed at intervals along the line and he had 12-pounder howitzers, which could be moved as needed on the battlefield. Orders were given, Grant wrote, for a platoon from each company to stack arms and fill canteens for the benefit of the rest of the companies. When they were back with filled canteens, the order to advance was given.

The Mexicans opened fire with their artillery, which fired only solid shot from six-pounder brass guns. "They hurt no one," Grant wrote, "because they would strike the ground long before they reached our line and ricochet through the tall grass so slowly that the men would see them and open ranks and let them pass. When we got to a point where the artillery could be used with effect, a halt was called, and the battle opened on both sides."

During the artillery exchange, grass tall as a man caught fire and smoke shrouded the battlefield. Taylor used this smoke screen to redeploy his troops. Gen. Manuel Arista attacked the left of Taylor's line, but was driven back by Taylor's field artillery, including the 12-pounder howitzers.

Near sunset, the Mexicans began falling back and Taylor's troops advanced to occupy the ground that had been held by the Mexican troops. There was a brisk fire from the Mexican artillery, and Grant saw a cannonball pass through their ranks, "not far from me," which took off the head of an enlisted man.

The first battle of the Mexican War ended as darkness fell. American casualties were nine killed and 47 wounded. Arista lost more than 200 men, killed and wounded.

Next morning, Arista retreated and Taylor moved in pursuit. In the middle of the afternoon on May 9, they reached a succession of ponds, an old channel of the Rio Grande called Resaca de la Palma.

Arista's forces formed on the opposite bank and moved brush and cut down trees to their front. Their artillery was placed to cover the approaches. As Taylor's troops advanced, Grant was with his company on the right wing. "The balls commenced to whistle very thick overhead, cutting the limbs of the chaparral right and left, and we could not see the enemy, so I ordered my men to lie down, an order that did not have to be enforced."

Grant saw a clear space between two ponds and advanced with his company. They met with no resistance and captured a Mexican colonel. Grant soon learned that the Mexican colonel had already been captured by another unit.

Grant said his exploit was equal to that of the soldier who boasted that he had cut off the leg of one of the enemy. "When asked why he did not cut off his head, he replied, 'Someone had already done that.' This left no doubt in my mind that the battle of Resaca de la Palma would have been won, just as it was, if I had not been there."

At Resaca de la Palma, the second major engagement of the Mexican War fought on Texas soil, Taylor lost 150 men to 1,200 Mexicans killed or wounded. The coming of war seemed to have an inevitability that the battles of Palo Alto and Resaca de la Palma and bombardment of Fort Texas merely confirmed.

At Fort Texas, the men thronged the ramparts and watched retreating masses of Mexican troops crossing the river a mile above the fort. They could see the pursuing infantry and charging dragoons, with the Stars and Stripes floating in their midst. The bombardment of the fort ceased.

The fort was soon crowded with Taylor's returning soldiers who, Whiting wrote, were astounded at the appearance of the fort, the grounds scarred and pitted from the bombardment. "When they left, the order and finish were complete, nothing obstructed the interior esplanade, which was smooth and even, and the slopes and grading of the parapet and bastions were perfect from under the supervision of the engineers who had constructed them. When now surveyed, however, the contrast was great. The whole interior was plowed and furrowed by exploding bombs, dug up and piled in heaps and ridges, amid battered rubbish and bursting baggage. Tents riddled by shot and shell were in tattered ruins while the torn parapets and ranged embankments testified to the vindictiveness of the siege."

On May 17, as Taylor prepared to cross the river and attack Matamoras, the city surrendered and was occupied by American troops the next day, while Mexican forces retreated toward Monterrey, 200 miles west.

Whiting visited Matamoras and saw the damage the American artillery had made throughout the city. "Entering some of the houses I found the city was crowded with wounded Mexican soldiers from the preceding battles. I returned with a sad heart to the fort."[20] Gen. Taylor proclaimed an order renaming the battered Fort Texas as "Fort Brown" in honor of the late Maj. Jacob Brown. The town that would soon grow up around the fort became Brownsville.

* * *

The legendary Great Western — Sarah Bourjett — was also in the battle of Fort Brown.

She was born in Tennessee about 1817. Her first husband enlisted in the 8th Regular Infantry at Jefferson Barracks, Mo. When Taylor's army landed in Corpus Christi in July, 1845, Sgt. Bourjett and Sarah were with it. She was a towering Amazon, 6-foot-3, weighed 200 pounds, and had flaming red hair and flashing blue eyes.

When she got off the boat at Corpus Christi, an awestruck soldier said she reminded him of the biggest and most famous ship of the day, with its twin smokestacks, a British steamer named *The Great Western*.

"Look at the size of her," he said, "she's as big as the *Great Western*." The name stuck.

Officially, she was a laundress. In the army, four women were authorized to wash and mend the clothes of each company. They had to be wives of soldiers or officially connected to the army. They were paid with wages deducted from the soldiers' pay. Unofficially, Sarah Bourjett was known to

---

[20] Capt. Whiting was in the battles of Monterrey, Veracruz and Cerro Gordo. The Mexican War veteran died on Aug. 2, 1892, at the home of his daughter in Washington at age 85.

run establishments for army men as a camp follower, operating under the official sanction of being a laundress and wife of a sergeant in the 7th Infantry.

Capt. Whiting wrote in his memoirs that during the winter he had a mess, composed of his company officers, which was conducted by the wife of one of his sergeants. "The Great Western she was called from being a gigantic woman of great strength and hardihood who afterwards became quite famous in connection with the service. I was one day attracted by hearing a noise in my campground, and looking out, saw her pick up a man who had offended her and, as if he were a child, set him down in her wash tub."

When the army moved to the Rio Grande in March, 1846, Sarah's husband was sent by sea to Point Isabel; perhaps he was ill, but he soon dropped out of the picture. Camp followers were not allowed to tag along but Sarah, as a laundress, was allowed to go. She bought a mule-drawn cart to make the trip. Her cart was filled with pots, pans and provisions to set up an officers' mess for men of the 7th Infantry.

Whiting's company reached the Arroyo Colorado on March 20, 1846. They ran into a company of Mexican cavalry. When the Mexican horsemen taunted them from across the river, the Great Western left her wagon and shouted that if someone would give her a pair of pants, she would wade the river "and whip any scoundrel who dares show himself."

During the siege and bombardment of Fort Texas, Sarah cooked and tended the wounded. The story was told that she was in the thick of the fighting and that a fragment of a shell tore a hole in her bonnet. One fanciful story had her taking the place of a dead soldier and manning a cannon. Other versions, however, say that she proved most useful during the bombardment by preparing meals and attending the wounded.

The account by Capt. Whiting is no doubt more accurate. "We had our merriment," Whiting wrote in his memoirs. "Mrs. Bourjett, the Great Western, abandoned our mess when the firing began and resorted with the other women and noncombatants to a shelter." Whatever her role was during the bombardment of Fort Brown, the Great Western became famous throughout the army for her part in the battle and her bravery at the Arroyo Colorado. She was the talk of the army.

When Taylor's army moved on to Monterrey, she went with it and opened a place called The American House in Monterrey, providing food and other comforts for soldiers. When the army moved to Saltillo, she opened a second American House there.[21] After Taylor's army was attacked by Mexican forces at Buena Vista, five miles from Saltillo, it was said that a soldier from

---

[21] A painting of her by Samuel Chamberlain, one of Taylor's dragoons, shows her in her Saltillo establishment.

Indiana ran into the American House and in a panic yelled that the army was all cut to pieces and that the Mexicans were headed for Saltillo. The Great Western cuffed the unfortunate soldier, sending him sprawling, saying, "You son of a bitch, there ain't Mexicans enough in Mexico to whip old Taylor. You spread that rumor and I'll beat you to death."

One of her favorite soldiers, whom she treated like a son, was killed while trying to rally an Illinois regiment at the Battle of Buena Vista. His name was Capt. George Lincoln. The story was told that she ventured onto the battlefield to recover his body, laid it out for burial, and removed his ring and a lock of hair to send his parents.

After the war was over and the Treaty of Guadalupe Hidalgo signed, elements of the U.S. Army were sent to take possession of California. Since the army's departure would have a depressing effect on Sarah's business, she packed up and was ready to leave with the army.

An officer described what happened, "She rode up to Major Buckner and asked permission to go with us. He informed her that if she would marry one of the dragoons, and be mustered in as a laundress, she could go. Her ladyship gave the military salute and then, riding along the front of the line, said, 'Who wants a wife with $15,000 and the biggest leg in Mexico? Come, my beauties, don't all speak at once — who's the lucky man?' A man named Davis stepped forward and accepted the offer."

The "marriage" lasted until they reached El Paso, where the Great Western opened a place called the Central Hotel in 1849. It was here that the legendary Texas Ranger Rip Ford ran into her and later wrote that "she could whip any man, fair fight or foul, could shoot a pistol better than anyone in West Texas, and at blackjack could outplay the slickest professional gambler."

She moved on to New Mexico and Arizona, operating places of business along the way. She died from the bite of a tarantula spider on Dec. 23, 1866 at Yuma, Ariz. She was buried with full military honors at Fort Yuma. Sarah Bourjett, the Great Western, was one of the most remarkable women of the Mexican War and the Old West.

CHAPTER 12

BILLY ROGERS,
MUSTANG GRAY
AND RETRIBUTION ON THE RIO GRANDE
1846 — 1848

We saw the remains of no less than seven of the unfortunate Rogers party.
The wolves and buzzards had done their work.

—George Wilkins Kendall

A t the start of the Mexican War, William Long "Billy" Rogers
survived a massacre near the Rio Grande on the Arroyo Colorado. In
later years, fantastic things were said about "Billy" Rogers, which
may be true.

Billy Rogers was born in Alabama in 1822. He was one of 10 children of
Patterson and Elizabeth Rogers. Patterson Rogers fought in the Seminole
Wars in Florida, where he became a friend of Zachary Taylor, then he ran a
hotel at Fort Jesup, La., that catered to the army. His son-in-law, Roswell
Denton, was an army sutler, a storekeeper authorized to sell goods on a
military post.

When Gen. Zachary Taylor brought half the U.S. Army to Corpus Christi in
1845, as Texas joined the Union, the Rogers family followed. When the army
moved to the Rio Grande in March 1846, a supply depot was established at
Point Isabel and Gen. Taylor authorized Roswell Denton to forward army
supplies. Denton prepared a wagon train to carry supplies to Point Isabel,
under the supervision of Patterson Rogers and his two sons, Anderson and
Billy. Once they were on the border, Patterson planned to open a hotel to
cater to the army.

While he was in New Orleans to buy goods, Roswell Denton wrote to warn
his father-in-law that it was too dangerous to move a wagon train to the
border without an army escort. There were reports of Mexican bandits and
guerrillas operating on the Texas side of the Rio Grande. Denton's warning
came too late.

The Patterson Rogers supply train left Corpus Christi on April 25, 1846. This was two weeks before the first battles of the Mexican War were fought at Palo Alto and Resaca de la Palma. Besides Patterson Rogers and his two sons, other members of the supply train were teamsters, with three women and four children. The wagon train followed the wide trail left by Taylor's army and arrived at the Paso Real on the Arroyo Colorado on May 1, 1846.

When they were four miles south of the arroyo, they were surrounded by 50 or more Mexican guerrillas. Patterson Rogers and the teamsters, taken by surprise, surrendered and were forced to head back to the arroyo. Two teamsters named Horton and Allenbrook were shot to death and a Mrs. Atwater was killed with a saber thrust.

At the Arroyo Colorado, 19 others in the party were bound and stripped of their clothes; the bandits wanted the clothes without bloodstains. The women were raped. The throats of men, women and children were severed, their heads pulled back and slashed from ear to ear and their bodies toppled from the high bluff into the river below.

All were killed except one. Billy Rogers missed death by an inch of the knife's blade. A deep gash severed his windpipe but the blade missed the jugular vein and he was still alive when his body was pushed into the river. He hid and watched as the bandits gathered their plunder.

After the guerrillas left, Billy Rogers wandered, semi-conscious, naked, and sunburned through dense brush. He stayed alive by eating berries and drinking rainwater. With his severed windpipe, he could only manage this by lying on his back.

On the fourth day, more dead than alive, he came to the ranch of Juan Corona, 30 miles from the site of the massacre. He was taken in and nursed back from the brink of death. While recuperating, Rogers started to learn Spanish, which would prove helpful when he began to search for the killers. The rancher Juan Corona was afraid that when word got out that someone had survived the massacre, attempts might be made on Rogers' life. Corona turned him over to the authorities in Matamoros.

War correspondent George Wilkins Kendall from New Orleans passed by the site of the Patterson Rogers massacre. "We saw the remains of no less than seven of the unfortunate Rogers party, so cruelly murdered here a few weeks since," Kendall wrote. "Five skeletons, one of them apparently a female, were lying upon the banks, where they drifted after their throats had been cut; two others were discovered near the wagons. The wolves and buzzards had done their work."

In Matamoros, Billy Rogers was thrown in jail. His wound was left untreated. When he was not among those returned in a prisoner exchange, other freed prisoners informed Gen. David Twiggs, a friend of Patterson Rogers. Twiggs threatened to bombard Matamoros, despite a truce that

90

protected the city, if Billy Rogers wasn't freed. He was released and his gaping wound treated by Army surgeon N. R. Jarvis. Gen. Zachary Taylor dispatched a ship to carry Rogers back to Corpus Christi. He recuperated at the home of his mother.

A healthy William Rogers later traveled to the border to wed Julia Corona, the girl who cared for him after the massacre. It was the patient returning to marry the nurse.

Rogers became a prominent man in Corpus Christi. He was elected sheriff of Nueces County in 1848. He bought a sheep ranch and made a fortune. He was elected to the Texas Legislature. He organized Corpus Christi's first volunteer fire department, the Pioneer Fire Company No. 1. Rogers was a well-known and well-respected citizen. What was not well-known, but was whispered about, was that he once prowled the border searching for the Mexican bandits who killed his father and brother and left him with a gashed throat.

A few names of the bandits were known. The leader was a man named Juan Balli, also spelled as Juan Baillie. The plunder that was taken from the wagon train showed up in Reynosa. "Mustang" Gray's Rangers, who were attached to Zachary Taylor's army, discovered that the Patterson Rogers' killers were on a ranch near Matamoros. Gray's Rangers attacked the ranch and killed two dozen men, which supposedly accounted for half the killers.

Of the others, it was said that the names and faces were committed to the implacable archives of memory and, one by one, their bodies were found on the border. These men were all killed in a distinctive way. They were stabbed in the chest and their throats cut ear to ear, almost symbolically.

The story was widely repeated that Billy Rogers and his brother Lieuen Rogers traveled up and down the Rio Grande on King and Kenedy riverboats. They would attend fandangos and when certain individuals were pointed out to them, they would be coaxed outside for a chat or a drink and once outside, in the shadows, they would be stabbed in the heart and their throats cut.

True? No one knows. But on the lower Rio Grande a slashed throat was called Billy's Mark and the general belief was that Billy Rogers got his revenge, murder for murder. Direct acts of retribution were understood and appreciated on both sides of the border.

Years later, Rogers told a friend that he and Lieuen accounted for all the cutthroat killers except a man known as Capt. Santos, who disappeared deep into the interior of Mexico. Billy Rogers died on Dec. 17, 1877. He was only 56 when he died, but his health had been poor, complicated by an old throat wound.

* * *

Billy Rogers was not the only Texan who sought retribution for the massacre of the Patterson Rogers' wagon train. So did the more sinister Mustang Gray, one of the more bloodthirsty figures in the history of South Texas. His real name was Mabry B. Gray.

The story of how he got his nickname — perhaps more legend than true fact — was that he lost his horse while hunting buffalo and alone, on foot, he captured a mustang pony. From then on he was known as Mustang Gray. He was said to be one of the finest riders in Texas and absolutely fearless in a fight. Gray's shadowy history reveals that he was a cold-blooded and remorseless killer.

When he was 19, Gray was with the Texas army at San Jacinto. As a veteran, he was granted a 640-acre land bounty by the Republic of Texas. This grant of land, called Gray's Ranch, was five miles north of Ingleside.[22]

After San Jacinto, Gray joined bands of Texans who were raiding Mexican-owned ranches in South Texas. Most of these ranches had been abandoned and the cattle left behind were rounded up and driven east to sell. The stock-raiders were called "cow-boys."[23] The author J. Frank Dobie described these cow-boys as "young men, mostly nondescript, un-uniformed, undisciplined, self-willed, and ready-to-die aggregation. Their great hunting ground was the area between the Nueces and the Rio Grande."

The notorious cow-boys expanded their activities to include robbery and killing in their attacks on caravans of peaceful traders from Mexico.

In 1842, with lower Texas in turmoil, seven Mexican traders from Camargo arrived at Victoria. They sold Mexican blankets and bought tobacco, bolts of calico, and other trade goods. On their way back, they camped near Goliad. They were sitting by a campfire cooking supper when Mustang Gray's party rode up. They were invited to share the meal and after eating, Gray's men pulled out their guns, tied the traders together, and told them they had a few minutes to make their peace with God.

Tied together, the Mexican traders were gunned down by the light of the campfire. The raiders hid the trade goods and took the horses to sell. One of the traders was still alive. He had been shot, but as he fell he landed beneath the body of the man tied to him.

When the killers left, the wounded survivor freed himself and walked to Refugio. He was nursed back to health. He has been variously identified as Manuel Escobedo or Manuel Escobar.

---

[22] John Dunn said he also owned a ranch at Grulla Motts near Corpus Christi.

[23] I use the hyphenated version to differentiate from later cowboys who worked the ranches and went up the trails to Kansas.

The survivor, Escobedo/Escobar, went to Victoria and told the story of the massacre to John J. Linn, a merchant and prominent citizen. While the people of Victoria were shocked, nothing was done to charge Gray and his band of killers, but the massacre made it hot enough for them around Victoria that they moved on to the area around Corpus Christi. They continued to prey on peaceful traders from Mexico.

In another incident, Mexican traders traveling to Corpus Christi camped on Oso Creek. Mustang Gray, Andy Walker and others disguised as Comanches attacked the camp at night, whooping and shooting. Several traders escaped into the brush while others were killed in the melee.

Corpus Christi founder Henry Kinney urged Texas President Lamar to crack down on the outlaw bands, which he called robber Texians. These outlaw bands were semi-legitimate since they were authorized by the Republic as ranging companies or, as they were usually called, spy companies. They received no pay, which no doubt justified in their own minds the taking of plunder from "the common enemy."

Attacks on peaceful Mexican traders invited reprisal raids from Mexico. These reprisal raids were mounted by a combination of cavalry and rancheros from the border region of the Rio Grande. They threatened Corpus Christi's existence. In 1844, Kinney was authorized by the Republic of Texas to field a company of rangers for the protection of his trading post. In trying to curb their activities, Kinney put some of the men he called robber Texians on his payroll, including Mustang Gray.

When Zachary Taylor's army arrived in Corpus Christi in 1845, Gray and some of his men joined Samuel H. Walker's First Texas Mounted Riflemen. This became the most famous unit of Texas volunteers in the war. As Taylor's army pushed into Mexico in the fall of 1846, there were reports (in error, as it turned out) that Corpus Christi had been nearly wiped out by Comanche raiders. Mustang Gray and the men who volunteered with him formed a new company, with Gray as the captain, which was sent back to protect Corpus Christi. After discovering that the reports of the Comanche raid were in error, Gray's company was ordered back to Camargo in early 1847.

Mustang Gray's rangers called themselves Mustangers after their commander. Among those in the company were Andy Walker, Reuben Holbein, David Hatch, Pat Quinn, and William Clark. Back with the army, they were assigned to escort and protect army supply trains traveling to Monterrey.

On Feb. 22, 1847, a supply train was attacked by Mexican guerrillas, the teamsters killed and their bodies mutilated. It was believed the raid was launched from a village named China, known as a center of guerrilla resistance.

On March 28, 1847, Mustang Gray's company attacked Rancho Guadalupe near the village of China. In the attack, 24 civilians were killed. S. Compton Smith, an army surgeon, wrote that Gray's company "in cold blood murdered almost the entire male population of the Rancho Guadalupe, where not a single weapon, offensive or defensive, could be found."

After the massacre, a proclamation in Mexico urged Mexican citizens to kill any American they encountered, civilian or military, armed or unarmed.

Gray's name was linked to other massacres during the war, real or imagined. One supposedly occurred at a place called Rancho San Francisco, according to Samuel Chamberlain, a dragoon with Taylor's army. Chamberlain, a Bostonian who loathed Texans, may have exaggerated an incident or passed on a rumor. At Rancho San Francisco, Chamberlain wrote, 36 men were tied to a post and shot by Mustang Gray's Rangers. Most of them were killed, said Chamberlain, by a man called "Greasy Rube." Chamberlain wrote that the names of "Old Reid, Captain Bayley (sic), Harry Love, Ben McCullough, and more terrible of all, Mustang Gray, will always remain fresh in the memory of Mexicans, as the atrocities committed by them now form a part of the nursery legends of the country."

Rip Ford, who was Jack Hays' adjutant in the war, defended the Rangers and by extension Mustang Gray as "killers by necessity, who had come to Mexico to settle a score and who were not going to be bothered by rules and regulations in going about it. They never made war upon any but armed men, when the field was open and the lists free."

After the Rancho Guadalupe massacre, Gray's Rangers were ordered back to the Mexican river town of Camargo. They were mustered out of service on July 21, 1847. Gray stayed behind in Camargo. He died in February, 1848, possibly of cholera. His body was taken across the Rio Grande and buried on the Texas side of the river, near Rio Grande City, in an unmarked grave.

After his death, a popular myth of Mustang Gray took its form in fiction written by Jeremiah Clemens of Alabama. Gray was also celebrated in a cowboy ballad that went: "There was a gallant Texan / They called him Mustang Gray / When quite a youth he left his home / And went ranging far away." The more accurate assessment of Mustang Gray was no doubt given by the South Texas merchant John J. Linn, who described him as a cold-blooded killer and moral monstrosity.

CHAPTER 13

CORPUS CHRISTI'S REEF ROAD, WETTEST ROAD IN THE WORLD
1840s — 1916

The Reef Road was about three miles long from shore to shore and was as crooked as a worm fence.

—*J. Williamson Moses*

It was near dusk when a Comanche raiding party struck Corpus Christi, one day in the early 1840s. Texas Rangers who were already in the vicinity chased the Indians to a spit of land stretching into the bay called the Rincon, which later gained the name of North Beach. As the sun went down, the Rangers had the Indians pushed up against the water, each side waiting for the other to attack. The Rangers were under the command of a Capt. Crouch. He decided to keep the Comanches hemmed in between them and the water while they sent to town, two miles away, for reinforcements. They could attack the Indians next morning.

When the sun rose, Crouch and his Rangers were astounded. There was not an Indian was in sight, not a pony, not a war bonnet. The Rangers followed the tracks which led into the water. They discovered that the water was scarcely knee-deep. The Indians escaped by following a raised natural reef of oyster shells that divided Corpus Christi Bay from Nueces Bay.

The oyster shell reef stretched from Rincon Point on the Corpus Christi side to Indian Point on the north side, near the later town of Portland. By sharp twists and turns, the reef led across the bay, connecting two natural sand spits, like fingers reaching out to touch, from the northern and southern shores. The Rangers' discovery led to what came to be known as the Reef Road.

When Zachary Taylor's army was concentrated in Corpus Christi in 1845 and early 1846, preparing for war with Mexico, Lt. Jeremiah Scarritt, an engineer, and a party of soldiers cut a passage-way through the reef. This allowed small boats to cross Nueces Bay and travel up the Nueces River to haul supplies to an outpost of dragoons at the village of San Patricio. The cut

95

in the reef was made on the southern end nearest the Corpus Christi shore. For years afterwards, at high tide, horses crossing the Reef Road had to swim across that stretch where Taylor's men cut a hole in the reef.

Two years later, the first work ordered by the newly created Nueces County Commissioners Court, on Jan. 11, 1847, was to mark the Reef Road so travelers in buggies and wagons and on horseback wouldn't stray into deep water. An overseer was appointed to "mark and designate by strong and substantial stakes the road across the reef." The overseer was given the power to call on all adult male inhabitants, who were legally bound to work on public roads or pay their share of the cost of the labor.

Within a year, the *Corpus Christi Star* reported, many complaints were being made about the stakes on the Reef Road having been thrown down or displaced. The paper later reported that the problem was fixed by Henry Gilpin and Thomas Parker, who crossed the reef in a wagon and drove in a number of stakes at the points where they were needed.

The county re-staked the marker posts when they rotted or when storms washed them away. The posts were about 12 to 14 feet apart and at low tide the water in most places was knee-deep. By 1850, travelers routinely used the Reef Road. They could cut off 40 miles from a trip by crossing over the reef rather than going around Nueces Bay and crossing the Nueces River at the Borden or Bitterman ferries. Crossing by the reef cut the distance to eight miles.

J. Williamson Moses, a former Ranger and mustanger, described the Reef Road. It was three miles from shore to shore, Moses wrote, and crooked as a worm fence. At high tide, traveling over the reef was dangerous; although it was marked with stakes in the water, showing the twisting path, it was easy to veer off the reef and into deep water. A traveler on horseback ran the risk of getting bogged down to the saddle in the mud of the bay bottoms or getting his horses cut up by oyster shells.

To people unused to crossing the reef, it looked like going to sea without a boat. Moses said it was quite a sight to see buggies and wagons and men on horseback slowly crossing the bay, from a distance looking for all the world as if they were walking on water as horses and mules felt their way along the Reef Road.

After the Civil War, one of the first acts of a newly reorganized county government was to replace the stakes marking the Reef Road. They had been removed for security reasons during the war.

During the violent times of Reconstruction, crossing on the Reef Road could be dangerous. One day in 1872, George C. Hatch made his regular banking run to Corpus Christi and was on his way back to Ingleside. Hatch, who rode with "Deaf" Smith at Jan Jacinto and was an uncle of James Bowie, was captured in San Antonio during the Woll raid in 1842. Hatch crossed on the Reef Road in his buggy and was robbed and murdered by bandits on what is now the Portland side, at Indian Point.

Not long after this, E.H. Caldwell, a young bank clerk, was returning from a trip to Refugio when he lost his bearings and reached Nueces Bay at White Point. He followed the shoreline until he reached the Reef Road at Indian Point. This was where Hatch had been killed. It was turning dusk when he saw two riders approaching. He had heard about the Hatch murder, and he was terrified, sure that the two riders were bandits.

He rode into the bay, following the stakes that marked the Reef Road, constantly looking behind him as the riders drew closer. They were still some distance away when he eased his horse into deeper water, well off the Reef, and moved away, with only his head showing above water. The riders passed by without seeing him. He remained convinced they were bandits. Caldwell contracted pneumonia and was in bed for two weeks.

In 1886, the San Antonio and Aransas Pass Railroad built a train trestle bridge across the bay. Boys would cross the bay on the trestle bridge to go duck-hunting on the Portland side. If a train arrived, they would drop down and hold on to the ties until it passed over.

The Reef Road continued to be used by travelers. Those coming in buggies and wagons from settlements and communities on the north shore to shop in Corpus Christi would cross at low tide and try to time their shopping excursion so they could return before dark. If they stayed too late, someone would lie down in the back of the wagon to try to see the marker posts by the phosphorous glow kicked up by the horses' hooves.

After the turn of the century, people still crossed the underwater Reef Road in horse-drawn wagons and buggies. Starting in 1912, the county began work on building a modern causeway bridge, which opened to traffic in January, 1916. Part of the fill used underneath the causeway was dredged material from the old Reef Road. The new causeway didn't last long. It was damaged by a hurricane in 1916 and destroyed by the 1919 storm that devastated the downtown and North Beach areas of Corpus Christi.

For more than half a century, Nueces County in South Texas had the only road in the world, marked and maintained at taxpayer expense, that was completely under water. It was surely the wettest road in the world.

CHAPTER 14

JOHN PEOPLES
AND THE CALIFORNIA GOLD RUSH
1849

A large number of the men were unfit to go to California and will be unfit to stay there unless they get a situation in the shade next to a cologne lake.
—John Peoples criticizing his fellow travelers

A carpenter named James Marshall saw something glinting in the water at the water mill. It made his heart thump. It was a gold nugget the size of a pea. An Indian worker yelled, "Oro! Oro!" It was Jan. 24, 1848 on the American River at Sutter's Mill in the new territory acquired from Mexico called California.

The news spread quickly. San Francisco almost emptied as residents took spades and wooden bowls and any implement at hand and headed for the American and Sacramento rivers to make their fortunes.

Headlines around the country shouted "Gold found in California!" Newspapers reported that gold nuggets could be picked up with no trouble at all. One story related that 20 gold hunters saw a glitter of gold dust in a ravine and each man threw himself down, spreading out arms and legs to lay claim to a spot. It was reported that miners in California could "open a vein of gold as cool as you would a potato hill."

The rush was on for El Dorado, the gold country of northern California. Like the carpenter Marshall when he picked up the nugget, the nation's heart thumped. Fields were left half-planted and houses half-built. Some small towns in the grip of gold fever lost half their population. A popular song had the lines — "I soon shall be in San Francisco and then I'll look around; and when I see the gold lumps there, I'll pick them off the ground." One man wrote that he planned to make $10,000 — "and it puts me in all sorts of good humor when I think of what a splash I'll make in silk."

In early 1849, some 15,000 gold-seeking emigrants made their way across the country to California. They went to mining camps marked by termite-like mounds of sifted dirt, camps with names like Gouge Eye, Loafer Hill, Jackass Gulch, Bedbug, Freezeout, and Chicken-Thief Flat. The songs of the miners became the hits of the time, songs like:

> *"Oh, what was your name in the States?*
> *Was it Thompson or Johnson or Bates?*
> *Did you murder your wife*
> *And fly for your life?*
> *Say, what was your name in the States?"*

Another popular miners' song went:

> *"Oh, don't you remember sweet Betsey from Pike,*
> *Who crossed the big mountains with her lover Ike,*
> *With two yoke of cattle, a large yellow dog,*
> *A tall Shanghai rooster and one spotted hog."*

Like the rest of the country, Corpus Christi was convulsed with gold fever. The town had a new newspaper, the *Corpus Christi Star*, which began publishing in September 1848. Page one was filled with gold news from California, which describes the geography of the gold fields, the techniques of extracting gold, and how to get there. There was a spoof ad for Gold Grease — "The operator is to grease himself, lay down on top of a hill, and roll to the bottom; gold and nothing else will stick to him." Price, $94 per box.

Corpus Christi's founder and leading booster, Henry Lawrence Kinney, saw an opportunity. Three years before, in 1845, he wrote letters to policymakers that resulted in Zachary Taylor bringing a 4,000-man army to Corpus Christi, a small trading post. After the army left in March 1846, the town dwindled to about 100 people.

When the U.S. and Mexico signed the treaty of Guadalupe Hidalgo on Feb. 2, 1848, ending the Mexican War, Kinney returned to find his town almost deserted. He set about trying to improve the town's fortunes and his own. With the nation's attention focused on California, Kinney placed ads in New York, Boston and other papers in the east claiming that Corpus Christi was the best place to start to reach the California gold fields. He argued that the route from Corpus Christi was safer and easier than taking the long hazardous voyage by ship around Cape Horn or the trek across the malarial jungles of Central America.

There was no easy way to get there. The main route overland, from Independence, Mo., was closed during the winter months. Another route by sea was 18,000 seasick miles around the treacherous Cape Horn. Another was

100

by ship to Chargres, Panama, then across the isthmus by pack mule and then aboard another ship on the Pacific side sailing to California.

The route promoted by Kinney was by ship or packet boat to Corpus Christi and from there overland across South Texas and the Mexican states of Chihuahua and Sonora to southern California.

With Kinney's newspaper ads touting Corpus Christi as the start of the best route to the West, across northern Mexico, Corpus Christi in early 1849 became the jumping-off place for companies of emigrants traveling to the California goldfields. Indianola on Matagorda Bay was also competing for the California traffic.

Gold seekers — or Argonauts — began to arrive in Corpus Christi in January 1849. The miners came aboard fast-sailing packet boats plying between Galveston and Corpus Christi.

The first group of 49ers arrived on Jan. 20 and the town began to stir with the kind of economic activity it hadn't seen since Taylor's army left in 1846. A dredging machine was put to work dredging a channel across the mudflats of the bay. Edward Ohler, a prominent merchant, built a wharf into the bay where goods and miners could be unloaded. The old Kinney House was reopened as the Corpus Christi Hotel. The wagons, horses and mules that were sold dirt cheap as army surplus after the Mexican War were suddenly in demand at high prices. Mustangs were caught and tamed for sale to the emigrants. Coopers, gunsmiths and blacksmiths set up shop.

Corpus Christi was a coming town again. Ships docked, unloaded, and headed back for another cargo. Each week brought new boatloads of miners with ready cash. They could get room and board at the Corpus Christi Hotel for $1 a day, for man or horse.

John H. Peoples' newspaper, the *Corpus Christi Star,* advised the arriving emigrants of the need to learn Spanish — "or they will be puzzled when they get into Mexican country, where even the mules understand no other language. One of a company who started out from Veracruz could not get his mule to budge, though he kicked, beat and cursed him in the choicest English. The mule only pricked up his ears at the strange sounds. A Mexican gave him the word — 'mulas, vamos!' — and away the mule went at top speed."

Groups of California-bound emigrants were organized into companies, with bylaws, judicial tribunals, and elected officers. Among the groups arriving in Corpus Christi in 1849 were the Mazatlan Rangers, the Essex Mining Company of Boston, the Carson Association of New York, the Kinney Rangers (named in honor of Henry Kinney), and the Holmes County (Miss.) Mining Company. The companies picked up Texans eager to make the trip.

John Coffee Hays, the famous Texas Ranger and Mexican War hero, joined the gold rush in 1849.[24]

Each issue of the *Corpus Christi Star* conveyed the excitement of the gold rush. For months the editor of the *Star*, Peoples, filled the paper with news about California. He came down with the fever and turned over his type trays and press to Charles Callahan, who would get the fever himself a year later and take off for the gold fields. Peoples joined the Mazatlan Rangers mining company under the command of Col. E. W. Abbott.

Peoples, a printer and newspaperman from Louisiana, knew Abbott from the Mexican War. Abbott led a Massachusetts volunteer regiment and Peoples was a war correspondent, one of the nation's first. During the war, Peoples followed the course of the American army. He published and edited the *American Flag* in Matamoros in 1847, founded the *Vera Cruz Eagle,* and the *American Star*, printed at Jalapa, Puebla and Mexico City.

Peoples left Corpus Christi for California with the Mazatlan Rangers in the first week of February 1849. As the *Star* described it, the Mazatlan Rangers took up a line of march for the Rio Grande, striking out from their encampment at Twelve-Mile Motts (Calallen area).

The trip across South Texas took 33 days, far longer than it should have taken. Pack-mule trains carrying trade goods from Corpus Christi regularly made the trip in nine or 10 days. Peoples wrote to the *Star* from the Presidio Rio Grande that reported favorably on the "Southern Emigrant Road to California," but he was scathing in his criticism of some of his fellow travelers.

Peoples said some Mazatlan Rangers paid their $150 fee to join the company at New Orleans and expected that nothing more was required of them. He said some deemed it below their dignity to do any physical labor. He said their wagons, when they left Twelve-Mile Motts, were weighted down with all kinds of unnecessary personal possessions and that many of the wagons were pulled by oxen and mules in poor condition.

On days when they should have been traveling, Peoples wrote, some indolent men refused to stir. They wanted to rest and take their leisure. "A large number of the men were unfit to go to California by any route," Peoples wrote, "and will be unfit to stay there if they ever arrive, unless they get a situation in the shade next to a cologne lake."

The Mazatlan Rangers, feuding between those who pulled their weight and those who didn't, broke up before they started across the arid regions of northern Mexico. The main group, with Peoples, continued across Chihuahua

---

[24] In California, Jack Hays was elected sheriff of San Francisco County and later was appointed surveyor-general of California. He became a wealthy man and one of the founders of Oakland.

and Sonora. It was not an easy trip. They ran out of water and suffered dysentery. Their most difficult undertaking was to cross raging rivers. They caulked the cracks of the wagon beds to turn them into rafts. They passed through deserted villages in Mexico, the inhabitants scared away by Apache raids.

John Peoples didn't make it to the California goldfields. He drowned while crossing the Gulf of California on the way to San Diego.

Capt. Parker French led a wagon train out of Indianola with 200 gold-seekers bound from New York to San Francisco. Each man paid $250 for the privilege of taking the shorter route to the goldfields, rather than the long trip around Cape Horn. By the time they reached Paso Del Norte (El Paso), several men had died en route and others decided to make it across Mexico on their own.

The word spread that the route from South Texas — whether starting from Corpus Christi, Indianola or Brownsville — was difficult and dangerous. Emigrants fell back on more established routes — sailing around the Cape, or sailing to Chagres and traveling across the isthmus, or by going overland from Missouri and Kansas. For South Texas by 1850, the gold rush was over.

CHAPTER 15

COMANCHES SACK LINNVILLE, INDIAN ATROCITIES AND FORT MERRILL
1840s, 1850s

What! Indians so near my post! I thought it was you Texans fighting among yourselves.

—*Capt. Plummer to Rip Ford*

A peace parley in San Antonio in 1840 erupted in gunfire, leaving 35 Comanche warriors and chiefs dead. This was the Council House Fight. Later that year, the Comanches retaliated when a war party variously estimated at 500 to 1,000 rode around Austin and San Antonio, avoiding settlements, and struck south. At Victoria, houses were burned and hostages taken. The Comanches headed for the coast. On the way, they captured Mrs. Cyrus Crosby, a granddaughter of Daniel Boone.

The attack on John J. Linn's growing town of Linnville, near the later town of Port Lavaca, came as a complete surprise. Town residents escaped to boats in the bay. The Indians plundered Linnville, a rich town, with warehouses filled with goods destined for San Antonio. The Comanches put on fancy top hats and tied ribbons on the manes of their ponies. They took books and tore out pages to use for rolling cigarettes. Others wanted the books read to them.

One hostage said the Comanches gathered around her when they camped and asked her to read to them and to explain the pictures in the books. Mrs. Crosby, Daniel Boone's granddaughter, couldn't read. The Indians beat her because she was illiterate. When she tried to escape, she was killed, with two arrows going through her.

A large force of Texans pursued the Comanches. They caught them at Plum Creek, which resulted in one of the worst defeats the Comanches ever suffered; 85 braves were left dead on the battlefield. That night, after the battle at Plum Creek, Tonkawa braves, who fought alongside the Texans, brought in the body of a dead Comanche and proceeded to cook him and carve him into portions. A man who observed the ritual said the Tonkawas, on eating the flesh of their mortal enemy, acted inebriated, as if they had been drinking whisky.

After the Comanche defeat at the battle of Plum Creek, Comanche war parties became smaller, and they struck more quickly, but the raiding didn't flag. During this time, Indian "depredations" were made against Corpus Christi and the surrounding region. Most of the attacks in the Corpus Christi area were made by Comanches and Lipan Apaches. Karankawas, the cannibals of the coast, were scarce.

* * *

In the midst of a state of war between Texans and Comanches, there were a few rare occasions when both sides could get along. One example occurred in 1844, four years after the Council House Fight, when a riding contest was held outside San Antonio between Jack Hays' Rangers, 50 Comanche warriors, assorted Texans and Mexican vaqueros. San Antonio residents gathered to watch the match on the prairie west of San Pedro Creek.

J. W. Wilbarger wrote that the Comanches were famous riders and so were the Mexican caballeros, and some of Hays' Rangers were equal, if not superior, to them.

The first prize for horsemanship went to Ranger John McMullen, second prize went to Corpus Christi's Henry Kinney, and third prize went to a Comanche chief named Long Shirt. The fact that Rangers and Comanche braves could gather in peaceful competition was a rare event.

* * *

Comanches loved a horse race. Col. Richard Dodge told of an unusual race at Fort Chadbourne near San Angelo. This was some three decades after the riding match in San Antonio. Some soldiers at Fort Chadbourne challenged a band of Comanches into a horse race. The Comanches seemed to be reluctant to compete against the soldiers' prized horses. They had to be coaxed into a race.

The Indians brought out this ugly and shaggy sheep of a pony ridden by an overweight Indian carrying a war club. The soldiers were amused. They thought — Why send out our best horse? They could race their third-best and have no trouble winning.

But the shaggy Comanche pony, ridden by a fat warrior brandishing a club, won the race. The Indians loaded up their winnings, which included sacks of flour, sugar and coffee that had been wagered. The soldiers wanted a rematch. With the knowledge that the Indian pony had just barely beat their third-best horse, they decided to send out their second-best. Once again, the

106

Comanche pony won. The soldiers were now serious and brought out a prized Kentucky thoroughbred that had never lost a race.

At the start of the race, the fat Comanche warrior threw away his heavy club, gave a war whoop, and the shaggy pony bolted ahead for a good 50-yard lead over the Kentucky thoroughbred. Before reaching the finish line, the Comanche turned in his saddle and rode backwards, making obscene gestures at the soldiers. Col. Dodge said they learned later that the Comanches had won a large number of horses from the Kickapoos by racing the same shaggy sheep of a pony.

* * *

Not long after the riding match at San Antonio, Corpus Christi came under attack, on May 27, 1844, by a war party of 25 Comanches. The Indians escaped, taking horses and mules with them.

Three days later, on May 30, the Comanches returned, trying to steal horses, but the residents of Corpus Christi were expecting them and had forted-up behind Kinney's stockade. After an exchange of gunfire, the Indians rode away, taking many horses with them. They were pursued by Henry Kinney and 11 other men, who caught up with the Indians 10 miles west of the settlement.

The resulting fight was described by J. W. Willbarger, who wrote that both sides dismounted and began shooting at each other from 50 yards. At this point, Willbarger said, the Indian chief rode to the front, holding up his shield of buffalo hide, and cursing (they assumed) the Texans. The Texans, already angry, fired repeatedly at him, but their bullets were stopped by the rawhide shield that seemed to be as tough as iron.

The Comanche chief's strategy was clear. His taunting antics were meant to stoke their rage and attract their fire. Before the Texans could reload, the other Comanche warriors charged. This classic Indian tactic would later be undone by the appearance of Colt's five-shooters, but the Colts were not widely available in 1844.

In this fight, a man named Louis Cook took an arrow in the eye. A young clerk at Kinney's store (identified as Mexican, but otherwise unnamed) was speared and his horse killed from under him. Kinney, on his horse, pulled up the young man behind him. A Comanche warrior speared the young man again, and the force of the blow sent the shaft through the clerk's body, wounding Kinney in the back. The clerk fell from the horse, dead.

The fighting was man to man, with Indians using spears, bows and arrows, tomahawks and the few guns they had, while the Texans tried to load and reload pistols and rifles. Of the 11 Texans, three were killed and the rest wounded. Among Corpus Christi's wounded were Kinney, Francisco Silva, and Henry W. Berry. Seven Comanches were killed and many of the remaining 10 were wounded.

Considering the small number of men involved on both sides, Willbarger said, the fight west of Corpus Christi was one of the bloodiest that took place between Texans and Comanches on the Texas frontier. After this attack, Kinney appealed to Austin for help and he was authorized by the Republic to raise a company of 40 men for the protection of the town.

* * *

In 1847, a surveyor visiting a Comanche camp saw a white man. He asked him if his name was Lyons. The man said it was. The surveyor told him his mother was still alive, living at the old place.

Warren Lyons had been captured by Comanches 10 years before. In 1837, he and his father, DeWitt Lyons, were working in a cow lot at their home in Lavaca County. Comanches killed and scalped the father and captured Warren, 11 years old at the time. The boy lived with Comanches for 10 years. The man who killed his father adopted him.

After the surveyor recognized him, Warren was able to escape from the Indians. When he reached home and rushed to embrace his mother, she collapsed from the shock. She had given up ever seeing him again. Warren found his old home had grown into a village, called Lyonsville.

Warren Lyons told about his life with Comanches and explained that his hair was cut short on one side of the head and left long on the other side as a mark of disgrace because he had run in a fight with Mexicans. He was torn between two worlds, yearning to return to life with the Comanches and his two Comanche wives. But he settled down, married a woman named Lucy Boatwright, and joined a company of Rangers commanded by Capt. J. S. Sutton. He remained a loyal and steadfast Ranger.

J. Williamson Moses, a former Ranger, said his friend John Duval loved to watch Lyons eat pecans. Duval said, "I wish I had a bushel of pecans so I could just watch Lyons chew them." Moses wrote that Lyons made a good Ranger and first-rate scout and was a valuable interpreter who knew and understood Comanches. "Rip" Ford described Lyons in one fight with Comanches. "Warren Lyons, the guide and interpreter, had been raised among Comanches. He came at his old *companeros* in true Indian style: jumping, stooping down, changing position in several ways. He wished his boots off; they were too heavy. He told (the Rangers) what the Indians were saying." It was said that Warren Lyons, in everything he did, from walking to riding a horse, looked and acted like a Comanche.

Not all the atrocities attributed to Indians were actually committed by Indians. In one example, renegades dressed as Indians went on a looting and killing expedition in South Texas. They attacked Roma and Rio Grande City, looted churches and killed travelers. Two of the "Indians" were caught and hanged on the Roma road with, as one account said, "their white skins exposed."

A killing in January 1850 near Corpus Christi was attributed to Indians. A boy named James Doyle was given a gun for his 16th birthday. He and a friend crossed over the reef to go hunting on the north side of the Nueces Bay at spring called Gum Hollow. At the spring, they were supposedly surprised by Indians. Doyle dropped his gun and ran while the friend hid in some bushes. The Indians picked up Doyle's gun and shot him to death.

Ranger Capt. Rip Ford was in Corpus Christi that day with a company of Rangers. They crossed over the reef and made an effort to follow the Indians, but, Ford said, there was no trail. Ford said that if young Doyle was killed by Indians, they were on foot and left no tracks. The spring became known as Doyle's Watering Hole.

Charles Bryant, an architect from Maine, was killed and scalped by Indians at Chocolate Bayou, north of St. Mary's, in 1850. Bryant, an architect in Bangor, Maine, designed some of that city's most famous buildings. In 1837, he became involved as a leader in a rebellion in Canada. When the rebellion failed, he was a wanted man in Canada and Maine for violating the neutrality act. He sailed for Galveston to start a new life.

When Zachary Taylor's army concentrated at Corpus Christi in 1845, Bryant moved to Corpus Christi and built the Union Theater to cater to the troops. In 1849, Bryant began work to restore the Union Theater; he planned to operate it as a hotel. He joined the Texas Rangers and was appointed mustering officer for three Ranger companies.

Bryant was summoned to Austin in January, 1850. On his way to Goliad, near John H. Wood's Ranch on the Chocolate Bayou, he was killed by a band of Lipan Apaches. As people from Wood's ranch watched (too few to go to his rescue), the Indians scalped Bryant. A company of Rangers commanded by Capt. John J. Grumbles[25] buried the body and took a lock of what remained of Bryant's hair. They chased the Indians for 300 miles, but couldn't catch them.

---

[25] Grumbles was a captain of Rangers in the 1840s and 1850s. He died in 1859.

109

Later that year, on Oct. 19, 1850, a Comanche war party raided the ranch of John Jacob Thomas (Americanized from Thommen). Thomas was an immigrant from Switzerland who got a job as a teamster with Zachary Taylor's army at Corpus Christi. After the war, Thomas bought land and settled on the Salt Creek, on the Lamar Peninsula, a few miles inland from where it empties into St. Charles Bay.

The Comanche raiders captured two daughters, Sarah and Eve, who were 10 and 11 years old. The girls were out bringing in the milk cows. They were captured in sight of their parents. Thomas raised his gun and took aim at an Indian, but his wife Verna begged him not to shoot for fear the Indians would take their revenge on the girls.

The Indians rode away with their two captives. That night, while they camped by the San Antonio River, Eve tried to escape. The Indians cut off her hair with their knives, stabbed her with knives and lances, and left her for dead. The Indians were heading for their camping grounds on the San Saba, 190 miles to the northwest.

The Indians tied Sarah to her horse to prevent her from escaping. She slept on the ground in a slip; they took her clothes when she was captured. She ate what the Comanches ate, horseflesh and pecans. Weeks later, an Indian agent swapped an Indian boy and some blankets for her. She returned home. Her sister Eve, left for dead by the Comanches, was found by a search party, which included her brother John Thomas. She recovered from her wounds, severe as they were.

In later years, Eve married Henry Kroeger, who ran a hotel at Lamar. Sarah married Anthony Strauch, who lived near the Thomas place on Salt Creek. They had five children and became a prominent family in Refugio. Sarah lived to an old age, known to all as "Grandma" Strauch, one of two little girls who were captured by Comanches and lived to tell about it.

* * *

Texas Rangers patrolled the country between the Nueces and Rio Grande in the 1840s, but the plan at the beginning of the 1850s was to turn over the task of protecting the Texas frontier to the U.S. Army. The army would build and man forts at strategic places. The Rangers would be mustered out and the expense of frontier protection would be shifted to the federal government. There was some overlap. The Rangers were still in the saddle while forts were being built.

In February 1850, two companies of the 1st U.S. Infantry under the command of Capt. Samuel Plummer moved up the Nueces River, 60 miles north of Corpus Christi. The site chosen for a fort was on high ground with a view of the stage road and a bend of the Nueces River. The fort's main purpose would be to protect wagon trains of supplies being hauled from Corpus Christi, the new army headquarters, to San Antonio and then on to frontier forts.

The soldiers lived in tents until planks and logs arrived. An Army bride, a Mrs. Grainger, went there in early 1850. Helen Chapman, the wife of an Army captain at Brownsville, wrote that at Fort Merrill "the site of the post had not been selected when the order was given to erect huts. Until they were finished, their only shelter was a tent." Pine logs were shipped from New Orleans to Corpus Christi then by wagons to the site. The soldiers built the fort themselves. They built officers' quarters, kitchens, a sutler's store, guardhouse, stables, and quarters for two companies. It was a concentration of buildings, not the kind of wooden palisade shown in old Westerns. They called it Fort Merrill.

After the fort was built, Rip Ford's Rangers stopped by on a scouting trip. They got rations from the fort and camped below it. They built a fire and made mesquite tea by boiling dark mesquite wood in water and adding sugar. The moon was full, a Comanche moon, and they could see motts of live oaks on the prairie and trees casting shadows on the river bottoms.

About 3 a.m., as they slept, a Comanche raiding party tried to steal their horses. There was a skirmish and as the Indians rode away, one of Ford's men, Mat Nolan, rushed barefoot through prickly pear to get a parting shot at the escaping Indians.

After the fight, Ford sent word to Capt. Plummer at Fort Merrill, telling him what had happened. Plummer yelled, "What! Indians so near my post! I thought it was you Texans fighting among yourselves." A loony soldier at the fort came out and cut the head off a dead Comanche. A Ranger ordered him to drop it.

Typically, soldiers at forts like Merrill waited for something bad to happen and when it did they didn't hear about it until the fight was over and the Indian raiders long gone. It was almost impossible to catch Comanche raiders, unless they wanted to be caught.

The Rangers were a different story for they had adapted to Indian tactics. They lived in the saddle and knew the land as no sedentary soldier ever could. As one Ranger once said, "We knew the rattlesnakes by their first names." And they could survive, said another, on nothing but tobacco juice, gunpowder, and whiskey.

Using the infantry at such forts, the historian Walter Prescott Webb wrote, was as much out of place in Texas "as a sawmill on the ocean." Comanche raiders traveled day and night on horse-stealing and scalping expeditions. They took extra horses for remounts. In one chase, Comanches rode 400 miles and stopped only three times to build campfires. Infantrymen mounted on mules — or even cavalrymen on big slow chargers — were no match for

Indian warriors riding lean ponies, the fastest horses of the prairie. Indian raiders went around forts, attacked with impunity, and returned to their refuge in Comanche territory. The contest was not even close.

The new state of Texas had to look to Washington for protection, but the inability of foot-bound regular Army soldiers to protect the frontier was a constant complaint from Texas to Washington. *The Ranchero*, a Corpus Christi newspaper, reported that a Capt. Dawson of the U.S. Army, with two wagon loads of clothing and a detail of six men, left under an escort of Rip Ford's Rangers. "Well," the *Ranchero* commented dryly, "Uncle Sam's men could not have fallen into better hands."

When sporadic Indian attacks continued around Corpus Christi in the 1850s, soldiers at the new army forts were rarely around. One exception occurred at a battle at Lake Trinidad, south of Ben Bolt, in 1854. Lake Trinidad was described as a pond in a wet year.

A wagon train carrying army supplies was attacked by Lipan Apaches between Fort Ewell and Fort Duncan. Patrols were mounted from every fort in South Texas, including Fort Merrill on the Nueces. The patrol from Fort Merrill rode west and at Lake Trinidad, the soldiers ran into a party of Indians that had just killed three mustangers. There was a standoff. The soldiers were joined by local ranchers carrying shotguns, but after seeing the size of the Indian war party, the ranchers left the task to the soldiers.

Lt. Blake Cosby, who was in charge of the dragoons, ordered his men to charge. The Indians fled into a skirt of mesquite timber and the fight continued until the soldiers ran out of ammunition and then became a hand-to-hand struggle. Three soldiers were killed and five wounded. Lt. Cosby was wounded. The Indians escaped.

Cosby led his battered detachment back to Corpus Christi, which was army headquarters for the region. There was a military hospital at Corpus Christi where the wounded were treated. We know the details of this fight because it was covered in a report by the Secretary of War to Congress. That report led Gen. Winfield Scott, in charge of the Army, to order soldiers at Army forts in Texas to be armed with Colt six-shooters and Sharps rifles.

Fort Merrill didn't last long. After its two companies of infantrymen were moved to Fort Ewell, the fort was closed in December 1855.[26]

The fort's beginning and ending coincided with the period when Corpus Christi was headquarters for the Eighth Military District. While the headquarters was at Corpus Christi, army supply trains moved along the stage road from Corpus Christi to San Antonio. When the headquarters' depot was moved back to San Antonio in 1856, there was little need for a fort to guard the Corpus Christi to San Antonio road.

---

[26] During the Civil War, Confederate cavalry units occupied old Fort Merrill for a time.

112

Fort Merrill and other Army forts in the 1850s were built and manned on the mistaken idea that the Army could rely on foot-bound infantry to control and contend with Comanches, the greatest warriors on horseback since the Mongols of Genghis Khan.[27]

---

[27] Nothing of the original fort remains. The state erected a granite monument in 1936, which incorrectly says it was named in honor of Capt. Hamilton W. Merrill. It was named for Maj. Moses E. Merrill of the 5th Regiment who was killed at Molina del Rey in the Mexican War.

J. Williamson Moses

CHAPTER 16

J. WILLIAMSON MOSES,
MUSTANGER IN SOUTH TEXAS
1850s

The furious thundering horses, clambering over their dead and dying companions, vanished in a cloud of dust.

—*J. Williamson Moses*

J. Williamson Moses wrote a collection of columns about his recollections of early Texas and Texans for the *San Antonio Express* between 1887 and 1890. He wrote under the pen name "Sesom," Moses reversed.

Moses was in the thick of things in South Texas in interesting times and he knew the great men of Texas history. He worked as a surveyor in the Hill Country, he was a Texas Ranger in the late 1840s, and then a mustanger in the Wild Horse Desert. He was a storekeeper in Banquete, a Civil War soldier, a postmaster and county judge. He was wounded by a Comanche arrow near Fredericksburg and almost hanged by a posse at Banquete. He was a Confederate officer in John Rabb's command on the Mexican border and, after the war, moved to Mexico with other Texas emigres. His memoirs, written in his last years after he had suffered a stroke, were never published.

Moses was born in 1825 in South Carolina on his father's plantation, Hopewell, near Charleston. He was nine years old and was playing with a young slave companion named Paul when they were attacked by a rabid dog. The slave boy protected Moses and was bitten in the process. He died a painful death. Moses wrote that every day of his life he mourned the death of Paul, the slave boy who saved his life.

Moses went to school in Charleston and Philadelphia then struck out on his own, moving to Florida and making his home near Apalachicola. He described a popular activity on the Florida coast of gathering bird eggs. They would visit remote beaches and on the first day they would destroy all the bird eggs they could find. Next day, they knew the eggs they found would be fresh.

Moses joined a group of Floridians who volunteered to fight in the Mexican War. They arrived in Galveston in 1846. Moses came down with a fever and was left behind when the group traveled on to join Ranger Sam Walker's command with Zachary Taylor's army on the Rio Grande.

Moses moved on to Houston. The winter of 1846-47 was cold, wet, and for Moses sickly. He recuperated while staying at the City Hotel. He became the pigeon of a group of card sharps and lost much of his money. After that plucking, Moses said, he had a heavy heart and a light pocketbook.

Moses found that the town of Houston was a hard-drinking place that lived up to the reputation of its namesake. It was raw and brash, but there were many luminaries there. Moses found that the town's favorite pastimes were drinking and fighting, followed by more drinking and fighting.

One day in Houston, David G. Burnet and Hugh McLeod sent Moses to find Sam Houston. He found the former president of the Republic of Texas in a saloon deeply engrossed in a bar bet. The bet was that Houston couldn't use one hand to pick up a heavy wooden chair by the lower rung and lift it without the chair wobbling. Houston approached the subject, said Moses, as if it was an affair of great public importance, making sure that all the details were agreed to beforehand. Houston wouldn't leave until he had lifted the chair and won his bet.

Moses tells another story about Houston. The fact that Houston had lived among the Cherokees was well-known and not always appreciated by his constituents. In one incident, Houston was visiting at a home in East Texas during a cold spell and the wind came whistling through cracks in the walls. Houston, joshing with the woman of the house, asked her, "Why don't you make that lazy husband of yours mix up some mud and moss and chink these openings?"

"Well, General," she said, "I have spoken to him several times about it, but I am afraid to be too importunate. He might leave me and take up with some Indian squaw like others have done." Moses said that Houston uttered not another word about chinking the walls.

On a trip to Bastrop, Moses stopped at a store/tavern called Hell's Half Acre, where he became the sport of four or five tough characters, one of whom was determined to bring on a fight. He backed Moses into a corner. Moses pulled his pistol and was about to use it when an old gentleman walked in and asked what the ruckus was about.

Moses said the saloon toughs slipped out like whipped hounds. The man who came to his rescue, as Moses soon learned, was Gen. Edward Burleson, who had been vice president of the Republic during Houston's second administration. Moses described Burleson as a man with little book learning and that he sometimes made laughable mistakes, but that he had an extraordinary mind and overall his acts were honest, practical and judicious.

116

Moses joined a group of surveyors who had been hired to survey land in the area of the Pedernales, Llano and San Saba rivers for German immigrants. Delaware Indians under a chief called Jack Harry were hired to supply game and protect the surveyors from hostile Comanches.

The surveyors often went for months without bread, Moses wrote, and there were almost no vegetables of any kind. They had all the bear meat, deer, antelope and wild turkey they could eat. They would use lean dried meat as bread and fresh fat meat as meat. It was a treat when they found sage or wild onions.

Another treat was honey. Above Fredericksburg they found one of the largest hives they had ever seen under a rock overhanging the Pedernales River. The surveyors wouldn't go near the hive for fear of being stung, but the Delawares walked up to the hive without hesitation and carted away three barrels of honey. The Indians anointed themselves with some kind of substance, said Moses, that calmed the bees and kept them away.

One day the surveyors went down to a stream for water and ran into a Comanche war party. Moses didn't see them until he was almost in their camp. They fired a shower of arrows as he whipped his horse toward a cedar brake. One arrow hit him in the side, pinning him to his saddle. The surveyors escaped to rejoin the rest of the party. They formed a defensive line and waited for the Comanches to attack.

The Comanches made a direct charge, but the surveyors and Delaware scouts put up a fierce fire and the Comanches, after shouting insults, rode away. Having been hit by a Comanche arrow and having his horse killed from under him, Moses' view of the Comanches lacked any sentimental nuance. Moses said the Comanches were treacherous, bloodthirsty, and murderous cowards. He said they would never fight with anything like equal numbers. When they met strong resistance, they would make tracks. Moses said the Seminoles he knew in Florida and the Cherokees and Delawares he knew in Texas would fight to the death. "Had it been either of those tribes that attacked us, it's doubtful if any one of us would have lived to tell the tale."[28]

At the time they were surveying the country was controlled by Comanches. "I remember being sent by Mr. James Giddings from where we were camped above Fredericksburg to San Antonio with a letter to Col. Jack Hays (who was then the surveyor of the district) for the purpose of making a plat of the territory we were to run over from the map on file in his office," Moses wrote.

---

[28] This contradicts Noah Smithwick's view, who lived among the Comanches and considered them the bravest of the brave.

"I started very early in the morning and though it was a long ride I intended to make it through, if it took me some time in the night. There was not single farm, ranch or habitation of any kind from where I started to the outskirts of San Antonio. My horse, Selim, was in fine order on the luxuriant pasture upon which he had been running. I knew his power of endurance. About midday I stopped for a short time at a clear and pleasant spring close to the trail and, slipping the bridle off, I let him graze and drink while I ate a frugal repast brought with me.

"I had stayed a little more than half an hour when, just as I was in the act of starting again, I saw coming over the hill some 18 or 20 Indians. It did not take me many seconds to tighten my girth and mount. But I was forced to make a detour or the Indians would have got within shooting distance. As it was, they did get in closer juxtaposition (to use the favorite word of a legal friend of mine) than was safe or agreeable. But there was no time lost from that moment.

"Selim showed them his heels. Though they pursued with yells, urging their ponies to their utmost speed for a considerable distance, I soon put a greater space between us, and not much grass grew under my horse's feet until I got to the suburbs of the city of the Alamo, which I did just before sundown — for the scare which the Comanches had given me caused the time to be shortened a great deal.

"When I rode up to Captain Crump's tavern they were just going to supper. When I told of being chased by the Indians, and where I had started from that morning, it caused a great deal of surprise. Cojo Young and one or two others went to look at my horse and prognosticated that he would be stiff and of no account for several days, if he ever got entirely over such a breakneck ride. In that they were mistaken. After being well rubbed down and cared for, on the next morning he was as sound and as bright as a new dollar.

"I never can call to mind old Selim, my favorite steed, without regret. Soon after this event, the Comanches stole him and several other good horses from our camp. After pursuing them for three days on the best animals we had left, our beasts were so jaded that when we overtook them, the Indians, after a pretty brisk skirmish, got away from us. We were compelled to return with two of our party wounded.

"Some of the horses were recovered at one of the trading posts and restored to their owners, but the last that I ever saw of my gallant steed two bucks were riding him off. One had his own pony shot and had jumped up behind the other who, to my infinite chagrin, was mounted on old Selim. I made strenuous efforts to get my horse back again, and even got Mr. Strubens, one of the Indian traders, to offer two or three good ponies, or their value, for his delivery at the post, but it was in vain. He was lost to me forever."

When the surveyors were camped on the Llano River, they visited a Comanche camp where they found an American captive who had been taken as a child. The blue-eyed young man pointed to a Comanche brave and said, "Him killee my father; now him my father." The captive's name was Warren Lyons. Although he had lived with the Comanches since he was a small boy he was finally convinced to return to his home.

"When I last saw Lyons he was a member of Capt. John S. Sutton's Rangers. He made a very good Ranger and a first-rate scout."

Moses himself joined Capt. Sutton's Rangers. They were posted to the Corpus Christi area and made their camp at the old village of San Patricio. During this time, a party of filibusters who called themselves Buffalo Hunters set up camp on Padre Island. They were mostly Mexican War veterans who planned to invade Mexico and establish a Republic of the Sierra Madre.

Moses wrote that war, like an indulgent mother, had spoiled many of her children and left them unfit for work. While the filibusters on the island were growing restless waiting for action, some of them hatched a plot to rob Corpus Christi's Henry Kinney. It was said he had $10,000 in gold in his house on the bluff. Kinney got word of the scheme and sent for Capt. Sutton's Rangers who were camped at San Patricio. The Rangers arrived before daylight just in time to convince the Buffalo Hunters to disband and return home.

Sutton's Rangers were moved to San Antonio in preparation to be disbanded. The task of guarding the Texas frontier was being turned over to the regular U.S. Army. Sutton's Rangers were mustered out without the pay they had coming. Some destitute Rangers sold their saddles and horses and spent their time at Capt. Crump's tavern, waiting for something to turn up.

In San Antonio at that time, Moses wrote, the Alamo was in ruins and the bridge over the river was not in much better condition. Few streets were paved. Moses thought San Antonio looked more like a Mexican cuidad than an American town. During siesta time, the streets were deserted except for gringos and burros.

After his Ranger company was mustered out in San Antonio, Moses next turned to mustanging — catching and selling mustangs in the Wild Horse Desert.

* * *

The deserted land between the Nueces and the Rio Grande was called the Wild Horse Desert because of its vast herds of wild horses — mustangs, or mesteños. How long had they been there?

Many accounts say they were the offspring of horses lost during Spanish expeditions to Texas in the 17th Century. They were left behind because they were lame or too weak to travel, but they recovered and adapted to the open grasslands of South Texas and spread across the coastal plains after generations of breeding.

That may be right, but there were wild horse herds in northern Mexico and it's likely they drifted across the Rio Grande, extending their range north and east and giving an identity to what the maps began to show as the Wild Horse Desert. For the horses, there were almost no predators and they multiplied like the rabbits introduced into Australia.

Spanish explorers noted the presence of wild horses. Blas de la Garza Falcón, governor of Coahuila, in 1735 saw huge herds of mustangs on his way to the Rio Grande. He believed they were descended from horses that had escaped during stampedes and turned wild. When Jose Escandon began establishing settlements on the Rio Grande in 1747 he found wild horses. On an inspection tour of missions in Texas in 1768, Fray Gaspar José de Solís saw herds of wild horses around Laredo. Father Juan Agustín Morfi, in another tour of inspection in 1777, saw mustang herds north of the Rio Grande "so abundant that their trails make the country, utterly uninhabited by people, look as if it were the most populated in the world." Manuel de Mier y Terán, who toured Texas in 1828, saw great concentrations of wild horses below the Nueces. "In these parts," he wrote, "it is necessary to post sentries to watch the packhorses and mules to keep them from running off with the wild horses."

Herds of wild horses were still prevalent in the region in 1845 when Zachary Taylor's army was encamped at Corpus Christi. Ulysses S. Grant, a second lieutenant, found that mustangs could be bought for a few dollars a head. When the army marched south in March 1846, Grant rode out to see the huge herds of mustangs, almost beyond number, too many, Grant thought, to be contained in the whole state of Rhode Island.

Hunting and capturing wild horses was a major occupation in South Texas. Thomas Dwyer, a lawyer from London, arrived in Corpus Christi in 1848 and went to work as a mustanger. He said the herds of wild horses stretched across the horizon and, when seen from a distance, the whole country seemed to be moving. Dwyer wrote that many Mexicans, whose families resided at Corpus Christi, Goliad, Laredo and San Antonio, supported themselves by catching wild cattle and by mustanging.

* * *

After Moses left the Rangers, he became a captain of a mustang crew in the early 1850s.

As Moses explained, the law regulating mustangers was that all branded animals when caught from the mustangs had to be returned to the owner of the brand, if known, and if not known they were presented at the county seat and the clerk of the county court took the brands and had them posted; if no claimant presented himself in a year they were sold at auction and one-half of the sale price went to the county and the other half to the mustanger. Each mustanging party had a captain who was held responsible for the good conduct of his men. They had to take out a license and give a bond with two or more good sureties to comply with the law.

Moses described the mustangers' methods. A crude pen, *corral de aventura*, was built with an opening that could be quickly closed. It was built of mesquite posts or any timber that could be found, built in a spiral shape, 50 or 60 feet in diameter, so that when the mustangs were run in at the gap, they continued to run round and round until they tired.

The fence was composed of stout pickets set firmly in the ground, inclining inward, and made as strong as possible to resist the heavy pressure often cast against it. It was braced from the outside and about two-thirds of the distance from the ground it had a stout pole lashed to the pickets to further strengthen the fence.

Leading to the *corral de aventura* were wings shaped like a huge "V" that stretched some 700 yards. The wings, built of brush, were not very strong or high. The object simply was to guide the horses for the gap of the corral.

The *aventurers* were the men who went round the mustangs where they found them grazing or watering and drove them as easily as possible in the direction of the open end of the wings.

When the herd was inside the wings, the receivers, or *recibidors*, moved in behind them. The *recibidors* would take them along the wings until the gradually narrowing in would bring the herd close together. About 30 or 40 yards from the entrance to the corral, hiding behind a blind of green bushes, one of the mustangers called the *enserador* was posted.

When enough horses were inside the corral, his job was to run into the entrance of the pen to keep the mustangs inside from running back out again. He would wave a sheet or white blanket before the frightened animals.

A little further off on the opposite wing would be another man, the *cortador,* whose job was to help the *enserador* by running into the wing and cutting off the mustangs when too many of them were crowding into the gap, then to help close the entrance of the corral and secure the pen. Once the gate was closed, the horses inside were trapped. They would run, frantic, their eyes white with fear, wheeling round and round the corral, looking for a way out, until they could not run any more. Then a catch, great or small, was secured.

The laborious work of taking horses, out at the side gap would begin. There would be no rest until the mustangs were roped, dragged out and side-lined by tying one fore leg to the hind leg on the same side, allowing about 12 inches of space to step. This side-lining was done with rawhide straps. When the mustangs caught in a run were so disposed of, they then had to be surrounded by mustangers and very carefully taught to step hobbled. They would be driven to water and grass until the rawhide straps could be taken off, gradually, one or two at a time, and they became gentle enough to drive. Then they were ready for market. Generally, the price was about $5 a head.

When a herd was being chased toward the corral, there was no telling how big the catch might be. What happened if it was too large for the corral was described by Moses at a place near Amargosa Creek, in today's Jim Wells County.

"We made such a large drove that when we got them going for the pen, the rush they made was uncontrollable. The *cortador*, whose job was to cut off the herd when the pen was full, was unable to do so. They went with such a rush he could do nothing. The animals in a wild stampede ran over one another. The bottom of the corral was covered with crippled and dying animals. Others in the herd rushed, crushing and bruising themselves against the pickets until the pen gave way. The furious, thundering horses, clambering over their dead and dying companions, vanished in a cloud of dust."

Mustangs were so numerous in Moses' time that no one would have believed they were already vanishing. The immense herds that made the horizon move were all but gone by the end of the 1850s. They were hunted like the buffalo almost to extinction. They were not natural to the land — they were as alien as those rabbits in Australia — but they were wild and beautiful and lent much to the character and spirit of early Texas.

* * *

Moses turned from mustanging to run for justice of Precinct 3 (Rockport area) and was elected. During this time, he wrote, Tom S. Parker, a former Nueces County sheriff, served as bailiff in district court in Corpus Christi. Parker one day stepped up to the bench and told Judge M. P. Norton, "Here is your venereal, judge."

Judge Norton said, "*Venire*, Mr. Parker, *venire*. Really, you must learn the law terms better."

Moses recalled a case being tried at Nuecestown, usually called Twelve Mile Motts. Benjamin F. Neal, the first mayor of Corpus Christi, represented the defendant. After the other lawyer quoted Sayles, Neal said, exasperated, "Sayles! Why, I am as good a lawyer as Sayles" and in reply quoted Lord Bacon.

The other lawyer said Bacon may have been an outstanding jurist in England but that he had no standing in a Texas court, while the venerable

Sayles did. At this point, Neal threw a law book, which hit the other attorney between the eyes, and he left the courtroom by jumping out an open window.

In 1854, Moses opened a store in Banquete and bought land on Banquete Creek. Around this time Moses was almost hanged by a posse. Some accounts say it was because some posse members riding through thought he was Jewish while other accounts say it because he was a fierce supporter of the open range. Whatever the cause may have been, he was rescued in the nick of time by John Rabb, a rancher near Banquete.

In about 1859, Moses wrote, "I remember a circumstance or two which illustrates the mode of living in those days by even our well-to-do, if not rich, ranchmen. There was a party of three or four of us — Col. Forbes Britton, Judge Benjamin F. Neal, and myself among the number — who started out from Corpus Christi with the intention of buying a drove of Mexican ponies.

"We went to the Olmos, the Bobedo and other ranches where we knew there was plenty of horse stock. We managed to supply our wants satisfactorily and at very reasonable figures.

"But the want of comfort and even respectable or decent way of living at the places where we stayed seems almost incredible. At the larger number of the ranches such a thing as a drop of milk was not to be obtained, though they had hundreds of cattle, and butter was an unknown commodity.

"We stayed at one ranch where the proprietor was very well off and had quite a large dwelling house built of stone, and which on approach looked to be of rather a better and more comfortable place than any we had seen.

"The old don, with whom I had very friendly relations, treated us with great hospitality. He insisted on our going to the house, where dinner was prepared for our party. When we got there we found that it consisted of a single room downstairs with a dirt floor beaten down hard. We were given small woolen cushions to sit on. When the midday meal was ready, one of his servants brought in a large well-dried beef hide which he spread in the middle of the spacious hall and put bowls around near the edge. Then he brought in a large iron pot nearly full of mutton broth, with which the portly and good-looking senora filled the bowls. We were then invited to draw up and fall to.

"After disposing of our soup as best we could with our tortillas, more tortillas were brought in and the ribs of the mutton, nicely roasted, were placed on them. Of these we were also invited to partake, and we made a most hearty meal, seasoned with the sauce of hunger after a hard ride. But there was not a knife or fork or spoon on the place that I saw, except the large wooden ladle with which the old lady so graciously dished out our broth. Nor was there a napkin or towel on the ranch. How they washed and wiped their hands and faces was a mystery I never solved."

At the outbreak of the Civil War, Moses joined the command of John Rabb. He was stationed at Ringgold Barracks, taken over by Confederates, at Rio Grande City. Among the officers there were Col. Augustus Buchel and Capt. Mat Nolan. In 1861, on the last night of the year, Moses wrote, a man named Segundo Garza was caught with three horses he didn't own. He was put in jail in Rio Grande City.

Some of the men in town repaired to the saloon to decide what to do with him. They figured the makeshift jail wouldn't hold him. They decided the best thing to do would be to take him some mescal to warm him up, then hang him. The man begged for mercy, but they hanged him anyway. Since he was taking a long time to die, they left two men to guard him and returned to the saloon to celebrate the New Year.

It went unnoticed during the hanging, but the slender limb had bent just enough to let the hanged man rest a big toe on a stump. When the two men left to guard him got tired of waiting and decided to cut him down, they found that he was not dead, just dazed.

The guards marched back to the saloon, leading the hanged man with the rope around his neck. In the saloon, one of the guards said, "Here's your dead man!" The shocked members of the lynch mob bought the hanged man mescal and made him promise to cross into Mexico and limit his horse-collecting on the other side of the river.

After the Civil War, Moses, like some other Texas Confederates, moved his family to northern Mexico. There were Texas emigre families living in Monterrey and Saltillo. Moses went to work operating a steam engine at a sawmill north of Saltillo. Moses loved northern Mexico, especially Saltillo, a gay city where you could buy some of the best fruit in the world, and Monterrey, a beautiful city. "I have yet to see an American who traveled or worked in Mexico," Moses wrote, "who will not freely admit that the people of Mexico are generally, almost universally, kind and considerate."

Moses moved back to South Texas and in 1871, he and his wife Victoriana built a cottage in Rockport looking over a salt marsh. He was elected chief justice (county judge) of Aransas County in 1871 and admitted to the bar. Moses moved to San Diego, where he became county judge.

Moses wrote that it was hard to believe that the area between San Diego and Corpus Christi was the same country where, not so many years before, he chased wild mustangs, lassoed wild cattle, and fought Comanches. Those were the days long gone, days when the sun seemed to shine with a brighter light. J. Williamson Moses died on April 28, 1893, at his home in San Diego. An obituary in the *Corpus Christi Caller* said, "Another old Texas landmark is gone."

Capt. Richard King

Henrietta King

126

CHAPTER 17

RICHARD KING,
LEGS LEWIS
AND THE KING RANCH
1853

You better run or the Mexicans will get you sure.
— *Bigfoot Wallace to Legs Lewis at Mier*

An eight-year-old orphan in New York City was apprenticed to a jeweler. His parents, Irish immigrants, died when he was five or six. He worked for the jeweler for two years before he ran away and hid in a ship bound for Mobile, Ala., the *Desdemona*. It was 1834. After four days at sea, he was found and taken to the captain of the *Desdemona*. He said his name was Richard King and he ran away because he didn't like looking after the jeweler's kids. The captain made him his cabin boy to earn his passage.

When the ship docked at Mobile, the captain found King a job on an Alabama steamboat. A few years later, the steamboat captain sent King to school in Connecticut, but he didn't like school and returned to the riverboat life, this time in Florida, where he met Mifflin Kenedy, captain of the steamboat *Champion*. Kenedy took the *Champion* to New Orleans and up the Mississippi. He was hired to select steamboats for Zachary Taylor's campaign in Mexico. Kenedy wrote his friend King and urged him to join him on the Rio Grande.

King arrived in South Texas in 1847. He became the pilot on the *Corvette*. King and Kenedy spent the war ferrying soldiers and army supplies up the Rio Grande. After the war, the two men formed a partnership with Charles Stillman and bought three surplus Army steamboats. On July 10, 1850, King celebrated his 26th birthday at Miller's Hotel in Brownsville.

In late April or early May 1852, King rode from Brownsville to Corpus Christi to visit Henry Kinney's Lone Star Fair. King was 27 years old. King and his companions probably followed the trail made by Gen. Santa Anna's army when it straggled back to Mexico after the defeat at San Jacinto, the same route followed in 1846 by Zachary Taylor's army as it marched to the Rio Grande at the start of the Mexican War. King's party would have passed the sandy alkali flats around the salt lakes, the *El Desierto de los Muertos*, Desert of the Dead, before reaching the rich coastal prairie.

Past the alkali flats, the land opened into a level prairie covered with stirrup-high grass. There were a few motts of trees on the horizon. Except for Manuel Ramirez's Bobedo Ranch, there was no habitation, no human sign anywhere, just vast herds of mustangs which gave this area its name, the Wild Horse Desert. Perhaps this is when King got the idea of starting a ranch or perhaps he already had the idea and the trip merely served as an opportunity to look over the land.

The Bobedo Ranch straddled the main route from Brownsville to Corpus Christi northwest of Baffin Bay. The *Corpus Christi Star* on March 26, 1849 reported — "Our correspondent en route to Brownsville writes from this well-known ranch: The Bobedo is owned by Manuel Ramirez (Elizondo) who has *manadas* of mares for breeding and between 2,000 and 3,000 head of cattle. Yet for all this stock — worth perhaps $20,000, he employs only one herder. I may as well remark, though, that the extent of the land, embracing 12 leagues, is so great as to isolate his stock from that of others."

One account says King stopped to visit the Bobedo Ranch and while there asked about land for sale. Ramirez told him about the Santa Gertrudis grant 12 miles to the north. That's where the party stopped to camp, on a slight rise about three-fourths of the way from Brownsville, 125 miles (where the city of Kingsville is today). They camped by a small stream called Santa Gertrudis, which had been named by Blas Maria de la Garza Falcón, who had a ranch in the area almost 100 years before.

The King party's campsite was a mile from Rip Ford's old Ranger camp. It was here, according to the family story, that King saw a pattern of the future, struck by the idea that this was ideal cattle country. King went on to Corpus Christi, a settlement with several hundred residents, to see the sights of the Lone Star Fair: horse-riding events at Maltby's Circus, fair exhibits, and a celebrated bullfighter from Mexico City.

When he returned to Brownsville, King talked over his idea of buying land and starting a ranch with Capt. Robert E. Lee, his friend. Lee told him it wasn't Virginia, but it was a country with a future. In July 1853, King bought 15,500 acres, part of the Santa Gertrudis grant, from the heirs of Juan Mendiola of Camargo, Mexico. He paid two cents an acre. Felix Blucher surveyed the land with King serving as a chain carrier. The deed was filed in Corpus Christi on Nov. 14, 1853.

King signed on a partner, Gideon K. "Legs" Lewis, a Ranger captain in Corpus Christi who could provide protection for the enterprise. Lewis, born

128

in Ohio in 1823, worked as a printer's devil in New Orleans and a reporter in Galveston. In 1842, when he was 19, he took part in the Mier raid into Mexico. At one point Bigfoot Wallace teased Lewis — "You better run or the Mexicans will get you sure."

The Mexicans did get him. The Mier raiders were taken to Mexico and imprisoned at Hacienda Salado. After they escaped and were recaptured, Santa Anna wanted to execute all the Mier prisoners but decided that one in 10 would be shot with the unlucky chosen by lot. The captives were forced to pick a bean from a clay pot filled with white and black beans. Those lucky enough to choose a white bean would live and those getting a black bean would die by firing squad. Legs Lewis drew a white bean.

After the captives were freed in 1844, Legs Lewis returned to Galveston to work as a reporter and when war with Mexico threatened, he took off for the Rio Grande. Lewis and Samuel Bangs started a newspaper called *The Reveille.* Lewis soon left the newspaper to join the Rangers. He was cited for bravery in carrying dispatches.

In 1852, Legs Lewis was in Corpus Christi helping Henry Kinney put on the Lone Star Fair. Kinney sent him to New Orleans to buy the engraved silver cups to be awarded as prizes. After the fair, Lewis was appointed captain of a Ranger company at Corpus Christi and then he signed on as Richard King's partner in the ranching enterprise on Santa Gertrudis Creek.

Richard King bought cattle in Mexico, at $5 a head, cheap because it was a drought year. King knew little about ranching but knew enough to get expert help. He hired all the vaqueros and their families from a small Mexican village, which some accounts identify as Cruillas, Tamaulipas. The vaqueros King hired were named Patino, Alvarado, Flores, Chapa, Ortiz, Villarreal, Cabazos, Villa, Ebano, and Cantu. They were called King's Men — *Kineños.* They were men who had spent their lives with cattle and horses and knew all there was to know about them. Along with King, they founded an empire of cattle and grass. King Ranch was as much their creation as it was Richard King's.

In Brownsville, King met Henrietta Maria Chamberlain, a preacher's daughter who ran a girl's school called the Rio Grande Female Institute. She was 18, a graduate of a finishing school in Mississippi, where she had learned needlepoint and flower arranging — skills not much in demand on the Texas frontier. Her father, the Rev. Hiram Chamberlain, came to Brownsville as a Presbyterian minister. He brought along his third wife and four children. Henrietta was the oldest.

When Rev. Chamberlain could find no suitable house to rent, he installed his family on a surplus riverboat. The dark-eyed Henrietta first met Richard King at the dock. King usually docked his freight boat, *The Colonel Cross,* where Chamberlain had tied up their houseboat. There was a sharp exchange of words between King and Henrietta, but King attracted to with the bright, pretty girl and got Mifflin Kenedy to introduce him.

They were an unlikely match. The churchy Henrietta was very much the preacher's daughter who shunned parties and abhorred alcohol. For entertainment, she liked to sing hymns and read the Bible. King, by contrast, was steeped in the rough ways of the waterfront. He liked to spend his leisure time with hard-drinking friends at the Noah's Ark Saloon.

Though King had gained wealth from the riverboat trade, he was far below Henrietta socially. But being in love with a preacher's daughter must have had some taming effects on King, taking off some of the rough edges, for he began to attend church services to see Henrietta. She was engaged to a Sunday school supervisor, but she called off the engagement to clear the way for King.

Henrietta Chamberlain married Richard King on Sunday, Dec. 10, 1854. That Sunday, she wore a peach-colored dress and sang in the choir. King waited in the pews with Mifflin, his best man, and after services the marriage ceremony was conducted by Rev. Chamberlain, who gave his daughter an inscribed Bible as a wedding present.

Henrietta was 22 and King was 29. He called her Etta and she called him Captain. King bought a carriage for their trip to his ranch on Santa Gertrudis Creek. Henrietta wrote of her honeymoon: "I doubt if it falls to many a bride to have had so happy a honeymoon. On horseback we roamed the broad prairies. When I grew tired my husband would spread a Mexican blanket for me and I would take my siesta under the shade of a mesquite tree."

* * *

In 1855, Legs Lewis, King's ranching partner, was accused of having an affair with the wife of Dr. Jacob Tier Yarrington of Corpus Christi. Yarrington found love letters between Lewis and his wife. Lewis was running for Congress and wanted the incriminating letters back.

When Lewis went to Yarrington's house and demanded the letters, Yarrington refused and warned Lewis not to come back. When Lewis returned on April 14, 1855, Yarrington shot him with a shotgun. Lewis fell against the house and died.

The slaying of Legs Lewis was big news in Texas. Most of the state's papers printed an account of the shooting of Lewis, "the boy captive of Mier." He had survived the Mier raid, the black-bean executions, the war in Mexico, only to be killed by a jealous husband in Corpus Christi. The husband was never tried for the shooting.[29]

---

[29] Yarrington and wife divorced. She became a teacher in Shubutu, Miss. He moved west and became a merchant in Oakland, Calif.

Lewis left no heirs, no known family, and his half-interest in the ranch was put up in auction. King asked Maj. W. W. Chapman to bid for the property for him by proxy. Chapman bought Lewis's share of the ranch and left word for King that he had to bid more than was expected because of the aggressive bidding by Capt. Fullerton. He signed a promissory note, which King paid. Long after Maj. Chapman's death, his widow Helen sued King, claiming she owned half the ranch. King lost the case and paid Chapman's heirs $5,000.[30]

After the death of Legs Lewis, the captain and Etta moved from Brownsville to the ranch. In 1860, King's steamboat partner Mifflin Kenedy joined him as a partner in the ranch.

When the Civil War broke out, King and Kenedy had 20,000 head of cattle and their longhorns were trailed east to help feed the Confederacy. As the North tightened a blockade on Southern ports, cotton was hauled down the Cotton Road to Mexico. The Cotton Road passed through King Ranch and the ranch became a headquarters and commissary, supplying the caravans of cotton with horses, mules and provisions and protection. At Brownsville, steamboats owned by King and Kenedy ferried the cotton to ships at the mouth of the Rio Grande. King and Kenedy put their boats under Mexican registry, flying the Mexican flag, and the two made a fortune hauling Confederate cotton down the Cotton Road and on the river to the Mexican port of Bagdad.

In late 1863, Union forces captured Brownsville. A few days before Christmas 1863, a rider arrived at King Ranch to warn King that a Yankee cavalry unit was headed that way to arrest him. King rode off in a hurry. When the cavalry arrived, shots were fired and a *Kineño*, Francisco Alvarado, ran out, yelling, "Don't fire on this house! There is family here!" He was shot dead on the porch. When the raiders didn't find King, they vandalized the house and rounded up cattle to drive to Brownsville.

A month later, Henrietta had her fifth baby, a boy, whom she named Robert E. Lee King after the Confederate general and family friend. King stayed busy moving cotton and served for spell as a private in James Richardson's cavalry.

After Robert E. Lee surrendered to end the war, King and Kenedy asked for and received pardons. Three years after the war, they divided their ranch holdings amicably and Kenedy bought the Laureles Ranch. The two men remained close friends and allies.

---

[30] A lawsuit in 2003 claimed that Chapman's lawyer, Robert Kleberg, was already under retainer by King. The Texas Supreme Court dismissed the suit, ruling that the claim was based on a conspiracy theory that could not be proved and there was no way of knowing 150 years later the true facts of the matter.

South of the King Ranch was the Bobedo Ranch.[31] King visited the ranch when he traveled to Corpus Christi in 1852 for the Lone Star Fair, before he started his own ranch. The Bobedo was a thriving, working ranch after the Civil War. In 1874, the owner of the ranch, Manuel Ramirez (Elizondo) died.

John McClane, Nueces County sheriff and close friend and retainer of Richard King, petitioned the court (the ranch was then in Nueces County) to be named administrator of the estate. McClane was appointed. Of the three appraisers of the estate, another was a close associate of King, his secretary and agent, Reuben Holbein.

The appraisers valued the estate at $56,000; cattle were valued at $3.50 per head, well below market value. King purchased all the land and cattle, paying Ramirez's sons. A King Ranch hand, Victor Rodriguez Alvarado, noted that the Bobedo cattle were trailed to Kansas and sold. "The money he (King) got from the steers was sufficient to pay the entire cost of the ranch." In that way, the older Bobedo Ranch was acquired by King.

* * *

Richard King's youngest son, Robert E. Lee King, died in St. Louis of pneumonia when he was 19. King started drinking his favorite bourbon "Old Rosebud" heavily after that and Henrietta stayed in St. Louis, perhaps to be away from King in his cups.[32]

During King's Rosebud years, daughter Alice Gertrudis King stayed at the ranch to look after her father. King was in bad health in 1885 and the whisky didn't help his growing stomach pains. Henrietta returned home to persuade him to go to San Antonio for treatment. Before he left the ranch, King's last instructions to his lawyer, James B. Wells, was to keep buying land and never sell a foot of "dear old Santa Gertrudis."

King died at the Menger Hotel in San Antonio on April 14, 1885. He was 61. Most of the family was at his bedside, along with Mifflin Kenedy, who had just buried his wife Petra. The eulogy of an old ranch hand who worked for King summed up the cattleman — "He was a rough man, but he was a good man. I never knew a rougher man nor a better man."

"How much land does a man need?" the Russian writer Tolstoy once asked. His answer was, "Just enough to be buried in."

---

[31] The name Bobedo is a corruption of the name of the Spanish grant, Rincon de la Boveda.

[32] Some years later, Henrietta would give strict orders that no liquor could be sold on King Ranch or in the town of Kingsville, which she controlled.

Richard King had more than enough to be buried in. He started with 15,500 acres and kept buying land until he owned 614,000 acres, which he left to Henrietta. He also left a debt of $500,000. Henrietta took over management of the ranch with the help of Robert J. Kleberg, who would marry Alice Gertrudis King the following year. After King's death, Henrietta always wore black. Her bonnets, gowns and gloves were black. Her iron-gray hair was parted and plaited in a severe bun. It was said her eyes were open and friendly, but there was a glint of steel.

At the ranch, she began the day by strolling through the vegetable garden. She would point out to a servant which vegetables to pick for dinner. She kept peppermints in her pocket to give grandchildren and carried a stout cane if they misbehaved. She ruled from a rocking chair, accessible to all, but no one ever forgot she was *La Madama.*

At King Ranch, dinner was announced by three bells: One to alert guests to get ready, which meant jackets and ties for men, corsets and gowns for women; the second to gather in the parlor; and the third started the progression to the dining hall, with *La Madama* leading the way. After dinner, they would retire to the music room to sing hymns, such as "Rock of Ages." She was still the preacher's daughter.

In 1893, Henrietta built a mansion on the bluff in Corpus Christi so Alice's children could attend school. She allowed only one subscription to the town's newspaper, the *Caller.* She would get it first, read all the news, then sit on the paper in her rocking chair and play a guessing game with members of the family about what was in the paper, who was getting married and so on.

The original ranch house, built in 1856 and enlarged over the years, burned on Jan. 4, 1912. The fire was believed started by a disgruntled gardener. Family and guests escaped the flames, but the old house was destroyed, along with family keepsakes. Mrs. King asked Kleberg to build a fireproof house that would be elegant yet comfortable enough for a man in boots. The result was the 25-room "Big House" patterned after a Mexican hacienda.

Henrietta King was an invalid in her last years. She died at age 92 on March 31, 1925. She died at the ranch where she had lived for seven decades. She lay in state in the front room of the great house as 5,000 friends filed by to pay respects. Some of the *Kineños* at the far end of the ranch rode two days to get there in time for the funeral. When her casket was lowered into the earth, horsemen waiting at the edge of the crowd rode forward and galloped around her grave, their hats removed and held aloft in a final salute.

She controlled the ranch that Richard King founded longer than he did. He ran it for 32 years; she controlled it for 40 years, with Kleberg's help, but with her making the decisions. She doubled the size of the ranch from 612,000 acres to 1.2 million acres. She promoted the growth of Corpus Christi and Kingsville with generous gifts of land for schools, for Spohn

Hospital, for the First Presbyterian Church. The skills she learned at a young ladies' finishing school in Mississippi, along with her rock-like moral standards, stood the preacher's daughter in good stead as *La Madama*, the matriarch of King Ranch.

Henry L. Kinney

CHAPTER 18

HENRY KINNEY,
WOULD-BE EMPEROR
OF THE MOSQUITO COAST
1854

I have a larger space to act in than I had at Corpus Christi and the result of my undertakings in Central America can hardly be imagined.
—Henry Kinney to M. P. Norton

One pattern in the character of Henry Lawrence Kinney, the founder of Corpus Christi, was revealed early. When he got into trouble, he took off for distant places. Kinney was born on the day Napoleon was exiled to the isle of Elba, on June 3, 1814. He was the third of six children born to Simon and Phoebe Kinney. They lived at Sheshequin, near Towanda, in the Wyoming Valley of Pennsylvania. His grandparents were killed in the last Indian massacre in Pennsylvania during the Revolutionary War.

Kinney's father Simon owned a store and Henry Lawrence worked as a clerk in the store. On the last day of 1832, the 18-year-old Kinney was attacked by a man who claimed that Kinney was paying too much attention to his wife. Even though Kinney did not start the fight with the husband, he was fined $1 for assault. After that, he left Sheshequin and made his way to New Orleans, then up the Mississippi River to Illinois. Kinney settled in the town of Peru, west of Chicago. He and a man named Ulysses Spaulding built a store in 1834 and Kinney speculated in land and built a small hotel in 1836. His family followed him to Illinois.

In 1837, the great statesman Daniel Webster came to visit his son Fletcher, who owned a farm near Peru, Ill. Kinney was in charge of the welcoming committee. He presented Webster with a carriage pulled by a matched team of cream-colored horses. Some accounts say Kinney fell in love with Webster's daughter Julia, proposed marriage and was turned down. This rejection, it was said, caused a broken-hearted Kinney to leave Illinois. While

137

he may have proposed to Julia Webster and was rejected, he likely left Illinois for financial reasons.

Kinney in 1837 took a contract to build part of a proposed Illinois-Lake Michigan Canal. This was during the great canal-building era. After the success of the Erie Canal, the country was in the grips of canal fever. Many ill-conceived canal projects turned into financial disasters, and so did the Illinois-Lake Michigan Canal. Kinney went bankrupt when the project collapsed and he skipped town, leaving huge debts and unpaid canal workers. Some accounts say that he left with the workers' payroll.

Kinney made his way to Galveston. Along the way he ran into a young Welshman who had been living in Alabama, William P. Aubrey, and the two former a partnership to open a store on the Texas coast. Kinney put up the capital. The partners arrived in the new town of Aransas City, on Live Oak Point, in 1838. Their store specialized in the Mexican trade.

Kinney quickly became a leader. Aransas City had Texas's first custom house, but Lookout Point, across Copano Bay, changed its name to Lamar to flatter Texas President Mireabeau Lamar, who ordered the custom house moved to his namesake. A meeting of citizens in Aransas City was called to protest the decision. The meeting was chaired by Kinney, who signed the declaration sent to the governor.

While Aubrey ran the store at Aransas City, Kinney hauled goods to an old Indian trading site near the west bank of the Nueces, the site that would become the town of Corpus Christi. In September of 1839, Kinney built a fort-like trading post at that site and moved into it with a few supplies. Kinney shifted supplies from the Aransas City store to the new place until the spring of 1840 when he and Aubrey closed the store at Live Oak Point and moved all their stock to the new location, which would become Corpus Christi.

Kinney's trading post was inside a stockade. He hired a force of armed men and had three cannons for protection. Mexican traders came over from west of the Rio Grande to buy goods at Kinney's trading post. The traders brought horses, mules, saddles, bridles, Mexican blankets, and pure silver bars and they carried away bolts of unbleached domestic cloth, guns and ammunition, and bales of tobacco. It was a lucrative trade. During the period of the Republic of Texas, the area between the Nueces and the Rio Grande was claimed by Texas and Mexico. Since both tried to collect import duties, goods were routinely smuggled to evade paying taxes to two separate governments.

Others saw there were huge profits to be made. In May 1841, a hero of the War of Independence, Philip Dimmitt and two partners, James Gourley Jr. and John Sutherland, began to build a trading post at Flour Bluff, 15 miles from Kinney's trading post. A company of Mexican cavalry from

138

Matamoros, which belonged to the command of Gen. Pedro Ampudia, a friend of Kinney's, raided Dimmitt's store. They carried away merchandise and seized Dimmitt and two other men, taking them with them. The Mexican force spent the night near Kinney's rancho, but Kinney's place was left unmolested.

In Mexico, Dimmitt committed suicide while he was held prisoner. The Mier prisoners in Mexico passed by the place where Dimmitt committed suicide, named Agua Nuevo (New Water) on their march from Saltillo to Hacienda Salado.

Since Dimmitt was a competitor, and since Kinney had influence in Mexico, Kinney and Aubrey were suspected of having a hand in the affair. They were tried in Victoria on charges of treason and were found not guilty, but the suspicion that they were somehow complicit in Dimmitt's capture and eventual death never went away. Another Kinney friend, Mirabeau Lamar, president of the Republic of Texas, may have played a role behind the scenes that resulted in the speedy trial and acquittal.

Kinney faced other troubles. The land he occupied was claimed by Mexican army captain Enrique Villarreal, who had a grant for ten leagues of the Rincon del Oso. Villarreal showed up with a small army to reclaim his 400 square miles of land along Corpus Christi Bay. To avoid a battle, Kinney agreed to pay him $4,000, about two cents an acre.

In 1844, a riding contest was held at San Antonio between Rangers, Comanches, Texans and Mexican vaqueros. Kinney won second prize. A man who knew Kinney said he could throw a dollar before him and with his horse in full stride pick it up while leaning from the saddle. "There was nothing which could be accomplished in the saddle he could not do on his favorite horse, 'Old Charlie.' "

In 1844, Kinney was elected to the Senate of the ninth Congress of the Republic. He represented San Patricio, Goliad and Refugio counties. He attended sessions in the old town of Washington, the capital of Texas after Sam Houston moved it from Austin. Kinney helped ratify the terms of annexation to the United States.

It was clear there would be a war between the United States and Mexico over the annexation of Texas, with the dispute centering on no man's land between the Nueces and the Rio Grande. As an American army was being assembled at Fort Jesup in Louisiana, Kinney began a successful campaign touting Corpus Christi as a base of operations for the army. When Zachary Taylor's troops landed in August, 1845, Corpus Christi was a small outpost with less than 100 people.

The conflict with Mexico showed another side of Kinney's character. He argued that neither Texas nor the United States had a legitimate claim to the land below the Nueces, that it had always been Mexican territory. Though he opposed the war, or said he did, he joined Taylor's army as a quartermaster and did his part to help win it. He had many contacts in Mexico and he had his own spy, Chipito Sandoval, and, while Taylor was in Corpus Christi, he was kept informed of Mexican army movements.

When Kinney rode south with Taylor's army, he left behind an all but deserted town. The inhabitants, men and women, followed the army south. Kinney returned two years later to a desolate and all but dead town. After the war, Kinney started a slaughterhouse on North Beach, where mustangs were killed for their hides and opened a beef packing house. When Brigham Young's Mormons were looking for a place to settle, Kinney tried to sell them some of his land outside Corpus Christi. He bought hundreds of surplus army wagons and advertised Corpus Christi as the best place to head for the California gold fields. This gave the town a temporary boost until the 49ers learned that the Chihuahua route was very hazardous. They sought easier ways to get to California.

Kinney in 1852 hosted the Lone Star Fair at Corpus Christi to help pay his debts. In the first week of May 1852, Corpus Christi was a crowded and exciting place. Hundreds of people were in town for Henry Kinney's Lone Star Fair, the first state fair held in Texas. The fair had been planned for months, perhaps inspired by the success of the Great Exhibition in London, the first world's fair that attracted some six million visitors.

Kinney, always optimistic, expected some 20,000 to 30,000 people would come to his Lone Star Fair. This was very ambitious considering that Corpus Christi was a remote and provincial place.

Kinney had no state or local funding to put on the fair so he financed it himself on money borrowed from friends. John P. Schatzel, wealthy merchant in the Mexican trade and former U.S. consul at Matamoros who moved to Corpus Christi, put up $45,000 for the fair. Forbes Britton borrowed $1,000 in gold to invest in Kinney's scheme. Other rash investors put up money.

Months before the fair was set to open, Kinney advertised the sale of livestock and land that would be held at Corpus Christi beginning on May 1, 1852. The *Texas State Gazette* at Austin reported that Kinney expected up to 30,000 people would come to the fair, though the editor thought this was an extravagant statement. Kinney, with infinite attention to detail, was doing everything he could to make the fair a success. Corpus Christi's newspaper, the *Nueces Valley*, reported he was "untiring in his exertions to make the fair worthy of himself and the masses who will be in Corpus."

Kinney distributed 20,000 handbills promising lavish entertainments and luxurious accommodations for visitors. He sent Reuben Holbein to London to promote the fair and encourage emigration. He wrote letters to state leaders and got prominent citizens to serve on the fair committee. He enlisted Gov.

Peter Hansborough Bell to open the fair and convinced one of the state's leading citizens, Ashbel Smith of Galveston, to preside. Smith also invested his own money in the fair.

Corpus Christi was buzzing with excitement. New buildings were going up and old buildings were refurbished. A race course was built. The *Nueces Valley* reported that, "Constant additions are being made to the already extended catalogue of amusements for the occasion, so that it is impossible that this feature of the fair can be a failure."

Kinney sent Legs Lewis, with $3,000 in his pockets, to New Orleans to buy silver cups and goblets to award as prizes. The *New Orleans Delta* reported that the 70 silver exhibit prizes — on display at the store of Hyde & Goodrich on Chartres Street — were of the "most highly wrought and elaborately finished specimens that we have ever seen." The *New Orleans Delta* also wrote that, "Extensive sales of land are to take place at the Corpus Christi Fair, and to capitalists this affords a fine opportunity for the profitable investment of money. Every species of amusement will abound, money will be plentiful, land cheap, speculation rife, and all the beauty and chivalry of Texas will be there."

As the day for the fair approached, the *Texas Republican* reported that every movement in and around Corpus Christi seemed to have some connection with the great fair. At the port of Indianola, ships departing for Corpus Christi included the sloops *Belle, California, Mary Ann, Wandering Willie* and *Major Harris*, a light-draft steamboat. The *Major Harris* was Kinney's own steam-powered packet boat, built at Cincinnati expressly for the shallow waters of Corpus Christi Bay. It began operating just in time to convey passengers to Corpus Christi from the New Orleans steamboats arriving at Indianola.

One of the early arrivals in town was Thomas S. Lubbock (for whom Lubbock would be named) with a letter of introduction to Kinney. Lubbock was seeking work as auctioneer at the livestock sales, and Kinney hired him. Many others were coming in. Henry Maltby's Circus arrived from San Antonio with its featured star, Ella Nunn. Ranger Capt. Rip Ford, veteran of the Mexican War, came to town. So did steamboat captain Richard King, riding up from Brownsville, and Sally Skull, known as a woman who carried a gun and was not reluctant to use it. She shot a man during the fair; Rip Ford said the man pulled a gun on her.

On April 17, 1852, the sloop *Wandering Willie* deposited 16 passengers at Corpus Christi and returned to Indianola for another load. Capt. McPherson told the *Indianola Bulletin* that a large of people had already assembled in the town, as well as a great variety of livestock, and "everything wore a promising appearance, and the committee of managers was engaged in arranging the plan of exhibition and distribution of premiums."

In Corpus Christi, streets were crowded with people with an out-of-town look, walking around, looking at the points of interest, visiting the warehouse where exhibits were displayed. They could stop for refreshments at stands with ice and lemonade throughout the town. The beach side of Water Street became a camping ground for families from the country. Many visitors stayed at the Union House on Chaparral, the old Union Theater built in 1845 when Zachary Taylor's army was concentrated at Corpus Christi. It had been converted into a hotel.

Maria von Blucher in a letter to her parents wrote that, "Corpus Christi is filling with people and animals of all kinds: jaguars, bobcats, bears, panthers, bullfighters and bulls, cocks — cartloads full, their purpose being fighting, the chief pleasure of the Americans — circus riders, fast runners, German girls and barrel organs. It vexes me that the women of our nation (Germany) sink so low here. For the prizes, Col. Kinney has bought magnificent and valuable silver things, worth many dollars, all the objects very tasteful . . . Kinney has also bought a steamboat, which transports the new arrivals promptly off the big schooners." Of all the excitement of the fair, Maria von Blucher was looking forward to the bullfight featuring Don Camerena, a celebrated matador from Mexico City. She wrote her parents that her husband Felix would take her to the bullfight "and I am indeed anxious to see it."

When the fair opened on May 1, 1852, Corpus Christi was crowded with visitors, but nothing approaching the 20,000 that Kinney expected. Somewhere between 1,000 and 2,000 people came. They came from New Orleans, Galveston, San Antonio, Brownsville and many from the Rio Grande border.

A New Orleans correspondent wrote that the arena was crowded each night with "elegantly dressed American and Mexican ladies, flirting their fans with the same coquetry that they would at an opera, officers of the army, frontiersmen of Texas, with their five shooters in their belts and the handle of a Bowie knife peeping from their bosoms, friendly Comanche and Lipan Indians, and Mexican rancheros." A band from New Orleans played each evening in front of Kinney's home on the bluff as leading citizens gathered for libations and music, puffing cigars and savoring the liquor.

Exhibits displayed in a warehouse included Mexican blankets, saddles, bridles, spurs, wool, cow hides. William Dinn showed off his agricultural products from his farm outside Corpus Christi. Auctions were held in the mornings with longhorn cattle bringing $5 a head, mustang ponies $20 and mules about $30 a head. At land sales, town lots sold for $100 and rural lands went for $1 to $3 per acre. Horse races were held in the day and circus acts in the evening, along with cockfights, riding contests, even lectures on philosophy and literature.

One featured performance was Mexico City's famed bullfighter Don Camerena. A young red bull named Colorado nearly gored the famous bullfighter; the match was declared a draw.

Don Camerena was not the only person from Mexico disappointed at the fair. Mexican revolutionary leader Gen. José M. J. Carbajal was a featured speaker at the fair. He was in Corpus Christi to drum up support. Carbajal, a longtime friend of Kinney's, was trying to separate the northern states of Mexico from the central government. Gen. Carbajal, who went to college in Virginia, set forth his cause and that of the people of Tamaulipas against the wrongs inflicted by the tyranny of the Mexican government, words that resonated with Texans who could remember their own revolution in 1836. But Carbajal attracted little support. His revolution dwindled into insignificance.

Near the end of the fair, on May 12, the prizes were awarded, later reported in the *Nueces Valley* on May 20, 1852. Richly embossed silver cups, chalices, urns, gravy bowls, brought back from New Orleans by Legs Lewis, were handed out for the best flock of sheep, the best herd of brood mares, the best herd of mustangs, and so on.

Gail Borden (of evaporated milk fame) won a prize for his canned meat biscuits. Transient English artist Thomas Flintoff won a prize for his paintings of Corpus Christi. John Dix won for the best flock of sheep. R. Clements won for the best herd of mustangs. Mrs. Manning was given a prize for two quilts. Henry Maltby was given an award for his "highly artistic feats of the ring and circus." Henry Kinney won three prizes, for a stallion, Mexican bridle, and milk cow. His wife Mary took a prize for the cotton grown on their Oso Ranch. Each prize bore the inscription: "From H.L. Kinney and General Committee of the Lone Star Fair, Corpus Christi, May, 1852."

On the last day, Ashbel Smith, chairman of the fair, spoke at the Maltby circus pavilion, praising Henry Kinney's enterprising character and noting the great expense he incurred in putting on the fair. He presented Kinney with two pieces of plate brought from New Orleans — a silver urn and a fruit basket — for his hospitality. Kinney spoke of past endeavors and chances taken in establishing a trading post at Corpus Christi, the dangers from Indian and Mexican raids, but he resolved, he said, pointing toward the bay, "to live or die on the spot."

After two weeks, the Lone Star Fair ended. Word spread from returning fair-goers that it was a flop. The sloop *Wandering Willie* arrived at Indianola with passengers returning from Corpus Christi. The *Indianola Bulletin* reported that the arrivals said the fair fell "infinitely short of what was expected, and in the main, is rather a failure. We can but suppose that the amusements and exhibitions were of a limited character."

143

A similar report was carried in the *Texas State Gazette* in Austin. "We learn from a gentleman just from Corpus Christi that the fair was considered rather in the light of a failure. There were present about 500 Mexicans, about 200 filibusters, including the renowned Carbajal, about 200 citizens from different parts of the country — being in all about one thousand persons. The sales of cattle, horses, and land, for which undoubtedly the fair had been gotten up, were meager to what was expected."

After the fair, the streets must have looked deserted. The circus performers, bullfighters, Mexican revolutionaries, soldiers, Indians, Very Important Politicians and "German girls of low moral" all left town. It was the first and last state fair in Corpus Christi. The failure of the fair wasn't bad management on Kinney's part, just bad logic. Corpus Christi was a long way from anywhere, far from population centers and travel was too difficult. So the expected 20,000 people did not show up to rescue Kinney from bankruptcy.

His creditors closed in, demanding payment, and Kinney was forced to give up his Mustang Island ranch and mortgage other holdings. Kinney later said he spent $50,000 on the fair, which attracted thousands of people, and that, "No such pageant had ever been known in this section of the country before." Of course, Kinney had a natural gift for self-promotion. While Kinney had a vast amount of land, there were no buyers. He had cattle on his ranches, but there was no ready market for beef. Kinney's solution was to light out for distant places. He made his friend Judge M. P. Norton his business agent and left Corpus Christi on Sept. 4, 1854, headed for the Mosquito Coast of Nicaragua.

Kinney planned to establish a colony in the Mosquito Indian region. Some said that his ultimate goal was to establish a slave state that would be annexed by the United States. Kinney's venture was one of two filibustering expeditions against Nicaragua in 1855. The other was mounted by William Walker of Tennessee. Sam Houston wrote that Kinney's scheme was financed by New York speculators. "He contracted for 30 million acres of land in the Mosquito territory . . . He planned to set up a new empire." In the language of the time, Kinney was a filibuster or freebooter.

In New York, Kinney wrote his friend M. P. Norton on Nov. 8, 1854: "The Central American Company met at my rooms last evening. Several of the great men of the nation attended and made speeches. All agree that I shall do down at the head of the New Government of Central America."

When rumors of Kinney's scheme reached Washington, Secretary of State William Marcy asked Kinney to put in writing the purpose of his venture. Kinney wrote that his aim was to occupy and improve the lands within the Central American Company's grant. Marcy replied that the government would not object if it were a peaceful enterprise, but that "it is assumed your colony proposes to take possession of a part of the Mosquito country for which Nicaragua claims jurisdiction." Marcy said that would represent an invasion of Nicaragua and would violate U.S. neutrality laws.

After this, Kinney parted ways with the Central American Company and concocted his own plans for Nicaragua. He borrowed money and formed a partnership with Joseph Fabens, the U.S. consul at San Juan del Norte. Fabens claimed ownership of a large tract of land at Lake Nicaragua. Kinney and Fabens called their company the Nicaraguan Land and Mining Company and they proposed to work the mines in the region, cultivate the lands and cut mahogany trees for export. They also planned to set up their own government with Kinney at its head.

Kinney chartered the steamship *United States*, but as the ship was made ready to sail Kinney and Fabens were indicted by a federal grand jury and charged with violating the neutrality laws. They were arrested and released on bond. The case against them was postponed several times. President Franklin Pierce ordered the commander of the Brooklyn Navy Yard to prevent the Kinney expedition from leaving port. Kinney's chartered steamship, docked in the East River, was blocked by four Navy warships.

On June 6, 1855, Kinney wrote his friend Norton that he was sailing that afternoon. He had secretly chartered another ship, the schooner *Emma*, and organized a demonstration to protest the blockade of the ship *United States*. While the attention of authorities was focused on the protest, Kinney sailed away on the *Emma* and was free on the high seas. In letters to Norton, he wrote that he expected to make a million dollars.

The schooner *Emma* wrecked on a reef off the Turks and Caicos Islands. The ship was a total loss. When the ship struck, passengers said Kinney took charge in a sensible and competent fashion, helping save lives and part of the supplies. After the disaster, Kinney sailed on the *Huntress* for Greytown (also known as San Juan del Norte).

On Aug. 17, 1855, Kinney wrote Norton: "I am at last on Central American soil with 100 men and more. This is a beautiful place and is to be the principal of the world. My force will be augmented in three weeks to 2,000 men, when I shall move up country. I have a larger space to act in than I had at Corpus Christi and the result of my undertakings in Central America can hardly be imagined."

Kinney's followers elected him governor. By his own authority, he could raise armies and establish martial law. He appointed a Cabinet, flew his own Mosquito flag, and established a newspaper called *The Central American*. Kinney's government survived 16 days before he resigned. He still struggled to establish control over the territory he claimed, but he was fiercely opposed by William Walker, who had become a real power in Nicaragua.

When Kinney went to meet Walker, he was a supplicant and he was lucky that Walker didn't have him hanged, as he had threatened to do. Kinney hauled down his Mosquito flag and with it his dreams of empire. He was broke, drinking, and lost any influence he had in Nicaragua. He gave up his residence in San Juan del Norte and in 1858 returned to Corpus Christi.

Back in his own town, he was hailed as a returning hero, despite the bad debts he left behind and the failure of his Mosquito Coast filibuster. Some who knew him well thought the Henry Kinney who came back was a shell of the man who left four years before. In 1861, bankrupt and in bad health, Kinney wrote Abraham Lincoln, offering his services as foreign minister to Mexico. Lincoln didn't respond, so he made the same offer to Jefferson Davis, who also turned him down.

Kinney and his wife divorced when he returned from Nicaragua; they had separated years before when she learned he had a mistress, Genoveva Perez, in Mexico. Early one morning in February, 1862, he was shot to death in front of the house of his old flame, apparently by her new husband. Henry Lawrence Kinney, the founder of Corpus Christi and an important figure in the history of South Texas, was buried in an unmarked grave in Matamoros.

CHAPTER 19

JEFFERSON DAVIS IMPORTS
CAMELS TO SOUTH TEXAS
1856

They were decorated with red blankets. My sisters and I ran after them.
—Amelia Lewis of the camels at Indianola

At the end of the war with Mexico, the United States acquired a vast new territory stretching to the Pacific. The new territory required a chain of forts to protect traders and settlers; carrying supplies to these far-flung outposts was a nagging problem. In 1855, Secretary of War Jefferson Davis decided that instead of using longer and longer mule trains, the Army needed animals that could carry more weight and travel greater distances over arid regions. Davis thought the solution was to import Arabian camels. He pursued the novel idea to use camels to carry supplies to frontier forts in the Southwest, between Texas and California. He convinced Congress in 1855 to spend $30,000 to study the practicality of using Arabian camels to haul Army supplies.

The expedition to the Middle East was commanded by Army Maj. Henry Wayne, who was to purchase the camels, and Navy Lt. David Porter, who was in charge of the store-ship *Supply,* which was to transport the animals to Texas.

Maj. Wayne and Lt. Porter spent months in Europe and the Middle East. They went to Balaklava, while the Crimean War was being fought, to see British Army camels in action. The British had a camel unit of 1,000 men mounted on 500 dromedaries, two men to each animal, sitting back to back. During a battle, the camels would kneel and the men would form a square behind the kneeling camels.

Maj. Wayne and Lt. Porter made their way around the Middle East buying camels. They bought 34 one-humped and two-humped camels and hired five handlers to make the trip.

After the animals were loaded, Lt. Porter wrote that the camels, housed between decks, were "all standing, cleaned up, side by side, their backs just clearing our deck." Lt. Porter reported that the camel deck was scrubbed daily and the whitewash brush kept going. The camels liked the salty taste of the whitewash. At the end of the trip, the camels were said to be in better health than at the beginning.

On May 14, 1856, the camels were unloaded at the port of Indianola. There were Arab handlers in flowing robes and 34 camels, including two-hump Bactrians, one-hump Arabians, and the cross-breed mule Bactrian-Arabian camels called "booghdee." Most of Indianola turned out to see the exotic creatures. It was as good as a circus.

The camels had been on the ship for three months. When their hooves touched dry land, they went wild with excitement, jumping and biting each other, crying out, breaking their halters, in their joy to be back on firm ground. Mrs. Amelia Lewis remembered the camels. "They were decorated with red blankets. My sisters and I ran after them. On Sunday, everybody looked at the camels. It was a great sight."

Maj. Wayne gave a demonstration of the camel's great strength. A one-hump Arabian was made to kneel and two bales of hay were strapped to his back. The people watching were amused. Together, the bales weighed at least 600 pounds. They expected the camel would topple over from this heavy burden. But then the officer directed that two more bales be added, giving the camel a load of 1,200 pounds. The crowd was amazed when the camel easily rose to his feet and trotted away.

"Lord almighty," said one man. "That would take two mules and a wagon, easy."

Another man said, "Hell, four."

Lt. Porter returned to the Middle East for a second shipment. Another contingent of 40 camels arrived the following year.

The first herd of camels left Indianola on June 4, 1856. Because the smell of camels frightened horses, a rider was sent ahead warning people along the road that "the camels are coming." In reports to Washington, Maj. Wayne wrote that the camels had found good grazing and they luxuriated in the rich grasses of South Texas.

The caravan stopped for a rest near Victoria. A rancher's wife on the Indianola-Victoria Road, Mrs. Mary Shirkey, collected camel hair and used it to knit a pair of socks for President Franklin Pierce. No mention was made of whether the president ever wore the rare camel-hair socks. From Victoria, the camels went to San Antonio and finally reached Camp Verde, three miles from Bandera Pass, near Kerrville.

From Camp Verde, the Army conducted experiments with the camels.

In one experiment, 3,648 pounds were carried by six camels from San Antonio to Camp Verde. A load that size normally would have required two wagons pulled by six mule teams.

Maj. Wayne was enthusiastic, writing Washington that, "The camels thrive in this climate. Two full mule teams played out on the San Antonio test-haul, but the camels sauntered ahead on schedule. Troopers are now accepting the camels (with less profanity). The mule is obsolete in the West."

In another experiment, camels were sent over mountainous terrain which wagons couldn't cross. Each camel carried 328 pounds and covered 60 miles in two days, with no sign of fatigue.

The one experiment that caused the camels problems was in the Big Bend country where sharp flinty rocks nicked and cut the soft pads of their hooves. In June 1857, a mission to survey routes to the West was ordered. The trip by camel covered 1,200 miles and lasted four months. These camels were kept afterwards in California and Arizona.

A Corpus Christi newspaper, *The Nueces Valley*, in January 1858 reported that, "The experiment of our government in introducing camels as beasts of burden has proved eminently successful. Lt. Edward Fitzgerald Beale, who has had charge of the wagon road from Fort Defiance in New Mexico to the Colorado River, says that over surfaces covered with volcanic rocks, across rivers, and under every conceivable hardship, they remained sound in foot and body, and elicited his admiration of their remarkable qualities. The experiment of our government in introducing camels as beasts of burden has proved eminently successful."

The experiment came to an end when Texas took over Camp Verde in the Civil War. The Confederates used some of the camels to carry cotton down the Cotton Road; each camel could carry two bales of cotton. But Col. Rip Ford, who acquired command of the camels, didn't have much use for them. In one report, he wrote, "The camels have been sent to Guadalupe for corn. Two are reported to have died on the way. They can live best on grass; it is not certain they will live on corn."

After the war, the remaining 80 camels at Camp Verde were sold at auction. Most of them were bought by a man planning to run a mail and freight operation from Laredo to Mexico City. The Ringling Brothers Circus bought five. Eventually, many were turned loose to fend for themselves.

It was said that the camels that were turned loose to live in the wild liked to feed on prickly pear leaves and mesquite beans, but would eat anything, one man said, from a well-rope to a wheelbarrow. For years, wild camels were hunted for sport in South Texas. Hunting parties were organized to track them down and kill them.

Dr. Oscar S. McMullen, a doctor in Victoria, said, "About 1891, I was out near where Kingsville is now located, on the sand dunes, hunting burros. The cattlemen wanted the burros killed out as they were there in great numbers and depleting the grass. I was not a little surprised to find two old camels

149

browsing around the sand dunes. Although I was there often after that, I never saw them again."

The lead camel driver who came over with the camels was a Syrian named Hadji Ali, which Texans shortened to "Hi Jolly." Hadji Ali died in Arizona in 1903. There is a monument to him at Quartzsite, Ariz., that reads: "The last camp of Hi Jolly, born somewhere in Syria about 1828, died at Quartzsite, Dec. 16, 1903. Came to this country in 1856. Camel driver, packer, scout. Over 30 years a faithful aide to the U.S. Government."

CHAPTER 20

BUFFALO HUNTERS
AND KNIGHTS OF THE GOLDEN CIRCLE
1848 —1860

The Buffalo Hunters are mustering strongly; many of them have started for the hunting grounds; more are preparing to follow.
                                        —The New Orleans Delta

A strange news item in the *Corpus Christi Star* on Sept. 19, 1848 reported that a party of 190 buffalo hunters departed St. Joseph's Island off the Texas coast. The men left on a schooner with the man in charge, Capt. L.A. Besançon, bound for New Orleans. The remaining buffalo hunters left for places along the Mexican border.

They were not hunting buffalo. No buffalo herds had been seen in South Texas in many years. They planned to invade Mexico to establish a Republic of the Sierra Madre. They were army veterans who were looking for some new adventure. There was strong sentiment that the Treaty of Guadalupe Hidalgo, which ended the Mexican War, gave away too much, was too favorable to Mexico, that the United States should have kept the northern states of Tamaulipas, Nuevo Leon, and Coahuila. They argued that "God ordained that Mexico should be part of the Union" or, at least, the northern and eastern slopes of the eastern Sierra Madres.

In August 1848, a large party of Mexican War veterans — the Buffalo Hunters — were brought by schooner from New Orleans to St. Joseph's Island, where they camped and prepared for an expedition into Mexico. They expected that the people of northern Mexico, with their help, would rise up and establish their own republic, one free of the government of Mexico City. *The New Orleans Delta* reported that, "The Buffalo Hunters are mustering strongly; many of them have started for the hunting grounds; more are preparing to follow."

J. Williamson Moses, a sergeant in J. S. Sutton's company of Texas Rangers, wrote that the Buffalo Hunters were camped on the island, with beef and supplies being sent over by Henry Kinney and other Corpus Christi merchants.

In time, the Buffalo Hunters grew restive with the tedium of waiting and some of them came up with a scheme to rob Kinney. They had heard he had a vast amount of gold at his home on the bluff. Kinney heard of the plan and sent word to Capt. Sutton, camped with his Rangers at San Patricio. When the Buffalo Hunters arrived at Kinney's house, they were confronted by a squad of Rangers and were convinced to leave peacefully. Kinney provided them with the means to leave.

On Oct. 13, 1848, the *Galveston Weekly News* reported that Capt. Besançon and most of his Buffalo Hunters had returned to New Orleans. Besançon wrote a letter to the *Democratic Telegraph and Texas Register* in Houston apologizing to Kinney. He wrote that he regretted "having brought down men for the purpose of engaging in what has been called the Sierra Madre Expedition. Had I been aware of your (Kinney's) opinion, and not relied upon Madame Rumor, I should have saved the expense of subsistence and transportation of a large body of men."

In the end, the buffalo hunt turned out to be a wild goose chase.

* * *

It was the age of filibusters. In July 1850, another group of 250 armed Texans left Galveston and Corpus Christi to join an expedition to invade Cuba. Many of these were followers of Gen. Narcisso Lopez and they would be executed when the invasion failed.

In another venture, Gen. Jose Maria Jesus Carbajal led a Mexican filibuster between 1850 and 1853. This is sometimes called the Merchants War because the merchants in Matamoros, Brownsville and Corpus Christi were angry that Mexican authorities were interfering with their smuggling operations and turned to Carbajal, who planned to establish a border republic that would be pro-American, pro-Texas, and pro-slavery. Carbajal spoke at Kinney's Lone Star Fair in 1852 and some 80 men, including ex-Rangers, joined the cause. Henry Kinney led his own filibustering expedition to the Mosquito region of Nicaragua. The venture failed and he barely escaped with his life.

* * *

One of the strangest of filibuster intrigues was that of the Knights of the Golden Circle. The organization was a Klan-like secret society that aimed to create an empire of slavery that would extend from Central America through northern Mexico and encircle the southern states of the U.S. The capital of this golden slave empire would be Havana.

Toward the end of 1860, groups of strangers began arriving in Corpus Christi by steamer from New Orleans. They left Corpus Christi on foot. Who were they? Where were they going? No one knew. It was very mysterious.

Corpus Christi's newspaper, *the Ranchero*, reported that the men belonged to the Knights of the Golden Circle. The Knights had a plan to settle the problems Southern slave-holders had with their arch enemies, the "abolitionists" of the North, and their arrival in Corpus Christi was connected to that plan.

The Knights of the Golden Circle organization was four years old. It was founded in Lexington, Ky., on July 4, 1856 by a man named George Bickley. The secret society spread across the South. Local units were called "castles." Members were formed in three orders. Those with a military assignment (most members) were called Knights of the Iron Hand. Those with a financial calling were Knights of the True Faith. Those with political and leadership skills were Knights of the Columbian Star.

The Knights' agenda was the opposite of abolition. They planned to "perfect" the institution of slavery in a new empire of slavery. This empire would be enclosed in a golden circle, with Havana as the capital, extending to Central America and including much of Mexico and the West Indies. In the United States, the empire would stretch from Kansas to Maryland and take in Texas and all the states of the South.

The empire, as the KGC envisioned it, would hold a monopoly on tobacco, cotton, sugar, rice, and coffee. The South would control an empire that would become a world power, one to rival ancient Rome. Havana, in fact, would be called New Rome. With this wealth and power, the cities of the South would no longer be dependent on the abolitionist cities of the North.

That was the long-term goal. Short term, the Knights would assemble a force to conquer Mexico. If Mexico could be conquered, carved into states and admitted to the Union, the added representation in Congress would make the South politically dominant.

It was a slave-owner's fairy tale, not to mention being morally repugnant, but the Knights had many followers in Texas who were men of political importance. Ranger Capt. "Rip" Ford was a member and so was Alfred Marmaduke Hobby, later a Confederate leader. A large number of state legislators were members. There were 30 "castles" in the state, including one in Corpus Christi.

In the fall of 1860, the Knights were on the march through South Texas. The mysterious movement of men toward the border was part of the plan to conquer Mexico. The venture was badly organized. Several groups of men arrived in Corpus Christi and left on foot, walking toward the border. One rendezvous point was Brownsville and another in Encinal County (this county was later added to Webb County), at Laredo.

One group of Knights reached Banquete and settled down to wait for an army of thousands. J. Williamson Moses had been a Texas Ranger when the Buffalo Hunters came through in 1848. He was a postmaster at Banquete when the Knights of the Golden Circle began to arrive. Moses was disdainful of what he described as a wild and hare-brained scheme.

"This magnificent order, at least in name," Moses wrote, "planned secretly to organize and when they had a sufficiently powerful host at their command, they were to swoop down on the land of Mexico, like Goths of ancient days. The leaders promised that the followers were to have a tract of 50 acres and five Mexican slaves, or peons, to till it for them. This was to be the allotment of privates. The officers, according to rank, were to get larger amounts of land and a greater number of slaves."

The country above Brownsville was filled with Knights. "Their campfires are increased every night by new parties arriving during the day," a Galveston paper reported. So many arrived at Gonzales that Gov. Sam Houston ordered them to disband and return home.

The *Ranchero* newspaper noted on Sept. 15, 1860 that a detachment of Knights passed through Corpus Christi and, a week later, another detachment arrived. "Those who passed through last week are at Banquete," the editor wrote. "It appears they are bound to suffer disappointment, as they expected to meet a large force subsequent to a march on Matamoros." The paper said there were no large concentrations of Knights in Encinal County "or at any point in this section, hence the disappointment."

The Knights who passed through were said to be "orderly and gentlemanly in their bearing, and one would suppose them not likely to be gulled by the prospect of a rancho in Mexico." But Henry Maltby, editor of the *Ranchero*, understood that they lacked the military force of arms to invade Mexico and he advised young men to stay home and forget the dreams of empire.

George Bickley, leader of the Knights, arrived in South Texas and cited difficulties in raising money, buying weapons, and organizing such a large undertaking. He said he was postponing the Mexican invasion to await the outcome of the U.S. presidential election in November.

The dispirited phalanx of Knights in South Texas headed home. Corpus Christi's "castle" turned out on the fifth birthday of the KGC on July Fourth, 1861. The *Ranchero* reported that the Knights "a numerous body, who have been regarded as a very mysterious order, marched through the streets, even as other members filed into Ziegler's Hall. George Pfeuffer made a telling speech and the Knights made a telling impression on the good things spread before them, and numerous pert toasts were made."

That was their last hurrah before the "castle" disintegrated. Some of the first Confederate militia units were formed from the ranks of the Knights of the Golden Circle and some secessionist leaders were high officers in the order. The KGC's dreams of preserving slavery in a new Empire of the Gulf became one of the first victims of the Civil War.

The Battle of Corpus Christ

The painting of the battle of Corpus Christi in August 1862 shows a
Confederate battery firing on Union ships in the bay. Thomas J. Noakes of
Nuecestown made a sketch during the battle and afterwards completed the
painting as a gift for Maj. Alfred M. Hobby, the commander of Confederate
forces defending Corpus Christi.

The Defence of Corpus Christi

The "Defence of Corpus Christi" (sic) was painted by Confederate Army Sgt.
R. H. Gamble. It shows Confederates repelling the Union troops.

156

CHAPTER 21

JOHN KITTREDGE
AND THE BOMBARDMENT OF CORPUS CHRISTI
1862

The enemy is now at our doors. We are in danger and should be prepared for any emergency.

—*The Ranchero*

Four months after the Civil War began with the bombardment of Fort Sumter, S.C., on April 12, 1861, an acting volunteer lieutenant, 45 years old, was ordered to report to the New York Navy Yard. That was in August. Lt. John W. Kittredge — a small native New Yorker with a sallow complexion — was given command of the bark *Arthur*, a three-mast warship fitted out for blockade duty in the Gulf of Mexico.

The blockade of the Texas coast had been underway since July, bringing maritime trade to a halt. The newspaper in Corpus Christi, the *Ranchero*, reported that, "The enemy is now at our doors. We are in danger and should be prepared for any emergency."

In December, Lt. Kittredge sailed the bark *Arthur* to Ship Island, off Biloxi, Miss., which was blockade headquarters in the Gulf for the Union fleet, and from there he sailed the *Arthur* to its assigned blockade station near the Aransas Pass channel on the Texas coast. Before his arrival, Texas ports on the western end of the Gulf had been so lightly blockaded that blockade runners could operate at will out of Indianola, Corpus Christi, and other seaports. This was about to change.

For the next few months, Lt. Kittredge caused havoc along the coast, capturing blockade runners and sending raiding parties ashore to pillage and burn. Frightened residents on Mustang and St. Joseph's islands moved inland. The year 1862 was a time of panic in towns and settlements within Kittredge's reach.

In the early morning of Jan. 25, 1862, the schooner *J. J McNeil*, a blockade-runner, stood in for Pass Cavallo and Indianola. It was loaded with a cargo of coffee and tobacco from Veracruz. After unloading, it was supposed to return to Mexico with sugar and cotton, but the *McNeil* ran into the *Arthur* and was

157

captured. Kittredge took the ship's owner, Judge Martin Talbert, as prisoner and sent the *McNeil* with a prize crew to Ship Island. The captured ship and cargo would be sold; the captain and his crew would receive their fixed shares in prize money.

In February, Kittredge captured a sloop, the *Bellefont,* inside the bar at Aransas. He landed marines and sailors at several places on the coast, including Mustang Island, where they burned the homes of the bar pilots who guided ships through the pass. They burned the wharf at the village of Aransas, across the pass on St. Joseph's, and made raids in the vicinity of the big Confederate bastion, Fort Esperanza, on Matagorda Island.

In April 1862, Kittredge took launches for a cutting-out expedition on Aransas Bay. The bays were too shallow for the bark *Arthur,* which drew 14 feet. Kittredge's men attacked three ships off Shellbank Island in Aransas Bay and captured two, which they were forced to leave behind when Confederate reinforcements arrived from Fort Esperanza.

Kittredge and his men, in their launches, were almost captured when they mistakenly took Blind Bayou on St. Joseph's for an opening to the Gulf. When they came to the end of the bayou, they scrambled out of their launches, ran across the island to the Gulf side, and signaled to the waiting *Arthur.* A cutter was sent to rescue the party just as the chasing Confederates arrived.

After this close call, Kittredge stayed inactive for two months, keeping to the boring routine of tacking back and forth on blockade duty in the vicinity of the Aransas Pass channel, between Mustang and St. Joseph's islands. He sent no raiding forays ashore. But Kittredge resumed the offensive in the summer. A coastal survey ship, the *Sachem,* was converted into a gunboat and added to his fleet, along with a yacht captured on Lake Ponchartrain, the *Corypheus.*

On July 9, 1862, Kittredge captured the schooner *Reindeer,* loaded with 45 bales of cotton, and the next day he captured the sloop *Belle Italia* and burned the sloop *Monte Christo.* The *Belle Italia* was loaded with corn and bacon and the *Monte Christo* was carrying medical supplies.

Kittredge now had the light-draft ships he needed to sail into Corpus Christi Bay. His target was Corpus Christi, which was lightly defended and had been a center for blockade runners. Kittredge's shallow-draft vessels included former blockade ships *Reindeer, Belle Italia,* the steam-powered gunboat *Sachem,* and the fast sailing tender *Corypheus.* Except for the *Arthur,* left to its blockade post near the Aransas Pass, the other four ships could easily operate on Corpus Christi Bay.

People in Corpus Christi knew that "the pirate Kittredge" was coming. The city's provost marshal, Charles Lovenskiold, ordered several abandoned shellcrete houses to be torn down and the rubble loaded aboard three old ships. They sailed to the Corpus Christi Bayou and the ships were sunk to block Kittredge's entry into the bay. Any large vessel crossing the bay to Corpus Christi had to use the Corpus Christi Bayou.[33]

The Confederate officer sent to prepare a defense of Corpus Christi was Maj. Alfred Marmaduke Hobby. The Hobby family — a widow and three sons, including Alfred M. — settled at St. Mary's in 1857 and opened a general store. Alfred M. Hobby was elected to the Legislature and when the war broke out he organized a battalion that later became the 8th Texas Infantry Regiment.

Hobby ordered the gunboat *General Bee* and dispatch boat *Breaker* to guard the Aransas Pass channel and sent a schooner to guard the shallower Corpus Christi Pass. Kittredge's flotilla arrived on Tuesday morning Aug. 12, 1862. The sunken sloops filled with shellcrete rubble hardly slowed them down. The gunboat *Sachem* tied on to each and towed them out of the way.

Kittredge sailed into the inner bay with the *Corypheus, Reindeer, Belle Italia,* and *Sachem.* Kittredge, on the *Corypheus,* chased the dispatch boat *Breaker,* which was manned by a Russian called Sam and Jack Hardin, who had been a pilot on Mustang Island. Seeing that the Yankees were overtaking them and that escape was impossible, they hastily prepared to abandon ship. To keep it from falling into Union hands, they planned to blow it up. They had a sack of gunpowder to do the job. They started a fire in the hold, threw in the sack of gunpowder, and grabbed a sack of sugar on the ship. They waded ashore, waiting for the explosion, which never came. In their excitement and haste they threw the sack of sugar into the fire and were carrying the sack of gunpowder. Kittredge's men put out the fire and captured the ship.

That night, Kittredge anchored in the bay. The lights of his ships were seen clearly from the town.

Next morning, Kittredge landed under a flag of truce and met Maj. Hobby and Henry A. Gilpin on Ohler's Wharf. Kittredge said he intended to inspect U.S. government facilities in the town. Hobby told him the U.S. government had no facilities in the town and, furthermore, he had the forces to prevent Kittredge from coming ashore. After an exchange of threats, Kittredge gave Hobby 48 hours to evacuate the inhabitants.

The people in town packed up the family silver and heirlooms and prepared to evacuate. One woman carried a heavy chest filled with valuables and buried it in her yard. After the crisis was over, she discovered that it was too heavy for her to lift. Another woman said you could see women and children running off to the country loaded down with chickens, pots, kettles, every

---

[33] A causeway from Aransas Pass on the mainland to Harbor Island now crosses over the old bayou.

159

imaginable article. One young woman carried a washtub and yelled back to her mother not to forget the looking glass.

Captain Andy Anderson, a young boy then, was on the wharf when Kittredge landed and saw old gray-haired Henry Gilpin, a former county judge, go to meet the federal officer. The Anderson family went to Flour Bluff in an ox-wagon and stayed in an old house they used to store salt.

Many of the evacuees went west of town or up the river to Nuecestown. Anna Moore (later Schwein), a young slave girl, said she remembered the evacuation and bombardment "as if it were yesterday. My mother was living in a little frame house north of the old Cahill building on Water Street. After the warning had been received that the town would be bombarded, Mrs. (Forbes) Britton came for us with an ambulance and took us out to Judge Cody's in the Mott — Nuecestown. From there we could hear the sound of the cannon just as well as if we had been in town.

"Judge Cody was not prepared for the crowd of people who arrived from town. People slept wherever they could, out under the trees. A few had blankets they spread on the ground. This was one of the most miserable experiences I ever went through. All next day we had only cornbread, black coffee and buttermilk. It was the first time I had ever eaten cornbread made with buttermilk, and the first time I had coffee. The Codys were Irish and their brogue amused me; I had never heard it before."

Three miles west of Corpus Christi, some evacuees set up quilts on sticks to escape the broiling sun. During the bombardment, the Rankin family camped out on the Gallagher sheep ranch west of town. "We stayed there a few days," William Rankin, a young boy at the time, said. "We could hear the cannon fire. One day, another boy and I went to FitzSimmons' store and got groceries and went back. The Gallaghers had plenty of meat and cornbread." The evacuees listened to the bombardment, wondering if their homes were safe, and the children chanted a popular schoolyard rhyme of the day, perhaps in jest and perhaps in earnest:

> *"Jeff Davis is our president,*
> *Abe Lincoln is a fool;*
> *Jeff Davis rides a big gray horse,*
> *Abe Lincoln rides a mule."*

In town, when the truce was over, three guns — an 18-pounder and two 12-pounders — were placed behind old fortifications that were put up by Zachary Taylor's engineers in 1845. At dawn on Friday, Aug. 15, 1862, Felix Blucher, a Confederate major, aimed the 18-pounder at the *Corypheus* and said, "I believe I'll take a pop at it."

Blucher fired and the shell hit near the ship. He fired another round and the shot passed through the mainsail of the *Corypheus*. Another shot went through the side of the *Sachem*. The ships returned fire, with the shells landing on the fortifications, throwing up sand. The exchange of shots from the ships and the shore battery continued on Saturday. On Sunday, the guns were silent.

On Monday morning, Kittredge sent the *Belle Italia* close to shore and the ship landed 30 men in launches along with a 12-pounder howitzer on North Beach in an effort to take the Confederate battery from the rear. The men were carrying rat-tail files to use to spike the guns. Maj. Hobby led a charge on the 30 men with the howitzer and they were forced to flee back to their launches, dropping the rat-tail files in the sand. One Confederate soldier, Pvt. Henry Moat, was shot in the head during the charge and killed.

After the shore party was rescued, Kittredge leisurely shelled houses for a while, firing some 500 to 600 solid shot and explosive shells at the town and, having satisfied himself with knocking holes in buildings he was not allowed to inspect, sailed away.

The weary evacuees returned home to find many houses damaged. Spent cannonballs were collected, which they called "Kittredges," and used as conversation pieces and door-stops for the front parlor. Later, it was told that some of the cannonballs were filled with whisky. The story was that Kittredge's private supply of whisky was stolen by his sailors and they hid it by taking the powder out of the cannonballs and refilling them with liquor. The story, more legend than fact, was that during the bombardment the sailors forgot which cannonballs were filled with whisky and thus unexploded cannonballs were found filled with liquor.

A month later, Lt. Kittredge returned to Corpus Christi under a flag of truce to remove the family of Union sympathizer (and later governor) E. J. Davis. He was told to come back in 10 days for an answer. Confederate authorities had some intelligence about what Kittredge's next move might be. The Union blockade commander had gone ashore before around Flour Bluff, south of Corpus Christi, to supplement his shipboard fare with fresh eggs and buttermilk.

This time, a trap was laid by Capt. John Ireland. Kittredge was captured, along with his gig's seven-man crew, without a shot being fired. He was taken to the town he had so recently bombarded and crowds of people came out to see "that pirate Kittredge." He gave his parole and was sent north.[34]

---

[34] Kittredge was later court-martialed and discharged for striking an ordinary seaman.

In December 1862, Kittredge was gone but the offensive striking power was still with the Union fleet off Aransas Pass and Pass Cavallo. Confederate forces were thin on the ground and seemed powerless against what they called "Abe's abolition fleet."

The Confederates hunkered down in earthwork forts on Mustang and Matagorda islands — Fort Semmes and Fort Esperanza — and in the port cities of Corpus Christi, Saluria and Indianola. Clashes between Union and Confederate forces occurred around the passes connecting the Gulf to the inner bays.

On Dec. 5, 1862, Confederate Capt. H. Willke and Capt. John Ireland (later governor of Texas) took a sloop, *Queen of the Bay*, to sound the depth of water at Corpus Christi Pass. Willke was the senior officer. They took seven soldiers from Ireland's infantry company, a captain of the sloop, Jack Sands, and three sailors. They measured the depth on the bar on the Gulf side of the pass (where Packery Channel is today) at 5½ feet and on the bay side at 3½ feet. Due to contrary winds, they spent the next two days in the pass.

On Dec. 7, they were chased by two launches manned by 22 sailors from the Union blockade ship, the USS Bark *Arthur*. The *Queen of the Bay* tried to escape, with the launches in pursuit, using sails and oars. The Confederates ran their ship ashore on Padre Island. The men of Ireland's company, crack shots from Seguin, clambered to the top of sand hills and opened fire on the Union men in open boats. The Union men, under fire, tried to escape by beaching their boats on Mustang Island, across the pass, and running for cover in the dunes. They fired back at the Confederates, who returned fire, killing one of the sailors.

As shots were fired, the wind blew the launches away from shore. Capt. Ireland secured one of the launches, in which he found a dead man, another wounded, heavy coats, arms and ammunition. The other launch, drifting toward the Gulf, was secured by Capt. Sands. On Mustang Island, the man in charge of the two launches, Acting Ensign Alfred Reynolds, had been shot twice. Reynolds and another wounded sailor began the slow march up Mustang Island toward Aransas Bay to join the federal fleet.

The Confederates recovered the body of the man killed in the dunes. Capt. Willke's command returned to Corpus Christi without the loss of a man. One wounded man they brought back had been helping guide the Union launches. He was a civilian from Corpus Christi named Peter Baxter, an immigrant from Scotland.

Andrew Anderson, whose family was known as Union supporters, was a teenager then. He had a different spin on the story. He said the Union launches arrived at Corpus Christi Pass by mistake, that after the initial outburst of shots from the Confederates they tried to surrender. "As the launches entered the pass," Anderson said, "the Confederates on the big hill some 40 or 50 feet high could look down into the boats and shoot the soldiers. There must have been much bitterness by the Confederates because the federals were helpless and made every effort to make them understand that they would surrender; but little attention was given this and a number of federals were killed and the others captured."

Anderson remembered that the wounded civilian, Peter Baxter, had a great ring on his finger. "He (Baxter) said they had wanted to surrender but were not allowed to; he died from his wounds and was buried somewhere in Corpus Christi, probably in Old Bayview Cemetery." The launches full of bullet holes lay on the beach near the Anderson home on Water Street.

Maria Blucher, whose husband Felix, a Confederate officer, was in charge of coastal defenses at Corpus Christi and Saluria, wrote her parents about the skirmish. "The other day eight of our soldiers took two boats from the Yankees in Corpus Christi Bay and killed three Yankees, who were buried here," she wrote. "Captain Ireland and Captain Willke were our leaders. They were in a small boat reconnoitering Corpus Christi Pass. Realizing they were being pursued by two launches (the Yankee blockade bark was near the mouth of the pass), they landed and lay in ambush until the 25 Yankees were near. Then they fired, killed three, wounded the officer, put the soldiers to flight, and returned to Corpus Christi, safe and sound, with the Yankee boats, three dead, and a great number of excellent arms and provisions."

The following May, there was another skirmish on St. Joseph's Island (across from today's Port Aransas). Confederate Capt. Edwin Hobby, with 28 men, hid in the sand dunes and attacked three Union launches carrying 40 men who came to load a cargo of cotton from a beached blockade runner. When Union sailors came in for the cotton on the morning of May 3, 1863, the Confederates, hidden behind the dunes, opened fire. Capt. Hobby in his report said, "We could distinctly see the men in the launches drop their oars and fall as we fired. Several bodies were floating in the water . . . I do not think I am mistaken in estimating the loss of the enemy as 20 in killed, wounded and prisoners."

Compared to the great battles in the East, the skirmishes on the islands toward the end of 1862 and in early 1863 were "affairs" in military terms. But more serious fighting was ahead with Gen. Banks' invasion of the Texas coast in late 1863 and the capture of Fort Semmes and Fort Esperanza, giving the Union control of the Texas barrier islands.

Cotton Lined the Banks of the Rio Grande opposite Brownsville

CHAPTER 22

SALLY SKULL
AND THE COTTON ROAD
1860s

She was famed as a rough fighter and prudent men did not willingly provoke her in a row.

—Rip Ford

S ally Skull rode, cursed, and worked like a man as a horse-wrangler and muleskinner. She was a crack shot and carried a rifle, two pistols, and a blacksnake whip she could pick flowers with. Her name was used to frighten children — "You better behave or Sally Skull will get you."

Her real name was Sarah Jane Newman. In 1833, at age 16, she married a man named Jesse Robinson and they lived near Gonzales. She bore him a daughter, Nancy, in 1834 and a son, Alfred, in 1837. They divorced in 1843; Jesse accused her of adultery and gained custody of the kids. Eleven days after the divorce, she married a gunsmith, George Scull, who disappeared. When asked where he was, Sally would say, "He's dead," with a look that shut off questions. She kept the name, though she changed the spelling from Scull to Skull. She moved to Banquete in Nueces County in 1852.

Texas Ranger Rip Ford saw her at Henry Kinney's Lone Star Fair in 1852. Ford wrote that, "The last incident attracting the writer's attention occurred while he was Kinney's (water) tank wending his way homewards (Ford adopted the curious habit of referring to himself in the third person). He heard the report of a pistol, raised his eyes, saw a man falling to the ground, and a woman not far from him in the act of lowering a six-shooter. She was a noted character, named Sally Skull. She was famed as a rough fighter and prudent men did not willingly provoke her in a row. It was understood that she was justifiable in what she did on this occasion, having acted in self-defense."

Sally Skull made her living buying horses in Mexico and selling them in East Texas and Louisiana, traveling as far east as New Orleans. Some said she got the horses by other than legal means, but they didn't say that in her hearing. One man learned this the hard way. Sally Skull heard that he had made some ugly remarks about her and when she ran into him, she whipped out a six-gun and said, "Been talking about me, huh? Well, dance, you son of a bitch!" and began shooting at his toes as he danced a lively jig.

In October 1852 she married John Doyle, husband No. 3. He died soon afterwards. Two versions have been told of his death. One said he drowned with a team of oxen in crossing a river, that Sally saw him drown and when a vaquero asked if he should retrieve the body, she said, "I don't give a damn about the body, but I sure would like to have the $40 in that money belt he had on him." The second version said Doyle and Sally spent a night carousing at a fandango in Corpus Christi and next morning he was anxious to gather their horses to leave and tried to wake her, without much success, so he dumped a pitcher of water on her. She came up shooting, killing him. She said she would not have shot him "had I knowed."

She married husband No. 4, Isaiah Wadkins, in 1855. She divorced him when he moved in with a woman named Juanita in Rio Grande City.

During the Civil War, she hauled cotton down the Cotton Road. When Union warships blockaded Southern ports during the war, the Confederacy opened a back door on the Rio Grande, which by treaty was an international waterway. Cotton was hauled by wagon, oxcart and mule cart down this trail — the Cotton Road — to Matamoros, which during the war became the greatest cotton market in the world. These were boom times in Mexico known as *Los Algodones,* the cotton times.

* * *

On the Cotton Road, wagons loaded with bales of cotton from East Texas and Louisiana plantations converged at Samuel Miller's ferry on the Nueces River at a little community called Santa Margarita. From Santa Margarita the road followed the route Zachary Taylor's army took when it left Corpus Christi in 1846. The next major stop was Banquete, west of Corpus Christi, where long trains of wagons and oxcarts passed day and night. Confederate troops camped on San Fernando Creek to guard this vital artery.

After Banquete, the next stop was King Ranch headquarters at Santa Gertrudis (at today's Kingsville), a receiving depot for the Confederate government. Teamsters could replenish their water and buy supplies at the ranch commissary. Richard King was an organizer of the Cotton Road and profited from the cotton trade during the war.

The Cotton Road branched into several directions, depending on the changing fortunes of war. For the first three years, the road ran south to Brownsville, following a wide track marked with snags of cotton caught in

166

the brush. After the Union army captured Brownsville in late 1863, the Cotton Road shifted upriver to Rio Grande City, where it crossed the river and made its way south on an old road running parallel to the river. Whichever route the road took, the cotton came down in a never-ending stream, with hundreds of wagons hauling thousands of bales, bringing back gold and war materiel on the back haul.

One traveler who described the Cotton Road was Lt. Col. James Arthur Lyon Fremantle of Her Majesty's Coldstream Guards. He made a three-month tour of the Confederacy in 1863. He arrived at Brownsville and traveled across the South, meeting Confederate generals and leaders, including Robert E. Lee and Jefferson Davis. He watched Pickett's charge at Gettysburg from the forks of a tree.

Fremantle kept a diary, filling it with trenchant observations about his experiences in Matamoros, Brownsville and traveling up the Cotton Road. When his ship arrived at the mouth of the Rio Grande, he saw some 70 ships from all nations waiting for cotton cargoes. Fremantle left the border with two colorful mule drivers much addicted to liquor. They rode in a four-wheeled carriage with a canvas roof that was pulled by mules and along the way they saw many wagons loaded with cotton. "Generally there were 10 oxen or six mules to a wagon carrying ten bales," Fremantle wrote. "They journey very slowly towards Brownsville."

* * *

At the beginning of the war, Sally Skull gave up buying and selling horses and bought a train of freight wagons and hired Mexican vaqueros to handle them. Fortunes could be made at the back door of the Confederacy with cotton that sold for a few cents a pound in east Texas bringing from 50 cents to a dollar a pound at Matamoros, paid in gold.

On her cotton-freighting trips, Sally Skull would visit her daughter Nancy Robinson in Bee County and her son Alfred Robinson at his ranch north of San Patricio.

On one trip, Sally Skull ran into a freighter who owed her money. She raised an ax and said, "If you don't pay me, I'll chop the front wheels off every damned wagon you've got." He paid.

John Warren Hunter was 16 when he drove a cotton wagon to Brownsville. He saw Sally Skull at Rancho Las Animas on the other side of the Big Sands. He said she was "superbly mounted, wearing a black dress and sunbonnet, sitting as erect as a cavalry officer, with a six-shooter hanging at her belt."

When she was 43, Sally Skull married her fifth husband, Christoph Horsdorff, called "Horse Trough," who was 20 years younger. The year after the war ended, in 1866, she disappeared. The general suspicion was that

Horsdorff blew the top of her head off with a shotgun to steal the gold she carried in a nosebag on her saddle horn. Whatever happened to Sally Skull, whatever the circumstances of her death were, she was never seen again. Horsdorff left South Texas and remarried.

One story said her body was discovered by a man named McDowell who found her boot sticking out of a shallow grave somewhere in South Texas. Another story said she changed her name and started a new life on a ranch near El Paso. Sally Skull may have killed two of five husbands, an assertion hedged with the usual caveat — she was never charged or convicted — they just disappeared, as she did herself.

What is not in doubt is that she made her own way on the male-dominated frontier of Texas at a time when gender roles were sharply defined and rigidly followed. It took a woman of exceptional character and inner strength to defy the conventions of a prejudicial time. She was mostly self-invented, with no role models to follow, one of a kind and well ahead of her time. The author J. Frank Dobie wrote that she was "notorious for her husbands, her horse trading, freighting and roughness." Pistol-packing Sally Skull with her blacksnake whip was truly one of the more remarkable characters in the history of South Texas.

The Rebels had Skedaddled Three Days Ago

CHAPTER 23

NATHANIEL BANKS
AND THE INVASION OF SOUTH TEXAS
1863

The flag of the Union floated over Texas today at meridian precisely.
—Gen. Nathaniel Banks to Abraham Lincoln

When he was growing up, Nathaniel P. Banks was a child laborer in a cotton mill. He was nicknamed the Bobbin Boy. In later life he made a fortune and was elected governor of Massachusetts. During the Civil War, Banks was one of Abraham Lincoln's important political generals, so-called because their rank was determined by political influence rather than military merit or experience.

The Bobbin Boy was given another nickname by Confederate soldiers in Virginia. His supplies were captured so often by Confederate troops under Stonewall Jackson that they called him Commissary Banks. He was transferred to New Orleans in 1862 and led a failed and costly effort to capture Port Gibson on the Mississippi below Vicksburg. After Vicksburg fell on July 4, 1863, a sizable Union army was available to disrupt the traffic in cotton going to Mexico on the Cotton Road in South Texas.

Cotton shipped through Brownsville and Matamoros was helping sustain the Confederacy. Gold from the sale of cotton bought guns and gunpowder, medical supplies, and military essentials. That was the reason for a Union invasion of Texas. But also there were fears that French forces propping up the Maximilian regime in Mexico might make common cause with Confederates; a strong Union presence in South Texas would discourage any such alliance.

The task of invading Texas was assigned to Gen. Banks. As he assembled his invasion forces in New Orleans, Confederate spies relayed the information to Texas. Texans knew the invasion was coming, but they didn't know where Banks would strike. Confederates expected him to make an overland assault from Louisiana, so they shifted forces to the Red River area. But Banks chose to make an amphibious assault, sending an advance force of

171

27 warships and transports carrying 6,000 soldiers to establish a beachhead at Sabine Pass, which drains water from Sabine Lake to the Gulf, near the Louisiana line.

Banks' objective at Sabine Pass was virtually undefended, except for one small Confederate fort that guarded the pass. The fort was manned by Richard "Dick" Dowling, a 25-year lieutenant, with a small artillery detachment of fewer than 50 men. The detachment was composed of home guard troops who were mostly Irish immigrant dockworkers from Galveston. They had half a dozen old cannons which, in their idle days, they had become proficient in using.

In the battle of Sabine Pass on Sept. 8, 1863, Dowling's Irish dockworkers fired at Banks' four Union gunboats that led the way for the Union invasion fleet. One of the gunboats was the *Sachem*, which had been involved in the bombardment of Corpus Christi by Lt. John Kittredge in August 1862.

At Sabine Pass, Dowling's gunners, with accurate fire perfected by long hours of practice, scored two direct hits, disabling two of the Union gunboats. Banks' invasion fleet limped back to New Orleans.

Banks next put together a 7,500-man invasion force made up of battle-hardened veterans from the Vicksburg campaign. They would be carried on transports escorted by Navy gunboats, but instead of trying to invade by the Sabine Pass he would go in through the Confederacy's back door on the Rio Grande.

Banks put this expedition under the command of Gen. Napoleon Jackson Tecumseh Dana, no stranger to South Texas. Dana, along with his brother-in-law Daniel P. Whiting, served in Zachary Taylor's army when it was concentrated at Corpus Christi in late 1845 and early 1846 preparing for the Mexican War.

Banks' army boarded 13 transports, escorted by three gunboats, on Oct. 23, 1863. Major units were the 13th and 15th Maine, the 94th Illinois, the 20th Wisconsin, and the 19th and 20th Iowa. There was also Battery B of the 1st Missouri Light Artillery. A soldier in the 13th Maine wrote that they marched to the levee in a pouring rain and boarded the steamer *Clinton*. They were packed so tight they couldn't lie down. They spent several days taking on fresh water. Once in the Gulf, a storm scattered the fleet and the expedition lost three steamboats, four schooners, all their horses and nearly all the artillery.

The weather finally cleared and a noonday sun was shining when the first units of Banks' forces landed without opposition. Soldiers of the 15th Maine raised an American flag and fired a volley in salute on the north end of Brazos Santiago Island, near the mouth of the Rio Grande. They landed at an abandoned Confederate salt works. Gen. Banks sent an exultant message to

Abraham Lincoln, dated Nov. 2, 1863 — "The flag of the Union floated over Texas today at meridian precisely."

The 13th Maine prepared to move on Brownsville. To keep their pants and shoes dry, a colonel ordered the soldiers to strip and wade. They crossed the shallow Laguna Madre with bare legs and feet. The razor sharp oyster shells on the bottom of the laguna cut up their feet and legs. At Brownsville, soldiers of the 13th Maine slept in an empty cotton warehouse. Next day, they moved into Fort Brown, Zachary Taylor's old fort that was bombarded by Mexican forces during the Mexican War. They found the water in the Rio Grande the sweetest they had tasted since leaving Maine. They met no Confederate opposition.

Gen. Hamilton P. Bee, in charge of Confederate forces in South Texas, known for his Hamlet-like indecisiveness, nearly set Brownsville on fire in his haste to destroy warehouses filled with valuable cotton so he could evacuate the city. Like Banks, Bee was a politician before the war. Also like Banks, he was militarily inept. He seemed to lack both the means and the will to fight. Before the war, he was a legislator and businessman in Laredo. Bee's forces retreated from Brownsville and stopped at Banquete, west of Corpus Christi. Bee worried about where Banks would strike next.

With Brownsville in Union hands, Banks prepared for the next objective. Advance units embarked on two captured Rio Grande riverboats — owned by Richard King and Mifflin Kenedy — and headed for Mustang Island. The units included the 13th and 15th Maine and elements of the 20th Iowa, under the command of Gen. T. E. G. Ransom.

The invaders landed at Corpus Christi Pass, the inlet dividing Mustang and Padre Islands. They waded through the surf at a place not far from where Bob Hall Pier is today. It was nightfall on Nov. 16, 1863 when they began marching the 18 miles to the head of Mustang Island, where Confederate Fort Semmes guarded the Aransas Pass ship channel.

On the march up the island, the Union soldiers carried 100 rounds of ammunition, guns, knapsacks, and three days' provisions. Their clothes and shoes were wet, their feet sore from the oyster-shell cuts they got in the Laguna Madre. They had to drag two heavy siege guns through the island's loose sand.

Early the next morning at daybreak they approached Fort Semmes, located near where Port Aransas is today. The Union skirmishers shot at Confederate sentries, driving them inside the fort. The Union gunboat *Monongahela* moved into the Aransas Pass channel, opposite the fort, and lobbed shells into the bastion.

The Confederates showed a white flag. When the white flag was raised, Cpl. Marvel McFarland came running out, waving at the Union troops, in what was meant to be a friendly gesture. But the gesture was mistaken and he was shot. His arm had to be amputated. The Union attackers captured three heavy cannon, one schooner, ten boats, 140 horses, nine officers, and 89 men.

While Fort Semmes was under attack, residents in Corpus Christi could hear the gunfire across the bay. Fort Semmes was manned mostly by Corpus Christi men and people in the city worried about their fate. Gen. Bee rode into Corpus Christi from Banquete and sent Lt. Walter Mann under a flag of truce to find out what happened to the men at Fort Semmes. The flag of truce was not honored — Mann was considered a spy and held a prisoner by the Union forces.

Trying to guess Banks' intentions, Bee withdrew the remainder of his forces from Corpus Christi. Before leaving, his men set a charge under the lighthouse on the bluff, but it only knocked down a corner of the building.

Bee's retreat was bitterly resented by the people of Corpus Christi, who were outraged by the apparent passivity of the Confederate commander. Bee reported to his superiors from Corpus Christi that, "About 3,000 of the enemy are now at the Aransas Pass. I shall virtually abandon this place tomorrow. There is nothing for the cavalry horses to eat and, from the latest developments of the enemy, he will either march up St. Joseph's Island and attack Saluria, or he will land at Lamar and cross over to Indianola, thus cutting off Fort Esperanza. I need not say that I find my position annoying. There are three points of attack for the enemy — Corpus, Lamar, and Saluria — the first is the least important to us."

Before Bee retreated in haste across the Nueces River, he ordered livestock and horses to be driven east of the Nueces, with nothing of value left behind. The draconian order also said that under no circumstances were male Negro slaves to be left behind. As a last resort, Bee ordered, they were to be shot, "for they will become willing or unwilling soldiers against us." There were no reports that the order to shoot male slaves was obeyed.

A Union garrison was established on Mustang Island and Fort Semmes was renamed Post Aransas.

The 20th Iowa was chosen for garrison duty, perhaps as a punishment detail because Maj. William Thompson of the 20th Iowa complained too loudly and too often about having to drag two siege guns through the sand on the march up Mustang Island. Gen. Ransom criticized Thompson for "constantly discouraging his men by complaining in their presence." Maj. Thompson, in a letter to his wife, wrote that he and the 20th Iowa were given the assignment as a mark of respect for the fine job they had done. Included in the garrison duty with the 20th Iowa were 200 African-American soldiers in the Corps d'Afrique who were assigned the task of building sand fortifications at the renamed Post Aransas.

The 20th Iowa was composed of farm boys from Marion, Iowa. They had fought in battles at Pea Ridge in Arkansas and during the siege of Vicksburg.

They settled in on Mustang Island. Union sympathizers came looking for food. Maj. Thompson said one man, a former slave-owner who had been worth $100,000 before the war, was reduced to begging for bread for his hungry children.

In letters to his wife, Maj. Thompson said there was plenty of beef on the island, but no trees for firewood, so his men roamed down Mustang and Padre Island looking for wood to build their huts for the winter. They made raids into Corpus Christi, as the residents looked on in helpless resentment, and pulled down vacant houses for planks and hauled away chests of drawers and fine-grained furniture to furnish their huts.

The regimental historian of the 20th Iowa wrote that, "Most of the men built comfortable quarters and furnished them with comfort, even luxury. The little frame huts contained mahogany and rosewood furniture of the richest description, procured during scouting expeditions by confiscation from houses abandoned by rebels."

Thompson wrote that his men always returned from their raids on Corpus Christi without having encountered any resistance. On one raid on Feb. 21, 1864, soldiers under Thompson's command searched the houses of prominent Confederates. They took away copies of Corpus Christi's newspaper — *the Ranchero* — which they found amusing because of its "rebel lies."

When the 20th Iowa was left to occupy Mustang Island, the remainder of Gen. Banks' invasion forces moved on to their third objective, the massive Fort Esperanza (meaning hope in Spanish) on Matagorda Island guarding Pass Cavallo. As a norther blew in on Nov. 19, 1863, Union troops were ferried across the Aransas Pass channel to St. Joseph's Island.

They reached Cedar Bayou, which separates St. Joseph's from Matagorda Island, on Nov. 23, 1863. A Confederate major appeared on the opposite side of the bayou, waving a white flag. He wanted to know what had happened to the Confederate soldiers manning Fort Semmes. A sergeant from the 15th Maine swam across the channel to talk. There was an angry exchange of words and the Confederate major shot the Union sergeant. From across the bayou, Union troops fired on and hit the major. He ran into the dunes, where his body was found. The sergeant was wounded.

The Union troops crossed Cedar Bayou on small flatboats they brought up on wagons, then marched 20 miles and camped at a deserted ranch house.

On Nov. 27, 1863, they gazed on the massive Fort Esperanza. At the beginning of the war, 500 slaves were put to work building this earthwork fort on the south end of Matagorda Island, near the town of Saluria. They built walls 12 feet high and 15 feet thick. The fort was armed with eight 24-pound cannons and one behemoth, a 124-pound "Columbiad," to guard Pass Cavallo.

As Union troops approached Fort Esperanza, they fired on Confederate pickets, driving them inside the walls. They prepared for a siege, digging rifle pits linked with trenches. Batteries were placed and cannon fire was exchanged with Fort Esperanza on Nov. 29. A Union soldier saw a cannonball rolling in the sand and foolishly stuck out his foot to stop it. It caused such damage his foot had to be amputated.

The Confederates inside the fort faced a strong force on their land side and Union gunboats in the pass. They spiked the cannons, set the powder magazines on fire, and evacuated before federal troops could close off their escape route. The federal troops set up camps and placed a regiment across the pass at Decrow's Point. By the end of November, it was bitterly cold. Union soldiers at Esperanza had no supplies and nothing to eat except beef from wild cattle butchered on the island. Since they had no tents, they sheltered in rifle pits dug for a siege, which were covered with the hides of slaughtered cattle.

Two captured riverboats that were being used to supply the Union soldiers, the *Planter* and the *Matamoros*, got too close to shore and ran aground. Both ships burned all their coal trying to get up enough steam to heave off. Soldiers were put to work collecting more fuel. They tore down abandoned houses, gathered driftwood and anything that would burn. The boats finally got clear by using kedge anchors to warp free. While this was going on, a sailor took aim at a cow and shot a captain in the head, killing him.

Frequent raids were made into Indianola and Port Lavaca. Indianola was occupied in December. By year's end, Union forces under Banks held possession of the lower Texas Coast, from Pass Cavallo to Brownsville. In February 1864 they were ordered back to New Orleans. Small garrisons were left at Pass Cavallo and Post Aransas at Aransas Pass, but these were also pulled out two months later.

Gen. Banks was not finished with South Texas. He led a Union army in one last attempt to invade the state from Louisiana. In the resulting battle in April 1864, badly outnumbered Confederates (12,000 Confederates to 40,000 federals) turned back Banks' superior forces in the battle of Mansfield (sometimes called Sabine Crossroads). The Confederate forces were under the command of Maj. Gen. Richard Taylor, son of old Zachary Taylor, one of two commanding generals in the Mexican War and former president.

Gen. Richard Taylor picked the site of the battle, 20 miles east of the Texas border. His forces included Brig. Gen. Thomas Green's brigade of cavalrymen armed with shotguns, Bowie knives, and swords. Green[35] was a hero of the Sibley expedition at Valverde, New Mexico. Taylor wrote of

---

[35] Gen. Thomas Green who fought at the battle of Mansfield should not be confused with Thomas Jefferson Green, one of the Texas leaders at the battle of Mier in 1842.

Green that, "I enjoyed watching his method of managing his wild horsemen." He said that Green's men, with shotguns blazing, "arrested the progress of a superior force of enemy horsemen."

The battle at Mansfield ended with the Banks' forces in full flight. Taylor's Confederates captured 2,500 prisoners and 20 pieces of artillery. After the battle was over, Taylor received a messenger from Gen. Kirby Smith ordering him not to bring on a general engagement with superior federal forces. Taylor swore loudly and sent Gen. Smith the message that the battle was already fought and won. That was Banks' last attempt to invade Texas.

Banks' earlier effort to invade Texas in late 1863 resulted in the capture of Brownsville and two Confederate forts on the barrier islands. The invasion disrupted the cotton trade but did not stop it. Strategically, Banks' invasion attempts in 1863 and the following year changed nothing. The new general of all the Union armies, U.S. Grant, who had been in South Texas in the run-up to the Mexican War, realized that Texas was too far out on the periphery to be of much concern. He knew that the war would not be over until Gen. Lee's army was beaten in the field in Virginia. For the rest of the war, South Texas was virtually left alone. The Confederates even moved back into Fort Esperanza, though there was little hope they could hold on to it if the federals ever decided they wanted it back.

CHAPTER 24

BENJAMIN F. NEAL,
CHIPITA RODRIGUEZ
AND HANGING TIMES
1863

I've had enough of this.

—Spectator at hanging

Benjamin F. Neal, Corpus Christi's first mayor, was a man of diverse talents. He taught school, practiced law, edited newspapers, rode with the Texas Rangers, presided as judge, and organized coastal defenses in the Civil War. He was the man who sentenced Chipita Rodriguez to hang.

Neal, born in Virginia, was trained as a lawyer. He came to Texas in 1838. He taught school at Live Oak Point, then was elected chief justice of Refugio County in 1840. He was holding that position when a band of Mexican irregulars pillaged and sacked Refugio. Neal was a member of John Reagan Baker's "spy" company which patrolled from Aransas City to Refugio.

He bought the *Advocate*, a newspaper across from Galveston, and moved the press to Galveston and established the *Galveston News*. He sold his interest in the *News* and established the *Galveston Daily Globe*. Neal moved to Corpus Christi in 1844 and became general counsel for the town's founder, Henry L. Kinney. In 1847, Neal was elected to the Texas House and in 1850 he established a newspaper at Corpus Christi, the *Nueces Valley*. In 1852, Neal was elected the city's first mayor.

In the late 1850s, Neal moved to Arizona, where he was appointed attorney general of the territory, but within two years he returned to Corpus Christi. At the start of the Civil War, Neal feared the Texas coast was open to invasion and wrote Jefferson Davis about the need for coastal artillery. Soon afterwards, he organized an artillery company to defend Corpus Christi.

Neal's company was stationed at Fort Semmes, on the northeastern tip of Mustang Island facing the channel. On Feb. 25, 1862, sailors and marines from one of the federal blockading ships landed on Mustang Island, burned homes, crossed the channel and burned buildings on St. Joseph's Island.

179

Before the landing, Neal withdrew his company and offered no resistance. This brought sharp censure from a Confederate major on Matagorda Island, who passed on a complaint that Neal acted "with cowardice and indecorum."

The sense of injury of the Mercers, Chubbs and other residents of Mustang and St. Joseph's islands — whose homes were burned and property plundered — was blamed on Neal. In his defense, he had no infantry support to repulse a landing force and his battery of two light six-pounders had little gunpowder. And of course he was not a soldier.

A few months later, when Neal was ordered to blow up the Aransas Pass Lighthouse, his men doubled the charge and the resulting explosion sent the spiral staircase inside shooting out of the top of the lighthouse, like launching a giant corkscrew. But the lighthouse was otherwise undamaged.

In 1863, U.S. forces under Nathaniel P. Banks occupied Brownsville and moved up the coast. Before they could reach Neal's Battery at Fort Semmes, Neal resigned his command; he had been elected judge of the 14th District. Lt. William Maltby, second in command, took over the battery in time to be captured by Union forces.

Judge Neal had a case to hear. That August, a horse trader named John Savage spent the night at Chipita Rodriguez's cabin on the Aransas River. His body was later found, his head split open with an axe. Suspicion fell on Chipita.

"Chipita" was a nickname probably derived from Josefa. Her father Pedro Rodriguez brought her to Texas from Mexico. He joined Texas forces and was killed in the fighting during the Texas Revolution. She settled down in a shack on the Aransas River. Her place became an overnight way station where travelers could get a meal and sleep on the porch. Savage, the horse trader, stayed at Chipita's place on the night of Aug. 23, 1863. He disappeared. Two women servants at the nearby Welder ranch were washing clothes in the river when they saw his body in a burlap bag. His head had been split open.

San Patricio County Sheriff Pole Means went to Chipita's, where he found blood on her porch. She said it was chicken blood. Chipita and her hired man, Juan Silvera, were arrested. Chipita and Silvera were charged with Savage's murder.

The trial was irregular. Neal was the presiding judge and the prosecutor was John S. Givens. Sheriff Means, who investigated the case, served on the grand jury that indicted Chipita. There was no jury panel for the trial — people were rounded up off the streets near the courthouse. Four members of the jury had been indicted for felonies, one for murder, and the jury foreman was a friend of the sheriff. The motive for the killing was supposed to be robbery but the horse trader's $600 in gold was found in his saddlebags.

180

Chipita would not help in her own defense; she offered no statements in the case.

The trial lasted most of the morning and the jury brought back a verdict by noon. Juan Silvera was found guilty of second-degree murder and Chipita was found guilty of first-degree murder. Because of her age and the weakness of the evidence against her, the jury urged clemency for Chipita. Judge Neal did not agree with the jury's plea and ordered her to be hanged on Saturday, Nov. 13, 1863.

The trial records were burned in a courthouse fire in 1889. What little survived suggests the evidence was not carefully considered. The case was circumstantial, with no witnesses and no motive. Why Chipita would not help in her defense is a mystery. Why Neal chose not to accede to the jury's request for clemency is another mystery. Many believed her to be innocent. Prominent citizens at San Patricio urged the sheriff not to carry out the sentence; the day before the hanging, he left the village, leaving the hangman to carry out the sentence alone. Judge Neal was not there, either; he was holding court in another part of the district.

Nov. 13, 1863 was Chipita's hanging day. When the hangman arrived in San Patricio, he tried to borrow a wagon, but was turned down. He was forced to confiscate it. They came for her in the wagon. She climbed up and sat on a coffin made of cypress planks that had been nailed together that morning. The wagon was pulled by oxen and people of San Patricio walked behind. One account said they were quiet — the only noise was the creaking of the wagon. They didn't have far to go from the courthouse and jail before the wagon stopped under a mesquite tree by the Nueces River.

The people watched as a new hemp rope was placed around Chipita's neck. She was wearing a borrowed dress and a woman in town had fixed her hair for the occasion. She showed no sign of fear.

At the hanging tree, there was a murmur when the wagon moved forward, the rope jerked, and Chipita dropped, her feet only inches above the ground. The oxen moved so slowly and her body was so frail that the fall didn't break her neck and she slowly strangled to death. A woman in the crowd fainted, a small boy ran away, and a man turned his back, saying, "I've had enough of this." The hangman cut her down and she was buried in the cypress coffin at the foot of the mesquite tree.

At the end of the war, in 1865, Neal was deposed as district judge by the military authorities. He was reinstated a few months later. In 1867, he was again removed by military order. Neal revived his old newspaper, the *Nueces Valley*, published from his house across from Artesian Park. He later sold the paper.

Neal married twice. After his first wife died, he wed Azubah (Zula) Haynes, a Quaker from Philadelphia. Neal died a relatively poor man on July

181

18, 1873. He was buried in Old Bayview Cemetery in Corpus Christi.[36] Where Chipita Rodriguez was buried is unknown, but it was somewhere under the limbs of the hanging tree on the banks of the Nueces River near the village of San Patricio.

* * *

This was an era of public hangings. Not long after the hanging of Chipita Rodriguez, a man named Jim Garner was hanged by a lynch mob in Corpus Christi. Garner had a reputation as a bad man and troublemaker. When he was 15, he killed a man named Bateman on Christmas Eve in a saloon in Helena, a rough town in Karnes County.

Ten years later, on May 15, 1866, when Garner was 25, he killed a storekeeper named Emanuel Scheuer in Corpus Christi.

Garner tried on boots and was leaving the store without paying when Scheuer said he wouldn't give him credit. Garner shot him through the heart, killing him instantly. Scheuer was laid out on the counter of his store. Garner was found and dragged along by a mob to an arroyo south of town lined with mesquite trees where he was hanged, all the time pleading, "Give me a trial, boys." Capt. John Anderson, a resident of Corpus Christi, said later — "A lot of us caught hold of the rope. The crowd was quiet as he kicked and kicked. Everybody left pretty quick."

* * *

Ed Singleton, a clerk in Bee County, had long sideburns and a reputation for violence. He worked for a man named John Dwyer. The two men left for Rockport to buy a load of whiskey and haul it to Dog Town (Tilden) where they planned to open a saloon. On the way back, they got to drinking the merchandise and Singleton killed Dwyer.

Dwyer's shirtfront had four gold buttons connected by a chain, a fashion of the time. Singleton cut off the shirt front to get the gold buttons. He was caught trying to board a ship at Indianola with Dwyer's money and those gold buttons on him. Singleton was tried, convicted, and sentenced to be hanged.

Some of his saloon friends made plans to free him from the Bee County Jail. The sheriff put out the word he was taking Singleton to Galveston for safekeeping. But he took him to a thicket outside town, chained him to a tree, and kept him under guard for two weeks, until the day before the hanging.

---

[36] A large granite monument in Old Bayview was dedicated to Neal's memory on April 7, 1935.

Back in jail, Singleton wrote his mother, vowing that he would never be hanged in public before a multitude of fools.

As the time drew near, Singleton wrote out his will and directed that somebody who owed him money should pay someone else that he owed, to square accounts. He said he wanted his body skinned and the skin to be given to the prosecuting attorney — named J. J. Swan — and that it be stretched over a drumhead and each year on the anniversary of his death the drum should be beaten on the streets of Beeville to the tune of "Old Mollie Hare."

The lyrics of the song included the lines: "Old Mollie Hare, what you doing there? / Running down the road as hard as I can tear. / Old Mollie Hare, what you doing there? / Running through the briar patch as hard as I can tear."

The night before the hanging, Singleton played cards all night with his guards. He was hanged on April 27, 1877. His last wishes, at least regarding his skin, were ignored.

* * *

In 1897, a man killed three members of a family near Floresville with an ax. He was arrested in Duval County, returned to Floresville, convicted and sentenced to be hanged. The events of hanging day were told years later to Bob McCracken, columnist for the *Corpus Christi Caller-Times*, by Ranger Capt. W. L. Wright, who assisted at the hanging. Another account was told by Jack Youngblood, justice of the peace at Floresville at the time.

On the day of the hanging, they gave the condemned man whisky in a tin cup, and kept refilling the cup. He made speeches and sang songs. The justice of the peace said the man drank whisky all day to fortify himself. The town was crowded with people who came to see the hanging.

A gramophone salesman played records and a fire extinguisher salesman erected a small model house in the street and set it on fire to demonstrate the efficacy of his fire extinguisher.

People who didn't know it was a demonstration began to run. One fellow yelled, "Keep your seat, folks, there ain't no fire!" Another man ran past him yelling, "You're a damned liar!"

At the scaffold, Capt. Wright put a black cap on the killer's head and fixed the knot in the rope. Wright said he forgot to move away from the trapdoor and had to jump away at the last second when it was sprung. Wright said it would have been like the two Rangers who hanged a man in Brownsville and forgot to move from the trap door. "When the trap was sprung, they went through it too, and fell six feet to the ground."

The *Corpus Christi Caller* noted that several other hangings were scheduled in the region. "This is good," said the newspaper, "but there is one thing about hangings that is objectionable. They do not occur often enough."

The body of Eunice Hatch, 18, who lived on a farm a few miles west of Corpus Christi, was found in her home on April 21, 1902. Her head had been split open with a hatchet. The body was found by John Priour, an uncle of her husband, James Marion Hatch, Jr. Her parents, Mr. and Mrs. W. H. Lindley, lived at Ingleside.

Hatch and his young wife had an infant daughter, Myrtle, who was crying in her crib when her mother's body was found. Hatch was the grandson of George C. Hatch, murdered of on the Reef Road in 1872.

In the murder of Eunice Hatch, suspicion focused on Andres Olivares, who worked on the nearby McCampbell place. He had been a guest in the house, but Eunice told her husband not to bring him back. "Jim, I don't want Andres over here anymore," she told him. "I don't like the way he looks at me."

Blood was found on Olivares' clothes and his shoes matched prints at the murder scene. Some men urged Sheriff John Bluntzer to let them have Olivares and turn his back. But the husband, Jim Hatch, stopped that. He walked up to the prisoner and talked softly to him for a time. People tried to overhear the conversation, but could not. Olivares hung his head and listened.

Though he pleaded guilty at the arraignment, Judge Stanley Welch ordered a not-guilty plea to be entered. The trial lasted one morning. That afternoon, the jury found him guilty. The judge ordered Olivares to be hanged on June 3, 1902. After the sentence, the newspaper printed Olivares' confession: "I did it but I do not know what was in me at that moment. I killed that woman, Jim Hatch's wife."

On the day of the hanging, Olivares was taken to a scaffold built at the 1854 Nueces County Courthouse and the jailer, named Ranahan, fixed the noose around his neck. Olivares said, "Adios amigos!" before Sheriff Bluntzer sprang the trap. Those who witnessed the hanging were Hatch, the husband, and the victim's father, W. H. Lindley. Like the murder of George C. Hatch on the Reef Road in 1872, the 1902 hatchet slaying of Eunice Hatch, followed by the hanging of Andres Olivares, was the talk of Corpus Christi for a long time.

Mat Nolan

CHAPTER 25

MAT NOLAN
AND THE DEFEAT OF CECILIO BALERIO
1864

Stand back or I'll shoot!

—*John Warren to Tom Nolan*

After the deaths of their parents, three Irish orphans — an older sister and two younger brothers — joined the U.S. Army. Mary Nolan, the older sister, was hired as a laundress. Her brothers Matthew and Thomas, 11 and 9 years old, were allowed to enlist as bugle boys in the 2nd Dragoons. The Nolans landed at Corpus Christi with Zachary Taylor's army in 1845.

Mary Nolan married a soldier. After he died, she became a nurse. During the Mexican War, Mat and Tom were at the battles of Palo Alto and Resaca de la Palma and served throughout Taylor's campaign in northern Mexico.

After the war, the three Nolans returned to Corpus Christi. Mary remarried and Mat, 16, and Tom, 14, joined the Texas Rangers. Ranger Captain Rip Ford cited Mat Nolan for bravery in a fight with Comanches near Fort Merrill on May 26, 1850. When the Indians tried to steal their horses, Nolan ran barefoot through prickly pear to get a shot as the Indians rode away.

When the Rangers were disbanded, Mat and Tom Nolan returned to Corpus Christi and in 1858, Mat Nolan, 24, was elected sheriff of Nueces County. He hired his younger brother as a deputy. During this time, the Nolans joined Ranger expeditions against Comanches and when trouble arose on the border. They were back in Corpus Christi on Aug. 4, 1860 when a drunk stabbed a saloon-keeper.

The Nolan brothers found the suspect, a butcher named John Warren, who pointed a gun and warned, "Stand back or I'll shoot!" When Tom Nolan reached for the gun, Warren shot him in the head. Warren was chased down and shot to death by Sheriff Nolan and several citizens who joined the chase. Tom Nolan died 11 days after he was shot.

When the Civil War broke out, Mat Nolan raised a company of volunteers, who enlisted at Banquete. His company served in South Texas and eventually he was back in the command of Rip Ford, his old Ranger captain. In the second year of the war, he returned to Corpus Christi to marry Margaret McMahon. Nolan and his company took part in the recapture of Galveston.

Mat Nolan was promoted to major and recalled to Corpus Christi to deal with Cecilio Balerio, who commanded an irregular Union cavalry outfit that rustled cattle on the King Ranch and other South Texas ranches and attacked wagon trains hauling cotton on the Cotton Road. Balerio's raiders lived in the brush and prowled the remote Wild Horse Desert.

Before the war, Balerio was a Nueces County rancher and horse-trader, who had a reputation for stealing horses. When the Civil War broke out, former Corpus Christi Judge E. J. Davis, who became a Union leader, enlisted Balerio to attack wagon trains carrying cotton down the Cotton Road to the Rio Grande.

Balerio's outfit was nominally under the command of John Haynes' Second Regiment of Texas Cavalry, but Balerio operated on his own, committing what the Confederates considered opportunistic marauding. Balerio, who turned 65 in 1861, was assisted by two sons, an older son named Juan and a younger son named Jose Mario.

Balerio was in contact with Union commanders in Matamoros and later in Brownsville. He supplied Union forces on the border with beef cattle rounded up from Texas ranches. He was also in contact with Union blockade ships standing to off the Aransas Pass channel. The ships supplied him with Burnside Carbines, Colt revolvers, blankets, and paid him in gold for his guerrilla activities against the Confederacy.

Balerio's cavalry was a persistent thorn for Confederates. His troops hid in the mesquite brush from which they launched surprise attacks against targets of opportunity, usually stray cotton wagons on the Cotton Road and unprotected ranches. Mat Nolan and other Confederate officers searched for Balerio without success.

In early March 1864 Balerio's cavalry raided the King Ranch and drove off 100 horses. Soon afterwards, Balerio's son Jose Mario slipped into Corpus Christi to visit his girlfriend and to gather intelligence of the movements of Confederate patrols. He was captured by Captain James Richardson, a Confederate officer, tried before a military tribunal, convicted of spying and sentenced to be shot by firing squad.

Major Nolan told Jose his life would be spared if he would lead them to his father's camp. Balerio refused but broke down when he was taken before a firing squad. He told Nolan that his father's outfit was camped 50 miles below Banquete at a place called Los Patricios (near the present town of Falfurrias).

Nolan assembled a makeshift force composed of some of his men and some from Richardson's company. Jose Balerio was placed on a horse, his feet tied to the stirrups and hands tied to the pommel. Behind him rode one of Nolan's men with orders to shoot Balerio at any sign of treachery. They rode southwest and halted before dawn on Sunday morning, March 13, 1864. The camp was unguarded.

At the last minute, before Nolan's men could attack, Jose gave a warning cry — "Cuidado!"

Balerio had 80 men and Nolan 62. The fight in a mesquite thicket lasted 15 minutes. Balerio's guerrillas charged and, Nolan wrote in his report, fought gallantly. Two of Nolan's men were killed and two wounded. Five of Balerio's men were killed, their bodies found in the brush, with blood trails indicating that others had been shot and dragged away. Wounded horses left behind had to be put down.

Balerio and his two sons got away. Jose, who had been tied to his horse, was allowed to escape as payment for leading the Confederates to his father's camp. After this narrow escape, the Balerios crossed into Mexico.

Cecilio Balerio went to see his nominal commander, Col. Hayne, and for some reason, Haynes refused to see him, a deliberate snub, coming after such a hard-fought encounter. Rip Ford, Balerio's sworn enemy, made note of this slight in his memoirs. Ford described Balerio in admiring terms as brave, crafty and resourceful, a tone suggesting he deserved better treatment from his Yankee commanders. "One thing is sure," Ford wrote. "After Captain Balerio's departure, no one came to take his place."

After the battle at Los Patricios, Nolan's company at Banquete played a cat-and-mouse game with Union forces on Mustang Island. Union soldiers would cross the bay to steal lumber and furniture in Corpus Christi. Nolan's soldiers would arrive the following day. This went on until Union forces were pulled back to New Orleans.

* * *

In August 1864, Nolan was re-elected sheriff of Nueces County, though he was a Confederate officer serving in the field. Rip Ford ordered him to arrest several known Union sympathizers, including Henry W. Berry, a former mayor of Corpus Christi, the first sheriff of Nueces County, who had served as a deputy sheriff under Nolan after his brother Tom was killed.

Ford's order to arrest Berry and other "perfidious renegades" could have led to their executions as traitors. Berry was on the list because he had been seen loading cotton on a Union ship off Padre Island. In a report to Ford, on March 6, 1864, Nolan wrote, "On the night of Thursday under the command of Captains Gray and Doolittle, with 45 men, the enemy returned in their boats, landing with them a number of Corpus renegades, among whom was H. W. Berry."

On Dec. 22, 1864 at sunset, Nolan was talking to a horse trader across the street from his house on Mesquite Street in Corpus Christi, a block south of the courthouse. Berry's stepsons, Frank and Charles Gravis, walked up, passed a few words, and shot Nolan with a shotgun. The horse-trader was chased down and killed with a pistol and left lying on the street with a hole by his left ear.

The wounded Nolan said the Gravis boys were the shooters. He said he knew why they did it, that they had their reasons, but he died before he could say more.

It was believed that Nolan was killed because of his intent to arrest Berry and other prominent citizens of Corpus Christi for treason. He was buried in Old Bayview Cemetery next to his brother Tom. Mat Nolan's headstone includes nothing about his high Confederate rank, but reveals his early days as a young Irish bugle boy in the Mexican War. It reads: "Matthew Nolan, Co. G, 2nd U.S. Dragoons."

A Confederate grand jury indicted Frank and Charles Gravis for murder, but nothing was done about the indictments in 1865 as the war ended. When Union occupiers took power in 1865, Berry was appointed sheriff and he hired his stepson Charles Gravis as a deputy. The indictments for killing Mat Nolan were relegated to a dark corner of the Confederate past.

For the Balerios, after Jose's near execution by firing squad at Corpus Christi and their defeat at Los Patricios, they crossed into Mexico and returned to Mier, Tamaulipas, where the elder Balerio was born. In 1868, Cecilio Balerio — Nueces County rancher and Union raider — died at 72. Two years later, Reconstruction Gov. E. J. Davis, the man who convinced Balerio to join the Union cause, awarded Balerio's heirs a quarter-section of land in South Texas for services rendered the Union during the Civil War.

Thomas Noakes

CHAPTER 26

THOMAS NOAKES' DIARY
OF DRY WEATHER AND HARD TIMES
1863 — 1865

I took our last sack of flour out of our secret hole.

—Thomas Noakes

Thomas Noakes left his home in Sussex, England when he was 16. He crossed the Atlantic as a cabin boy, reached South Texas in 1845 and got a job as a ranch hand for Corpus Christi founder Henry Kinney. Noakes was well-educated and he had a talent for making things. He developed skills as a carpenter, saddle-maker, gunsmith, musical instrument repairman, farmer, and storekeeper. He taught school for a time. He also kept a diary. The first volume was lost, but the second volume, which begins in 1858, and later volumes tell us much about life in South Texas during the Civil War.

Noakes lived outside Nuecestown, near today's Calallen, up the river from Corpus Christi. He lived with his wife Marie and, in time, they had seven children. Because his right lung was useless and he suffered from consumption, he was given a certificate of disability by Confederate military authorities, which allowed him to stay with his family. Noakes served, more off than on, in a local Confederate militia and may have been on hand for the bombardment of Corpus Christi when U.S. warships under Lt. J. W. Kittredge attacked and shelled the city. Noakes later painted a watercolor of the battle.

On Feb. 11, 1861, Noakes wrote about his wedding day in his diary. "I have been helping to plough fields for Mr. Ludwig (his future father-in-law). I rode to Corpus with Mr. Ludwig, bought some seed, a barrel of flour, procured a marriage license at the county clerk's office and left notice of my marriage at the office of the Corpus papers, then returned home to Mr. Ludwig's. After supper I took the horses, riding one and leading the other, and went home and dressed. And then it being quite dark, I took the horses to

Mr. Taylor's in the town (Nuecestown), he being the justice of the peace, and fetched him to Mr. Ludwig's and there Mary and I were married, unknown to anybody but the old folks and Mr. Taylor, as we did not wish to have any fuss. And for my part, I could not have had a party if I had wished, as 30 cents was the most cash I possessed. I had not even the money to pay for a license, but Marie (he alternately called her Mary and Marie) being willing to take me as I am, I thought it a waste of time to wait for better times."

Noakes' diary reveals the terrible times during the war when a drought and a bitterly cold winter afflicted South Texas. The land was stripped of grass and even the hope of grass. In June 1863 Noakes and two friends went to the Salt Lagoon (today's Baffin Bay) to get a load of salt, which could be traded inland for meat and other foodstuffs. On the way, they found a place where women were living without their husbands, who had deserted them and gone over to the Yankees.

"One of the women had a child die on the previous evening and there was not a man or boy big enough to make the coffin and dig the grave, so we offered our services," Noakes wrote. "I made the coffin — there being tools and lumber there — while Stevens and Harrison dug the grave. We buried the child and headed home at sundown."

Noakes went to Banquete to get paid "for a beef which the quartermaster had on his books, it having been killed for the Confederate troops. The beef was worth $15, but I was paid $2, and that is the first pay I have had for several they killed. Before we were in any danger, we had to feed the soldiers with our beeves. As soon as danger threatened, we were abandoned. Now that we are once more out of danger, the troops are being sent back to live again on our beeves." Such hardened cynicism toward Confederate authorities was a sentiment shared widely by the end of the war.

From Noakes' diary at the end of 1863 — "I took our last sack of flour out of our secret hole. I went to Corpus to get some sacks. I succeeded in getting some sacks and a little bread, soda and black pepper. Corpus looks more desolate than ever." Dec. 31, 1863 — "The last day of a miserable year. Bitterly cold. I sat by the fire mending Mary's shoes." Next day — "Water froze, milk also. Stayed in and boiled soap. I drove the cart to Taylor's and borrowed two bushels of corn." Jan. 5, 1864: "Exceedingly cold, water froze close to the fire. I put my horse in the house to keep him from perishing."

* * *

The Union blockade shut off supplies, causing acute shortages of food and necessities. Since it was all but impossible to get manufactured goods, stores closed and the economy collapsed. Clothing, shoes, flour, sugar and coffee were scarce, very expensive, or not available at all. Texas, overrun with longhorns, had plenty of leather but no shoe manufacturers. It was a cotton state, but had no cotton mills. Tools used for making things came from the North or from Europe. Now these were unavailable.

People had to improvise and adapt. They had to relearn old skills. They made looms to weave cloth. They used indigo plants to make blue dye. They collected indigo weeds which were packed into barrels and filled with water. After a few days, the water and weeds were dumped, leaving a cake of blue dye at the bottom. The cloth woven on homemade looms inspired songs about "homespun dresses, like Southern ladies wear."

They ground acorns to make ersatz coffee. There was no white sugar, but people who could travel could get a crude yellow cane sugar from East Texas, at great expense. People around Corpus Christi would travel as far as San Antonio and Austin to obtain flour or corn meal, but it was risky. A man on the road with a wagon and horses was always in danger of having his team and wagon confiscated by Confederate authorities for use in hauling cotton down the Cotton Road.

* * *

In times of scarcity, Noakes showed a genius for improvisation. He burned cow dung for ashes to make lye soap. He tanned cow hides to make what he called "square buckets" and leather sacks. Everything had to be made by hand and it was all but impossible to buy tools. He made saddles for extra income and made his own shot to kill small game by beating lead into thin sheets and cutting it into small squares, which he found "answers very well."

The bad times brought on by war turned even worse with a severe drought, which plunged them into deep misery. Death and destruction spread across the land. Noakes wrote that there had been no rain "worth mentioning" for a year, since July of 1863. Cattle and sheep were dying along the dried-up creeks and rivers.

Noakes said dead animals met one's gaze in every direction. He counted 163 head of cattle and three horses dead in the mud at one watering place. They bogged down in the mud by creeks and rivers, the last place where grass could be found, and then they were too weak to get out and died by the thousands mired in the mud.

Noakes saw a team of work steers yoked together, one dead and the other standing quietly by its side. "Go which way you will go," he wrote, "you see dead horses, cattle and sheep. All the creeks stink with them."

Across the desolate countryside, denuded of grass, wind blew dust and sand, filling the sky with a haze that limited visibility. What you could see was parched and brown — "There is not a green thing to be seen."

195

Noakes traveled far in an exhausting hunt for corn and flour. Because there was little grass, his horses wandered off seeking forage. He would spend days trying to find his cart horses. Then he would travel to the Salt Lagoon, 50 miles away, to get a load of salt to trade for corn, sweet potatoes and other staples. These were hard trips for Noakes. He had one lung and was often spitting up blood and running a fever.

In March, 1864, on the way to Goliad, he and a neighbor, Ned Taylor, cut down trees so their horses could eat the moss from out-of-reach limbs. "As soon as we began cutting down the trees, crowds of cattle came running up and only with great difficulty could we get any moss for our horses, as the starved cattle fairly took it by storm. We could not drive them away. Very sad. They ate the moss and leaves and then the branches, eating everything under 1½ inches in diameter."

On his trips, Noakes found houses empty, yards overgrown with weeds, and ranches that were semi-derelict because of a shortage of manpower. On a trip down Banquete Creek, out of 12 or 14 houses, "I only saw one or two that were occupied, the rest having been abandoned; everything has fled east."

He found Corpus Christi "in a state of desolation, everything gone to ruin and hardly a living soul to be seen," the pall of neglect and abandonment seen everywhere. He thought that Goliad, where he went to trade salt for corn, had "a substantial look about it. Unlike most Texas towns, a good many houses were built of stone and in very good taste."

Beeville, wrote Noakes, "was a poor, deserted-looking place, nearly every house standing on the bare prairie without a fence and having the general appearance of so many wooden boxes standing about at intervals." Helena was a "tumbled-down-looking affair," with the men gone to war and farms abandoned. If it had not been for wartime, he thought Seguin "would have been a lovely and interesting neighborhood. There are some very nice-looking houses and the fine school house is a tasteful building."

He was surprised to find New Braunfels so big. "The principle street must be three quarters of a mile long with some very fine buildings." The streets were lined with chinaberry trees and the houses were clean, with nice, shady gardens. Noakes walked all over New Braunfels trying to trade his salt for flour and he found the prices "ridiculously high. We had to pay 15 cents for a small glass of beer and everything else in proportion."

Near the end of Noakes' diary for 1864, he wrote, "I was working on my saddle tree and killed two large rattlesnakes, taking their fat, but having nothing to put it in, I had to skin one of the snakes without ripping the skin and of that I made a bag in which I brought home the fat, by tying a knot at each end."

In an entry on Oct. 28, 1864, Noakes wrote — "I took a ride up the river, giving myself a Texas holiday, which consists in riding a broken-down horse all day, in search of game that you never find, and having nothing to eat."

* * *

After the war, in the fall of 1865, rancher George Reynolds asked Noakes to teach school at Nuecestown. Noakes didn't want to teach, but he needed to provide for his family. He went to Corpus Christi to see William Carroll, called "Little" Carroll, a teacher at the Hidalgo Seminary. Carroll told Noakes how he organized his lessons and next day Noakes audited Carroll's class.

Most of the exercises were written on the blackboard, Noakes wrote. "The writing lesson is copied on the board, from the grammar or the arithmetic, by the teacher and recopied by pupils. After which, every pupil recites what he has written to the teacher, who examines the writing at the same time, thus the pupils learn to write, cipher or speak grammar at the same exercise." This was followed by spelling, geography, and arithmetic, in which pupils went over multiplication tables and Carroll copied sums on the blackboard.

"Commencing with the top of the class," Noakes wrote, "each boy does his part, the teacher doing the figuring on the board, as the pupils direct him, each pupil holding his slate and copying the sum when it goes on. When the sums are completed, the pupils take their slates to the teacher, who inspects the manner in which they are written. In the reading lessons, each pupil reads a short passage, while the pupil next to him stops him (as they term it) that is, at a comma, he exclaims, 'comma one' and so on."

After spending the day in Carroll's class, Noakes went to see the postmaster Horace Taylor, the former teacher at Nuecestown, to borrow a blackboard. Now he was ready to conduct school.

Noakes began teaching on Oct. 1, 1865. He started school at nine, went to lunch at 12, and quit at 4 p.m. "I experienced much less difficulty from my students than I expected and found them anxious to learn. I experienced the greatest difficulty for want of books, slates, everything required to carry on a school. I found the schoolhouse deficient as much as the pupils, the windows being gone, sashes and all."

After school, Noakes had chores to do until dark, such as rounding up cows, butchering meat, digging a well, tanning a hide. Noakes settled in to his new pursuit. He noted that teaching required more patience than education. He made a deal with a parent named Stevens to teach his children without paying a fee in return for him providing Noakes with lunch each day. The Stevens' place was near the schoolhouse.

197

On Nov. 13, 1865, a freezing norther blew in. The windows of the schoolhouse being out, "the wind and rain made it very disagreeable. After dinner, I made a fire, but it was very cold and most of the children being thinly clad, I dismissed school at 3 p.m." On Saturday, he fixed the windows of the schoolhouse.

On Nov. 29, there was an explosion at a neighbor's place, the Hinnant home. A bottle filled with gunpowder was being used as a candle holder. When the candle burned down, the gunpowder exploded. "My best pupil, a young lady of 16 (Mary Hinnant) was hit in the face and arm by fragments of glass and badly cut, besides being much burned." Noakes visited her and was distressed to see "what was once a pretty face all burned, cut and swollen. I now have four pupils sick with fever and one wounded from a gunpowder explosion."

On Dec. 5, 1865, Noakes kept a fire burning at the schoolhouse. "Some days, school-teaching goes very much against me, and this was one of the days. I sometimes feel as though I must get on my horse and ride off somewhere to get away and leave everything and then again there are moments when I feel more satisfied."

When his friend John Williams died, Noakes wanted to be executor of the estate. This would entitle him to a percentage of the sale. But George Reynolds and James Bryden, influential stock raisers, sought that for themselves. Noakes was furious, writing that Reynolds and Bryden "hate to see me make a cent and if they can keep me poor, I will be dependent on them. By allowing me to keep a small school, they intend to keep me from starving while they get their children educated."

Noakes tried to prevent Reynolds and Bryden from "their contemplated self-appropriation of John Williams' estate" but had no success. On Dec. 22 he told his pupils he was giving up the post of schoolteacher. He bid them farewell. "I did intend to say more, but so many sorrowful looking faces being turned on me at the same time quite unmanned me. I had to thank them for their attention during the short time we had been together."

He rode into Corpus Christi to buy groceries for Christmas, paying 60 cents a pound for coffee, 50 cents a pound for sugar, and $1 for a small tin of preserved peaches, "those things being considered the height of luxury." Noakes, amid mental turmoil, was depressed on Christmas Day, feeling that "everything was crooked and everybody corrupt."

Two days after Christmas he rode into Corpus Christi and withdrew his application to become administrator of the Williams' estate. He saw that Bryden and Reynolds were in town. Back home he vented his spleen in his diary — "In these people we see the old adage verified, that if a beggar gets on horseback he will ride to the devil."

A Mr. Doke (perhaps the name was Doak), a short-tempered man from Louisiana, took Noakes' place as schoolmaster. On Dec. 31, 1865, Noakes summed up his brief tenure as a teacher. His income for the year did not exceed $4 and he noted that, "The only gain I made has been confined to experience and that may be good pay for future purposes, but it's a very poor article to live on."

Noakes later opened a store in Nuecestown. It was plundered and burned when Mexican bandits raided Nuecestown on Easter weekend 1875. Thomas John Noakes, an Englishman who made a new life for himself in South Texas, died in 1878. He was buried on his farm outside Nuecestown.

Rip Ford

CHAPTER 27

RIP FORD
AND THE LAST BATTLE OF THE CIVIL WAR
1865

You can retreat and go to hell if you wish. I am going to fight.
—Rip Ford to James Slaughter

John Salmon Ford missed the battle of San Jacinto — he arrived a month too late — but he didn't miss much else in the next 50 years of Texas history. He was a major participant and keen eyewitness to the main events of his time. His Confederate Cavalry of the West, operating in the borderlands of South Texas, fought and won the last land battle of the Civil War.

Ford was trained in Tennessee as a teacher and doctor. When he arrived in Texas in 1836, he practiced medicine and did surveying work. He fought in several Indian skirmishes in east Texas, including the battle of the Neches in 1839 when Cherokee Chief Bowles was killed, still wearing the red silk vest given him by Sam Houston.

Ford, elected to the Ninth Congress of the Republic, introduced the legislation to allow Texas to join the United States. That year, 1845, he became editor of the *Austin Texas Democrat.* When war broke out with Mexico he joined Jack Hays' regiment of Rangers.

Ford fought in battles from Veracruz to Mexico City. One of his duties as adjutant to Jack Hays was to send out death notices. He would write "Rest in Peace" at the bottom of the list. He shortened it to "R.I.P" and someone started calling him "Old Rip."

Ford in his memoirs described the Rangers' entry into Mexico City, writing that the inhabitants turned out to see the hated Texas devils, "*Los Diablos Tejanos.*"

After the war, Ford led an expedition to El Paso to find a practical overland route to California during the gold rush. In El Paso, he ran into Sarah Bourjett, the Great Western, a camp follower who had been with Taylor's army in Corpus Christi and was in the bombardment of Fort Brown. She owned a bordello-hotel in El Paso.

Ford, appointed to head a company of Rangers, stationed his company at Henry L. Kinney's ranch on the Oso near Corpus Christi. Another of Ford's camps was on the Santa Gertrudis Creek, the site that would become headquarters of the King Ranch.

For the next few years, Ford pursued Comanche raiding parties in the valley of the Nueces. In 1849, his company of Rangers patrolled an area between the Nueces and the Rio Grande, above the road from San Antonio to Laredo.

Ford wrote in his memoirs that any move by a Ranger toward dandyism or affectation in dress was bound to be put down by other Rangers, who would not tolerate affected airs. On a trip in 1849, a Ranger named Henderson Miller, troubled with sunburn and a blistered nose and lips, bought an umbrella to protect his sensitive features. On the second day out, when Ford left camp with two men to go hunting, they were only a mile or so away when they heard a sharp exchange of firearms coming from the camp. The men with Ford wanted to rush back, thinking the camp was being attacked by Indians.

Ford was not excited. He explained that the camp was not under attack. "The boys are just shooting Henderson Miller's umbrella."

When they returned to camp later that day they found the umbrella had been shot to pieces. Ford said he let matters pass without notice since he could not remedy the affair and decided that silence was the best course of action. Ford doesn't say, leaving us to guess, but we suspect that Henderson Miller never went out with an umbrella again.

* * *

A year later, after Fort Merrill was built overlooking the Nueces River north of Corpus Christi, Rip Ford's Rangers stopped by to camp. There was a skirmish during the night when Comanches tried to steal their horses. In another fight with Comanches near Fort Merrill, Ford yelled to a Ranger — "Level, what is the matter?"

"Damn them," he said, "they shot my horse."

"Oh, is that all?"

"No, damn them, they shot me, too."

Rip Ford was elected to the Texas Senate in 1852. He went back to newspapering, then joined Carbajal's revolution in northern Mexico, which failed.

In 1858, Ford was appointed to head another command of Rangers to deal with hostile Comanche tribes on the Canadian River. Ford and Shapley Ross led a combined force against Comanches under Chief Iron Jacket. He was called Iron Jacket because he wore a Spanish coat of mail into battle. It didn't help him this time. He was killed in the fight with Ford's Rangers.

When Texas seceded from the Union, Ford was given a desk job as chief of the bureau of conscription for Texas. He pursued draft-dodgers for two years. In December 1863, Gen. John B. Magruder, commanding the District of Texas, ordered him to command a regiment of Texas cavalry composed of volunteers too young or too old to be drafted. Ford called his unit the Cavalry of the West. It operated in South Texas, from Corpus Christi to Brownsville to Laredo. Ford was promoted to brigadier general of Texas state troops in 1864.

* * *

In March 1865, Union Gen. Lew Wallace[37] came to Brazos Santiago on a diplomatic mission from Abraham Lincoln. Wallace sent a message to Confederate Gen. James Slaughter at Brownsville, seeking a conference. After some delay, caused when a norther blew in, Slaughter agreed to meet Wallace at Point Isabel. Slaughter took Rip Ford, also a brigadier general, with him, while Wallace had his staff.

The subject of the meeting was the possibility of concluding an informal, limited peace between the Union and Confederacy in South Texas.

Lew Wallace, according to Ford's memoirs, said it was useless to continue to fight on the Rio Grande. Slaughter and Ford said they had no authority to act unless they received instructions from their Confederate superiors in the Trans-Mississippi Department. This included the states of Louisiana, Arkansas, Texas and the Indian Territory, the area severed from the Confederacy proper when the Union gained control of the Mississippi River.

Rip Ford left the meeting with the understanding that there would be a peaceful co-existence, at least unofficially, along the border at Brownsville, based on nothing more than a gentleman's agreement reached with Wallace.

Confederate superiors in the Trans-Mississippi Department, especially Gen. John G. Walker at Houston, were furious that Slaughter and Ford had discussed reaching an understanding without proper authority. Walker insisted the war was far from over and that they would fight on.

The following month, on April 9, Gen. Robert E. Lee surrendered at Appomattox. The news didn't reach South Texas for some time — exactly when has been a point of contention. The states in the Trans-Mississippi continued to resist until they finally surrendered a month later, on May 6.

Despite the surrender, the fighting wasn't over.

---

[37] Gen. Lew Wallace would later gain fame as the author of "Ben Hur."

On May 11, Col. Theodore Barrett, commander of the federal encampment at Brazos Santiago on Brazos Island, sent a Union detachment, about 300 men, on a foraging expedition or to take possession of Brownsville. The detachment was comprised of black soldiers from the 62nd U.S. Colored Infantry and Company A of the Second Texas U.S. Cavalry. They were under the command Lt. Col. David Branson.

On May 12, Branson's soldiers surprised and routed a Confederate outpost at Palmito Ranch, 12 miles east of Brownsville (18 miles by river) near the old Palo Alto battlefield.

In the skirmish at Palmito Ranch, three Confederate prisoners were taken and a number of horses. The outpost was manned by Confederate cavalry under the command of Capt. George Robinson. That afternoon, after their initial defeat, Robinson's troops began to skirmish back toward their former position. The federals, assuming the Confederates got reinforcements, fell back four miles east to San Martin Ranch.

When Rip Ford got word that Union forces attacked Capt. Robinson's regiment he ordered Robinson to hold his ground until he could bring reinforcements. Over supper in Ford's quarters, there was a disagreement between the two Confederate commanders, James Slaughter and Ford, about the course of action. There is no hint in Ford's memoirs that they knew the war was over. While both were brigadier generals, Slaughter was senior in rank. Ford asked Slaughter — "General, what do you intend to do?"

"Retreat," Slaughter said.

"You can retreat and go to hell if you wish," Ford told Slaughter. "These are my men and I am going to fight. I have held this place against heavy odds. If you lose it without a fight the people of the Confederacy will hold you accountable for a base neglect of duty."

Slaughter reluctantly agreed to move to the front to resist the federal advance. They decided to meet next morning at the parade grounds at Fort Brown and march out to repel the enemy.

The next morning, Ford waited until almost noon with no sign of Slaughter. Ford, with 70 men and a battery of six 12-pounders, marched to San Martin Ranch. He observed the federal position a half a mile below the ranch, placed his batteries to block the road, and deployed his forces to flank the federal position. He told his troops, "We have whipped them before. We can do it again."

Artillery fire was directed at the Union position. Skirmish firing became brisk and some Union skirmishers were captured. As Confederate troops charged, the Union troops began to run and continued to run for seven miles until they reached Brazos Island. Ford, in a wry understatement, said the Union soldiers left the battlefield "in a rather confused manner." Ford ordered a halt near Boca Chica Pass. When Slaughter arrived and took command, he wanted Ford to resume the pursuit. Ford declined to do so, explaining that their horses were jaded and they were near the Union garrison at Brazos Island, from where the retreating Yankees would gain reinforcements.

It was nearly dark when Confederates and Yankees moved out in skirmish formation. A Union soldier, John J. Williams, a private in the 34th Indiana, was killed. His family later received a medal honoring him as the last soldier killed in the Civil War.

By the last light of the day, an artillery shell from the Union guns struck near the Confederate position. A Confederate soldier still in his teens — using "very profane expletive for so small a boy" — fired a random shot from his Enfield rifle at the darkening dunes of Boca Chica. This may have been the last rifle shot fired in the Civil War.

In this affair, said Ford, the federals lost 25 to 30 men killed and wounded and 113 prisoners were taken. Confederate losses were five wounded, none seriously. Ford may have understated his losses, but the official record is vague. Later accounts said Rip Ford and the Confederates only learned of the surrender of Robert E. Lee and Joseph Johnston and the downfall of the Confederate government from the Union prisoners taken in the battle at Palmito Ranch (also called Palmito Hill). The federals said they thought the Confederates knew the war was over, that they were sent to take possession of Brownsville, not expecting any resistance on the way.

News of the Confederacy's demise had reached the border before the Palmito Ranch fight. A passenger on a steamboat threw a newspaper, *The New Orleans Times,* to Confederate soldiers camped along the riverbank at Palmito Ranch. The newspaper included accounts of the surrender of the Confederate generals and the assassination of Abraham Lincoln. Whether Rip Ford knew it is another question. Some believe the last battle was fought because Ford didn't like the idea of his men surrendering to black soldiers in the Union Army. It has also been pointed out that if Ford's command continued to resist, a valuable consignment of cotton could be moved across the river, into Mexico, to avoid confiscation by Union troops. Richard King and Mifflin Kenedy, the ranchers and Rio Grande steamboat owners, had an interest in the cotton. The two men piled up fortunes from cotton traffic during the war.

The author Tom Lea wrote that there was a considerable quantity of cotton in Brownsville and that Yankee speculators persuaded the Union commander at Brazos Santiago, Col. Barrett, to capture Brownsville so that the Union quartermaster could sell the cotton as perishable contraband with a good profit for the Unionists involved. The plan, wrote Lea, "took no account of Rip Ford, who still sat in Brownsville, caring very little about the fate of CSA cotton but a great lead about any violation of the pledged word of the (Lew) Wallace truce."

Whether Ford knew the war was over — whether the fight was a result of a misunderstanding on both sides — whether it was calculated to give the Confederates time to move valuable cotton to safety across the river — or whether it was the result of a violation of a gentlemen's agreement — are questions we leave open until more evidence is found. But the skirmish at Palmito Ranch on the Rio Grande, between Rip Ford's "Cavalry of the West" and Union soldiers from Brazos Island, was the last land battle of the Civil War.

* * *

Four years after the war, in 1869, Ford was approached by a goat rancher named Champini. He wanted Ford to represent him before a congressional committee meeting in Brownsville. The committee was hearing claims for reparations based on losses due to cross-border bandit raids. According to Ford's memoirs, bandits from Mexico had stolen 150 goats from Mr. Champini over a five-year period. Ford's task was to present a claim to the congressional committee for Champini's 150 goats, plus whatever their natural increase would have been. Champini's claim was for all the goats that were and all the goats that would have been.

At the hearing, Ford made a case for Champini's goat losses, actual and hypothetical. Members of the committee were puzzled. How many goats were they talking about? Ford figured, scratched his head, and figured some more. A goat has three kids in March, two in September, and the March goats have their own kids when they are 18 months old, and these in turn have their own kids, and the September goats have their kids, and so on. As he figured, the hypothetical goats began to multiply. Ford put down his pencil, agitated. Champini's original 150 goats, if left alone, would have increased to two million, five hundred and twenty-one thousand and eighteen goats.

At this point, Ford forgot about trying to obtain reparations for Mr. Champini and became more concerned about the goat crisis.

"Lord help us," said Ford, "if figures don't lie, and if this goat business isn't stopped, in 10 years, sir, the state of Texas won't be able to hold all the goats." Ford may have shown the committee that Mr. Champini was entitled to be reimbursed for 2.5 million goats, but the committee decided he should be paid for 150 goats and no more.

* * *

Ford continued to play a role in Texas affairs during the dark times of Reconstruction. He led a march on the governor's mansion that helped force Reconstruction Gov. E. J. Davis of Corpus Christi to give up his office to the

206

duly elected new governor. The author T. R. Fehrenbach captured the essence of Ford in a passing incident — "Observers note how old Rip Ford, weathered but not withered in his last years, squinted carefully down both sides of a San Antonio street — the famous, careful, Southwestern stare, evaluating the men, the weather, and the land — before he emerged into the sun."

Ford was a legendary Ranger, doctor, statesman, newspaperman, historian, Indian fighter, Confederate officer, and quintessential Texan. As Fehrenbach wrote, he loved a horse, the brush country of South Texas, and the smell of danger. He not only helped to shape Texas history but also wrote about it. After years of fighting Comanches, Mexican soldiers, border bandits, and Yankee cavalry, John Salmon "Rip" Ford, the old gray ghost of the border, died in his bed after a stroke on Nov. 3, 1897.

CHAPTER 28

CONFEDERATES LEAVE FOR MEXICO; OCCUPATION OF SOUTH TEXAS BEGINS
1865

If we go out on the streets, we see nobody but the colored troops. I believe there is over two regiments here now and more coming.
    —*Thomas Noakes on occupation forces in Corpus Christi*

After Robert E. Lee surrendered at Appomattox on April 9, 1865, a group of Confederate officers asked for volunteers to cross the Rio Grande, conquer the country up to the Sierra Madre mountains and form their own government.

The officers asked Gen. Simon Bolivar Buckner to command them. As Buckner delayed in giving his answer, the Confederate troops drifted away, most of them returning home. There were few volunteers for the Sierra Madre venture. Several Confederate officers decided to go anyway.

In Austin, Gov. Pendleton Murrah, the 10th governor of Texas, discussed a plan of exile with Gen. Alexander Watkins Terrell on June 17, 1865. They feared the victorious Yankees would exact revenge against Confederates of high rank. During the war, Terrell led the 34th Texas Cavalry — Terrell's Texas Cavalry — in the Red River Campaign in northern Louisiana. He was promoted from colonel to brigadier general at the end of the war.

When Terrell's party left for Mexico, Gov. Murrah went along, though he was in bad health. He died of consumption at Monterrey on Aug. 4, 1865. At San Antonio, Texas Confederates joined others fleeing into exile from Louisiana, Kentucky, and Missouri. Refugees included prominent politicians, such as Gov. Henry Allen of Louisiana, Thomas Reynolds of Missouri, former Governors Trusten Polk of Missouri, Charles Morehead of Kentucky, Thomas Moore of Louisiana, and Edward Clark of Texas, who completed Sam Houston's term as governor in 1861.

Besides Terrell, the Texas refugees included several Confederate generals and colonels — John B. Magruder, William Hardeman, Wilburn King,

209

Hamilton Bee, P. N. Luckett, and many prominent families, some with their slaves. Others who chose to leave the land of their birth rather than accept life under Yankee terms were Sterling Price, E. Kirby Smith, Thomas Hindman of Arkansas, and William Preston of Kentucky.

When Terrell's party reached Roma on the Rio Grande, they learned that Union cavalry was approaching with orders to capture or kill any Confederates trying to enter Mexico. They rode at a furious pace to reach a ford on the river above Roma.

Henry Maltby's newspaper, *The Ranchero*, which had been at Corpus Christi but relocated to Matamoros, reported on July 23, 1865 that "a large number of distinguished Confederates have passed through Monterrey for the city of Mexico."

Before he died, Gov, Murrah gave Terrell a letter of introduction to Maximilian, the French-imposed emperor of Mexico. Terrell carried the letter, wrapped in oilcloth, in one of his boots. In the letter, Murrah asked Maximilian for consideration for Terrell and William Hardeman, who were under orders to look for a suitable location in Mexico where Confederate exiles could settle.

Gen. Terrell rode to Mexico City where he was granted an audience with Maximilian at the emperor's residence at Chapultepec Castle. Maximilian gave him the rank equivalent to colonel in the French army in Mexico. Gen. William Hardeman, known as "Gotch," George Flournoy, and John B. Magruder served in Maximilian's army.

To aid Terrell's mission, Maximilian opened Mexico to colonization by former Confederates. The emperor by order granted them freedom of worship, exempted them from paying taxes for a year, and offered each head of family 640 acres of land. He even allowed them to keep their slaves in an "apprenticeship."

Confederates in exile turned their hand to various occupations in Mexico. Wilburn Hill King, who had fought in the Red River campaign, started a sugar plantation. Gov. Henry Allen of Louisiana established an English-language newspaper called the *Mexican Times*. Matthew Maury, the first naval officer of the Confederacy and the founder of oceanography, was appointed commissioner of colonization. John Henry Brown, the later Texas historian, surveyed lands for a colony. Hamilton Bee planted cotton. Sterling Price built a bamboo house and tried his hand at becoming a coffee planter. Thomas Hindman also started a coffee plantation.

They learned the hard way that farming was difficult in a land overgrown with bamboo and banana. Growing coffee beans, they discovered, was hard because it took years for the plants to reach maturity.

One Confederate colony settled at a place called Villa Carlota, named for the Emperor's wife. It was west of Veracruz on the road to Mexico City, described as a poverty-stricken little village of clapboard houses and crumbling adobe, with destitute families scratching out a bare living. Many Confederate expatriates lived in the vicinity. Another Confederate colony was at Tuxpan, between San Luis Potosi and Tampico. Other Texas families settled in Monterrey, Saltillo and Mexico City.

A number of Texans also emigrated to British Honduras (Belize). George C. Hatch, a landowner near Corpus Christi in San Patricio County, freed his slaves and went to the Hatch Colony[38] in British Honduras.

The transplanted Southern planters in British Honduras had a hard time adjusting to the hot, humid climate and to the soil, which grew crops they were not familiar with and would not grow crops they understood. They tried to grow cotton, but found it unreliable. They discovered that sugarcane was the best crop. After a couple of years in British Honduras, Hatch,[39] like most Confederate exiles, returned to Texas.

In Northern Mexico, J. Williamson Moses, a former Ranger and a mustanger in South Texas, got a job operating a steam engine at a sawmill near Saltillo. Moses later wrote that there were many Texas families living in Mexico after the war. "We did sometimes hear the English language and could bring up home subjects."

It was a difficult time in Mexico.

"In those days," Moses wrote, "traveling was not unattended with danger," on account of the distracted state of the government, when it was hard to tell where the empire ended or the republic commenced. The peaceful inhabitants themselves were often at a loss to know what response to make when, as often happened, an armed party would suddenly ride up to a house in a village or ranch, and give this usual greeting of *"Quen vive."* If the reply was *"Viva republica,"* when the party were imperialists, it was apt to go hard with the poor citizens. The same would be the case if the response was *"Viva el emperio,"* when the party were *Chinacos* or liberals.

"A party rode up to a house on a ranch where the old man, the owner, was very cautious in giving expression to his opinion. The party gave the customary *'Quen vive,'"* Moses wrote. "The old man for a moment was dumb, but his wife, more ready witted, replied without hesitation, *'Viva nuestra Senora de Guadalupe'* (Live our Lady of Guadalupe). The old man at once caught on, and cried, *'Que viva nuestra Senora y todas los santos, pues'* (Live our Lady and all the saints, of course). The officer in command, a good fellow in the main, took in the situation and laughingly took up the refrain, *'Pues que viva nuestra Senora de Guadalupe y todas los santos, y santas!'*

---

[38] The Hatch Colony was later renamed the Toledo Settlement.
[39] George C. Hatch was taken prisoner in San Antonio during Woll's raid. He was killed by bandits in 1872 on the Reef Road near Corpus Christi.

which was heartily joined in with by his men. . . The ranch was left unmolested, at least for that time."

During this time, Maximilian's regime, backed by French forces, was under attack by Benito Juárez and his ally Porfirio Diaz. Confederate exiles like Moses and Terrell had to move cautiously in the conflict.

Terrell heard that an agreement had been reached between U.S. President Andrew Johnson and Napoleon III of France. Napoleon, they heard, agreed to withdraw French forces in Mexico supporting Maximilian if the United States would not seek to intervene to enforce the Monroe Doctrine.

That would leave Terrell and other Confederates in Maximilian's army with the choice of leaving with the French or becoming subject to the tender mercies of the Juárista soldiers flush with victory. The Confederates were also dismayed by Maximilian's Black Decree by which the army was ordered to shoot all armed Juáristas within 24 hours of their capture.

Maximilian was captured at Querétaro and died on June 19, 1867 before a firing squad at Cerro de las Campanas — "Hill of the Bells." His imperial reign lasted three years. His execution brought an end to the French attempt to rule Mexico by proxy. Most Confederate exiles returned to the U.S. Having backed Maximilian because he offered them protection, they were the losers in another civil war and forced into exile a second time. Terrell slipped out of Mexico posing as one Colonel Monroe, wearing a sombrero and a faded gray uniform. He returned to Texas.

* * *

Only a few Confederates escaped to Mexico at the end of the war. Most stayed behind to face occupation and hard times. Corpus Christi was one of the few Texas cities subjected to prolonged occupation.

When Gen. Phil Sheridan took possession of Texas for the Union, he ordered the 25th Army Corps to occupy Galveston, Indianola, Brownsville and Corpus Christi. Some 52,000 Union troops were stationed along the coast, out of 70,000 total in the state. Small cavalry detachments were sent to San Antonio and Austin. Other units camped at Refugio and Goliad.

Corpus Christi, with 400 residents at war's end, was occupied by 3,000 Union troops. The sheer numbers were bound to cause trouble.

Texans wondered why such a large force was sent to occupy a defeated and demoralized state, which was as low, one said, as the tail of a whipped cat. But the Union occupation troops were sent to Texas at least partly as a show of force, in response to French intervention in Mexico.

In June, Gen. Charles S. Russell was ordered to take a regiment to Corpus Christi. By July, two regiments were in town. Russell occupied the home of Judge R. C. Russell (no kin) at Chaparral and Taylor. Because Confederates

212

had to come to this house to take the "ironclad" oath to the Union, it was called the Ironclad House. In Matamoros, editor Henry Maltby, who moved his newspaper *The Ranchero* there before the end of the war, scoffed at all the oath-taking — "The Yankees are the greatest people for oaths that we have ever seen."

Most Texans acquiesced to the new order. Thomas Noakes, an English immigrant farmer who lived at Nuecestown near Corpus Christi, wrote that, "I met Mr. Staples and some others and we went into a discussion regarding the taking of the oath that is required of us by the Yankee, when we came to the conclusion that, being whipped, we have to conform to their measure sooner or later, and we considered it the best policy to do so at once."

Corpus Christi was occupied off and on by three Union regiments — the 10th, 28th and 36th — for more than a year. The 122nd may have been stationed there for a short time. The regiments, designated as United States Colored Troops, were under the command of white officers.

This wasn't the first time that area residents saw African-Americans in blue uniforms. When the barrier islands were captured by Union forces in 1863, two companies of black soldiers in the Corps d'Afrique were garrisoned on the island. They were auxiliary soldiers employed to dig fortifications.

By contrast, the black soldiers that came in the occupation were combat veterans seasoned by the hazards of war. They had fought in battles in Virginia, around Petersburg and Richmond, in the last year of the war. The Union soldiers set up tents on the beach and the bluff. Noakes, visiting Corpus Christi, wrote in his diary in late July, 1865, "If we go out on the streets, we see nobody but the colored troops. I believe there is over two regiments here now and more coming."

Trouble quickly arose between residents and soldiers. *The Ranchero*, reporting from afar in Matamoros, wrote on July 28 that the troops plundered empty houses. Among the houses sacked was that of Conrad Meuly, a Union supporter who had died a few days before in Brownsville. "The furniture and all fixtures, including a rosewood piano, were carried off," reported the *Ranchero*. "The soldiers went into the backyard, broke open the family vault, and entered the coffin containing the remains of an infant and scattered the bones on the ground."

When Margaret Meuly, Conrad's widow, complained to Gen. Russell about the occupation troops wrecking her house, he said there was nothing he could do. *The Ranchero* reported that the white officers feared their own troops — "They are afraid to ascend the bluff (where many of the soldiers camped) in open daylight and after six o'clock in the evening they are afraid to walk the streets." Soldiers were accused of drunkenness and vandalism. Helen Chapman, a Unionist, noted in her diary that there was "a good deal of bitter feeling about the colored troops."

J. B. (Red) Dunn said the Union soldiers subjected people to all kinds of humiliation and insults. He wrote that two soldiers broke into his uncle's home and stole clothing and guns. When the Dunns returned home, they found the uniforms abandoned and army weapons left behind.

"One of the boys, Matt Dunn, reported the theft to the officer in charge. The officer denied that any of his men were involved. But next morning, Matt got there before roll call and saw that two names were not answered. He called the officer's attention to the matter, but the officer flew into a tantrum. He told Matt that if he was so sure about it, to go get the deserters and not come bothering him about it.

"Matt found them by Nueces Bay. When they saw him coming they pulled out their pistols and told him to stay back. Matt opened fire on them and when all his loads were gone but one, he charged and killed one of them. At that, the other one ran into the bay and got bogged down in the mud. Matt roped him and dragged him to shore. He turned him over to the commanding officer."

Maria Blucher wrote her parents in Germany — "The federal troops have been ordered away; Corpus Christi will be rather lonely with 2,000 fewer men. We have gotten along very well with the officers, and upon closer acquaintance they have done all in their power to protect us from inconveniences and incessant thefts."

In November, soldiers of the 28th Regiment, from Indiana, were shipped to Brazos Santiago where they were mustered out. They were welcomed home in Indianapolis as returning heroes.

The departure of the 28th Regiment did not end the occupation of the city. Other units were shunted in from Brownsville and Indianola. On Dec. 1, 1865, Noakes wrote in his diary that, "Some nigger troops passed through the motts (Nuecestown), being generally very saucy in their behavior."

The conjecture later that Union regiments of black soldiers were removed because of friction with local citizens is dubious. It is doubtful that tough Union generals like Phil Sheridan cared much about the sensibilities of defeated Confederates. Sheridan didn't much like Texas anyway. It is more likely that the regiments were transferred because it was time for them to be mustered out. The vast Union army was being disbanded and sent home, unit by unit.

By January, 1866, Noakes was writing in his diary that, "The colored troops are nearly all withdrawn and Corpus Christi begins to look very much as it used to do before the war."

It would be a long time before Texas recovered from the war, the occupation, and Reconstruction. Of immense importance were the trail drives. Former Confederate soldiers home from the war were among the first to organize and conduct the cattle drives to Kansas, which helped to revive the shattered Texas economy.

Many of the Confederate exiles who went to Mexico at the end of the war returned to distinguished careers. Alexander Watkins Terrell was elected to the Texas Legislature, authored legislation to build a new state capitol, served as U.S. envoy to the Ottoman Empire and as a regent of the University of Texas. He died in 1912 and was buried in the State Cemetery in Austin.

Edmund J. Davis

CHAPTER 29

GOV. EDMUND J. DAVIS
AND RECONSTRUCTION
1869 — 1873

*Would it not be prudent, as well as right, to yield to the verdict of the people
as expressed by their ballots?*

—U. S. Grant to E. J. Davis

Edmund Jackson Davis was a brigadier general in the Civil War on the Union side. He became the most despised governor in Texas history. He hated his former enemies the Confederates and they hated him, calling him the devil with red whiskers. His implacable hatred of former Confederates was reciprocated in full measure. The Confederates even came close to hanging him during the war.

The interpretation of Davis's time in office has been subject to revision. Was he a dictator who wielded dictatorial powers? He was. As governor of Texas during Reconstruction, E. J. Davis was a dictator by any meaning of the word, though revisionists have focused disproportionate attention on his good points.

Davis came to Texas from St. Augustine, Fla., with his widowed mother when he was 11 years old. They arrived in Galveston in 1838. Ten years later, Davis moved to Corpus Christi to study law and he practiced in Laredo, Brownsville and Corpus Christi. He was appointed deputy director of customs at Laredo, then appointed federal judge of the Lower Rio Grande Valley. He rode a judicial circuit that stretched from Corpus Christi to Laredo to Brownsville.

Judge Davis married Anne Elizabeth (Lizzie) Britton of Corpus Christi on April 6, 1858 at the bride's home.[40] "Lizzie" Britton was the daughter of Sen. Forbes Britton, a state legislator who was a veteran of the Mexican War.

---

[40] The place is still standing in Corpus Christi today. It's called Centennial House.

After the marriage, a house on the Britton Ranch on Oso Creek was moved to town to become the home of the newlyweds.

In the time leading up to the Civil War, Davis opposed the move toward secession. When the issue came up for a vote in February 1861, Davis spoke at the Nueces County Courthouse against Texas leaving the Union. Like his father-in-law Forbes Britton, who died two months before, Davis was an ardent Unionist. He spoke at the courthouse in reply to pro-secessionist speeches.

When the war broke out, Lizzie Davis's twin brother, Edward Britton, a surgeon, enlisted in the Confederate Army. Her husband went to Matamoros to organize the First Texas Cavalry, U.S.A., made up of Unionists like himself. Confederates called them renegades. Davis was commissioned a colonel of volunteers.

Confederate commanders in Brownsville learned that "renegades" Davis and his aide, Capt. W. W. Montgomery, were staying at the Imperial Hotel in the port city of Bagdad, across the mouth of the Rio Grande on the Mexican side. They were waiting to board the steamer *Nicaragua*.

In a cross-border raid by Confederates that violated Mexican territory, Davis, Montgomery and four U.S. Marines were captured and taken across the river to Clarksville on the Texas side.

The Confederates hated Capt. Montgomery, who was known to taunt them from across the river. He was promptly hanged. E. J. Davis was next. The Confederates were putting a rope around his neck when Confederate Gen. Hamilton P. Bee rode up and ordered him returned to the Mexican side. Official apologies were made to Mexican authorities for the territorial violation.

Some accounts said Davis escaped hanging because he and Bee belonged to the same Masonic Lodge. It was also said that it was a gallant gesture by Gen. Bee since he had courted Lizzie Britton before she married Davis. Whatever the reasons, Confederates would regret not having hanged E. J. Davis when they had the chance.

A British army officer saw the evidence of the hanging of Montgomery. Lt. Col. James Arthur Lyon Fremantle of Her Majesty's Coldstream Guards made a tour of the Confederacy in 1863. Fremantle arrived by ship at the mouth of the Rio Grande and crossed the river to Brownsville, where he found half a dozen officers at a fire "contemplating a tin of potatoes."

They were bragging about a Yankee they hanged some time before (Montgomery). Fremantle saw the body. "He had been slightly buried, but his head and arms were above the ground, his arms tied together, the rope still around his neck, but part of it still dangling from quite a small mesquite tree. Dogs or wolves had scraped the earth from the body, and there was no flesh on the bones. I obtained this, my first experience of lynch law, within three hours of landing in America."

A Confederate colonel named Duff told Fremantle that the Montgomery affair was wrong, but "my boys meant well."

In the Union invasion of the Texas coast in 1863 by an army under the command of Gen. Nathaniel P. Banks, Davis' cavalry unit was ordered to disrupt Confederate supply lines in South Texas. Afterwards, Davis and his men were transported to Louisiana to take part in the last Union invasion of Texas, which was turned back in the Battle at Mansfield.

In March 1864, Davis led an expedition up the Rio Grande to capture Laredo, 210 miles from Brownsville. With Union forces in control of Brownsville and the mouth of the Rio Grande, the Confederacy's vital cotton trade shifted upriver to Laredo and Eagle Pass, where trains of wagons loaded with cotton made their way downstream on the Mexican side of the border, safe from attack.

The intent of the expedition led by Davis was to seize Laredo and eventually Eagle Pass to stop the cotton traffic.

Davis's Second Texas Cavalry and other troops left Brownsville in the middle of March. Some troops were carried on the steamboat *Mustang* while the cavalry rode along the river.

At Laredo, Confederate Col. Santos Benavides, the highest ranking Mexican-American in the Confederate Army, learned of the federal expedition. He took his regiment and three other companies out to intercept Davis's force.

The steamboat *Mustang* could not proceed past Guerrero. The river was too shallow. Davis sent an advance guard of 200 men ahead to Laredo, with plans to bring up the main body as quickly as possible in support. The advance guard was under the command of Maj. Alfred Holt. Their orders were to seize 5,000 bales of Confederate cotton stacked in Laredo's main plaza.

Laredo was lightly defended by Confederates, with less than 100 men. They had deemed it unlikely that Union forces at Brownsville would venture so far from their home base.

Mexican guides took Davis's advance force over little known roads. They were almost to Laredo when a Mexican ranchero sounded the alarm. With Col. Benavides' forces scattered in other places to protect the cotton routes, Laredo citizens were mustered to defend the town. They built barricades in the plaza.

Col. Benavides took 42 men to the outskirts of Laredo. He divided them into squads and posted them in houses. Maj. Holt's Union soldiers, 200 men, arrived at three in the afternoon. When skirmishers were in range, Benavides' men began firing, forcing the federals back. The federals dismounted and advanced on foot.

"My men maintained a steady fire," Benavides wrote in his report to Brig. Gen. Rip Ford. "The brave Major Swope and a Mexican named Juan Ivara charged right upon an advancing squad of 40 Yankees and compelled them to retreat. Major Swope stood there until he emptied the last shot of his six-shooter, which compelled him to retire for the purpose of reloading. While doing so his horse was shot three times and also Juan Ivara's. The enemy advanced again, but was repulsed by the vigorous fire of my gallant men, who were full of fight. The firing was kept up until dark when the Yankees thought best to skedaddle in their own peculiar style and give up the intention of walking into Laredo that day."

When Benavides' reinforcements arrived the following day, Laredo celebrated with the ringing of church bells throughout the city. That ended the battle of Laredo on March 19, 1864. Maj. Holt was forced to retreat and rejoin E. J. Davis's main body. They made their way back to Brownsville.

Davis was promoted to brigadier general in the Union Army before the end of the war.

* * *

After the war, E. J. Davis returned to Corpus Christi to open a law office. His clients were Union supporters whose property had been confiscated by Confederate loyalists during the war, such as Helen Chapman, a Unionist who came back to Corpus Christi from New York to reclaim her family's property.

In 1867, an outbreak of yellow fever claimed Corpus Christi's two doctors. A former slave, Anna Moore Schwien, recalled that E. J. Davis sent to Havana for a doctor and brought him to Corpus Christi at his own expense to treat the sick.

Another account said Davis carried a sick woman three blocks so she could visit her sister before she died. Mean things were said about Davis, Anna Moore Schwien said, "but he deserved credit for what he did for Corpus Christi during that dreadful epidemic."

Davis was elected to the constitution convention of 1868-69. Before leaving Corpus Christi for the convention, he gave his wife Lizzie a fan decorated with diamonds and mother-of-pearl. He was elected president of the convention, where he argued in favor of the disenfranchisement of all former Confederates, unrestricted Negro suffrage, and he urged the fragmenting of Texas' future political power by dividing it into three states.

In November 1869, the duties and responsibility of governing Texas were under the control of the military. By order of Gen. Joseph Jones Reynolds, an election was held for governor and state offices. Davis, six years after he was spared death by hanging, was elected governor. He beat Andrew Jackson

Hamilton by 800 votes out of 78,993 cast. Many believed it to be the most fraudulent election in Texas history. Hamilton thought he won. After the election, the ballots were taken to Louisiana, where they disappeared. Fraudulent or not, Judge Davis was declared elected and he became governor on Jan. 18, 1870.

After the election, Davis and his wife Lizzie left Corpus Christi for Austin. Their coach stopped at the small village of San Patricio on the Nueces River and they pulled up at the home of Mrs. Eliza Sullivan. The newly elected governor of Texas sent in his respects. The reply came back — "Mrs. Sullivan is not at home to the traitor."

In office, Davis was a virtual dictator. He was empowered to appoint more than 8,000 state, county and local officials, including judges and sheriffs. He pushed through a State Police bill in the House that gave him dictatorial power. When it failed in the Senate, he had senators who opposed it jailed until they agreed to pass it. The State Police force was under Davis' personal command. Through state printing contracts, he could reward newspapers that supported him, thereby creating his own propaganda machine.

Davis was considered personally honest, but he can't be judged solely on his personal traits since he was the head of a corrupt, brutal, self-serving dictatorship. His State Police broke up Democratic (big D and little d) meetings. They entered homes without warrants. They made false arrests. They carried out summary executions that were tantamount to officially sanctioned murder.

Davis's term from 1870 to 1874 was the most tumultuous in Texas history. A corrupt Legislature plundered the treasury. Officials sold votes and stuffed ballot boxes. With power unchecked by courts or higher authority, the State Police terrified law-abiding citizens.

Davis ran for re-election in 1873. His opponent was Richard Coke, a barrel-chested Democrat who had been a private in the Confederate Army. This was another fraudulent election with widespread voter intimidation and ballot-stuffing. Despite the voting irregularities by the Davis machine, the former Union general lost to the former Confederate private by more than two to one.

After the election results were certified, Davis refused to give up power. He barricaded himself in his office, with a company of state militia to guard him. He sent a telegram appealing to President U. S. Grant to send federal troops to keep him in office. Grant minced no words when he wired back — "The call (for troops) is not made in accordance with the Constitution. Would it not be prudent, as well as right, to yield to the verdict of the people as expressed by their ballots?"

Grant's refusal to send troops infuriated Lizzie Davis. She reportedly took down Grant's portrait from the wall and put her foot through it. Davis had to vacate the governor's office or risk civil war. Spitefully, he locked the office door and left no key behind. Coke, the new governor, had the door broken down as Austin celebrated with a 102-gun salute. Coke sent a telegram to President Grant, thanking him for his non-intervention.

This marked the end of Reconstruction in Texas. It also marked the end of Davis's political career. Back in power, the former Confederates rewrote the Texas Constitution to make sure that no future Texas governor would ever wield as much power as had E. J. Davis.

Davis died in Austin on Feb. 27, 1883. His monument, an ostentatious obelisk, was the tallest in the State Cemetery. One former Confederate said the size of the monument was very appropriate since E. J. Davis was "the biggest son of a bitch Texas has ever seen." Even death doesn't square some accounts.

CHAPTER 30

THE SUTTON-TAYLOR FEUD
1867 — 1875

What do you find so interesting, you damned rebel?
—Union soldier to Hays Taylor

The bloodiest feud in Texas history started after the Civil War. In a way, it continued the war at the family and local level. The Sutton-Taylor feud was centered around the towns of Clinton and Cuero in DeWitt County in South Texas. After the violence spilled over to adjacent counties, a Texas Ranger said, "It takes five large counties to bound DeWitt — and it is an awful strain to hold it all in."

William Sutton, his brother James, their allies, and the military and civil authorities that ruled Texas after the war were on one side. Former Confederates Creed and Pitkin Taylor, their sons and friends, including gunslinger John Wesley Hardin, were on the other.

The Suttons were aligned with the law, or what represented the law, and the Taylors with the lawless. Both sides were violent and treacherous and not reluctant to resort to ambush, assassination and execution to pursue their vendettas. Those not connected to the Suttons and Taylors kept a watchful neutrality and tried to stay out of the way.

Who knows what set it off? Some say it started when Creed Taylor hanged a Union man who refused to grind corn for Confederate wives. Others say it started with a dispute over unbranded cattle. Some say it started when a Taylor stole cattle from a widow and William Sutton took her cause as his own. Others think it began when a Taylor killed two black Union soldiers in a shootout in front of a saloon.

Creed Taylor fought at San Jacinto, rode with Jack Hays and named his first son John Hays Taylor. Creed and his brother Pitkin, diehard Confederates, were among those after the war who had not been reduced to a humble and obedient state by defeat.

The feud with the Suttons may have already been in progress or a violent encounter in Mason County may have lit the fuse.

Creed's son Phillip Dubois Taylor — called Do'boy — was drinking in a Mason County saloon on Nov. 14, 1867. Do'boy's brother John Hays Taylor, known as Hays, took a newspaper outside and sat squatting against the wall to read it. He was not as partial to liquor as Do'boy. A squad of black U.S. soldiers, part of the occupation forces after the war, strolled by. As Hays Taylor was squatting against the wall, reading his paper, one of the soldiers jerked up Hays' hat brim and said, "What do you find so interesting, you damned rebel?" Hays kept a dead silence and resumed reading. The soldier pushed Hays' hat down over his eyes.

Hays got to his feet, pulled his pistol and shot the soldier through the heart. He then shot a sergeant who tried to intervene. A reward was posted for Hays and Do'boy Taylor.

On Christmas Eve 1868 in the town of Clinton, DeWitt County, "Buck" Taylor, Creed's nephew, called William Sutton a horse thief. Sutton killed Buck and his cousin Richard Chisholm.

In 1869, William Sutton led a posse that laid an ambush and killed Hays Taylor. Do'boy, riding with Hays, escaped (he was killed later in an affray not related to the feud). After the killings of Buck and Hays Taylor, the feud was heating up.

In 1869, Jack Helm, an ally of Sutton, led the "Regulators" that were authorized under military authority. Helm and his men gained a reputation for arresting men, shooting them, and claiming they tried to escape. Reports of executions by Helm and his Regulators attracted attention by the press. One paper reported that in July and August 1869, Helm's Regulators killed 21 men "attempting to escape."

On September 14, 1869, the *Galveston News* wrote: "This thing of putting down civil government and then employing 'regulators' under military authority to hunt up and execute people, according to their own notions, is not the best thing in the world."

Helm's Regulators rode into San Patricio County and killed Taylor allies John and Crockett Choate. A neighbor, F. O. Skidmore, was wounded in that attack. Skidmore wrote a letter of complaint printed in the *Victoria Advocate*. He said the Regulators "conducted themselves in an extremely boisterous manner while at the (Choate) house, appropriating whatever they desired, as if they had killed a robber chieftain and had a right to appropriate his effects. They left me nothing, not even my clothing and pocket change. They stole my saddle, six-shooter, and other things of less note."

When Gov. E. J. Davis created the State Police force to replace the Texas Rangers, he appointed Jack Helm as a captain, despite Helm's reputation for executing prisoners.

Helm's company of State Police soon lived up to past form of Helm's Regulators. On the night of Aug. 26, 1870, a posse led by Helm and William

Sutton arrested Henry and William Kelly. These two men were Pitkin Taylor's sons-in-law. The Kelly brothers were shot to death near their home. Amanda Kelly, Pitkin Taylor's daughter and Henry Kelly's wife, witnessed the slayings from a hiding place. She said she saw William Sutton shoot William Kelly, who was filling his pipe, and another man shoot Henry, her husband.

After these killings, State Sen. B. J. Pridgen, considered a Taylor ally, wrote a lengthy criticism of Helm in the Nov. 30, 1870 *Austin Republican:* "I know of at least twenty cases of murder by Helm and his party. For example, Helm with his men went to the house of a Mr. Bell of Goliad County — arrested him — took him off in the woods — killed him and left him to the mercy of scavengers generally and reported that 'he attempted to escape.' He arrested a Mr. Moore on the same day, treated him as he did Bell, and made the same report. They went to the house of a Mr. Jones, tore him from the embrace of his distressed wife and children, and when a little way from the house gallantly dispatched him in the presence of crying little ones, who had doubtless followed along in anxious expectation of what would be done. He, too, 'attempted to escape.' They then arrested a Mr. Pool, took him off in the woods and left him lying in a pool of blood and alleged that he, too, attempted to escape."

The Austin Republican commented on Pridgen's report, writing, "It is a little remarkable that Jack Helm's victims surrender at discretion, no matter whether he goes to their houses by night or by day, they lay aside their weapons and rely on him, as an officer, to look after their personal safety. But it seems that once in his possession a change quickly comes over the spirit of their dreams and they 'attempt to escape.' "

Not long after this, at the end of 1870, Jack Helm was dismissed from the State Police. Gov. E. J. Davis yielded to the growing complaints about Helm's violent and extra-judicial methods of law enforcement. However, Helm was soon elected sheriff of DeWitt County and resumed his career as an officer of the law and ally of the Sutton forces.

After the killings of the Kelly boys, Pitkin Taylor swore to get revenge for the slayings of his two sons-in-law, but the Suttons got him first. Members of their gang slipped into his cornfield in the night and waited. Pitkin Taylor had an ox with a bell and one man set the bell to tinkling. When Pitkin went out to see what was bothering the ox, he was shot and killed. At the funeral, Pitkin's son Jim swore to wash his hands in Bill Sutton's blood. This wasn't bombast. At the scene of the funeral with family and relatives looking on, the responsibility to carry on the feud was passed on within the family.

Jim Taylor and his cousins Bill Taylor and Alf Day shot William Sutton in a Cuero saloon, though Sutton was not slain, only hit in the arm. The two Taylors and Alf Day were jailed, but John Wesley Hardin freed them. The

Taylors mustered their allies and ambushed Sutton ally Jim Cox, shot him and slit his throat.

"Some of us schoolboys were in Cuero when the Taylor-Sutton feudists came into town armed to the hilt," wrote John D. Young. "There must have been a hundred on each side. While we boys watched from behind a log, one side backed the other into some cow pens. Had a shot been fired, hell would have broken loose in Georgia. The leaders recognized this fact, a flag of truce was raised, and the crowd disbanded. Three days later they were shooting each other again from ambush."

On May 17, 1873, Jack Helm's career of shooting prisoners "attempting to escape" was brought to an end when he was shot to death in a blacksmith shop by John Wesley Hardin and Jim Taylor.

That December, a truce was signed to end the feud, but it didn't hold. The Taylor camp once again bent their minds to a day and time and method of getting revenge. The Taylors learned that William Sutton was planning to send a herd of cattle up the trail to Kansas and that he and his wife would depart Indianola by ship to New Orleans then travel by rail to Kansas. On March 11, 1874, Sutton, his wife Laura, and Gabriel Slaughter, a friend, were boarding the steamship *Clinton* at Indianola. Jim and Bill Taylor opened fire, killing William Sutton and Slaughter.

After killing William Sutton, Jim Taylor left on a trail drive. Bill Taylor, who stayed behind, was arrested by the Cuero town marshal, "Rube" Brown, while trying on a pair of boots. Three cowboys linked to the Taylors were arrested and charged with rustling. A mob broke into the Clinton jail and hanged the cowboys. A Galveston paper said they were lynched "by the Sutton party, as they have an old feud with the Taylor crowd."

The day Indianola was almost destroyed by a hurricane, Sept. 15, 1875; the trial of Bill Taylor was set to begin. He was charged with killing William Sutton and Gabriel Slaughter. As storm waters flooded Indianola, Taylor and two other prisoners were taken to a place of safety. They overpowered the guard and escaped.

While on the run, Bill Taylor wrote letters to "Rube" Brown threatening to kill him for arresting him and for being a leader of the Sutton faction. At a saloon in Cuero on Nov. 17, 1875, Brown was playing cards when five men linked to Bill Taylor dragged him outside and emptied their guns into him.

Bill Taylor was tried and acquitted of killing William Sutton, then accused of the rape of the daughter of a "peaceable colored man." After that, he left the area. Jim Taylor and two friends went to Clinton on Dec. 27, 1875. When they appeared in Clinton, one paper reported, "the Sutton party surrounded them and shot to death all three."

The feud was over. The people in DeWitt County, especially those linked to the Sutton and Taylor factions, were at last able to sleep at night.

The Sutton-Taylor feud lasted a decade and left many widows and fatherless children. It claimed untold numbers, though no accurate count of the victims can be made since many killings were feud-related but some were not and sorting out the difference is all but impossible. Estimates put the number at more than 200. William Sutton and several of his allies were killed. His brother James Sutton, with an instinct for self-preservation, moved to West Texas. Of the Taylors, Hays, Pitkin and several sons and sons-in-law, assorted cousins and nephews, were killed. Creed Taylor, the old Texian who rode with Jack Hays, lived to be more than 100. He died in his bed on Dec. 27, 1906.

* * *

Another blood feud in South Texas, less violent and of short duration, pitted the Garner and Means families in San Patricio County. Unlike the Sutton-Taylor feud, there is no doubt about the origin of this one.

In 1876, ranchers around Meansville, a small community in San Patricio County near the present town of Odem, agreed to have their cattle dipped to control ticks. The agreement stipulated that the cattlemen would pay the cost of the treatment.

All the cattle in the area were treated except for those owned by Col. William Means, a former sheriff and the founder of Meansville. He refused to have his cattle dipped. San Patricio County Sheriff Ed Garner hired cowboys to round up Means' cattle and have them dipped, after which the colonel was billed $35 for expenses. He refused to pay.

Soon after this, three of Means' six sons shot up a dance at the community of Papalote. Sheriff Garner led a posse to arrest them. The sheriff's posse surrounded the Means' ranch house and ordered the hell-raisers to come out and give themselves up. Instead, Col. Means came out with a rifle. Garner said, "I wouldn't do that if I were you."

Shots were fired and Col. Means was killed. The three Means boys were taken to jail.

In retaliation, Garner was shot and killed as he came out of church at Meansville. The shooter was believed to be John Means, a crack shot, but his brother Alley took the rap and went to prison for it.

After Garner was killed, the people of Meansville encouraged the Means clan to leave. One day in 1879, the Means family packed up, bag and baggage and branding irons, and left San Patricio County, departing in 23 covered wagons. That brought an end to the Garner-Means feud.

Trail drives

228

CHAPTER 31

TRAIL DRIVES
TO LOUISIANA AND KANSAS
1770s — 1880s

Served with me four years on the Goodnight-Loving Trail, never shirked duty or disobeyed an order, rode with me in many stampedes, participated in three engagements with Comanches, splendid behavior.
     —Charles Goodnight of black cowboy Bose Ikard

Trailing cattle to Louisiana is much older than trailing cattle to Kansas. Thousands of Texas longhorns from herds belonging to Spanish missions in South Texas were driven to Louisiana to feed the Spanish army of Bernardo de Gálvez.

Gálvez, governor of Spanish Louisiana, was commissioned by Spain to mount a campaign against the British to assist the Americans in their fight for independence. During the American Revolution, 10,000 longhorns were trailed across bayous and through swamps with cypress trees to New Orleans. In the summer of 1779, a herd of 1,000 head, with 20 men from San Antonio hired to drive them, were attacked by Comanche warriors. The Indians killed one drover, wounded two others, and slaughtered some cattle.

Before the Texas Revolution, Victoria's Martin De Leon took a herd to New Orleans, traveling over what became known as the Opelousas Route. From New Orleans, cattle could be shipped to markets in the north. In 1835, a steer that would sell for $5 in Texas would fetch $35 in New Orleans. The author J. Frank Dobie noted that at the time the battle of San Jacinto was fought a herd of Texas cattle was being trailed to New Orleans "which for decades continued as a market, cattle being shipped thence north by boat. Shreveport and Vidalia (opposite Natchez on the Mississippi) and New Iberia were other loading points."

After the Texas Revolution, veterans of San Jacinto rounded up cattle abandoned by retreating Spanish rancheros and drove them east for sale. They became known as "cow-boys."

James Taylor White, an early rancher near the present town of Liberty, drove cattle to market in New Orleans during the 1830s and early 1840s. Some ranchers would put their cattle together in a big herd and drive them to New Orleans. In their absence, women and children would "fort up" in one of the ranch homes, giving them the security of numbers, until the men returned from the drive, which would take several weeks. Raising cattle, it was said, was easy; getting them to market was the hard part.

For cattlemen along the coast, it was faster to ship by sea, but not cheaper. A man named James Foster of Indianola began buying and shipping cattle to New Orleans on Morgan Line ships. By 1851, he controlled the stock-carrying capacity of steamboats plying between Indianola and New Orleans. The longhorns made the journey in pens built between decks and on deck. It's not clear whether their horns, which could stretch up to five feet from tip to tip, were sawed off to accommodate tight quarters.

A cattleman named William Grimes objected to the high shipping rates charged by the Morgan Line. He decided in 1855 to send a herd over the Opelousas Route to New Orleans. One of his ranch hands, Abel Head "Shanghai" Pierce, was in charge of the herd. Pierce was 20 years old at the time. He would go on to become one of South Texas' greatest cattlemen.

During the Civil War, Texas cattle were trailed east to feed Confederate armies. M. A. Withers, a trail hand, was 16 when he helped take a herd from Lockhart to Shreveport in 1862. On another drive to Shreveport, the drovers found the buffalo flies so bad "the cattle would run off, crazed with misery, and it was hard to drive them back to the herd."

W. D. H. Saunders was 17 when he was hired to drive a herd of 1,100 longhorns from Goliad to Mississippi in October 1862. When they reached the Mississippi River, a thousand of the herd "took to the water and easily swam across." About 100 cattle, quite sensibly, were unwilling to jump into the river. They were sold on the Louisiana side. The drovers and owners were arrested and detained on both sides of the river by Confederate authorities, who thought they were trying to take the herd to the Union Army besieging Vicksburg. Most of the herd was sold below Natchez, while some of the cattle were trailed across Mississippi to Mobile, Ala., to be sold.

Trailing cattle across snake-infested swamps, bayous and marshy bogs of Louisiana was difficult. The drive Shanghai Pierce made to New Orleans in 1855 for William B. Grimes became the basis for one of his famous campfire stories. His ability to elaborate on a story was legendary. His story of the Louisiana trip was told in the cowboy fashion of tall tales.

"The mud and water of the Louisiana swamps compelled us to pick every step," Shanghai would say. "The public roads — where there were any — would bog a saddle blanket. My steers were nice, fat, slick critters that knew how to swim, but they were used to a carpet of prairie grass. They were mighty choosy as to where they put their feet. They had a bushel of sense and pretty soon over there in Louisiana they got to balancing themselves on logs in order to keep out of the slimy mud. They got so expert that one of them would walk a cypress knee to the stump, jump over it, land on a root, and walk it out for another jump. If there was a bad bog-hole between cypresses you would see a steer hang his horns into a mustang-grapevine and swing across like a monkey. The way they balanced and jumped and swung actually made my horse laugh."

Pierce was a regimental butcher in the Confederate Army, a position he compared to brigadier general — "always in the rear on an advance, always in the lead on a retreat."

Like Shanghai Pierce, the cattlemen who organized and conducted the trail drives after the Civil War were former Confederate soldiers. So were the cowboys. Men who came back from the war after four years of fighting had learned to endure hardship — sleeping on the ground, spending long hours in the saddle or on the march, pushing on through a storm. These former Confederates were among the first to go up the trail after the war.

When the war ended, returning soldiers were broke. Their Confederate pay was worthless. Though Texas did not suffer as much as Southern states where the fighting was heaviest, there was still almost no industry, few jobs, few prospects of jobs, and very little money. Commercial ties had been disrupted or sundered.

The men in gray had to start over. They had to make something seemingly from nothing. But the state was overrun with cattle. Inside Texas, the price of cattle had dropped to about $1 a head, the value of the hide, but in the great packing-house cities of Kansas City, St. Louis and Chicago, the value of cattle ran from $20 to $40 a head. A few Texas cattlemen began exploring ways to get their cattle to that high-dollar market.

Small herds of a few hundred head went north in 1866 for Baxter Springs in southeast Kansas and Sedalia, Mo. They ran into trouble from bands of armed men called Jayhawkers and Redlegs. As the men driving the herds north from Texas were mostly former Confederate soldiers, the Jayhawkers and Redlegs were men who fought on the Union side. They used the fear of Texas tick fever as a pretext to ambush men with herds and steal their cattle. But the herds that did get through sold for high prices.

Texas cattlemen could see a way forward. They learned that the Union Pacific Railroad had reached Abilene, a small town of log-hut buildings, but a railhead nevertheless, in western Kansas, far away from the trouble in eastern Kansas and western Missouri. Herds could be sold in Abilene and shipped by rail to the stockyards of Kansas City, St. Louis and Chicago.

Drovers turned their herds toward Abilene. They followed the most famous of all cattle trails, the Chisholm Trail. An estimated 75,000 head reached

Abilene in 1867. Every year after, the herds grew larger as trail-driving became a science and progressively easier, though there would always be flooded rivers to cross, stampedes on a stormy night, and unexpected trouble along the trail.

Stories of the men who went up the trail can be found in "Trail Drivers of Texas," stories like that of W. F. Cude, a Confederate soldier who was captured and released on parole. "Four of us left Jackson, Miss.," Cude wrote, "and walked to Beaumont in 16 days. My shoes had worn out. When I got to Houston, I went to a store and got a new pair of shoes. I told the clerk to charge them to Jeff Davis." Cude signed on as a trail hand to take a herd to Kansas.

R. G. "Dick" Head enlisted when he was 16 and spent four years in the Confederate Army. After the war, he got work as a trail hand with pioneer drover John J. Meyers, who led the first herds to Abilene.

T. M. Turner, nicknamed "Louisiana," was a Confederate scout who always wanted to be a cowboy. After the war he went to Goliad and started with a herd for Abilene.

D. C. Rachal (his name was Darius Cyriaque, but he went by D.C. for obvious reasons) enlisted in the 5th Texas Infantry in Hood's Brigade. He was in battles from the Wilderness to Gettysburg. After four years of hard fighting, he started a ranch at White Point across Nueces Bay from Corpus Christi and began to trail herds to Kansas. In Rachal's case, "drive" is the right word. He was known for driving the herd at a fast pace and then to let the cattle eat and fill out when they got to Kansas. The technique took his name. A trail boss hurrying his herd along would say, "Rachal 'em, boys, Rachal 'em."

In "Trail Drivers," there are no typical stories — each being different in its own way — yet they are all typical. Like this one. A cattleman named Randolph Paine bought cattle at $12 a head and drove 3,000 steers to Abilene. He sold them for $30 a head and brought the money back to Denton County in a wagon.

That's the essence of the story. Cattle went north in a flood and gold came back to a destitute land. Except for what the cowboys spent in the cow towns of Kansas — raising hell and waking up the sheriff — the money came home to become the economic mainstay of Texas during lean times of Reconstruction.

The men in gray returned to Texas after the war and, almost by accident, devised a great industry, one of the greatest of the 19th Century. The trail-drive era lasted two decades, from 1866 until the late 1880s, when fencing and railroads ended the practice. Before it was over, 10 million cattle were driven north and sold for $250 million, money used to sustain and develop Texas. It was a tremendous enterprise.

In the first five years after the war — from 1865 to 1870 — the cattlemen, trail bosses and trail hands were trailblazers in every sense of the word. Many of them, if not most of them, were former Confederate soldiers and, like the longhorns they trailed to market, they were a tough breed.

* * *

Many of the large herds trailed north started from South Texas. A Corpus Christi paper reported that James Bryden, trail boss at King Ranch, "starts off with the first drove of cattle for the Kansas market, his herd consisting of 4,120 head from Nueces County." "Quite a number of our young men are starting for Kansas with cattle," reported the *Nueces Valley*. In 1873, a steer worth $8 in Corpus Christi would bring $23 in Abilene.

Some ranchers made their own drives while others sold cattle to a drover, who would gather herds in the spring. The drive would take some four months; they wanted to get them to market before cold weather set in. The cattle were fattened on the way, except for those who would hurry them along, like D. C. Rachal, and fatten them in Kansas.

For about 1,000 head on the trail, there would be 10 or more cowboys, called waddies or screws. They were paid $30 to $40 a month. The drive would include a trail boss, horse wrangler, cook, and some had a scout to find bedding ground and good river fords and hunt for wild game to vary the diet.

The chuck wagon carried bedding, yellow slickers and provisions, which included beans, flour, sugar, bacon, lard, and coffee beans. The coffee was usually Arbuckle's, which put a peppermint stick in every bag and which usually went to the hand who volunteered to grind the coffee.

The two top hands rode point. Near the front were swing riders, followed by flank riders. At the rear were drag riders, eating the dust of the herd.

In the early days of a drive, the cattle were driven hard to break them to the trail and speed them away from their home range. After they were trail-broken, a typical herd walked 10 to 15 miles a day at a leisurely pace. Trail-driving was pleasant when the skies were clear and there was grass and fresh water. With a herd idling along, grazing as they walked, the cowboys dozed lazily in the saddle.

They went up the Texas, Western and Chisholm trails. The trails out of South Texas joined to form the Chisholm Trail. One trail, the McCoy Trail, began near Corpus Christi. The routes shifted — overlapped and spread apart — depending on grass and water and how many herds had gone before.

While many trail hands were former Confederate soldiers, some were former slaves who learned to handle cattle while others were away fighting. Black cowboys have been largely overlooked in the popular myth of the cowboy era.

Cattleman Charles Goodnight wrote a tombstone inscription after the death of Bose Ikard, one of his black cowboys — "Served with me four years on the Goodnight-Loving Trail, never shirked duty or disobeyed an order, rode with me in many stampedes, participated in three engagements with Comanches, splendid behavior."

One woman from South Texas went up the trail to Kansas. She was Amanda Burks of Banquete in Nueces County. She went up with her husband in 1871. She rode in a buggy and slept in a tent. She thought the drive was pleasant until they ran into "the worst electrical and hailstorms I ever witnessed. The lightning seemed to settle on the ground and creep along like something alive."

When the herd was sold, the Burks traveled by rail to New Orleans and took passage on a ship to Corpus Christi. "I arrived home in much better health than when I left it nine months before."

Trail hands worked long hours. In the evenings they played poker by the light of a bull's-eye lantern and told tales of their own concoction by a dying fire. They slept in the open on a blanket with a saddle for a pillow, which some called a Tucson bed. Cowboys' colorful expressions, their parody of moral codes, their self-deprecatory humor and earthy wit, set them apart. Walter Prescott Webb wrote that cowboy language took on the character of the land, close to primal elements.

On a trail drive, every man had his own job or, in cowboy parlance, every bull had to carry his own tail. A lazy hand was as useful as a three-legged horse or he was said to be quicker at the pot than on the job. A cattleman with a small herd was a little feller. A farmer was someone who turned the grass upside-down. Men of like character were made of the same leather. Someone you could depend on was good to ride the river with. A waddy with experience had wrinkles on his horns.

No hand was more important than the cook, called Coosie or dough wrangler or biscuit shooter. Cowboys tried hard to keep the cook in a good humor. One cowboy said, "This damned biscuit is burned on the outside, raw in the middle, and salty as hell." Then, after a long pause, "Just the way I like it."

The chuckwagon had a large box divided into shelves at the back with a hinged drop table that folded up to cover the shelves. The chuckwagon was called crumb castle, mess wagon, or pie box. Many of the trail drive cooks kept sourdough starter to make biscuits, which were cooked in a Dutch oven nestled in a bed of hot coals with hot coals heaped on top. Hot biscuits were spread with a mixture of sorghum syrup and bacon grease called "Charlie Taylor." A cook on a special occasion might make pancakes, which the hands called "splatter dabs."

234

Meals varied little. There was chili, beans, son-of-a-gun stew, fried bacon called "chuckwagon chicken" and fried salt pork called "Kansas City fish." Dessert, a rare treat, was sometimes an old Navy dish called "spotted pup," made of rice, raisins and cinnamon. One cook, short of supplies, discovered that Copenhagen snuff made a reasonable substitute for cinnamon. Another favorite was a dessert of dried fruit and dough called son of a bitch in a sack.

The meal was finished with Arbuckle's coffee. If a cowboy got up to replenish his cup, and someone yelled, "Man at the pot!" camp etiquette required him to refill all the other cups before his own. Cowboys would wait for someone to make the first move, then yell, "Man at the pot!" If the man at the pot was lucky, there might be enough left to fill his own cup.

Trail-driving was dangerous when a herd stampeded or when flooded rivers were crossed. "We took the river route," one wrote in disgust, "since we must have crossed every damned river in the country, and every one was wet."

Worse than crossing a swollen river was a stampede, from the Spanish "*estampida*." [41] In one storm, a cowboy could see lightning skipping across the tips of the ears of his horse. One was so sure he would be killed by lightning he wrote his own epitaph — "George Knight, struck and killed by lightning, 20 miles south of Ogallala on July 20, 1879." Some died on the trail, by lightning or drowning or other mishap. They were wrapped in blankets and buried in shallow graves. One wrote that the saddest sight he had ever seen was a mound of fresh earth topped with boots, the last resting place of some unfortunate cowboy.

On the way home, cowboys nursed hangovers and memories, sometimes riding back over the same trail. They would arrive in South Texas in the fall, often broke, having spent their wages on saloon women, fancy clothes and presents for the folks back home. One returning trail hand said he was so tired of excitement he wouldn't give a nickel to see an earthquake.

But by the next spring many would be ready for another trip up the trail, repeating the cycle. One cowboy said after a drive he would never forget the feel of the saddle, the weight of the six-gun pulling on his belt, or what a blessing on a rainy night was the yellow slicker the cowboys called "fish."

* * *

One of the most colorful of cowboys hailed from South Texas. Charles Angelo Siringo grew up in the 1850s and 1860s on Matagorda Island. In 1885, Siringo published the first cowboy autobiography, "A Texas Cowboy," which sold a million copies during the author's lifetime. It remains a classic.

---

[41] The writer J. Frank Dobie said the old Texian word was "stompede."

Siringo's father was an Italian immigrant and his mother was Irish. After his father's death, Siringo worked as a cowboy for "Shanghai" Pierce and became a trail driver in the 1870s. From there he worked as a cowhand on a Panhandle ranch. During this period, he met Billy the Kid and later led a posse into New Mexico in pursuit of the Kid and a herd of rustled cattle. He tracked Billy the Kid across New Mexico, but gave up when he lost his traveling money playing three-card monte.

In 1886, Siringo — an "old stove-up cowpuncher" — moved to Chicago and went to work for the Pinkerton Detective Agency. He tracked down wanted men all over the West, from Alaska to Mexico and became almost as famous as a detective as he was as a cowboy. He was known as a dogged tracker who always got his man. In one chase, he paddled a dugout canoe through icy Alaskan waters until he captured two gold thieves.

Siringo in his lifetime knew Billy the Kid, Bat Masterson, Pat Garrett and many others. He died in Los Angeles in 1926. If you wanted to find someone to blame for creating the popular myth of the Texas cowboy, you could start with Charlie Siringo.

Another noted cowboy author was Andy Adams, who wrote "Log of a Cowboy," which is filled with sharp observations that only someone who had lived the experience could have written. It was published in 1903.

Adams' book is a novel, not an actual account of a real drive, but it's a novel based on Adams' first-hand experiences as a trail-hand in the 1880s. The protagonist in the book is a cowboy named Thomas Moore Quirk who could play the fiddle and thought nothing of riding 30 miles to a dance.

In Adams' novel, Quirk signed on for a drive to move 3,000 Circle Dot cattle from Brownsville to Montana. They traveled up along the Laguna Madre; it took them a week to cross the Kenedy and King ranches. They passed west of San Antonio and then took the Old Western Trail. Pointing north, the herd was strung out like a mythical serpent.

The cattle walked and grazed, taking their time, and the narrative was pushed along like the cattle, at a natural pace. The Circle Dot cowboys deal with thieves, stampedes, cattle bogged in quicksand, and when they reach Dodge City, they're warned about shooting up the town. An old hand tells them — "Don't get the impression you can ride your horses into a saloon, or shoot out the lights in Dodge. It may go somewhere else, but it don't go here."

Of course they did not heed that advice. What's the point of having a gun if you can't shoot up the town? They had a few drinks at the Long Branch, until their heads swelled up bigger than their hats, they lost money playing faro, and after a nasty encounter with a rude bouncer at the Lone Star Dance Hall, they shot out the lights and for good measure shot up the town as they rode out of Dodge. Cowboys called this "Waking up the sheriff."

The South Texas author J. Frank Dobie wrote that if all the other trail-driving books were destroyed, you could get an authentic picture of trail men and cow country from Andy Adams' "Log of a Cowboy."

* * *

Behind the cowboys were the men who hired them, the cattlemen, the men who created the cattle kingdom of Texas, which was founded in that rough triangle of South Texas from San Antonio to Corpus Christi to Laredo. The South Texas cattlemen learned from the Spanish rancheros and vaqueros who came before them. The author O. Henry called these Texas cattlemen grandees of grass, barons of beef and bone.

Texas's most famous cattle baron was Richard King. As an orphan in New York, King stowed away on a ship and became a cabin boy on Alabama riverboats. He met Mifflin Kenedy, a steamboat captain, and the two were hired to run boats on the Rio Grande for the U.S. Army during the Mexican War. After the war, Kenedy and King became partners in the riverboat carrying trade. In July 1853, King bought 15,000 acres of the Santa Gertrudis grant for two cents an acre. He didn't know how to handle cattle, but he hired expert vaqueros from a village in Mexico.

A year after King began the King Ranch, a young man from Rhode Island, Abel Head Pierce, stowed away on a schooner bound for Indianola. He was discovered at sea and put to work handling cargo. They called him "Shanghai" because he walked like a Shanghai rooster, but he was not rooster-sized. He was 6-foot-5 with a megaphone voice that carried across distant pastures. He went to work as a cowboy and during the Civil War he enlisted in the Confederate Army. After the war, he established Rancho Grande on Tres Palacios Creek.

"Old Shang" was described as uncouth as the cattle he owned but "infinite in wit and anecdote." When he went to buy cattle, he had a pack horse loaded with gold and silver led by his black cowboy, Neptune Holmes. Shanghai Pierce would spread a blanket on the ground and count out the gold and silver.

Another beef baron was Mifflin Kenedy, a Pennsylvania Quaker. Like Richard King and Shanghai Pierce, he also went to sea as a young man, shipping out on a vessel bound for Calcutta. He worked on a riverboat and obtained his pilot's license. A well-worn cliché compares the vast prairies of South Texas to the sea — the land described as a green ocean covered with waves of grass. The metaphor seems fitting considering that three of the greatest cattlemen of the coastal prairies of South Texas were men of the sea — King, Kenedy and Pierce. As young men, they were all more familiar with the deck of a ship than the saddle of a horse.

When Richard King bought Santa Gertrudis in 1853, Mifflin Kenedy chose to stay with the steamboats. Then he joined King in ranching in 1860. When the Civil War broke out, King and Kenedy had 20,000 head of cattle. Their longhorns were trailed east to help feed the Confederacy. The two took a close interest in the Cotton Road. King used his ranch as supply headquarters for the wagon traffic and Kenedy shipped the cotton on their steamboats on the Rio Grande. The war made them wealthy.

After the war, King and Kenedy divided their holdings and Kenedy bought the Laureles ranch. It included 130,000 acres on a peninsula at Baffin Bay (the old Salt Lagoon). Kenedy sold the Laureles in 1880 and bought 450,000 acres to the south. He called his new ranch La Parra for wild grapevines. King continued to expand the King Ranch. When he died, it took in about a half million acres.

By contrast, the open-range cattlemen often owned just enough land for their ranch houses and working headquarters. Some called them range pirates. But they began to realize that the future would be in fenced pastures. Some of the open-range cattlemen in South Texas included Martin Culver, whose headquarters was at Rancho Perdido on the Nueces River.

Another was John Rabb, who lived near Banquete. Rabb was said to have more cattle with his Bow and Arrow brand than King and Kenedy combined, but he owned only 100 acres of land. After his death, his widow Martha began to buy land and soon acquired 30,000 acres of pasture in Nueces County. It was said she would sit on the top rail of the corral fence to watch the branding and cutting out of stock. She smoked little cigarillos and always carried a box of them with her. They called her the Cattle Queen of Texas.

The era of cattle barons and open-range cattlemen reached its apex in the two decades following the Civil War. Like their half-wild longhorns, the old barons of beef and bone were tough as rawhide and wonderfully adapted to the thorny brush land of South Texas.

The age of the cattle kings lasted little more than one generation, roughly from the 1850s to the 1890s. Times changed. The open range was converted into fenced pastures and semi-wild longhorns were replaced with improved breeds of cattle. The era of the author O. Henry's "grandees of grass, kings of the kine, lords of the lea, barons of beef and bone" came to an end. The cowboys who rode up the trail, and the cattle barons they worked for, were a special breed. We will not see their like again.

Indianola

CHAPTER 32

KILLER STORMS
SEALED THE FATE OF INDIANOLA
1840s — 1886

The 'sea lions' gave us as much trouble in the water as wild cattle ever gave anybody in the brush.

—John D. Young

In the summer of 1840, a Comanche war party of 500 braves headed for the settlement of Linnville on Lavaca Bay, where they plundered stores, burned the town, and took captives. A large force of Texans caught them at Plum Creek, where the Comanches suffered a crushing defeat. After Linnville was sacked, its commerce moved south to Lavaca, where residents rebuilt their homes on a bluff overlooking the bay.

Lavaca ("the cow") got its name when it became a shipping point for cattle. Charles Morgan, the New York shipping tycoon, made it a port of call for his Morgan Line ships. Lavaca was changed to Port Lavaca to reflect its growing status as a seaport.

Prince Karl of Solms-Braunfels, head of the German Immigration Society, picked a spot to land 200 German families 12 miles down the shore from Port Lavaca. The immigrants landed at Indian Point, which was renamed Karlshafen (Karl's Harbor). The strip of beach along Lavaca and Matagorda bays was surrounded by lakes, bayous and marshes.

A tent city emerged on the sandy shore as thousands of German settlers arrived at Karlshafen. From there they moved on to New Braunfels and Fredericksburg. One immigrant wrote that their oxcarts carried supplies of every kind imaginable — "complete machinery for a mill, a number of barrels of whisky, and a great many dogs. We came prepared to conquer the world."

Up the coast, Port Lavaca made a fateful decision to raise its wharf fees. Shipping tycoon Charles Morgan was quick to react. He built a wharf 12 miles below Port Lavaca on Powderhorn Lake, down the beach from Karlshafen. He established regular steamer service between his new docks and New York. The community that sprouted up around Morgan's docks was known as Powderhorn, then Indianola.

Indianola became a center of considerable commercial activity. Wharves stretching into the bay were piled high with hides, pecans, oats, corn, cotton, gold bullion destined for the U.S. Mint at New Orleans. Longhorns were driven to the docks for shipment east. John D. Young helped drive longhorns, which the cowboys on the coast called sea lions. "Our route to Indianola," Young wrote, "was across bayous and along lakes and the 'sea lions' gave us as much trouble in the water as wild cattle ever gave anybody in the brush."

The growth of Indianola created a huge shipping business. Goods arrived at the port and were freighted up the trail to San Antonio. The heavily traveled trail was known by several names — the Cart Road, the Old Freight Road, the Goliad Road, the Mexican Cart Trail. The Cart Road ran from Indianola to Victoria to Goliad to Runge and Helena, in Karnes County, to Floresville and San Antonio. The exact route shifted, depending on the availability of grass and water for the freight teams.

There was a steady stream of wagons and carts pulled by mules, horses and oxen moving up and down the Cart Road. The trip to San Antonio — depending on weather and mud — took from four to six weeks. Many Cart Road freighters lived at Goliad or Helena, stopping places in between. Helena, the last major stop on the Cart Road, was a rough town. It was named for Helen Owings, wife of one of the town's founders. The town was known for what was called the Helena Duel, fought by two men whose left hands were lashed together, leaving enough distance to slash at each other with Bowie knives, but not close enough for fatal stab wounds. The Helena Duel, it was said, usually ended in one or both fighters bleeding to death. Helena was headquarters for Cart Road freighters.

In the mid-1850s, San Antonio merchants sought a cheaper way to get their freight hauled from Indianola. The going rate was $3 for 100 pounds. The merchants recruited Mexican cartmen — *carreteros* — from Chihuahua, who began to haul supplies for the San Antonio merchants and the U.S. Army at reduced rates. The *carreteros* lived at a settlement on the San Antonio River. The competition between Chihuahua *carreteros* and Texan Anglo freighters created a bitter rivalry. The Texas freighters, idled by the competition, reacted with violence. In 1857, the Cart War broke out on the Old Cart Road.

Men with blackened faces slipped into the camps of the Mexican cartmen at night. They cut the spokes of the wagons almost but not quite through, creating mayhem on the trail when the wheels collapsed. As the feud intensified, ranchers and settlers along the Cart Road sided with the Texas freighters, claiming that Mexican cartmen slaughtered their cattle and encouraged their slaves — especially young women slaves — to run away.

242

In July 1857, a train of Mexican carts loaded with U.S. military supplies was attacked near Helena. One Mexican cartman was killed. In September, another train of 17 Mexican carts was attacked by men with blackened faces. Two Mexican cartmen were killed and several wounded. Other attacks on Mexican cartmen were mounted near Goliad and on the Cibolo Creek in Karnes County. Gen. David Twiggs, commanding the Eighth Army Department in Texas, ordered Army escorts for wagon trains hauling government supplies. The stream of commercial goods moving from Indianola to San Antonio slowed to a trickle. The merchants complained to Gov. E. M. Pease, who called out a force of 75 men to put an end to trouble on the Cart Road.

Two instigators of violent attacks against Mexican cartmen — a man named Wardick and another named Brownin were hanged in Goliad. There may have been other lynchings. With the show of force by the Army and civil authorities, the harassment and killing of Mexican *carreteros* ended. But the violence succeeded in driving them away. After 1857, there were only a few Mexican cartmen still hauling freight on the Old Cart Road.

* * *

Secretary of War Jefferson Davis launched an experiment to study using Arabian camels to carry Army supplies. The first shipment of camels arrived at Indianola on May 14, 1856. Not long after the camels landed, another ship docked at Indianola, claiming to have camels for sale to private individuals, but the cargo consisted of smuggled African slaves who were sold from the ship.

During the 1850s, which were bustling times for Indianola, a man named D. A. Saltmarsh ran a stagecoach line from Indianola to San Antonio. One passenger found that the roads were so bad he had to walk most of the way and he had to help pull the coach out of mud holes — "the hardest and dirtiest work I have ever done."

Capt. Peter Johnson ran schooners from Indianola to Saluria on Matagorda Island and from there ran a stagecoach line down Matagorda, across Cedar Bayou, to the town of Aransas on St. Joseph's. His line carried the mail from Indianola to Corpus Christi.

In the Civil War, Indianola was occupied when Union forces captured Galveston in 1862 and again in 1863 after Gen. Nathaniel P. Banks' army captured Brownsville, Fort Semmes on Mustang Island, and Fort Esperanza on Matagorda Island. Indianola was held briefly by Union forces before they were withdrawn, ending Banks' campaign in Texas.

After the war, Indianola — the Queen City of the West — passed Galveston as a port and became one of Texas' greatest cities. Then it was nearly destroyed when a storm struck on Sept. 16, 1875. The Signal Service, the forerunner of the U.S. Weather Bureau, called it one of the most perfect types of tropical storms since the tracking of hurricanes began.

Indianola was terribly vulnerable. Its location was low and exposed, at near sea level, and almost surrounded by water. When the storm surge hit, the streets turned into rivers. Trains couldn't run with the tracks underwater and people were trapped in wooden buildings that collapsed in the storm surge. They clung to lumber and cotton bales. A four-year-old girl, her hand caught in a rooftop, was found 15 hours later, alive, but half-crazed from the ordeal.

Huck's Lumber Yard, the Casimir House hotel, the *Indianola Bulletin* newspaper, Louis de Planque's photo studio, and three of every four buildings were destroyed. The storm cut 12 new bayous through the devastated town. Some 200 lives were lost. But people began to rebuild. They were not beaten.

History repeated itself on Aug. 20, 1886. Indianola was hit by another powerful hurricane. Some who experienced both storms said the sequel in 1886 was worse. It was followed by a fire that consumed what the storm left standing. The last disaster sealed the fate of Indianola. People didn't have the heart to rebuild the ruined city. Buildings were salvaged, the lumber removed and hauled to Port Lavaca, Victoria, Beeville and other towns where homes and stores were rebuilt. Commerce moved on to Rockport and Corpus Christi. The two catastrophic storms a decade apart spelled the end of Indianola. Today, it is a small fishing village, with a store or two, and the large graveyard of a once thriving city.

CHAPTER 33

JOHN DUNN
AND THE NOAKES RAID
1874 — 1875

It is sometimes amusing to hear people say that the murderers were never caught. Well, ignorance is bliss.

—*John Dunn*

John Dunn's father Matthew, a native of Ireland, came to Corpus Christi in 1845 with Zachary Taylor. He was a sutler[42] with the army. After the first battles of the Mexican War at Palo Alto and Resaca de la Palma, Matthew Dunn became a teamster. He survived the massacre of a train of supply wagons ambushed by guerrillas in northern Mexico.

When Matthew Dunn returned to Corpus Christi after the war, Henry Kinney, founder of the town, gave him 100 acres on the old San Patricio Road, five miles from town, to settle on. He married Sarah Pritchett and they had three sons — John, Matthew, and James. The father suffered a sunstroke, which affected his mind. While hospitalized in New Orleans he became lost and was never found again. With the outbreak of the Civil War, Sarah Dunn took her three sons to Gonzales on the Guadalupe River to stay with relatives. After the war, they returned to the homestead northwest of Corpus Christi.

In a yellow fever epidemic that decimated Corpus Christi in 1867, John Dunn[43] came down with the fever. He sweated it out by sleeping between two sick cousins. "I threw myself down between the two cousins I was

---

[42] A storekeeper authorized to sell goods on a military post.
[43] He was called "Red John" to distinguish him from a cousin also named John Dunn.

nursing," he wrote, "and threw my arms across them to keep the covers on. I went crazy. I crawled across the room, struck my head on a table hard enough to make it bleed. That let the hot blood out. It saved my life."

After the epidemic, Dunn went to Rockport to look for work. He arrived at night and slept under a live oak. The next morning he spent a quarter on sardines and crackers. He found a job hauling lumber for a man named Powell. He worked for him until 1868 when he got a job as a fireman on the side-wheel steamer *Reindeer*.

After a trip to St. Louis, Dunn returned to Corpus Christi where he found a new development — three beef packing houses, also called "hide and tallow" plants, or packeries. He went to work in a packery on North Beach outside Corpus Christi owned by Bill Brunwinkel and Henry Ball.

After working in the packing house, Dunn, with his brother Matt, joined a company of Texas Rangers. Dunn wrote that the other 60 men in the company were "the worst mixed lot of men that ever came together in one organization."

One man had ridden with Quantrill's raiders and another man, called "Three-Fingered Jack," was wanted for murder in California. They worked the borderlands of South Texas where a different kind of war had raged for decades, where raiding across the Rio Grande shaped a generation of tough, violent hombres. The Rangers were disbanded when Gov. E. J. Davis established the State Police Force.

After the Rangers were disbanded, Dunn tried various jobs. He worked at King Ranch for three months, cut hay for U.S. troops in San Antonio, and hired on as a trail-hand to take a herd of cattle to Kansas. When he returned from Kansas, he joined volunteer posses, "Minutemen" they were called, after an upsurge in violence during Reconstruction.

On Sept. 5, 1872, George Hatch, an old pioneer Texan, was shot to death in his buggy on the north end of the Reef Road. Eli Merriman, a reporter, saw Hatch's body in the shot-up buggy, with the old man slumped over, his pockets cut out and horse stolen.

A posse rode into Mexico looking for the killers. They found a man riding Hatch's horse. He was killed, but they lost the trail of the other two men who were believed involved.

John Dunn, riding with the posse, indicated that the murderers were dealt with in time. "Outside of five or six persons," Dunn wrote, "no one knows whether they were caught or not." Dunn said that the names of the killers had been made known to them and were written down and put in their hats. "It is sometimes amusing to hear people say that the murderers were never caught," he said. "Well, ignorance is bliss."

During this lawless time, bandits robbed, killed, stole cattle, attacked and burned ranches. The bandits were a mix of outlaws from Mexico and bad

246

men on the run. "The situation is truly deplorable," said the *Nueces Valley* newspaper. "There is no security for person or property between the Nueces and the Rio Grande." Stolen cattle were driven across the Rio Grande and hide peelers skinned cattle — often while the bawling animals were alive. Ranchers in South Texas hired gunmen to track down rustlers and hide peelers.

People did not dare to travel, even for short distances, without being heavily armed and constantly alert. On Aug. 19, 1872, William Murdock, who lived on the Santa Gertrudis Road outside Corpus Christi, was tied up, a heavy plow placed on top of him, and burned alive.

* * *

One of the worst crimes of a lawless decade was committed on May 9, 1874, at Peñascal, a one-store settlement 60 miles south of Corpus Christi on a point of land at Baffin Bay. Store owner John Morton, 24, his brother and two customers were killed in a cold-blooded and brutal robbery.

It was near dusk when a cook returning with a bucket of water from the well hid and watched as 11 bandits dismounted. He heard shots and saw a man named Herman Tilgner, a customer in the store, come running out vomiting blood. He watched as the killers finished him off. From his hiding place, the cook saw the bandits shoot Michael Morton, brother of the store owner, four times in the head. They tied up a customer named F. M. Coakley and executed him. They shot the store owner in both arms and forced him to carry out their plunder, then shot him six more times. His body was found behind the counter, one leg bent under him, a prayer book nearby covered with blood.

The killers stayed all night, drinking whisky and trying on store clothes. They left at dawn, wearing new store clothes and leaving their own clothes in the wrecked and blood-splattered store.

The alarm spread. Several posses rode to Morton's store. One was made up of John Dunn, his brothers and some of his cousins. In examining wagon tracks near the store, Dunn noticed a brown powder, which turned out to be brown sugar that had leaked from one of the bags the bandits had taken. The trail of brown sugar ended a few miles from Peñascal, but it revealed that the bandits were riding not for the border, as might have been expected, but north toward Corpus Christi.

They scoured the country looking for the bandits. A man told the posse he had seen sheepherders looking for work who were staying in an old jacal. The posse found the hut empty, but came across a rider who tried to get away. He was cut off and a member of the posse stuck a rifle in his ribs. The man said he saw armed men camped in a sheep pen on the Nueces River. The posse reached the sheep pen at midnight.

"The hard south wind had blown the big gate open," Dunn wrote, "and we charged right in among them before they knew we were there. I happened to dismount beside a blanket where two men were asleep. One of these was Hypolita Tapia. The other was Andres Davila (he learned their names later).

"After satisfying ourselves that these were the only men implicated in the murder and robbery, we took them back to Mean's village (Meansville). We placed the prisoners in a room under guard.

"First, we took Hypolita Tapia out and told him we wanted him to tell us all about the murder but he stated he would confess nothing. We took him to a tall mesquite tree, strung him up, and let him kick a few chunks out of the horizon. After that, he stated that he was ready to divulge everything."

Andres Davila confessed before he received similar treatment. Tapia in his confession said he was a vaquero and sheepherder who lived in Corpus Christi. He said that a Corpus Christi policeman named Tomas Basquez had been in Buckley's wool store in Corpus Christi and overheard that there would be a large consignment of goods and money going to Peñascal. Basquez wanted to get 10 men to go down and get it. Tapia said he agreed to do it and he got 10 men to go with him, including Andres Davila and an Anglo named Joe. The man named Joe became the ringleader of the bunch.

When they arrived at Peñascal, Tapia said, the boat on which the goods had been shipped was sighted some distance from shore. They assumed that the boat had already landed the money and goods, but it had not. When they hit the store, the raiders found only $12 or $13 in the cash drawer. Tapia told how the four men at Morton's store were killed.

As the posse questioned the suspects, word spread of their capture. Ranchers who lived nearby showed up with ropes and plans to use them. The Dunn brothers convinced them that if they lynched Tapia and Davila, it would destroy any case against the policeman Basquez and the Anglo-American named Joe, if they ever caught him. Tapia and Davila were delivered to Nueces County Sheriff John McClane.

During the trial, the prosecutor told the jury that Hypolita Tapia made a voluntary confession. Tapia jumped up, pointing to rope marks around his neck and shouted, "That's the voluntary confession!"

Tapia and Andres Davila were found guilty and sentenced to be hanged on Friday, Aug. 7, 1874. A third suspect identified as the man who shot the storeowner Morton was taken out of the San Diego jail and lynched. The policeman Basquez and the Anglo named Joe were never brought to justice.

Tapia, days before his scheduled hanging, asked to marry his common-law wife, who lived in Corpus Christi. The day before the hanging, the two prisoners were shaved and dressed in white shirts and black pants. Tapia's friends and relatives attended the wedding at the jail. The bride wore a calico dress and black shawl. The ceremony was performed by Father Claude Jaillet.

The next day, Father Jaillet returned to escort the two men to the scaffold. Tapia and Davila were still wearing the white shirts and black pants from the wedding. Tapia's last words were — "My friends, I am here today to die by hanging. I have killed no person nor helped kill anyone. The people forced the party that was guilty to swear against me; but it is all right. Goodbye." Davila stood with downcast eyes and said nothing.

After the hanging, two of Tapia's brothers swore vengeance. John Dunn, the man responsible for his capture, took to sleeping in his cornfield, away from his cabin. One night, when he went back into the house to get a drink of water and absentmindedly lit a lantern, shots were fired at him from the darkness. After that, for safety, he rejoined the Rangers.

* * *

When the Rangers were camped on the Santa Gertrudis, Dunn related, it was customary at morning roll call to detail a squad to bring in firewood. The Rangers rode out on horseback to the woods along the creek and used their ropes to drag broken tree branches back to camp. They would have a huge pile in a short time. At nightfall, if it was cold, they would set the whole pile on fire to keep the camp warm.

Dunn noticed an old bull was slipping into the camp late at night. When the men settled down to sleep, the bull would find a place near the fire to keep warm. One cold night, the bull came in, sniffed around, and stretched out a few feet from where Dunn had spread his bedroll. The bull made his bed too close to the fire, Dunn said, and during the night he got burned by a spark. The bull went up like a rocket, snorting and bellowing and raising a ferocious commotion. With the bull in panic, all hell broke loose. The Rangers, startled from their sleep, began firing their guns in every direction, thinking they were under attack. The bull in his frenzy scattered the coals of the fire and some of the bedrolls went up in flames, before things finally settled down.

The Rangers took inventory. There were two wounded men, several burned blankets, a broken bridle bit, a broken wagon tongue, and a saddle shot full of bullet holes. Next morning, the old bull was seen three miles from camp. Dunn reckoned he was a sensible animal who learned from his mistakes, for he never returned to claim a warm spot by the fire.

* * *

249

In the last week of March, 1875, a band of 150 bandits gathered at Las Cuevas below Rio Grande City. They were followers of Juan Cortina, "The Red Robber of the Rio Grande."

The bandits separated into four groups for raiding forays into Texas. After some indiscriminate killing of travelers and lonely shepherds, three of the bands crossed back into Mexico. The fourth group of 33 men rode towards Corpus Christi. They arrived about dark on Thursday, March 25, 1875 and camped on the Oso nine miles from town.

After sunrise on Good Friday, the bandits showed up at the ranch of Joseph Campbell, a sheepman with a large family who lived near the Juan Saenz community. They went on to the S. H. Page ranch near Tule Lake. They ransacked the Page home and some of the bandits switched their worn-out saddles for better ones they found at Page's. The bandits took the men at the Page ranch hostage, forcing them to run ahead as they rode up the road to George Frank's store at Juan Saenz.

At the store, a bandit yelled "Viva Cortina! Viva Mexico!" They put on store clothes and swapped old boots for new ones and found $80 in the cash drawer. They killed an elderly Mexican man who worked for Frank who recognized one of the bandits.

Outside the store, traffic on the road was heavy that Good Friday with people on their way to church in Corpus Christi. The bandits took people they encountered hostage.

One party captured included sheep rancher George Reynolds, his two teenage daughters, their governess, Adele DeBerry, and ranch hand Fred Franks. The bandits told Reynolds to take off his clothes. He was indignant. "You're not going to make me take off my pants here before my daughters and this young lady?"

The bandits didn't force the issue, but they made Franks, who was courting Miss DeBerry, take off his boots and trousers.

The bandits stopped Henry Gilpin and Miss Laura Allen, who were heading for Corpus Christi. Another man captured was Sidney Borden, founder of Sharpsburg on the Nueces River, cousin of the inventor of condensed milk.

They took Mrs. E. D. Sidbury, wife of a Corpus Christi lumber dealer, and her daughter hostage. The two women were on their way to pay the ranch hands at Mrs. Sidbury's Rancho Seco.

The bandits took the captives' horses and made them walk or run as they headed for Nuecestown. One bandit who knew Henry Gilpin shouted, *"Andale! Don Enriquez! Andale!"*

A man named Joe Howell complained about having to run in his bare feet so they made him put on Miss Allen's slippers and he tried to run for a bit, then stretched out on the road and refused to move. There were shouts and curses in Spanish and the bandits jumped their horses over him, but left him behind, unharmed.

They herded the remaining hostages along the Up River Road. Some of the captives, like Gilpin, were elderly. They were quirted to make them run faster. Since they did not shoot Howell for his defiance, other captives refused to budge. The bandits argued about whether to shoot them, but finally decided to leave them behind.

Four Texans trailing the bandits were led by John Dunn. They came across the stragglers the bandits left behind. "I shall never forget how miserable Fred Franks looked," Dunn said. "He had been wearing a good suit of clothes and shop-made boots, but the bandits left him with nothing but his underclothes."

As the Dunn posse rode on UpRiver Road, they saw 10 bandits a little way down the road. They had Sidney Borden on foot ahead of them and were forcing him up the road at a trot. One of the bandits was riding Borden's prized dapple gray race horse. Near Frank's store, members of the Dunn posse and the bandits watched each other, keeping their distance. The bandits were too many for the Dunns to attack and the bandits were not disposed to initiate the action. Each group kept a wary eye on the other. John Dunn recognized his brother Mike's horse and buggy and realized he had been captured.

Word that Mexican bandits were terrorizing people nine miles from the city reached Corpus Christi before noon. The alarm was spread by James M. Hunter, who owned a livery stable on Water Street. Hunter barely escaped capture when Sidney Borden was taken.

Guns were taken down from gun racks as men in town prepared to face whatever dangers were bearing down. They expected a horde of bandits to come riding in at any moment.

Sheriff John McClane lathered his horse riding up and down the streets, urging people to stay inside, bar their doors, and mothers to collect their children. A class of school girls was on a picnic on North Beach. Since the men in town were standing guard, awaiting the raiders, boys were sent to bring the girls in. Women and children boarded the steamship "Aransas" and a lumber schooner in port. The vessels left the wharf and anchored out in the bay.

William Rankin was at work painting the upstairs of the McCampbell Building at the corner of Mesquite and Peoples. "Charles Vandervoort, Chris Yung, James McKenzie and I were painting together, when John McClane (the sheriff) rode by shouting, 'Mexican raid! Mexican raid!' We locked up the house and ran out. I had never carried a gun up to that time in my life, but I was assigned, with others, to guard the outskirts of the city and was part of the armed patrol."

251

A meeting was held on Mesquite Street. Several men agreed to ride to Nuecestown to take on the bandits. Sheriff McClane tried to stop them, pleading that he needed every able-bodied man to protect the town. Jim Dunn, another of John's many relatives, had a few words for the sheriff. John Dunn said, "What Jim Dunn said to him would not look good in print."

At Nuecestown, Thomas Noakes' store sat on a hill up a slope from the Nueces River. Noakes was waiting for the mail rider to bring the mail when a man called "Lying" John came in to buy flour. As Noakes was getting the flour he saw three bandits ride up. He grabbed his Winchester and seeing a bandit raise a pistol to shoot "Lying" John, Noakes fired first, hitting the bandit in the chest. Noakes' wife ran from the store with their five children. When the mail rider, William Ball, rode up, the bandits took the mail and the mail rider. Noakes and "Lying" John scuttled through a trap door at the back of the store and hid in a trench under the floor.

The bandits plundered the store, then started a fire. Mrs. Noakes, who had returned after seeing the children to safety, poured water on the fire. Several times a bandit restarted the fire only to have her put it out before the flames finally took hold. With the store on fire, "Lying" John ran for it. He was hit and then shot as he lay on the ground. As the fire became intense, Noakes made a run for it. He had his Winchester and was ready to shoot. Mrs. Noakes yelled that the bandits were gone. As the store burned, Mrs. Noakes ran inside to save her prized feather bed.

Three miles away, at Juan Saenz, the men from Corpus Christi rode up, their horses sucking wind. Among them were George Swank, a hot-tempered roofer, Pat Whelan, a brickmaker, "Wash" Mussett, Pat McManigle, who ran the Gem Saloon, Clem Vetters, and Jesus Seguira. They could see the smoke rising from Nuecestown. When the posse arrived at Nuecestown, Noakes' store was in smoldering ruins. He was sitting on the ground with his Winchester.

The roofer Swank told Noakes to give him the gun, that all he had was a six-shooter with which to go up against the bandits. Noakes refused, saying the bandits might come back and he would have no protection. Swank pulled his revolver and threatened Noakes, "Hand over that rifle or I'll shoot you myself." Noakes gave Swank the Winchester.

The bandits took their plunder and remaining captives on a wagon and camped in the brush outside town. When Swank and one of Dunns rode up, a shot was fired, killing Swank, as the rest of the Dunns and the group from Corpus Christi arrived.

Shots were exchanged between the posse and the bandits. "The bullets were singing around us," John Dunn said. "We could recognize the sound of Mike Dunn's sharpshooter, which the bandits had stolen from him. The lead in the end of the cartridges had been split down to the brass shell and their scream was like the wail of a lost soul."

As the posse prepared to charge, the bandits took off, leaving their plunder and prisoners behind. Sheriff McClane arrived and took Swank's body. They found a wounded bandit — the man Noakes shot — who was placed in a two-wheeled cart to haul to Corpus Christi. "Lying" John, shot four times, survived to claim that he had been shot eight times.

* * *

On Saturday morning, the day before Easter, 1875, Sidney Borden, who was captured by the bandits a day earlier, arrived with a posse he had raised at Sharpsburg. Someone had asked what kind of men he wanted and Borden replied, "I'm looking for men with strong nerves and weak minds." News of the raid brought "Minutemen" militias riding at a hard gallop from all over.

They gathered at Banquete and divided into three groups, each group heading in a different direction. Borden's group rode toward San Diego. About 20 miles away they found a campsite where the bandits had barbecued a goat. In another 20 miles they reached the ranch of Jorge Alanis, who joined the posse.

Past E. H. Caldwell's Borjas Ranch, they captured two men. Some of the posse members wanted to hang them while Sidney Borden, Marion Garner, and another man argued that there was nothing to link these two men to the Mexican raiders.

"Nothing more was said," Garner said of the pro-hanging faction, "but we could see by the frowns on their faces that it didn't set well." Those who wanted to hang the two men rode off into the brush, taking the prisoners and two long stake ropes. They came back without the prisoners. It was later determined that one of the hanged men was a Laredo merchant and the other his servant. Neither man had any connection to the bandits that raided Nuecestown.

The posse tracked the bandits to the Rio Grande, then gave up. Borden told the posse, "Boys, I've brought you on a wild goose chase. We'd better head for home."

In Corpus Christi, the wounded bandit was brought to town on a wool cart. They took him up on the bluff, looking for a place to hang him and began to loop a rope around the steeple of the Catholic Church.

Cattleman Martin Culver stopped them, telling them not to desecrate God's house. The mob went down Leopard Street to a gate with a cross pole. William Ball, the mail rider who had been captured at Noakes store the day before, put the hangman's noose around the bandit's neck. They drove the cart under the cross pole, a rope was thrown over it, the bandit was lifted into the air, and the cart drove on. The body was left hanging that night and not taken down until Easter Sunday morning.

Mrs. E. D. Sidbury and her daughter were found Easter morning. They had escaped from the bandits on Friday and hid in the brush. They were lost for two days. In the aftermath of the raid, George Reynolds spent two years tracking down his team of stolen horses. He found them in government stables in Saltillo, Mexico, and got them back. Thomas Noakes built a new store a mile from the old site and the town moved with him. Militia companies made retaliatory raids against those suspected of being in league with the bandits. Armed bands roamed throughout the violent triangle of South Texas, hanging vaqueros and burning the homes of Mexican-Americans, with or without cause.

John Dunn joined a militia group headed by Hines Clark of Banquete and served as a Texas Ranger. He later became a farmer and dairyman after he married Lelia Nias. He opened a private museum at his place on Shell Road outside Corpus Christi to display his large collection. Among other items, he had hundreds of guns from frontier times that had belonged to famous Texans, including the pistol taken from Hypolita Tapia when he was captured at the sheep pen. Dunn died at age 89 on the last day of September 1940.

Henry Scott

CHAPTER 34

CAPT. HENRY SCOTT,
LEADER OF VIGILANTES
1874

*They tracked down and liquidated skinners, rustlers, bad men, desperadoes
and common criminals.*

—*Judge W. L. Rea of Henry Scott's Minutemen*

In the lawless 1870s, citizens banded together to impose their own idea of
law and order. Bodies were found hanging from mesquite limbs all over
South Texas. Some were reported — "Archey Reeves at Ingleside found
a Mexican hanging in the Nine-Mile Mott near Corpus Christi reef.". . .
"James Hart was present at Corpus Christi when they took a Mexican boy
and brought him to the mott (at Doyle's Water Hole) and five of Dan
Doughty's company were seen to go into the mott with the Mexican who was
found hanging. The Mexican boy formerly lived with Tom Welder."

Several vigilante outfits rode out of Refugio. One vigilante leader was
Capt. Henry Scott, rancher and former Confederate officer. Henry Scott's
family came to Texas from New York when he was two and joined the Power
colony at Mission Refugio. Scott was six when Texas prisoners were
executed in front of the mission on March 16, 1836 by Gen. Jose Urrea's
troops. The 20 or more executed men were members of Amon King's
company. Scott watched as the Texans were marched in front of the mission,
tied two by two, and shot.

Four years later, 10-year-old Henry Scott was riding with his father, Capt.
John Scott, on the trail of a party of Lipan Apache raiders. They caught the
Indians near the border, where the city of Brownsville is today, and in the
fight Capt. Scott was killed. Young Henry Scott was captured by the Lipan
Apaches, who took him deep into Mexico. One night, he slipped away and
escaped on a pony, riding alone through a rugged area, living on berries and
roots, until he came to a rancho, and from there made his way back to Texas.

During the Civil War, Capt. Scott's company of Confederate militia was stationed near the King Ranch to guard the Cotton Road. After the war, Scott enlarged his ranch from the original 4,000 acres (outside today's Woodsboro) to 35,000 acres between Medio Creek and Chocolate Bayou.

Scott's Minutemen were organized in Refugio in 1873 to protect against Mexican bandits. John Young said he joined Coon Dunman's regulators, a vigilante committee, which were absorbed into the larger company commanded by Capt. Scott.

Young said the members of Scott's company rode their own horses and paid their own expenses. "However, this expense did not amount to much as every home was open to us for anything we needed, without price. There was nothing for us to do except to put those criminals across the Rio Grande where they belonged, but too many of them would take their chances on being killed rather than return to Mexico where they would be lined up against a wall and shot. Where the evidence warranted, we gave them the choice to swim or fight."

Refugio's Judge W. L. Rea said Scott's Minutemen restored order in Refugio County, but they also ranged into Goliad, Bee, San Patricio, and Nueces counties. "They tracked down and liquidated skinners, rustlers, bad men, desperadoes and common criminals," Rea said, and added that extraordinary times demanded extraordinary measures.

A Minuteman related one encounter. "One night a band of Scott's men surrounded a gang of 15 Mexican horse thieves in a thicket. Captain Scott called the men about him and said, 'Boys, don't fire too quick. Get as close as you can and aim at the middle of their bodies. Just keep it in mind that Mexicans can't hit you.' Within an hour, Texas had a dozen fewer horse thieves within its borders."

On May 9, 1874, four men were killed at Peñascal on Baffin Bay. A store owner, his brother and two customers were shot to death in a robbery. After the Peñascal slayings, a Committee of Public Safety was formed in Corpus Christi and an order was issued that all adult males had to register. Each man was given a certificate. Failure to produce the certificate was a serious matter.

One of Scott's friends was a deaf sheep rancher named Thad Swift. His place was on the Saus Creek in Refugio County near Scott's own ranch. Thad Swift took his wool clip to the town of St. Mary's and sold it for $700. The payment came in small leather sacks filled with silver dollars. That was on Saturday, June 7, 1874.

On Sunday, Swift, who was deaf, was murdered in his bed, cut to pieces in horrible ways. His wife was stabbed 25 times, her throat cut, and her body left in the yard, where it was mangled by hogs. The Swifts' three girls knew nothing of the slayings until they woke on Sunday morning and found the bodies of their parents. The oldest girl, who was eight, took her younger sisters, leading one and carrying the other, to their uncle's house three miles away. The news spread and riders came from all over. Men turned pale at the grisly sight at the Swift place.

Henry Scott's Minutemen were in the saddle after the news spread of the Swift murders. The Minutemen split up. Part of Scott's company, under the command of a ranch hand named Edward Fennessey, went after a man named Marcelo Moya, who lived in Goliad County. Scott and the rest of his Minutemen chased a man named Juan Flores, who had been with Swift to sell the wool and knew about the payment of silver dollars. Flores was considered a prime suspect in the slayings. Scott took his posse toward Laredo, following the trail of Flores.

John Young was with the Fennessey posse. Young was responsible for steering the posse toward a ranch near Goliad, telling the Minutemen he knew of a "bad Mexican" named Moya who might have been involved in the killings.

The suspicion linking the name Moya to the Swift murders apparently was based on the report that someone had seen one of the Moyas riding from the direction of the Swift ranch and that he owned a very sharp knife. Then someone remembered that old man Moya had remained loyal to Mexico during the Texas Revolution.

The Fennessey posse was soon riding toward the Moya Ranch in Goliad County. Their ostensible purpose was to arrest one of the Moya boys, the one described by Young as a "bad Mexican." Their real purpose was left unsaid, but it became clear the Minutemen were not looking for suspects but victims. John Young said, "What I saw when I arrived at the Swift ranch changed me from a simple-hearted country boy to a hard-nerved man boiling for revenge."

The posse found the Moya ranch house was built of palings, daubed with moss and mud, with chink holes here and there. The Moyas were locked inside and refused to come out. One yelled, "What do you want?" A member of the posse named Dan Holland peered into a chink hole and yelled, "We want you."

The answer was quick in coming. One of the Moyas fired through a chink hole and shot Dan Holland in the head, killing him instantly.

The posse laid siege to the ranch house, firing at random into the chink holes, trying to hit the shadowy Moyas barricaded inside. While the Moyas were forted up and both sides shooting through the chink holes, the sheriff of Goliad County, Phil Fulcord, arrived and took charge. He urged the Moyas to come out, telling them they would be safe under the full protection of the law.

They came out. There were two Moya brothers, Antonio and Marcelo, and their aging father. The sheriff convinced the Refugio Minutemen to let him and his posse take the Moyas on to Goliad.

After the sheriff and his prisoners left, the Minutemen changed their minds. John Young described what happened. "A lot of us did not propose to put off a punishment that we knew the Mexicans deserved," Young said. "The guard and prisoners (Fulcord and his men) had only gone about three miles when we surrounded them. The guard offered practically no interference. In the melee that followed, Marcelo was shot dead. Old Moyer (Moya) was wounded and down on the ground. A maddened ranch boy rode his plunging horse over him, at the same time emptying his six-shooter at him. Another man dismounted and cut the Mexican's throat."

All three of the Moyas were killed and their bodies left lying on the road. They were never implicated in any way with the Thad Swift murders.

In Refugio County, Mexican-Americans suspected of complicity in the Swift murders, or of being in league with bandits from Mexico, or somehow supportive of their activities, were rounded up and chained in the old wooden courthouse at Refugio. One night, a lynch mob took three prisoners and hanged them from a tree at the Swift ranch on Saus Creek. Like the Moyas, they were in no way connected to the Thad Swift murders.

On the Rio Grande near Laredo, the posse of Capt. Henry Scott trailed the prime suspect of the Swift murders, Juan Flores, who had crossed into Mexico. Scott sent a Minuteman named Frank Boggus across the river to make a deal with Mexican authorities. Some accounts say Scott paid $1,000 out of his own pocket to bribe officials to return Flores across the river.

Flores was brought back to Refugio, tried, and convicted. Before he was hanged on the outskirts of town, he admitted his guilt from the scaffold and expressed remorse. No evidence ever surfaced that implicated any others who were killed or lynched for the Swift murders.

People of Mexican descent began to leave Refugio County. Accounts say the roads west were filled with oxcarts and wagons and when Minutemen stopped the wagons, they found only women and children. When they searched, however, they found men hiding beneath bedding in the wagons. Some of the men were taken back to Refugio. What happened to them? Who knows? Lynch mobs kept no records.

Conditions were near anarchy. Armed bands killed travelers and lonely shepherds and burned remote ranch houses. Roads were too dangerous to travel. Posses of Minutemen responded with their own brutality. As the retaliation following the Swift murders showed, the Minutemen were not particular about whether their victims were guilty or innocent. The author T. R. Fehrenbach wrote that the raiding and posse lynchings kept blood feuds and mutual hatred alive throughout South Texas. Racial or ethnic memories of the bloody times would be passed down through the generations. Blood memories die hard.

Capt. Henry Scott, the old vigilante, died at Corpus Christi on Feb. 27, 1891 when he was 61. He had spent much of his life chasing border bandits during violent times when raiders struck across the border and Minutemen rode in deadly pursuit. They cut a furious swath across the land.

Longhorns

CHAPTER 35

PEELING CATTLE
AND THE SKINNING WAR
1870s — 1880s

Shoot the first gringo son of a bitch who comes here and attempts to look at a hide.

——*Hide dealer in Matamoros to employees*

At the end of the Civil War, Confederate soldiers returned to South Texas to find huge numbers of almost wild, unbranded longhorns. They took those not branded and drove them to Kansas railheads where they were shipped to growing Northern cities hungry for beef. So many Texas longhorns went up the trail in the five years after the war it glutted the market.

Cattle prices fell to almost nothing. The value of the longhorn was reduced to the value of its hide, the tallow that could be rendered for candles, the horns and bones that could be used to make buttons and knife handles. Almost overnight, beef slaughter houses sprang up on the Texas coast, mainly from Padre Island to the Rockport area, but also as far east as Galveston.

Such slaughterhouses — also called packing houses, packeries, and hide-and-tallow factories — were not unknown before. Henry Kinney, the founder of Corpus Christi, opened a slaughterhouse on Corpus Christi's North Beach in the 1840s where mustangs and longhorns were killed and stripped of their hides. In the 1850s, C.R. Hopson, with Kinney as his partner, operated a beef packing house in the center of town, at Peoples and Water streets. After the Civil War, in 1866, rancher Richard King built a packing house inside the city limits and John Wade operated another packery at Nuecestown 12 miles away.

Other packing houses were built on North Beach and at Flour Bluff. All that was required was an outlay of capital to set up packing sheds with great iron tanks, then to hire cowboys to round up cattle and butchers to slaughter and dismember the animals. Huge fortunes were made from the hide and tallow factories.

The owner of a slaughterhouse at Flour Bluff, James M. Doughty, relocated to a rocky point on Aransas Bay, which became the town of Rockport. William Hall, a Maine Yankee, built a packing house nearby, which was followed by a dozen others. The Coleman-Mathis-Fulton Pasture Company built a packing house at Fulton, just up the coast, and there was another large packery at Frandolig Point. Still another was at what is now an exclusive residential development called Key Allegro.

Rockport packing houses would pay $4 to $7 a head for any longhorn that would pass the brand inspectors. A packery employing 40 workers could process up to 250 head of cattle a day. The men were paid well to work in the muck and blood — from $1 to $4 a day, top wages then.

One Rockport packing house hired 10 cowboys to supply it with 1,000 steers every two weeks. The cowboys chased half-wild longhorns from the brush country all over South Texas. At Rockport's Big Wharf, ocean-going ships loaded salted hides, barrels of tallow, and huge cargoes of horns and bones. The ships brought nail kegs filled with silver dollars for exchange. Stories were told that kegs of silver coins were so common they would be left sitting on the pier unguarded and untended.

"Red John" Dunn worked in a packery owned by Bill Brunwinkel and Henry Ball, one of three packing houses on North Beach, across a shallow bayou from Corpus Christi. Another packery on North Beach was operated by Alonzo DeAvalon, a man who wrote poetry in his spare time.

Dunn described the process at the packing houses.

Cattle were driven into a small chute. A man with a sharp spear — he was called a sticker — stood on a plank walk above the cattle and stabbed them expertly in the neck, severing the spinal column. Before going into boilers, the horns were removed, the skin cut around the neck, then the feet removed, and the head was hooked to a ring bolt. A mule pulled from the tail and the skin came off like a shuck — peeled right off, which is why they called it "peeling cattle." The enterprise itself was called "peeling and tanking."

The carcasses were hauled on to the main floor by a block and tackle pulled by a mule. There the butchers went to work with the gut man cutting the carcass open, the marker cutting hams and shoulders, the ax man breaking the bones where they were marked. The meat was pitched onto platforms until there was enough to fill the iron tanks, where it was boiled. The tallow, the fat, was scooped off with huge ladles. Dunn was a fireman. His job was to keep a fire going under the tanks where the meat was boiled.

In the early years, the meat was pickled and sold by the barrel, much of it to the Army. But in the great packing house era so many thousands of longhorns were killed that there was little market for pickled beef. After it had been boiled and the tallow scooped away, the meat, without value, was dumped in huge hills of putrefying flesh that attracted coyotes, vultures, flies and seagulls. In the heat of Texas summers the mountains of decaying flesh gave off an unbearable stench.

At a slaughterhouse owned by John King and W. N. Staples on Padre Island, the waste meat was dumped into Packery Channel, one of the channels dividing Padre and Mustang Islands. On North Beach, it was dumped into Hall's Bayou, where the Port of Corpus Christi's ship entrance is today. The packeries on North Beach were within smelling distance of Corpus Christi.

Capt. John Anderson in his vessel *Flour Bluff* hauled salted and dried hides and barrels filled with tallow from Mifflin Kenedy's packing house at Flour Bluff to Rockport. Andy Anderson, one of his sons, said on one trip that Capt. Kenedy told them, "'You can have all the tongues you want, boys, but don't get in the way.' They were big tongues, and made good eating."

Within a decade of the beginning of the packing houses, winter "die-outs" and summer droughts depleted the longhorn herds of South Texas. Beef prices climbed so high that it was no longer profitable to slaughter cattle for their hides, tallow and horns. Slaughtering at the beef packing plants dwindled until they were finally closed. The iron boilers were hauled away, some to be used as water tanks for stock. The peeling and tanking era came to a close.

* * *

South Texas suffered a searing drought in 1871 and 1872, followed by a bitterly cold winter. So many weak and undernourished longhorns died that it was said a man could walk for miles on longhorn carcasses without his feet touching the ground. Cowboys called this wholesale death of cattle a "die-up." Following the die-up winter of 1871, the spring of 1872 brought the skinning season. Ranch hands carried long sharp knives to strip the hides of dead cattle on the range.

After the die-up, E.H. Caldwell of Corpus Christi noted that every man with a horse and a skinning knife went out into the country looking for cattle that, if not dead, soon would be — and quite often these would be helped to die by unscrupulous skinners. For honest skinners, brands served to identify the owner, who was due the value of the skin less the amount owed the skinner for his work.

Cattlemen hired skinners and used their own ranch hands for this odious task. But many skinners working the ranges were thieves — bandits from below the border, freebooters, veterans of the Civil War, wanted men on the run. The skinning season brought on the conflict between ranchers and outlaw skinners called the Skinning War.

For hide thieves, it was easier to haul away wagonloads of hides than it was to drive a herd of stolen cattle across the border. They worked the ranges, killing cattle and skinning them where they fell, leaving mounds of rotting flesh across the prairie. Some thieves used a long knife fixed to a pole to cut the tendons of the cattle to immobilize them, then shot or stabbed them to death and skinned them at their leisure. Sometimes they cut the brand out, leaving a hole in the hide.

Bands of hide thieves worked the ranges, killing cattle and taking hides by the thousands. Two of the main hide thieves on the ranchers' black list were a man named Pat Quinn and another named Alberto Garza, also known as "Segundo" Garza. "Red John" Dunn's company of Rangers tracked "Segundo" Garza around Lagarto, but couldn't catch him.

The Nueces Valley newspaper under the heading "Killing and Skinning" reported — "We learn of the wholesale slaughter of cattle by Alberto Garza and his party. At one place there were 275 carcasses, at another 300, and at another 66. These robbers seem to be well-supplied with ammunition, rodeo the cattle, and shoot them down in their tracks, until a sufficient number is killed for the day."

It was reported that Segundo Garza had 60 men killing and skinning in Nueces and Duval counties. In one account, he sent a taunting message from his camp to the town of San Diego demanding that they bring enough money to buy the hides his men had collected or send enough men to fight. Several cattlemen — Jasper Clark, James F. Scott and nine others — took up Garza's challenge and attacked his camp. Garza and his bunch of hide thieves escaped in such a hurry they left saddles, bridles and bloody hides behind. Near the camp the posse found the carcasses of 80 cattle that had been killed and skinned.

The winter of 1873, another die-up year, kept the hide thieves busy. One major market for stolen hides was at Brownsville and Matamoros. Dunn wrote that American merchants built stores to deal in stolen goods. Cattlemen who tried to track down their stolen property found a dead end along the border. One hide dealer in Matamoros told his help, as quoted in "King Ranch" — "Shoot the first gringo son of a bitch who comes here and attempts to look at a hide."

Cowboys described this lawless time as "hell with the hide off." Rustlers, hide thieves, and robbers rode in heavily armed gangs — from 10 to 100 men — and with brazen confidence they knew they could take on just about any force they ran up against. If truly threatened, they could run for the border and find sanctuary across the Rio Grande.

Conditions were so dangerous during the Skinning War that people were afraid to travel. John McCampbell, a Corpus Christi lawyer, quit practicing law for a time because it was too risky to attend courts in other towns. Rancher Richard King traveled with a heavily armed escort, yet he was attacked by eight men waiting in ambush in August, 1872. A young German riding with him in the coach was killed.

Washington and Mexico City sent separate commissions to investigate the lawless conditions in South Texas and northern Mexico. The commissioners took thousands of pages of depositions, but it came to nothing. The grisly attacks on ranch houses, rural stores and unwary travelers did not abate. During this era, some outrages included the mutilation murders at the Swift Ranch near Refugio, the Morton store killings at Peñascal on Baffin Bay, and the Nuecestown raid above Corpus Christi.

With South Texas convulsed by violence, people reacted with alarm. The depredations provided a ready-made excuse for extralegal actions. The violence of the border marauders and hide thieves during the Skinning War was reciprocated by the reactive violence of the posses and Minutemen. Innocent people were caught in between.

Robert Adams

William Adams

CHAPTER 36

ROBERT AND WILLIAM ADAMS
AND THE GREAT SHEEP ERA
1850s — 1880s

I went through a lot of hardships the early part of my life. People don't know what hard times are; they think they do, but they don't.

—Robert Adams

The Adams' brothers, William and Robert, came to Corpus Christi in 1852 as children of English immigrants attracted to Texas by Henry Kinney's land promotions. The brothers hauled cotton down the Cotton Road and became sheepmen and cattlemen in Nueces and Jim Wells counties.

Henry Kinney, founder of Corpus Christi, distributed handbills in Britain and Ireland offering 100 acres of land for one dollar an acre. With the purchase of 100 acres, Kinney would throw in a horse, yoke of oxen, 10 cows and a lot in Nuecestown. Robert Adams Sr. put down his money for 100 acres. He and wife Maria and four children, including William and Robert, Jr., boarded the *Essex* for the trip across the Atlantic.

William, the oldest son, was six when the family left Liverpool. His brother Robert Jr. was five. They sailed on the *Essex* bound for New Orleans. William said the captain gave the boys raisins. The voyage lasted seven weeks. At New Orleans, they took an old black steamer, the *Mexico*, to Galveston and boarded a stern-wheeler for Indianola. From there a small mail boat carried them to Corpus Christi.

They landed in November 1852 at Ohler's Wharf. Rube Holbein met them when they landed. Holbein's father was Kinney's land agent in London. It was a new and strange place. The handbills portrayed Corpus Christi as a major city, but "Corpus Christi was a little ordinary place," William said. "It extended only about as far up as Artesian Square. There may have been one or two houses up towards the hill, but not much was built up."

269

Robert's recollections were similar. "There were three little stores. Old lady Hart had one on the beach. Old man Noessel had a small store on Chaparral Street; and Norris had a store on the hill. There was a meat pickling plant on North Beach, then called the Rincon."

Robert Adams, Sr. had been a railway inspector in England. He wanted to farm, but the land he put a down payment on was not farmland, as farmers would discover half a century later. Adams didn't take up the land and lost his down payment. He got a job as a hired hand and moved the family to a farm near Nueces Bay at Avery Point.

It was beautiful country. From the Oso to Agua Dulce, William recalled, it was rolling prairie with no brush or timber except along the creeks, where hackberry and live oak grew. The prairie continued nearly to San Diego. William said you would think nothing of saddling up a horse and wherever night found you, unsaddle and go to sleep. He said he slept out many nights using his saddle for a pillow.

As oxen plowed the fields, Robert Jr. would lead them, resting when the oxen were turned. Maria Adams, a former seamstress, brought her feather bed from England, a silk shawl, and two cherished dresses. She was homesick; to cheer her up, Robert took her to visit English families at Nuecestown. When the Adams lived at Avery Point, west of Corpus Christi on Nueces Bay, Army headquarters were located in Corpus Christi. Supplies were freighted on mule trains to forts on the frontier. Army sentries patrolled the edge of town on the lookout for hostile Indians. Robert remembered that his mother would hear coyotes howling and think Indians were on the prowl.

In 1855, Robert Jr., who was 8, went to work for Samuel Colon, a freighter at Nuecestown, 12 miles upriver from Corpus Christi. "Quite a bit of Colon's freight went to San Patricio and to Rancho Grande (across the river)," Robert said. Robert's job was to handle the oxen that pulled Colon's wagons. "One time Colon broke my leg," Robert said. "There were five or six yoke of oxen hitched to the wagon, and some of them weren't very gentle. Colon told me to unhitch them. I didn't go to do it and he picked me up and threw me down on the floor so hard it broke my leg. I crawled under the porch. They didn't set my leg, just bandaged it. After a while I would walk with one crutch and a cane, but my leg would break time and again."

When he was living with Colon, Robert worked gathering loads of salt at the Laguna Madre. "When the water came in high, it filled all the shallow lakes, and when it receded the salt could be gathered. It was in small grains about the size of peas. You had to take it out of the water, which was about two inches deep. We would pile the salt on the bank and let it drain, and later put it into sacks or buckets. The wagons used for hauling salt were drawn by six yoke of oxen. We would go up the old salt road, which ran to Nuecestown. Here it was stored in a small house to be sold. Most of it was exchanged, not sold. All of North Texas came to Corpus to get salt (during the war) for home use and for stock."

Maria Adams died in 1861. William, the oldest son, inherited her feather bed. Robert Jr. left Colon the freighter in 1862 to work at the Holthaus Bakery in Corpus Christi. That winter, when he was 15, he was sent to Victoria to get a supply of yellow sugar used to make cookies. They took two oxcarts, with a man named Long driving one and Robert driving the other. "The road wasn't very good, and we had to ford all the rivers. One river was the Guadalupe at Victoria. It was all I could do to keep on my feet, the current was so swift. Of course I walked alongside the oxen to drive them across. You had to whip them."

During the war, Robert and William hauled cotton to Brownsville. With ports blockaded, cotton was taken down the Cotton Road and sold at Matamoros, providing cash to buy war materiel for the Confederacy. Robert and William each had four yoke of oxen to handle. They were paid $10 Confederate a month.

In 1863, Robert Sr. arranged for Robert Jr. and William to tend sheep for Henry Gilpin and Frederick Belden on Penitas Creek. This was during the great sheep era in South Texas.

* * *

Like the cowboy and the vaquero, the shepherd was at home in South Texas. Flocks of sheep grazed the ranges from Corpus Christi to Laredo. Oxcarts loaded with wool, from as far away as Mexico, lumbered into Corpus Christi, one of the world's great wool markets.

The sheep era began about 1850 when William Chapman, an Army officer, was transferred from Brownsville to Corpus Christi. Chapman realized that the area's rich grasslands made ideal sheep country. He set up a sheep camp on Santa Gertrudis Creek and brought in purebred Merino sheep from Pennsylvania.

While the Merino sheep was unmatched for the quality of its wool, it was too delicate for the harsh climate of South Texas. Mexican sheep could take the heat, but produced coarse wool.

Chapman figured that fine-wooled Merinos bred with tough Mexican sheep would produce a hardy breed with a fine fleece. His Merino cross-breeds became the standard breed in South Texas. Chapman was soon joined in the sheep business by cattle ranchers Richard King and James Durst, and later Mifflin Kenedy. They were convinced that the prairies of South Texas made great sheep country.

Immigrants from England, Scotland and Ireland — many attracted by Henry Kinney's land promotions — became the sheepmen of the Nueces

Valley. James Bryden, a sheepman from Scotland, was hired by William Chapman to handle his sheep. In payment for watching the flock, Bryden was given part of the natural increase of the flock and a share in the wool profits. Bryden grazed Chapman's sheep along Santa Gertrudis Creek.

The following year, Richard King bought 15,000 acres to begin his ranch along San Gertrudis Creek near the Chapman sheep camp. King bought 50 merino bucks from Ebenezer McClane, of Chartiers Township, Washington County, Pa., below Pittsburgh.

Ebenezer McClane sent his son John with the sheep down the Ohio River to the Mississippi. The sheep were lost in a riverboat fire near New Madrid, Mo. John McClane got another 75 bucks and delivered them in 1856. He stayed in Texas and went to work for King, who was building up his flock on the Santa Gertrudis.

John McClane soon had his own flock on the San Fernando Creek. Besides working for King, McClane was an agent for his father, importing merinos for sale in Texas. Richard King, from his initial purchase of 10 Merino bucks and 42 Mexican ewes, within a decade had some 40,000 sheep. His main sheep camp was called Borregas.

Word spread that South Texas was sheep country. Sheepherders came to South Texas to make their fortunes by tending sheep on shares. John Buckley came to Duval County from Ontario, Canada, to raise sheep.[44] A man named Oscar Edgerly arrived from New York to tend sheep for William Headen, one of Corpus Christi's wealthy wool merchants.

Edgerly recorded the routines of a sheepherder in a diary. He stayed busy moving the sheep and setting up new camps. When the sheep ate all the grass near watering places, they were driven out in search of greener pastures, then brought back for water. Edgerly once moved the flock to San Fernando Creek. Richard King rode up and told him to move. Oscar moved up the creek. King told him to move again. "As I thought I was not on his lands, I did not move," Edgerly wrote. "I stayed there until the grass gave out, then took them up on the Aqua Dulce."

Edgerly's daily tasks included taking the sheep to water or grass, cooking meals, and keeping a close watch for coyotes and other predators. He said that sheep, unlike cattle, had to be lived with.

* * *

That was something Robert Adams, Jr. quickly learned. The deal that Robert Adams, Sr. arranged for his sons with Gilpin and Belden was that the brothers would get a share in the wool profits and they would get half the

---

[44] John Buckley was the patriarch of the William F. Buckley family.

increase in the flock. William Adams soon went back to hauling cotton on the Cotton Road while Robert, Jr. stayed with the sheep for three years.

"William stayed only one year, when he quit and went off," Robert once said. "That left it all on me. I stayed the three years out. One time I didn't have any clothes or shoes to wear. I dressed some sheep skins and made me a pair of buckskin pants and some shoes. I made them with my hands. Buckskin is warm until it gets wet. But if it gets wet, if a norther comes in, you do get cold.

"I never saw a house for a year, and was not inside a house for over two years. The elements were my roof and the wilds were my house. I did most of my own cooking for four years, and had nothing to eat but meat. I had no bread and didn't know what a vegetable looked like."

In the fall of 1866, the father, Robert Adams, Sr., returned to England for a visit. He took the youngest son John with him. On the return voyage, the steamer *Raleigh* caught fire off the coast of South Carolina and Robert, Sr. and John were lost at sea.

After four years tending sheep, Robert's share of the increase gave him 750 sheep. Robert Adams, Jr. married Lorene McWhorter and they moved into a jacal, or hut, built of mesquite posts with a palmetto roof.

William Adams built his own jacal when he married Sarah Dodson. William brought his mother's most prized possession, her feather bed, to the jacal. William and Robert formed a partnership on a sheep ranch on the Barbon Creek, a partnership that continued for 26 years. Robert and William became prominent sheepmen in what then was the northwestern part of Nueces County. The brothers soon had 15,000 sheep.

* * *

After the Civil War, there were 1.2 million sheep in Nueces County, which had more "fleecies" than any other county in the country. Tax rolls for Laredo's Webb County in 1878 recorded that that county had 8,000 cattle and 239,000 sheep, so many sheep that one cowman said he was afraid to ride through the place wearing a wool shirt.

In shearing season — April to June and August through September — big two-wheeled oxcarts loaded with bags of wool came to Corpus Christi to sell to the wool merchants on Chaparral.

Chaparral would be crowded with oxcarts at the wool-buying stores of Doddridge, Lott & Company, Bryne & Buckley, Norwick Gussett, Headen & Son, John Woessner, J. B. Mitchell & George Evans, and Edey & Kirsten, later bought out by Uriah Lott. Gussett, the town's richest wool merchant, was a former muleskinner in the Mexican War. In 1873, he purchased three million pounds of wool. Gussett's store, topped with a rooster weathervane, was called *"la tienda del gallo."* Perry Doddridge's place, with the symbol of a ram, was *"la tienda del borrego."*

The Weekly Democratic Statesman in Austin reported on May 24, 1877 — "Corpus Christi is controlling a large wool trade. It is thought that four to five million pounds will be handled this year." Sheepmen returning to Mexico after selling their wool clip in Corpus Christi carried back merchandise for sell, so they made a profit coming and going. Returning sheepmen who had sold their wool clips were often targeted by bandits. Those returning to Mexico would drill holes in the wooden axles of their oxcarts, then the holes were packed with silver dollars and sealed with wooden pegs.

Several things happened almost at the same time to bring the sheep era to an end. A parasite decimated the flocks in South Texas. In 1884, Grover Cleveland was elected president and he lowered the tariff on cheap Australian wool, a devastating blow to Texas sheepmen. And a third factor was the end of the open range. Sheepmen needed free grass and when cattle ranchers began to fence their pastures, the days of the sheepmen were numbered. The convergence of all three factors brought the sheep era to a close, which also ended Corpus Christi's importance as a wool market.[45]

When the sheep era came to an end, the Adams brothers, like other sheepmen in South Texas, turned to cattle. They fenced their land and brought in purebred cattle and soon knew as much about cattle as they did sheep. In 1892, William bought a ranch near Alice and, two years later, the partnership came to an end. Robert kept the Tecolote ranch. William served as a county commissioner in Nueces County for 16 years and played a role, with his brother, in establishing Jim Wells County.

William Adams was interviewed about the early years in Texas when he was 93; he died a month later. Robert was interviewed when he was 94, between 1938 and 1940; he died in 1944, at age 97. His younger sister, Mary Ann Adams, who married Henry Monroe Hinnant, lived to be 108 and was known at the end of her long life as the "Queen of the Brush Country." In his 1940 interview, Robert Adams said, "I went through a lot of hardships the early part of my life. People don't know what hard times are; they think they do, but they don't."

---

[45] During World War II, Corpus Christi, the once-great wool market, received millions of pounds of Australian wool, which were stored in warehouses at the Port of Corpus Christi for the duration of the war.

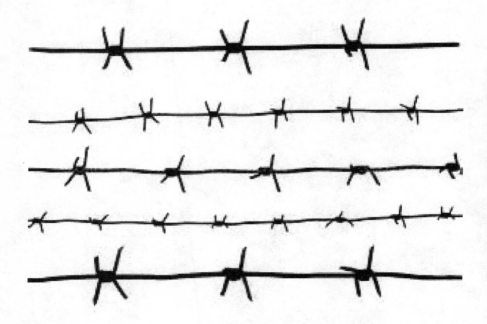

Barbed Wire

CHAPTER 37

BARBED WIRE
AND THE FENCE-CUTTING WAR
1860s — 1890s

If you don't make gates, we will make them for you.
—Note to rancher, punctuated with bullet holes

Before barbed wire came to South Texas, Mifflin Kenedy built a 36-mile fence of pine boards and cypress posts across a peninsula, from the Oso to Laureles Creek, which closed the Laureles Ranch in 1868. Capt. Andrew Anderson recalled that when the fence was being built he hauled "a million feet of lumber" to the Laureles aboard the *Flour Bluff*.

Isom H. Thomas, the caporal of Laureles, said Kenedy took a lively interest as the fence went up. "He would look down a long line and if he saw the slightest deviation from a straight line, the kink had to be straightened out before he would pass it."

The *Nueces Valley* reported in May, 1871 that Kenedy's Laureles Ranch, comprising 94,150 acres, was assessed at $231,675. The article said the fence was 37 miles long and cost $1,000 per mile to build. Three years later, much of Kenedy's fence was ripped up by the hurricane of 1874.

After Kenedy enclosed Laureles, his friend Richard King began to fence King Ranch. Like Kenedy, he used planks and cypress posts treated with creosote. Within three years, by 1874, King had 70,000 acres fenced.

The Coleman, Mathis and Fulton Pasture Co. began fencing in 1871. One fence, north of Fulton, stretched from Puerto Bay (also called Port Bay) to Corpus Christi Bay, and another from Chiltipin Creek to Nueces Bay.

Another early fencer was S. G. Miller, who put up a 15-mile mesquite fence on his ranch where Lake Corpus Christi is today. This fence was made of mesquite posts set vertical against each other. The fence angered Miller's neighbors because it blocked a road between Corpus Christi and Gussettville. Mrs. Miller said the fence "caused a great deal of trouble with all the residents. Nearly every day we would find the fence cut some place. As the old road ran through the place (their ranch), travelers did not hesitate to tear down this fence and leave it down for yards instead of going a little out of the way to the gate." Miller finally got fed up and had a deep trench dug just on the inside of the fence. One dark night, several wagons ended up in the ditch and Mrs. Miller said "such cursing and swearing you never heard, but that was the end of the trouble." This was a preview of fights to come when fences closed off what had been seen as a public right-of-way.

After a bad drought and severe winter in 1873, ranchers in South Texas lost thousands of head of cattle. They starved and froze to death, helped along by their weakened condition. Mifflin Kenedy, with his grass protected on the fenced-in Laureles, didn't lose a single head. Other cattlemen took notice. Martha Rabb, called the cattle queen of Texas, enclosed her Banquete ranch — sometimes called "Rancho Flecha" for the Bow-and-Arrow brand — with a plank fence made of pine boards nailed to cypress posts. The fence was 40 miles long and took a fence-rider two days to ride it.

In 1874, patents for barbed wire and for the machine for making it were granted to Joseph Farwell Glidden of De Kalb, Ill. Barbed-wire fences soon stretched across the land. But not in South Texas, for several reasons. South Texas ranchers distrusted anything from the North and barbed wire had another strike against it, being invented by a farmer. They also feared the "thorny wire" would wound cattle and give entry to the deadly screw worm.

While barbed wire was slow to catch on in South Texas, it did catch on. An event that helped it gain acceptance was staged in San Antonio in 1878 by one of Glidden's top traveling salesmen, a man named John W. Gates. He was better known as "Bet-a-Million" Gates.

Gates talked San Antonio city officials into letting him put up a demonstration barbed-wire corral in Military Plaza. When the fence was up, he had longhorns driven into the enclosure. As cattlemen watched, the longhorns shied away from the sharp barbs. When two men entered with flaming torches, the cattle still refused to get close to the thorny wire. Many who saw the demonstration became enthusiasts of Glidden's wire.

Once ranchers had their own barbed-wire fences, they discovered that cattle and horses learned to avoid it. After cattle had a brush with the wire, it was said, you couldn't drive them between two posts, whether there wire there or not. "Bet-a-Million" Gates couldn't fill all the orders for barbed wire that was "light as air, stronger than whisky, and cheap as dirt."

New fence lines of barbed-wire angled their way across Texas. The historian Walter Prescott Webb wrote, "Barbed wire was cheap to buy and easy to erect. It did not obstruct view nor did it waste any ground. It stopped and held livestock without danger."

There were still some holdouts. Mifflin Kenedy sold his Laureles Ranch to a Scottish syndicate in 1882 (investors in Britain were buying ranches across the West). Kenedy then bought La Parra — "Grapevine" — in the Big Sands.

278

He had fenced Laureles in 1868 with expensive heart-of-pine planks. At La Parra, he used cypress posts and five strands of galvanized round wire. A fence of 60 miles enclosed roughly 400,000 acres. Nearby Armstrong Ranch followed suit when a fence was built to separate Armstrong and Kenedy lands. The ranch used cypress posts with smooth wire and there were turning devices at half-mile intervals to tighten the wire.

Another South Texas rancher, Abel Head 'Shanghai' Pierce, distrusted barbed wire. He was afraid his cattle would cut themselves on the barbs and die of screw worms. Gradually, though, barbed wire caught on and fences that were "horse-high, bull-proof and hog-tight" spread across the land.

Barbed wire intensified conflicts between ranchers and farmers, cattlemen and sheepmen, free-range men and enclosed-pasture men, small stockmen and big ranchers. They began to cut each other's fences.

Prowlers in gunnysack hoods with fence-cutters in their pockets roamed at night snipping wire. Ranch hands rode fence lines on guard for fence-cutters. The result was the Fence-Cutting War. It was, at least in part, a revolt against change and modernization. Beyond that, there were real injustices at the root of the conflict. Some fences closed what had been public right-of-ways and some fences shut off access to vital communal watering holes.

Before the coming of windmills and artesian wells, in the 1890s, access to watering holes was a life-and-death issue. The conflict became bloody. A headline in a Chicago paper said, "Hell breaks loose in Texas."

Texas Rangers were sent to quell the violence. Ranger Ira Aten, ordered to track down wire-cutters, said he upped his life insurance and oiled his six-shooter. Rangers hated the duty. It required them to infiltrate gangs of known cutters, to get inside information, and then stake out lonely stretches of fences at night, concealed in the shadows, waiting for armed cutters to show up and start snipping.

Ranger Aten wrote his superiors in Austin — "I will ask it as a special favor of the adjutant's office never to ask me to work after fence-cutters again for it is the most disagreeable work in the world."

Almost every county in the state reported fence-cutting crimes. In Nueces County, the *Corpus Christi Caller* reported that James McBride's fence, five miles from town, was cut in a number of places and said "the perpetrators of this malicious act should be caught and punished."

In Live Oak County, wire-cutting saboteurs destroyed a fence then dug a grave and left a rope dangling in it with a note — "This will be your end if you rebuild this fence."

Near Castroville, a rancher found a note on his fence, punctuated with two bullet holes — "If you don't make gates, we will make them for you."

In Coleman County, in west central Texas, night-riding fence-cutters destroyed a man's fence then left an empty coffin on his porch. He turned it into a water trough and rebuilt his fence. One rancher, longing for an end to the conflict, said he wished "the man who invented barbed wire had it wound around him in a ball and the ball rolled into hell."

The crisis was made worse by a drought in 1883. Water holes dried up and some cattlemen and sheepmen found fences standing between their thirsty livestock and water. The fences were cut.

Gov. John Ireland called the Legislature into special session in January 1884 to deal with the crisis. Laws were passed making fence-cutting a felony; it was a crime to carry fence-cutters in a saddlebag. It was a jailing offense to be caught at night with a pair of nippers.

With these new laws, the Texas Rangers began to gain the upper hand. But there was still sporadic violence. Near Brownwood in Brown County, Rangers fought a gun battle with cutters; two fence-cutters were killed and two wounded.

In Navarro County, near Corsicana and Richland, Ranger Aten in 1887 devised what he called a "dinamite boom" (dynamite bomb), a shotgun primed with dynamite and set to explode when the fence was cut. He bought shotguns, 50 pounds of dynamite and dynamite caps and set his "booms" along several fences. He went to Austin to report his activity. He was ordered to go back and remove the bombs. Instead, he exploded them; the blasts were heard for miles. That was the end of Aten's "dinamite boom racket."

In 1893, a county judge in Uvalde County, between San Antonio and Laredo on the upper Nueces River, John Nance Garner[46] wrote Austin for help — "Francis Smith & Co. some weeks ago fenced their pasture on the Nueces River with a splendid four-wire fence. It had only been up some four weeks when one entire side was cut between every post. They rebuilt it at once and in less than 10 days it was cut again. They rebuilt it again and last Friday night, it was cut a third time, just as before. What we want is about three good Rangers to come here and catch these lawbreakers."

Barbed wire divided the land into controlled pastures. It changed the land and the landscape forever. In a symbolic sense, barbed wire fences separated the old and new Texas. Before the coming of fences, it was said a man could ride a thousand miles — from the Rio Grande to the Canadian Rockies — without encountering wires strung between posts or having to go through a gate. Barbed wire changed the land. In doing so, as Bigfoot Wallace said, "It sure played hell with Texas."

---

[46] Garner was later elected vice president when Franklin D. Roosevelt was elected president.

Uriah Lott

CHAPTER 38

URIAH LOTT,
THE GRINGO WHO BUILT RAILROADS
1875 — 1905

What, do away with our wagon trade! Never!

—Newspaper editorial

Uriah Lott, a native New Yorker, started a wool-buying business in Corpus Christi in the late 1860s. But his ambition was to build railroads and within three decades, from 1875 until 1905, Lott became, as a book by J. L. Allhands called him, "The Gringo Builder."

He was born on Jan. 30, 1842 in Albany, N.Y. He had a common school education and was innocent of any college or university. When he was in his early 20s, he was hired at the Chicago & Alton Railroad station. After the Civil War, he traveled to Brownsville and then to Corpus Christi, where he learned to grade wool and hides.

Uriah Lott opened his own commission house in 1869, but he began to invest his energy and savings in the dream of building a railroad from Corpus Christi to Laredo. He got financial support from ranchers Mifflin Kenedy and Richard King, wealthy and influential men in South Texas.

Lott promoted a railroad bond issue in 1875. It failed because some feared it would ruin the lucrative oxcart trade. Bales of wool arrived in Corpus Christi on huge Chihuahua carts with big round wooden wheels pulled by teams of oxen. The carts brought wool and hides from as far away as Chihuahua, Mexico. After 1871, some of the heavy carts brought cargoes of copper, lead and silver ore from mines in Mexico that were shipped from Corpus Christi to smelters in Hamburg, Germany.

"Some idea of the importance of Corpus Christi as a wool market may be gleaned from the fact that a deluge of wool poured into this market," Allhands wrote. "A single caravan brought Doddridge, Lott & Company 200 bales of wool, along with a fine lot of baled goat skins and up to November, Norwick Gussett had loaded boat-load after boat-load for New York, until he had cleared 14 large schooners of wool for that 11-month period, and for that year Corpus Christi handled three million pounds (of wool), forwarding principally to New York and Philadelphia."

The long trains of oxcarts were almost a daily sight in Corpus Christi. On the return trip, the oxcarts carried merchandise of all kind back to Mexico. The kind of goods that were sold by the wool dealers and taken back to Mexico can be seen from a listing of the goods received by George F. Evans, dealer in wool and hides and commission merchant. He received by schooner from New York in December, 1874: 75 cases assorted jellies and preserves; 700 cases of assorted canned goods; 300 five-pound pails of Goshen bitters; 30 cases of imported macaroni; 50 cases Florida water; 50 cases condensed milk; five boxes of oatmeal in 14-pound tins; 100 barrels of crushed sugar; 300 cases of soap; 50 cases of raisins; 50 cases of Old Tom gin; 20 chests of choice tea; 50 cases of vermicelli; 100 barrels of Rosedale Cement; 20 barrels of Portland Cement; 50 cases vinegar bitters; 100 barrels of cigar vinegar.

Lott ran into stiff opposition based on fears that a railroad would ruin the oxcart trade. "What, do away with our wagon trade! Never," said a newspaper editorial. Others argued that inevitably railroads would be built across the state and that without a railroad to the Rio Grande Corpus Christi's trade with the interior of Mexico would be cut off anyway.

On Jan. 30, 1874, a special meeting of the stockholders of the Corpus Christi, San Diego, and Rio Grande Narrow Gauge Railroad was held at Market Hall. Perry Doddridge, Uriah Lott's partner in the wool business, presided. Among other stockholders in attendance were William L. Rogers, Thomas Beynon, and John McClane.

An election called in 1874 on a proposed county bond issue of $200,000 was called off before it could be voted down at the polls. But within a year, Corpus Christi began to realize that its oxcart trade in wool and hides was already being diverted to San Antonio and Brownsville. The amount of wool arriving at Corpus Christi in 1874 had dropped to a third of what it had been in 1871.

The project of building a railroad was revived and Lott and the stockholders revised their plans and came back in 1875. Lott was able to sell bonds for his railroad — chartered as the Corpus Christi, San Diego, and Rio Grande Narrow Gauge Railroad — and he received land grants from the Legislature. For every mile of railroad tracks built, he would get 16 sections of state-owned land, but it was land of little value at the time, worth about $100 per section.

Lott, with $6,500 he borrowed from Richard King, bought a new steam locomotive from the Baldwin Locomotive in Philadelphia. When it arrived in Corpus Christi one day in September 1875, Fogg's Bar and Billiard Room, usually packed in the middle of the day, stood empty. Fogg's patrons left the bar to see the engine unloaded from the steamship *Mary*. The locomotive bore a shiny brass legend that read "Corpus Christi."

On Thanksgiving Day 1875, people gathered at Cooper's Alley and Mesquite Street to watch Uriah Lott drive the first "golden" spike of the Corpus Christi, San Diego and Rio Grande Narrow Gauge Railroad. The spike was gilded by James McKenzie to look like real gold. It was stolen that night. Grading began next day with one man using a pick and shovel.

A man named J. P. Nelson arrived in Corpus Christi with plans to ask Lott if he could get the grading contract. Lott told Nelson he already had a man at work grading the right-of-way on the Hill. After Nelson went to look at the work, he told Lott that no railroad could be built on such a poor grade. He said he would go out and grade a piece and let Lott see the difference.

When Lott came by a few days later to inspect the work, he found Nelson fixing his big silver watch with the sharp end of his grading hoe. After looking at the grade, Lott told Nelson, "A man who can fix his watch with a grubbing hoe can have the grading contract of this railroad."

A month after the spike was driven, Lott advertised his first schedule in the *Corpus Christi Weekly Gazette*. Excursion tickets to the end of the track cost 50 cents. Passengers sat on home-made wooden benches to ride 18 miles to Martha Rabb's pasture, where the town of Robstown is today. Construction was slow. By Jan. 1, 1876, only 25 miles of track had been laid and opened for operation.

The line had one wood-burning locomotive and 14 cars. "This dinky little engine," Allhands wrote, "with its odd-looking funnel shaped stack, would pull up to a mesquite wood yard, where all hands would proceed to smother the tender under a pile of wood."

When the tracks reached Banquete, a pipeline was laid to Agua Dulce Creek for water. To make steam, mesquite logs were burned in the locomotives; they threw off dangerous sparks that set a few range fires.

At Banquete, Indians attacked the work crew, killing all but two. In another incident, Lott and a man from Pennsylvania, J. J. Dull, who made the iron rails, hired a buggy and team at John Fogg's Livery Stable. They traveled to San Diego to meet influential citizens at the office of N. G. Collins.

The next morning, Lott and Dull were on their way to Corpus Christi. Two miles east of San Diego, they encountered a band of Mexican bandits who had a dozen captives tied to trees. They stripped Lott and his guest of their valuables and took all their clothes, down to their underwear, and tied them to a bush with pieces of rawhide.

One of the captives worked his way free and ran to San Diego and raised the alarm. Forty men rode to the scene. The robbers fled. Lott and the man from Pennsylvania were freed and they drove their carriage to W. W.

Wright's ranch house at Banquete, where they obtained some clothes and a fresh team of horses, and rode on to Corpus Christi.

As the railroad was slowly progressing, a party came to look over the work, camping near the Borjas Ranch, halfway between Corpus Christi and Laredo. Included in the party were Richard and Henrietta King, Mifflin Kenedy, Lott, and several others. The grading contractor, Nelson, said, "They expected to have a good breakfast in the morning but were much disappointed, some cows coming in the night and eating all the bread."

Construction was delayed in 1878 when the port was under yellow fever quarantine. A year later, Lott ran out of money and construction was halted at San Diego. He sold the assets to the Palmer-Sullivan Syndicate. In 1881, the Texas Mexican Railway acquired the project and finished the line.

When the tracks reached Laredo in 1881, the new company allowed the former owners to celebrate the inaugural run. Richard King, Mifflin Kenedy and Uriah Lott invited a hundred friends to ride to Laredo in a private car named "Malinche." On the way, they quaffed lemonade spiked with champagne and Rose Bud whisky (King's brand). They were in fine spirits when they reached Laredo. The train's arrival set off the largest celebration in Laredo since the Civil War, when Col. Santos Benavides' Confederates beat back an attack by Union raiders.

The name of the railroad was changed to the Texas Mexican Railway. The headquarters were moved from Corpus Christi to Laredo in 1890. Lott's iron rails were replaced with steel rails shipped from England and the wood-burning locomotives were converted to coal-burners then later to oil-burners. In 1902, on the night of July 17, every employee of the railroad and another 450 hired hands were put to work converting the line from narrow-gauge to standard-gauge. The 162-miles of track had been prepared and the operation was accomplished overnight.

The Tex-Mex — Lott's Railroad — gained a reputation as the friendliest and most unusual railroad in the world. If an engineer spotted a buck grazing by the tracks, he would stop the train and let the passengers take a few shots. He would stop the train for a cowboy who needed a ride to the next station. Ranch wives would give conductors shopping lists to be filled in Corpus Christi or Laredo and brought back on the return run. In the early days, passengers would toss up mesquite and ebony cordwood to the tender to help speed things along. On almost every trip to Laredo, the train would have to stop to wait until herds of cattle got off the tracks. In the early years, half a dozen armed men rode "shotgun" to guard against bandits.

All of this made for a rather leisurely schedule. A Corpus Christi newspaper, *the Crony,* on March 8, 1902 observed that the Tex-Mex, which it jokingly called the "Till-Mañana," "has almost arrived on time twice this week." The paper noted later, on July 5 that year, that there were no accidents

286

on the Fourth — "except the Till-Mañana came in almost on time, only five hours late."

* * *

Even though he ran out of money and had to sell the Corpus Christi, San Diego, and Rio Grande Narrow Gauge Railroad, Uriah Lott didn't give up on railroads. He helped build the San Antonio and Aransas Pass Railroad, the SAAP, which reached Corpus Christi in 1886. He was the driving force behind the St. Louis, Brownsville and Mexico Line, the "Brownie," which reached Brownsville in 1904.

Lott built the first mile of the San Antonio and Aransas Pass Railroad with old rails that were given to him by another railroad. He built the next three miles with old streetcar rails. As the line began to take shape, Mifflin Kenedy put up $4.4 million to pay for the rails, spikes and hardware. After this, Kenedy was so strapped for cash that his grocery dealer, William Rankin, carried his account on the books without interest. The people of Corpus Christi subscribed $100,000 and Bee County $50,000.

In completing the SAAP line, one of Lott's biggest obstacles was to build a trestle bridge across Nueces Bay. The original plan was to build it from White Point to where the port turning basin is today, but the mud was almost bottomless on that line across the bay. The trestle bridge was built over the old Reef Road.

The completion of the SAAP line to Corpus Christi in 1886 had unexpected consequences. The Morgan Line, which dominated Gulf shipping, had served Corpus Christi with ocean-going freighters since the Morris & Cummings channel was dredged across the bay in 1874. The Morgan Line had a monopoly on the carrying trade out of Corpus Christi. With the coming of the SAAP and the loss of that monopoly, the Morgan Line stopped its ships from coming to Corpus Christi. Merchants in Corpus Christi were forced to buy a small steamer to carry cotton bales and other cargo to the port at Galveston.

After building the SAAP, Lott began building a railroad from Corpus Christi to Brownsville, which was still served by a stagecoach line. The St. Louis, Brownsville & Mexico Railroad — known as "The Brownie" — was chartered in 1902. Principal backers included wealthy ranchers in the region, Robert Kleberg of King Ranch, Robert Driscoll, John G. Kenedy, and John B. Armstrong.

The railroad made its inaugural run from Brownsville to Corpus Christi on July 4th, 1904. It took nine hours to make the 160-mile trip. Afterwards, passenger runs were made daily between the two cities, except on Sunday. Before the Brownie, there was not a sizable settlement or post office from Sinton to Brownsville. Today's cities and towns between Corpus Christi and Brownsville — Robstown, Kingsville, Ricardo, Riviera, Raymondville —

owe their founding to the Brownie. The first town to spring up was at the junction of the Brownie and the Tex-Mex. This was on the old Palo Alto Ranch that belonged to Robert Driscoll. The new town was called "Rob's Town."

The last of four railroads to reach Corpus Christi in the great railroad era was the San Antonio, Uvalde and Gulf Railroad. The SAUG was known jocularly as the Sausage Line. It was the only major railroad line in the Corpus Christi area not built by Uriah Lott.

The railroad-building endeavors of Uriah Lott changed the landscape of South Texas. They brought him fame, but no wealth. The old "Gringo Builder" died almost penniless in Kingsville in 1915.

CHAPTER 39

DROUGHTS, RAIN BATTLES
AND AN ARCTIC NORTHER
1892 — 1899

As long as this wind keeps steady out of the west, it won't do any good to pray.

—Preacher on praying for rain

Droughts are no strangers to South Texas. In 1534, during Cabeza de Vaca's sojourn in South Texas, Indians begged him, as a powerful medicine man, to make it rain so they could plant their corn. They said there had been no rain for two years.

Closer to our time, during the Civil War, a two-year drought compounded the war's miseries. Thomas Noakes at Nuecestown above Corpus Christi wrote in his diary on Jan. 24, 1864 — "No rain worth mentioning since the 10th of last July. Dead animals meet your gaze in every direction, look where you will; the atmosphere is quite oppressive on account of decomposition."

Severe droughts afflicted South Texas in almost every decade of the last half of the 19th century. During those times, grass burned up, creeks dried up, water holes filled with sand and cattle died by the thousands. Cowboys called these times "die-ups."

The author and folklorist J. Frank Dobie, who grew up in Live Oak County, wrote that during a drought you could hear the pitiful bawling of cattle day and night. "No more distressful sound can be made."

Another "die-up" hit in 1872. A long drought opened gaping cracks in the land. Cattle caught in the cracks had to be pulled out or they would die. The drought was followed by a bitterly cold winter. Cattle drifted away from the bitterly cold norther and bogged down along the creeks. That's where they died — bogged down in mud where the river receded. They were just too weak to pull themselves out.

Another bad drought hit Texas again in 1886. Dobie wrote that it was a year without a spring, a whole year of August weather. "The only winds were whirlwinds — the sign of more dry weather. The grass roots had died; the

289

bull nettles in the fields were runty and withered. Drought cracks seamed the black land everywhere. Dry, dry, dry, and not a cloud to try."

Dobie wrote about another drought that occurred in 1888. Several ranchers thought it would be a good idea to consult an old preacher who had lived through many droughts, to get him to pray for rain, to intercede with the Almighty in their behalf.

"He listened to them sympathetically, then said, 'As long as this wind keeps steady out of the west, it won't do any good to pray.' "

A severe drought in the 1890s led to an unusual experiment. A book titled "War and the Weather" by Edward Powers noted that concentrated artillery fire in the Civil War would quite often bring rainstorms. He theorized that clouds could be bombarded into dropping moisture. It sounded plausible enough that the U.S. Department of Agriculture conducted several cloud-bombarding experiments in South Texas.

On Sept. 26, 1891, experimenters took two howitzers outside Corpus Christi. They fired the shells timed to explode at 500 feet. After the shells exploded, a few scattered raindrops fell. By the time the last shot was fired, people at the experiment were soaking wet. Did that prove the theory valid?

Skeptics pointed out that on the day of the exercise there were thunderclouds over the city and that it had rained the day before. The skeptics argued that the howitzer shots had nothing to do with making it rain. Others pointed out that the skeptics missed the point. There had to be clouds to bombard for the experiment to work. They would certainly get no rain by bombarding a clear blue sky.

It was decided that another test was needed. The experimenters went to San Diego. This time, they tried something different and pulled out all stops. Besides an artillery battery consisting of mortars and cannons, they used 10-foot balloons filled with gas and carrying explosive charges. The plan called for synchronized explosions with the artillery fired to coincide with balloon explosions.

One of the onlookers, Judge James O. Luby, carried an umbrella just in case.

The mortars and cannons thundered. The balloons exploded at one-minute intervals from 9 p.m. until midnight. After most of the local observers gave up and went home, at about 4 a.m. the last balloon was sent up and exploded. After a few more artillery shots, a heavy rain began to fall. San Diego was ecstatic.

The San Diego test was followed by an experiment conducted in the Alamo Heights area of San Antonio. The first shot took off the top of a mesquite tree and concussions from the cannon shots shattered the windows of the Argyle Hotel.

But there was no rain in San Antonio. However, there was a violent downpour in Laredo. A telegram from Laredo, sent in jest, thanked the man in charge in the San Antonio experiment, John T. Ellis, for the rain. That ended the experiment of bombarding clouds until 20 years later.

C.W. "Charlie" Post, the man who invented Grape Nuts and founded the West Texas town of Post, near Lubbock, set up dynamite blasting stations to make it rain. He called his bombardments "rain battles." After one exercise in 1911, it rained for 10 days. A man sued Post for damages for the heavy downpour.

The idea of firing cannons at clouds may seem odd, but when pastures dry up and bake under a merciless sky, when green grass turns brown and dies, when thirsty cattle bawl night and day, desperate ranchers and farmers look for any solution — whatever the chance of success — to make it rain.

* * *

On the subject of weather, what is a norther?

Weather forecasters rarely use the term, preferring to say cold wave or cold spell, but it is familiar to all Texans. Northers, said J. Frank Dobie, blow the world inside out and freeze the lining. Northers bring weather cold enough to freeze the horns, or something more precious, off a brass billy goat. Another Texas writer from the 19th Century, Alex Sweet, said the thermometer can fall rapidly during a norther, sometimes 40 degrees in an hour. A man in Austin, wrote Sweet, "saw the thermometer fall three feet in two seconds — off a nail."

Whether they are called cold waves, northers or blizzards, the worst to hit Texas, in the recorded memory of man, came in the middle of a Saturday night on Feb. 13-14, 1899. It swept down into Texas and within hours temperatures dropped to the lowest the state had ever seen.

It was fiercely cold. The temperatures are hard to believe, but they were well-reported at the time. In the Panhandle, temperatures plunged to 31 degrees BELOW zero at Tulia, 23 degrees BELOW at Abilene, 16 degrees below at Denison, 11 degrees below at Dallas, and four below at San Antonio. The oasis of warmth in the state was Corpus Christi, which registered a balmy 11 degrees above zero.

The entire country was stone cold. Freight trains were stalled, causing "coal famines" in the frozen cities. "There is great suffering," the *Corpus Christi Caller* reported, "especially among the poor in New York and other large cities where the cold is the worst known in decades."

Some people were found frozen to death while others were burned to death. Big pot-bellied stoves, the main source of heat in many homes, were loaded up with coal, if the occupants had it, or wood and the fires were stoked until

291

the stoves glowed red-hot. Tragic accidents resulted when people tried to get warm by crowding in too close. A slight brush against a red-hot stove and clothes burst in flames.

In Corsicana, a 10-year-old girl burned to death when she stood too close to a hot stove. In Alice, a woman burned to death when her dress brushed against a stove and ignited.

Out in the fields, many thousands of lambs and other livestock were frozen to death on the range.

The San Antonio Express reported that "for the first time in human memory, the San Antonio River was turned into a cake of ice of sufficient thickness to hold human weight."

Capt. Andrew Anderson of Corpus Christi, who made his living as a bay pilot, got caught in that terrible blizzard. "We were 50 miles down the Laguna Madre when the storm hit. We were iced in. The Laguna had frozen over. That night, it was snug and warm in the cabin (of their boat, the *Flour Bluff*), but in the morning we couldn't get the cabin door open. By chopping with a hatchet we were finally able to open it, and what a sight we saw.

"There was snow and ice over the sails and rigging. It was impossible to move them. After much beating and shaking of the canvas, however, we were able to hoist the sails. Then we went to work on the anchor, and finally got that loose. It was so intensely cold we had to stop every little while and get a drink of hot coffee. Finally we started out with a head wind. We got up 25 or 30 miles, as the wind was rather favorable, and anchored at sundown. We had to climb the hoops around the masts to get the sails down that night. It was about noon when we reached the bay and the wind died down. We had to pole in from the beacon to the wharf.

"During this same terrible cold," said Capt. Anderson, "a fellow in an open boat with vegetables from Ingleside landed in front of my house (on Water Street). There was so much steam from the water he couldn't see anything, so he anchored. He was so cold he didn't see how he could live if he remained on the boat. So he jumped overboard, thinking he would just as soon freeze to death in the water as in the boat.

"After swimming a ways he was able to walk. Reaching shore, he asked me to go out to the boat and get another fellow off, who had remained behind. The bay was frozen out 30 or 40 feet from shore; my skiff was on top of the ice, and the oars were about six inches thick with the ice. We found the man on the boat nearly gone, just sitting huddled up, covered with canvas; he didn't respond when we called to him. We pulled him off the boat and tumbled him into the skiff and made for the shore in a hurry. He just lay there in the skiff, appearing to be dead. But on shore they put some whiskey in him first, and then some coffee, and brought him to."

292

The *Corpus Christi Caller's* correspondent at Alice reported that it dropped to five degrees above zero. At Tarpon (later renamed Port Aransas) the boat harbor froze over and people walked on the ice between the boats. Thousands of frozen fish, stunned by the cold, lined the shore.

At Corpus Christi, according to the *Caller*, the blizzard killed all the cabbage and garden truck around the city. It killed the city's oleanders. It froze meat in the market and saws had to be used to cut it. It froze vinegar in bottles, ink in ink stands, and blueing in the stores. It froze the red combs off chickens and froze "a bunch of goats to death back of town." It froze the river solid at Nuecestown and people could walk from bank to bank across the river. It froze Nueces Bay from shore to shore, allowing a man who delivered the mail from Rockport to Corpus Christi to ride his horse across the rock-hard Nueces Bay. It even froze the much deeper Corpus Christi Bay well out past the piers; the fishing boats tied to the wharves were encased in ice and people could walk on the ice as far as the Central Wharf bathhouse. It froze seagulls, which fell to the ground like stones. From Amarillo to Corpus Christi, the blizzard of 1899 was the coldest weather Texas has ever seen.

George H. Paul and homeseekers

CHAPTER 40

GEORGE H. PAUL
AND THE SOUTH TEXAS LAND RUSH
1907 — 1924

"Field after field of rich black soil so pleased Henry that I began to fear I was going to have to call out some of the ranchers to lasso him to keep him from buying a team of mules, donning his overalls and going to work at once."

—*Etta Doherty, homeseeker*

M ost of the old cattle barons were dying out. They would not be around to see their grazing land turned into plowed fields. They would not be around to see the passing of an era when the birthplace of the cattle industry in South Texas was turned into farm tracts.

Toward the end of the 19th Century, ranches with hundreds of thousands of acres found it unprofitable to run cattle on land that could bring up to $10 to $20 or more an acre. Vast tracts of ranchland were subdivided and sold for small farms. This was the beginning of the land rush and homeseeker era. It started with the coming of the railroads.

The Texas-Mexican Railroad was completed from Corpus Christi to Laredo in 1881. The San Antonio and Aransas Pass Railroad reached Corpus Christi in 1886. The St. Louis, Brownsville & Mexico Railroad made its first run in 1904.

Ranchers could get their beef to market with this network of railroads, but railroads needed people and a greater density of population to make a profit. South Texas, covered by rangeland and cattle, was sparsely settled. For the railroads, no people meant no passengers and, except for cattle, no freight.

In the late 1880s, during a prolonged drought, ranchers began to sell some of their vast acreage. With fencing and stock breeding and improved range management, they didn't need as much pasturage. They could recover some of their drought losses by selling excess acres, which brought more than they could make by grazing cattle.

There was a strong confluence of shared interests at work. Ranchers needed land promoters to sell their excess acreage. Railroads needed farmers and settlers to make a profit on lines built on speculation. Farmers needed the railroads to get their crops to market. They all worked together to create the great land rush. Railroads helped the land promoters by offering low-cost passenger rates to homeseekers. Land promoters, buying the land outright or working on commission, subdivided large tracts of virgin ranchland into small farm-sized plots and then brought in hundreds of farmers and would-be farmers, mostly from the Midwest, to make the sale.

In the Coastal Bend area of South Texas, the sale of ranchlands began with the Coleman Fulton Pasture Company. The Texas Land and Cattle Company and King Ranch quickly followed suit. The Benton pasture lands near Alice, part of the old Galveston Ranch near Falfurrias, the N.G. Collins properties around San Diego, and chunks of the Welder Ranch were also sold for farming.

In San Patricio County, the Coleman Fulton Pasture Company (later known as the Taft Ranch) was the first to turn to tenant farming. This began in 1886 and intensified in the 1890s. The ranch brought in a man named Frank Ayers to supervise land sales. A house was built for Ayers at a railroad stop called Corpus Christi Junction. Ayers' house was the first structure in the coming town of Gregory.

The 300,000 acre Coleman Fulton Pasture Company sold 2,000 acres to Midwestern farmers from $10 an acre up to $25 an acre for smaller tracts. Prospective buyers were invited to come look at the soil. The selling job was made easy when a party of prospective homeseekers found a stray stalk of cotton that had grown accidentally from dropped seed. The stalk contained 80 cotton bolls.

Part of the sell-off resulted in the founding of Portland, the first of the land-rush towns in the Coastal Bend area. Two syndicates from Portland, Maine, bought land from the Coleman-Fulton Pasture Company and sold home sites across Nueces Bay from Corpus Christi. A Kansas firm, the Portland Harbor and Improvement Company, bought 640 acres next to property owned by the eastern syndicates. In 1890 and 1891, the Kansas firm developed a town site under the management of John G. Willacy.

The *Corpus Christi Caller* in July 1891 reported the sale for lots in Portland. "The steamer *Mascot* carried a good many people over to Portland on Friday, making more than one trip." In two days, $33,000 worth of town lots were sold. The area around Portland was one of the first to turn to truck farming. Grocery storeowner William Alexander McHarry built the first frame building in a town of tents in Portland.

In 1895, the Texas Land & Cattle Company sold acreage around Flour Bluff. This syndicate in Scotland had bought Mifflin Kenedy's Laureles

Ranch. The syndicate sold land in the Encinal and Garden tracts outside Corpus Christi. Flour Bluff lands were sold in the early 1890s by E. B. Cole, who would load up the buggies with ice, beer and picnic lunches and pick up his prospects at the Steen Hotel. They would spend the day driving around Flour Bluff looking at land.

In 1904, 8,000 acres of the Grim Ranch southwest of Corpus Christi were sold to Stanley Kostoryz, a Czech newspaper publisher from Nebraska. He paid $52,000 for the tract, which he renamed the Bohemian Colony lands. He sold small plots to Czech farmers from around the country.

Even the King Ranch, surprisingly, began to sell land, despite the dying words of Richard King to his lawyer, James B. Wells, to never sell a foot of "dear old Santa Gertrudis". In 1906, King's widow Henrietta sold 20,000 acres in the Rincon Bovedo (or Bobedo) tract to Theodore Koch, a banker from St. Paul, Minn. Koch sold farm tracts and founded two towns, Riviera and Riviera Beach. At Riviera Beach, he built the Buena Vista Hotel, with a view of Baffin Bay, for prospective land-buyers.

The author T.R. Fehrenbach noted that all Texas is connected to a land rush. He was referring to pre-revolutionary Texas. Much of South Texas is connected to the second great land rush that began just before the turn of the 20th Century and continued for the first decade afterwards. This land rush took off with the arrival of young man from Iowa named George H. Paul.

Paul grew up near Washington, Iowa. He worked on a farm for $18 a month until he began selling land in Canada. He heard about ranchlands opening up in South Texas and came down to see what was going on. He arrived in Corpus Christi on Jan. 3, 1907 and stayed at the Seaside Hotel.

The land that stirred Paul's interest was part of the Driscoll Ranch north of the Tex-Mex Railroad, land once owned by Martha Rabb. But it was under contract to land agents from Central Texas. Paul agreed to sell land around Hebbronville and soon had carloads of homeseekers arriving. He was approached about the Driscoll land and he met Robert Driscoll in the law office of G. R. Scott in Corpus Christi. Paul agreed to sell the Driscoll lands north of Robstown.

There were other land agents working the area, but the 30-year-old Paul set the standard. He put together an organization and developed a strategy for selling the lands. He had two salaried employees at the start, but within a year he had 1,200 agents around the country.

George H. Paul was running a multi-million-dollar company that would have an immeasurable impact on the future of South Texas. He bought four Pullman cars, one with kitchen facilities, to serve as the homeseekers' hotel for the 10-day trip from Kansas City until their return. With the Pullman cars, Paul was able to bring in 200 people and feed them. He would rent extra

Pullman cars when he had more than 200 people. He charged $1.50 per day for bed and meals, below his expenses.

Paul's homeseeker trains started at Kansas City. Paul once said that if a state agent had enough people to have a car from his state, they would have a Pullman car located for him. "This way we sometimes had several cars all converging on Kansas City to join our train," he said. The railroads gave special Homeseeker Excursion Rates — $23 for a round trip from Kansas City or St. Louis.

In late 1907, Paul hired an Iowa contractor to build what became the State National Bank Building in Robstown. "People asked where we were going to get customers for the general store we established on the first floor of the building, Paul said. "We explained that we expected to bring them in and settle them on the lands in the vicinity of the town."

The sale of 12,000 acres of Driscoll lands north of the railroad started in 1907. Paul started selling another 60,000 acres south of the railroad and began selling Taft Ranch lands in San Patricio County.

For the Nueces County lands, the prospective buyers arrived in Corpus Christi every two weeks. The homeseeker train was switched to the Tex-Mex Railroad line for the short run to Robstown. They would reach Robstown on Friday morning and spend two days looking at land. Paul's Pullman cars were parked on a siding south of town.

All the carriages and buggies were assembled to take the prospective buyers to see the land. Hiring enough vehicles was a great problem. Paul's agents would hire buggies and spring wagons from the three livery barns in Corpus Christi, one in Alice and one in San Diego.

On the trips, the buggies would make a long caravan, sometimes 50 or more, traveling slowly and stopping often. Each agent carried a map showing lands for sale. Men on horseback would ride back and forth with questions for the agents. Paul's salesmen would show the land, answer questions, and let the customer decide whether to buy. They would say, "If you haven't been given the picture as it exists, Mr. Paul will refund the money for your trip."

On one trip, when the caravan reached a point south of Robstown, an Iowa woman signed a card to buy a 40-acre tract. Before her card was filled out, horsemen came back with orders for the next tract of 880 acres and another for 160 acres. "Before the teams moved again," wrote Paul, "we had signed cards covering 3,000 acres." On average, 85 percent of those who made the trip bought land. But not always. Mrs. O. E. Smith, whose husband sold land for Paul, recalled when 200 prospective buyers arrived just after a heavy rain. "The mosquitoes were so bad," she said, "we didn't sell an acre."

On a typical excursion, they would look at land on Friday and Saturday and return to Corpus Christi for church services or an excursion on the bay aboard the *Pilot Boy*.

A woman named Etta Doherty and husband Henry arrived in February 1909 to look over land near Sinton. She wrote a letter to her hometown paper in Fairmount, Ind.

"We joined the George H. Paul Company's special car at Kansas City," Etta Doherty wrote. "From Kansas City on our trip was made without any change, as the engine, sleepers and diner were under control of the company. There were about 160 passengers. The evenings were spent in entertainment, consisting of music and speeches; the days of becoming better acquainted and seeing new countries.

"On reaching Sinton," Mrs. Doherty wrote, "we found Waldo Haisley and family well and enjoying their new home (they came the year before). We took a drive in the morning, passing a beautiful grove of live-oak. We came to a magnificent home owned by a wealthy rancher, which is certainly all that could be desired in the way of a country house. In the afternoon we went to Taft.

"Field after field of rich black soil plowed and harrowed, waiting for cotton seed, so pleased Henry that I began to fear that I was going to have to call out some of the ranchers to lasso him to keep him from buying a team of mules, donning his overalls and going to work at once. It was a very interesting afternoon spent there. We met and talked with some of the farmers, who seemed very prosperous and contented."

A woman named Flossie Harrop married Harvey Dunlap on July 1, 1908 in Lincoln, Neb. They arrived in Robstown 10 days later, on a bright sunny day. They came on a George H. Paul homeseekers' train. Harvey Dunlap had bought a tract for a farm the year before. On their first night in Robstown, the Dunlaps stayed in the Kuehm Hotel, a combination hotel, post office and saloon. About midnight, they heard an uproar and stuck their heads out to investigate. They were told it was only the Driscoll cowboys coming into town.

Next day, when they went to see their farm, three miles from town the bride met with a rude shock. "I was amazed at the chaparral and mesquite brush on the farm," Mrs. Dunlap said. "Mr. Dunlap assured me this brush was easily plowed out, that it just had surface roots, but it cost 30 dollars an acre for men to grub it out with grubbing axes; the roots were sometimes three feet deep."

As the bride had feared, their toughest task was to "grub out" the deeply rooted and thick growth of running mesquite. They hired family crews from Mexico to dig out the roots. They camped on the farm until they built a two-room house and spent $87 on furnishings. The Dunlaps would take a horse and buggy the three miles to town almost every day to get the mail because they were homesick.

What brought people from Nebraska, Iowa, Kansas and Missouri to Texas was the deep longing for their own piece of land. In the Midwest, land prices were out of reach for many, but subdivided ranchland in Texas was cheap, on average $15 to $35 an acre, so homeseekers came here by the thousands. After buying their plots, they went back to get families, farm equipment, and livestock. Railroads leased special boxcars (called immigrant cars or Zulu cars) that were separated for household goods and livestock.

Dr. Alfred T. Hightower, who bought a tract near Odem, put the family furniture, a wagon, horses, and his Reo automobile in an immigrant boxcar. The family camped under a mesquite tree while their house was being built.

Life was not easy as they struggled to adapt to a harsh land of brush, cactus and rattlesnakes. Some lived in barns or tents until a house could be built and a well dug. Pasture fences and two-story "Kansas barns" for livestock were usually the first priority.

Some homeseekers thought the land was ready to plow but, as the Dunlaps discovered, the land had to be cleared of brush and a tenacious underground growth of running mesquite.

Underground mesquite was located by small switches that showed above ground. The mesquite roots spread far. People in South Texas, it was said, had to dig for their wood. The dense network of roots had to be dug out with grubbing hoes, mattocks and axes. Thousands of "grubbing crews" came up from Mexico to clear land. Some crews were entire family units. They were paid by the acre; the rate was $12.50 an acre in 1910, which jumped to $25 an acre or more.

S. J. Vickers, who bought a tract near Sodville, hired Mexican laborers to dig out the roots. They lived in tents on his land and worked to clear the running mesquite. The grubbed-out roots were burned in huge piles.

Root plowing was also done with huge steam tractors. Some steam tractors burned the mesquite roots they dug up. Plowing out the roots was made easier when a root plow was invented by a Moravian blacksmith named Tom Mrazek, who came to Robstown in 1908.

People wielding grubbing hoes and the powerful steam tractors moved across virgin pastureland until what had once been a grazing range for cattle was converted into farmland. Cowboys called this activity "turning the grass upside-down."

Homeseekers met with difficulties and hardships. Many went back north, especially in the drought years that began in 1914. More hardy ones, determined to make good, survived and learned how to farm in South Texas. These hardy Midwestern farmers were grafted onto the ranch and cattle culture of South Texas.

"As we showed the lands we always stressed the need for more people and that with plenty of people this would become a very beautiful and prosperous section of the country," George H. Paul once said. "I remember talking to a young, single man from Nebraska. I think he was quite impressed by what I told him, for he bought a tract of land, then went back to Nebraska and got married and brought his new wife to Robstown. I believe they added eight children to the population, and now I am told that one of their sons has started off with twins, so the populating of Texas goes on. This young man from Nebraska was named Harvey Dunlap."

Paul had a powerful influence on the future of South Texas. Following the conversion of grazing land into farmland, new towns were built. Robstown, Bishop, Sinton, Taft, Gregory, Orange Grove, Premont, Falfurrias, Riviera, and others owe their existence to the turn of the 20th Century land rush.

In 1907, Paul sold 56,000 acres of Driscoll land. In 1908, he sold 56,000 acres of Coleman-Fulton Pasture Company land in San Patricio County. In 1910, Paul sold 70,000 acres of John Welder's ranchland. In two years, he sold 200,000 acres in Nueces and San Patricio counties. Before the land rush was over, he sold half a million acres of Texas ranchland.[47]

* * *

The promotion of farming in the Coastal Bend area of South Texas continued long after the end of the great land rush era. One unusual promotion was called the Black Land Special, an excursion train that left Corpus Christi on Nov. 9, 1924.

On board the train were 110 prominent farmers, businessmen and civic leaders — all wearing pearl-gray Stetsons — on their way to cities across Central and North Texas to promote the fertile black land farming region of South Texas. The man credited with organizing the Black Land Special was Maston Nixon, a young cotton farmer from near Robstown.

Nixon was born in 1896 in Luling. When his father died, he was sent to boarding school in San Antonio. His first job was to harness a mule to the ice wagon, for which he was paid $5 a week. He invested his money in Dixie Oil and Refining. He eventually owned 10 percent of the company.

Nixon enlisted in the army in 1917 and, as a second lieutenant, was drilling recruits when two men came to see him about his stock in the oil company. They offered him $46,500 in cash or the same value in stock in a new company. He took the cash and long regretted that decision. The new company became Humble Oil.

---

[47] George H. Paul made a fortune selling South Texas ranchland to farmers. After business reverses in later years he lived in extreme poverty in a shabby basement apartment in Omaha, Neb. He died on August 22, 1965. He was 88.

Nixon served as an artillery captain in France at the end of World War I. After he was discharged in 1919, he moved to a cotton farm at Petronila and married Hallie Fincham of San Antonio.

The inspiration for the Black Land Special started with Nixon after he helped establish the Robstown Chamber of Commerce. He had a survey run on black land farm acreage unfarmed but available for sale in Nueces, Jim Wells, Kleberg, and San Patricio counties. He learned that while there were several thousand farms in the four-county area, hundreds of thousands of acres were available.

Nixon cast about for a way to encourage farmers in other parts of Texas to settle in the black-dirt farm region of South Texas. Rather than trying to bring prospective buyers to South Texas, as Paul did during the land-rush days, they would go to them. They would hire a train and take farmers and farm products to show them what could be grown in the black-land region of South Texas.

Maston Nixon enlisted the help of Missouri Pacific, Southern Pacific and Tex-Mex Railroads, which helped cover expenses for the 12-car excursion train. He got Texas A&M University to prepare the exhibits. He got the 20th Infantry Band at Fort Sam Houston to make the trip.

The Black Land Special departed the San Antonio & Aransas Pass depot on Saturday, Nov. 9, 1924. Farmers, businessmen and civic leaders were ready to carry the message of prosperity to Central and North Texas.

An editorial in the *Corpus Christi Caller* said the train was a revelation. Even people who had spent their lives in this section were surprised, the paper said, by the variety of products in the exhibit cars. They knew the products were grown here, yet the massing and grouping of them in four cars "could not fail to make one feel proud that he was a part, no matter how small, of all this wealth."

At the first stop on Monday morning at Lockhart, 800 people visited the Black Land Special. At Taylor on Tuesday, 1,500 people saw the film "Land of Plenty" and visited the exhibits. At each stop, the 20th Army Band, followed by the delegation in their pearl-gray Stetsons, would parade through the downtown to the theater. There people would see the film "Land of Plenty" about the farming techniques and products of the Coastal Bend, then they would visit the exhibit cars.

The first was the cotton car. One end of the car was a miniature cotton field, with real stalks and a typical cotton wagon. The other end featured manufactured cotton products. The second exhibit was the grains car, with all the varieties of corn and grain and a map of the four counties made of various grain seeds. The third railroad car included pecans, date palms, among other trees. The fourth car showed all the varieties of fruits and vegetables grown in the region, including flapper cabbage, Bermuda onions, "carrots that made your hair curl and beets that put roses in your cheeks."

Everywhere they went — Sherman, Paris, Ennis, Mexia, Corsicana, Waco — they were greeted by large and enthusiastic crowds. An estimated 55,000 Texans saw the movie and 65,000 saw the exhibits. The trip was judged to be a wonderful demonstration of the farming fertility of the black land soil of the Corpus Christi area. Within five years after the trip, 100,000 new acres were brought into production in the Coastal Bend, in large part a direct result of the seeds planted by the Black Land Special, called the greatest promotion ever devised for any section of the state.

Patrick F. Dunn, D.P.I.

CHAPTER 41

PAT DUNN,
THE DUKE OF PADRE ISLAND
1879 — 1929

If the Lord would give me back the island, wash out a channel in Corpus Christi Pass 30 feet deep, and put devilfish and other monsters in it to keep out the tourists, I'd be satisfied.

—Pat Dunn after he sold his island ranch

Patrick F. Dunn was the duke of Padre Island. His domain was an empire of sand, cattle and 112 miles of Gulf beaches. Over a 50-year span — 1879 until 1929 — he developed the island into a unique ranch, with white-faced cattle wading in the surf, with corrals made of driftwood that washed ashore. He patrolled his 135,000 acre island ranch in a spring buggy pulled by two white mules.

Dunn gave himself the title of duke. He received a letter from some fellow in England whose name was followed by a string of titles and initials for one honor or another. Dunn in reply stuck D.P.I. after his name. Edward Kleberg, his lawyer, asked him what the letters stood for.

"Duke of Padre Island."

It seemed to fit.

Many years before, when Pat Dunn was six years old, his family lived near his uncle John Dunn, five miles from Corpus Christi on the way to Nuecestown.

"Us kids used to go over to Uncle John's and play," Dunn once told a reporter. "He was building a well. In those days, they would dig a hole about eight feet square and go down until the sand began to cave in before they put in curbing. He had some ox chains and bows and things he did not want to get pressed (confiscated) by Confederate authorities.

"So he took all the best chains and bows and the wheels off the wagon and hid them in the well. Some soldiers came to confiscate Uncle John's things. They looked at the wagons and harness and there was nothing but junk. One said, 'Why, Dunn, you're a teaming contractor; you've got better stuff than this. This stuff is just junk; we can't use it.'

"I heard that and said, 'Why, there's a good harness down there in the well.' Uncle John slapped me and I ran into the house crying. I told my aunt that Uncle John slapped me when I was telling about the harness in the well. She said no wonder I got slapped."

The following year, when Dunn was 7, his father (Thomas Dunn Sr.) died. "We had just loaded our wagon with cotton when my father passed on. The oldest boy was 12 and the oldest girl was 13, so my mother (Catherine Hickey Dunn) decided to haul the cotton to Brownsville herself. She took me along. We never got further than Santa Rosa, though, when the war ended."

Pat Dunn was 21 in the drought year of 1879. This was near the end of the free-range era and Pat and his brother Lawrence were looking for a place to move their cattle. The brothers and their mother were partners in the cattle business.

When they moved their cattle to Padre Island, on July 7, 1879, Dunn called it the greatest cattle ranch in the world. He bought out his brother and mother and would later call his ranch "El Rancho de Don Patricio."

Dunn wasn't the first to use the island as a ranch. Padre Nicolas Balli, for whom the island was named, began a cattle ranch on the island's southern end. Balli built a ranch house of driftwood and called his ranch Santa Cruz (Holy Cross). The island had been called Santiago, but it began to be called Padre Balli's island.

Balli found freshwater under the dunes and ran cattle on the island from 1806 until he died in 1829. His nephew took over after that and the Balli ranch continued to flourish until the Ballis moved to the mainland after a severe hurricane struck in 1844.

On the heels of the Ballis came John Singer, whose brother Merritt invented the sewing machine. The Singer family was shipwrecked on the island in 1847. The family saved what they could from their wrecked ship, made a tent out of one of the sails, and began running cattle in the same area of Padre Balli's Santa Cruz ranch, 20 miles up from the island's southern tip.

At the beginning of the Civil War, Singer, a Yankee, was afraid his wealth would be confiscated. He put some $62,000 in jewelry, gold coins and silver bars in a big clay jar and buried it in a sand dune. After the war, he returned to reclaim his treasure, but storms had erased the landmarks. He dug in the dunes around the old Santa Cruz ranch headquarters for a long time, but never found his buried cache.

About that time, several families settled 17 miles south of Corpus Christi Pass at what would be called the Settlement, or the Curry Settlement. The patriarch was Carey Curry, an Alabama preacher. His sons Joe and Uriah ("Coot") Curry, former Confederate soldiers, lived nearby.

After the war, a Yankee schoolteacher named Lively came to teach at the Settlement. The first day of school, one of the Curry boys said, "Mr. Lively, I want to see your belly. Grandpa says it's blue."

During the yellow fever epidemic of 1867, several Corpus Christi families moved to the Settlement, where the fever never reached.

In 1874, John King and W. N. Staples established a beef packing house next to a deep channel at Corpus Christi Pass. This part of the pass became known as Packery Channel. But the packery was long gone when Dunn began grazing cattle on the island in 1879.

In the years that followed, Pat Dunn didn't just build a ranch on the island. He built a way of life. Dunn acquired grazing rights on the island from the Corpus Christi law firm of McCampbell & Welch.[48]

The year after Dunn moved to the island, in 1880, he bought 400 cows at $8 a head from D. C. Rachal at White Point, across Nueces Bay. Dunn and his hands herded the cattle from White Point to Flour Bluff, where they forded the Laguna Madre near Pita Island. The Laguna was shallow enough for the cattle to wade, but at the deeper end, near the island, they had to swim for a short distance.

In the next few years, Dunn began to build up one of the most unusual ranches in the world. His El Rancho de Don Patricio was a remote, enigmatic place. Dunn established four cattle stations, with corrals and holding pens, about a day's journey apart down the island. Number one was at the head of the island. It was called Owl's Mott, where owls once roosted before the grackles took possession. This station included a house for Dunn, one for his foreman, and a bunkhouse for hands. Number two was called the Novillo station. Number three was at Black Hill, sometimes called Boggy Slough. Number four was at Green Hill, the highest elevation on the island. Between these four stations were several camping places, such as Campo Bueno and Campo Borrego.

At roundup time, in April and October, the hands moved the cattle up from the southern tip, at Brazos Santiago. Dunn built traps and cutting chutes to virtually eliminate the practice of roping, which he thought was cruel. "Roping is unnecessary," he once told a reporter. "You run a cow down, rope him and brand him, and he'll be afraid of you as long as he lives." When calves were branded, they were not roped, but "mugged." That is, they were caught in the pen and thrown down by hand. "When an expert thrower goes

---

[48] This has long been in legal contention by descendants of Padre Balli, whose family was granted the island by the Spanish crown and confirmed by the government of Mexico. I won't try to trace the spaghetti history of the claims and counter-claims of who owned or bought or sold the island.

to work," said Dunn, "it just looks like he lays his hand on the side of the calf and it falls over."

The white-faced cattle on the island grew fat from what was called beach or sedge grass — vegetation that was about the same as in the sand belt on the mainland. Dunn's cattle would wade in the surf and eat sand crabs and dead fish. Their hides showed spots of tar (asphaltum that washes up from the Gulf floor) from lying on the beaches. There was plenty of fresh water. Three to four or five feet down on the island is a layer of fresh water, which rests like a cushion on the heavier saltwater underneath.

"You can find good water in most places within a few feet of the surface," Dunn told a reporter. "Usually, you can find freshwater near the shore when you cannot find it near the center of the island. The storms brought in saltwater and it stood in lakes for a long time. If you dig in those places, you'll find saltwater. But nearly everywhere else, you can find good water."

Dunn had 75 water tanks dug in the sand. These were long trenches shored up on the sides and ends with ship hatch covers and other salvage material to keep out the sand. The cattle would kneel to drink. "We watered our cattle at these cow wells," said Dunn. "We called them tanks. Those things had to be kept clean."

Five years after he moved to the island, in 1884, Dunn married a widow, Mrs. Clara Jones, and he adopted her daughter Lalla. The Dunns moved 17 miles down the island to the Curry Settlement. They had a small house at the Settlement; some of the Curry family members still lived there.

In 1890, after Dunn's daughter May contracted scarlet fever, he moved the family to Corpus Christi and later built a new home on the bluff, at 317 S. Broadway. This became the home of his daughter May after she married Jack Chilson.

Pat Dunn still spent most of his time on the island, except during the time when he served in the Texas Legislature and had to live in Austin during the legislative sessions. He told a reporter he never felt easy when he got too far away from the island's salt air that smelled of the sea.

Over the years, Dunn was a diligent beachcomber. He and his hands built corrals and bunkhouses from pine and mahogany logs that washed ashore during storms. Dunn once told the story of one of his hands who thought he was going to die.

"You can't die," Dunn told him. "There's no wood to make a coffin."

After this, a storm hit the Louisiana coast, washed out a graveyard, and a coffin landed on the beach on Padre Island. Dunn told the man, "Well, your coffin has come in." But, when they went down to look at it, there was a skeleton inside. Dunn told the fellow that since the coffin was occupied, he'd have to postpone his dying a bit longer.

The island was a remote place. Fishermen and hunters who wanted access had to get permission from one of Dunn's agents at Point Isabel or Corpus Christi. Time stood still on the island, with little news of events from the wider world. One day in April, 1906, Dunn rode into Corpus Christi and stopped at the Ben Grande Saloon on the bluff. Dunn saw a friend sitting in front.

"Sam, what's new?" asked Dunn.

"San Francisco's still burning," said Sam.

"San Francisco burning? How come?"

"They had an earthquake about seven or eight days ago and it started a fire."

A man who didn't know Dunn walked out of the saloon and picked up on the conservation.

"Where the hell have you been, that you haven't heard about the San Francisco earthquake?"

When Dunn was in town, he liked to stop by the St. James Hotel where, in the evenings, Pat Whelan, the McCampbells, and other citizens would gather on the porch and talk about the events of the day.

In 1907, Dunn built a two-story house at the head of the island, facing east on Packery Channel. The house, never painted, was built of driftwood that had washed ashore. Dunn told a reporter that the house was made two-story because the lumber that washed up was too long and he had no saw to cut it with. "I just set the timbers upright and they were high enough for a two-story house. If I'd had a saw, I would've built a one-story house."

The house was furnished with door hinges from ship refrigerators, chairs from a wrecked steamer; a wooden cask with Japanese letters served as a washbasin, and whisky barrels were used to catch rainwater.

On the south porch by the kitchen was a long table made of driftwood, unpainted and weathered gray like the house. Ranch hands were served their meals there, prepared by Dunn's cook named Aurelio. They would sit on the south porch, in the long purple evenings, and wait for night to close in.

One Christmas, one of the hands picked up oranges and lemons that had washed up on the beach. Dunn sent the man back to look for a coconut. "He went down to the beach," said Dunn, "and came back a few minutes later with some coconuts. And we had some of the finest ambrosia you ever tasted." Another time, they were craving sausage. As if delivered by Providence, they found a sausage grinder on the beach. They rounded up a wild pig and soon had sausage.

Dunn once said schools of redfish would jump in the shallow waters of the Laguna Madre stampeding the cattle grazing on the shore. Cowhands could rope a couple of redfish for dinner, as if it were no trick at all.

Dunn always had a fund of strange stories about the island. After the 1916 hurricane, a bad one, Dunn noticed that a ranch hand named John Brumfield kept muttering to himself and prodding the sand with the toe of his boot, looking for something. He had lost his false teeth in the storm. Brumfield continued to scratch in the sand to the amusement of Dunn. Then Brumfield gave a whoop. Incredibly, he had kicked up the sand in the right spot and found his dentures.

After the 1916 hurricane destroyed the two-story ranch house on Packery Channel, Dunn built a one-story house a mile and a half away. He didn't live there long. In 1926, Dunn sold his title to El Rancho de Don Patricio to Col. Sam Robertson, who planned to develop the island into a tourist resort. Robertson built the Don Patricio Causeway in 1927, which opened up the island to visitors from the mainland. Dunn retained grazing rights for his cattle and mineral rights. He moved into town and put up at the Nueces Hotel.

Dunn knew the island would never be the same, and he regretted selling out. It wasn't the livelihood he missed; it was the life. "I want to find another island, one that no one can reach," he told a reporter. But he really wanted to get the island back, the lonely, inaccessible place that it was, a place where the world could intrude only with his permission. He said later, "If the Lord would give me back the island, wash out a channel in Corpus Christi Pass 30 feet deep, and put devilfish and other monsters in it to keep out the tourists, I'd be satisfied."

Dunn died of a heart attack on March 25, 1937 in his room at the Nueces Hotel. He was 79. No one ever possessed the island more completely than Patrick F. Dunn, the Duke of Padre Island.

CHAPTER 42

RANCH LIFE WITH THE MILLERS, TRUITTS, AND DOBIES
1790 — 1930

The hills could hardly be so lush with buffalo clover — as we used to call the bluebonnet — and the red bunch grass, so soft and lovely, as they are in the eyes of memory.

—J. Frank Dobie

Sylvanus Gerard Miller moved to the Nueces River Valley to start a horse ranch in 1859. He settled on land bordering both sides of the river. When the Civil War broke out, he joined Terry's Texas Rangers and saw a lot of action with Nathan Bedford Forrest's hard-riding cavalry.

After the war, Miller's ranch was in ruins, the horses gone. He set about restocking the ranch and building a house with lumber hauled from Corpus Christi. To get ready cash, he cut down trees to make a ferryboat for Chihuahua wagons traveling to Mexico. Miller's Ferry became a major crossing place on the Nueces River.

In 1869, Miller took horses to sell in New Orleans. In Louisiana, he met Susan Frances East, 19-year-old daughter of a plantation owner. They married on Jan. 31, 1870. They bought a buggy and a mare named "Lady Morgan," which cost $300.

At Brashear (Morgan City), they took a steamboat to Galveston then a mail boat to Indianola. They left Indianola with the horse and buggy. After riding 30 miles, and getting on toward dinner time, they came to a log ranch house where they spent the night. There were two rooms, one with beds lining the wall and another with a fireplace used for cooking. For supper, they had beef, biscuits, and black coffee; for breakfast they had fried eggs, bacon, biscuits, and black coffee.

When they reached the ranch, the bride thought it beautiful.

"It was vivid green in tall, waving mesquite grass," she wrote. "Added to this was a splash of wildflowers spread like colored lace over the green." Many Mexican families lived on the ranch. The women, dressed in black with shawl-like *rebosos,* were curious about the newcomer. They would pat her hair to see what she was made of and say, *"Muy bonito!* and they would bring me pots of chili and prickly pear with eggs." Mrs. Miller saw them often as they came to the ranch store to get supplies. Miller's store was about a mile from the ferry.

Mrs. Miller wrote about her life on the ranch. She told about the legend of Casa Blanca, the old Spanish ranch house built of white caliche blocks that dated back to the 1750s. It was located on the banks of Pinetas Creek, a mile from where the creek joins the Nueces. This later became part of the Wade Ranch near Sandia.

This was the legend: Long before Texas was a republic or a state, when it was still part of the Spanish empire, a wealthy rancher in South Texas planned to return to Mexico with his two sons and daughter. He packed up his goods, along with 10 kegs of gold and silver. The day before they were to leave, a Comanche war party was seen nearby. The rancher hid the kegs by submerging them in a small lake near a lone mesquite.

That night, the Indians attacked. The rancher and his sons were killed; only a daughter survived. She returned to Mexico. Many years later, the daughter, an old woman, returned to Casa Blanca to search for the treasure. But she couldn't recognize a single landmark. Where the lake had been was a mesquite thicket and the one tree was one of many. She never found the buried kegs. Other people over the years searched for the lost treasure of Casa Blanca.

On Miller Ranch, the Millers' first child was born in 1871. A year later another child was born. It was a busy nursery. The sequence of births came regularly. In 19 years, from 1871 to 1890, Mrs. Miller gave birth to 13 children — Vivian Gerard, Ernest Elmer, Rollo Lee, Demrie Buford, Eilleen, Dean, Zenna Hortense, Adlia Lamar, Callie Lena and Susie Natalie. Three others died young or at birth. As the family expanded, the valley was being settled. Lagarto across the river was growing. Their ranch was located midway between Lagarto and the coming town of Mathis.

Miller put up a mesquite fence that angered some because it blocked the Corpus Christi-Gussettville road. Travelers would tear down sections of the fence rather than go through the gate.

In November 1876, Mrs. Miller returned from Louisiana on the sidewheeler *Mary.* The ship arrived as a norther hit. The *Mary* ran aground and pounded her bottom out as immense waves, black as pitch, lashed the sinking ship. With distress flags flying, bar pilots from the Mercer settlement tried to reach them in a pilot boat, but couldn't get close in the crashing seas.

"Trial after trial was made to get to us, but each time the great waves carried our rescuers beyond our reach," Mrs. Miller wrote. After several hours, the pilot boat was lashed to the *Mary* by her gangplank. "To reach this gangplank, we waded through water waist-deep on deck. As I started across the gangplank, the *Mary* broke away and down I went into the sea. As I fell, the heel of my shoe caught on one of the slats. This broke my fall and enabled me to catch hold of the plank. Scrambling to a sitting position on the gangplank, I bobbed up and down as each wave struck. It seemed an eternity before sailors caught hold of it and I was helped into the rescue boat." The passengers, numbed by the cold, went to the Mercer cabin to dry out before a roaring fire. When Mrs. Miller reached Rockport, she learned that her husband was in Corpus Christi "crazed with grief" after reports that all on the stricken ship were lost. "There are no words to describe our happy meeting, after he had mourned us as dead and we had given up hopes of seeing our loved ones again."

At the ranch, she was shown her husband's improvements. He put up an Eclipse windmill and built a gristmill to grind corn, living up to the family name of Miller. He drilled artesian wells, put in an irrigation system, planted fruit trees, imported rose bushes from Alabama, and planted crops of cabbages, onions and watermelons. In 1907, Miller and his son Ernest bought a 110,000-acre ranch near Durango, Mexico. Ernest had married Gertrude Wade and after John Wade died, she inherited part of the Wade Ranch. Her inheritance helped finance the operation in Mexico. Ernest imported the first Herefords into Mexico and was supplying cavalry horses for the Mexican army when he was murdered by his American partner in 1908. That year, S. G. Miller died after a bout of typhus fever. He was 76. Another son, Adlia Lamar, called "Top," died in the Mexican Revolution of 1912.

Susan Frances Miller described the ranch's demise to make way for a reservoir and dam — "Eight thousand acres of the fertile land of the Nueces Valley is soon to be submerged in a great reservoir which the city of Corpus Christi is creating. A dam is being built below our ranch. The beautiful valley I have known for half a century will disappear beneath the water."

Where the Miller Ranch had been became a lake. The vivid green of mesquite grass, the splash of wildflowers, the roses brought from Alabama, much of what comprised the old Miller Ranch lies beneath the waters of Lake Corpus Christi.

* * *

Another vivid picture of ranch life in South Texas comes from Maude T. Gilliland's "Rincon." Her family, the Truitt family, packed up and left Corpus Christi in the summer of 1902. They were moving to Rancho Capisallo owned by Brownsville political boss James B. Wells, who was also the attorney for King Ranch. Alfred Levi Truitt had been hired to manage Wells' ranch.

313

The Truitts left with two wagons, a buggy, eight mules, two buggy horses, and four saddle horses. From Corpus Christi they traveled west for 10 miles, then turned south and followed the same route Zachary Taylor's army took when it left Corpus Christi in 1846. After they passed King Ranch headquarters, they came across a flock of geese and the vaqueros accompanying them raced among the geese, using long rawhide whips to bring down several as they took flight. The popping of the bullwhips sounded like gun shots. The mother, Molly Truitt, cooked the geese, seasoned with salt and pepper, flour and water, in a Dutch oven covered with hot coals. For supper they ate roast goose with pan gravy, camp bread and coffee.

Going south, the Truitts passed cattle bones bleaching in the sun, skeletons from an old drought, and watched as the Alice-to-Brownsville stage passed and at one point saw the stagecoach driver change horses at Encino del Poso. They traveled through isolated country; there was not a village or post office between Sinton and Brownsville in 1902, before the coming of the "Brownie" railroad.

They stopped at El Sauz, a division of King Ranch, where they were guests of "Uncle Josh" Durham, the ranch foreman and former member of the famous McNelly's Rangers.

They turned southwest to reach Rancho Capisallo, which straddled Hidalgo and Cameron counties. It was 100 miles from the nearest railroad.

Not long after they arrived, the ranch was sold and the Truitts moved on to another ranch owned by Wells, the 146,000-acre ranch in Starr and Hidalgo counties named Rincon Medio. The ranch house at Rincon, Gilliland wrote, was in the shape of a T. It had 18 rooms but no indoor plumbing. Each bedroom had a washstand and white enamel chamber pot. When the weather was cold, the Truitt children bathed by the fireplace.

On the ranch, everything stopped for siesta at 2 p.m., the hottest time of the day, when horses stood under a big mesquite, lazily switching at flies. At 3 p.m., they would awake to the sharp smell of mesquite smoke mixed with the odor of roasted coffee beans coming to a boil.

They got mail by horseback from Sam Fordyce 35 miles to the south. They would get the Sears Roebuck catalogue and the *Kansas City Packer*. For entertainment, they had a gramophone on which they played the songs of Caruso and the music of John Phillips Sousa. A salesman whose mission in life was to sell pianos to Texas ranchers sold them a piano. Mrs. Truitt could play; she had taken music lessons from the Catholic sisters in Corpus Christi. She would play "Give My Love to Nell" and "A Package of Old Letters." They got books for Christmas, Kipling's works, "The Light That Failed," "Captains Courageous," "Kim."

Ranch days began early, at 4:30 or 5, with the sound of the coffee mill grinding, followed by the smell of freshly brewed coffee. The coffee mill was

314

nailed to the wall. Green peaberry coffee beans came in 100-pound sacks. The beans were roasted in black bread pans.

They had venison, cabrito and beef. The beef was cut in thin strips and hung on clotheslines to dry in the sun to make beef jerky. Crusty loaves of bread were baked in an old wood stove. There were tortillas, *pan dulce* and *bunuelos*.

On wash day, mesquite wood fed a fire under a big black wash pot in the yard. Shavings from a bar of Crystal White soap were added to the boiling water. As clothes boiled in the pot, they were punched down with a broom stick. For ironing, flat black irons were heated on the wood stove. Even after washing and ironing, the clothes gave off a strong odor of mesquite smoke.

A frequent visitor was a neighbor rancher from Hebbronville, W. W. Jones, who would ride over in a two-wheeled cart pulled by mules. It had broad-rimmed wheels for pulling through the sand. In crossing through pastures, he would take down fences and tell Mr. Truitt where he took them down so fence riders could make repairs. Jones would sit on the porch gallery and chew black-horse tobacco and spit into the yard. The tomcat learned to keep his distance. Jones would stay several days until he was talked out or ran out of tobacco.

Those were the ranch times described by Maude Gilliland in "Rincon" (Remote Dwelling Place) about her life when she was Maude Truitt, the daughter of Alfred and Molly Truitt. Mrs. Gilliland wrote that those who have never lived on a ranch missed something in life.

"It is nice to have ranch memories stored away to draw on when the looking-back period comes — memories such as the lace-like shadows of the mesquite under a noonday sun — the paisano folding back his wings as he skims across the road — the yip-yip of coyotes — thirsty horses drinking from a wooden trough — the sound of creaking saddle leather and the clinking-clanking of spurs — all these make looking back a pleasure."

* * *

Looking back to when Spain still held title to Texas (though it hardly knew what to do with it), there was a fortified ranch house on the south bank of Ramireña Creek in today's Live Oak County.

A later name for this fortified ranch house was Fort Ramírez. It was not a fort, but the headquarters of a rancho. This was at the turn of the 18th and 19th centuries when Spanish rancheros received large grants of land on the west side of the Nueces River. One of the first was at Casa Blanca, where Juan José de la Garza Montemayor and his sons started a ranch between the Penitas Creek and the Nueces River. To the north was Fort Ramírez, which

315

was built between 1790 and 1802, about the same time that Casa Blanca was founded.

What little we know about Fort Ramírez was that it was built by Don José Antonio Ramírez and his son Don José Victoriano Ramírez, who came from Camargo. The ranch house was built of white caliche blocks (called "sillares") quarried from a caliche hill not far away. The Ramírezes filed for title to eight leagues (35,000 acres) on Ramireña Creek. In their claim, they said they had cleared fields, built corrals and ranch houses, and had herds of cattle and horses.

The Ramírezes, like the Montemayors at Casa Blanca, built ranch houses for defense. They began stocking the Nueces Valley with cattle and horses long before people named Wright, McNeill and Dobie came along. But the story of the Ramírezes and the Montemayors is not often told because the details that make a story worth telling have been lost and the land keeps its own secrets.

The bare bones of the story can be found. The people at Rancho Ramírez constantly had to be on guard for Indians. Getting too far away from the protective stone walls could be fatal. The rancheros were attacked and their herds of horses and cattle stolen. In Mexico, the revolt against Spanish rule led to Spanish soldiers being withdrawn from Texas. This left the ranches in the Nueces Valley even more unprotected than normal.

In one Indian attack in 1812, many people were killed at Fort Ramírez. The ranch was abandoned. Livestock and even household goods were left behind. The surviving members of the Ramírez family fled to Mexico, back to Camargo. Similar Indian attacks occurred at Casa Blanca and other Spanish ranchos on the Nueces River.

While the Ramírez heirs did not return, they did not abandon their claim to the eight leagues of land between the Nueces and Ramireña Creek. In 1828, Leandro Ramírez petitioned the state of Tamaulipas to confirm the Ramírez grant. The grant was approved in 1834. After the Texas Revolution, the Republic of Texas did not confirm the title, but the state of Texas finally confirmed the claim in 1858. Over the next twenty years the heirs sold off the land parcel by parcel, probably for little more than pennies an acre.

One sale cited by J. Frank Dobie showed how much the land was valued. In 1866, the year after the Civil War when there was little money in Texas, a section of land (640 acres) that included old Fort Ramírez sold at auction because of 60 cents owed in back taxes.

The 640 acres were sold to Peyton McNeill for $6, less than a penny an acre. The walls of Fort Ramírez still stood back then, a reminder to new settlers that others had come before. In a few years, the old walls of Fort Ramírez were torn down by people searching for hidden treasure, then the rubble was hauled away and only the faint traces of Fort Ramírez remained.

J. Frank Dobie grew up near Fort Ramírez on his father's ranch, which Dobie wrote about in "Coronado's Children" and in a newspaper article in 1959. He recalled that the Dobie house was in a mott of live oaks overlooking the valley of Long Hollow.

Dobie recalled — How the house had a paling fence around it, with flowers, and a dirt yard swept bare to show snake trails . . . How the wild buffalo clover reached the stirrups of his saddle . . . How the horses would stamp on the caliche at their stables to knock off red ants crawling above their hooves . . . How the stillness of the day was broken by the lonely sound of windmill lifting rods . . . How coyotes serenaded at night in stereo . . . How fresh and green the mesquite looked in the early spring . . . How his horse Buck would point his ears when Dobie walked into the pen to rope a mount, seeming to ask if he was going to ride him or Brownie.

In "Coronado's Children," Dobie wrote — "All I regret now is that the stones of Fort Ramírez have been carried away. I should like to stand on them once more in April and gaze across the winding Ramireña upon the oak-fringed hills beyond. Yet the hills could hardly be so lush with buffalo clover — as we used to call the bluebonnet — and the red bunch grass, so soft and lovely, as they are in the eyes of memory."

BIBLIOGRAPHY AND SOURCE NOTES

1. *Cabeza de Vaca: Slave and Medicine Man in South Texas*
There is a wealth of material on Cabeza de Vaca's extraordinary journey and travails. Most accounts are based on his own *"Naufrágios"* published at Zamora in 1542. I relied on translations by Fanny Bandelier, published in 1905, and Buckingham Smith, published in 1851 and 1871. Other books and articles include Harbert Davenport and Joseph Wells, article in the *Southwestern Historical Quarterly*; Harbert Davenport on Oviedo's account in the *Southwestern Historical Quarterly*; F. W. Hodge, "Spanish Explorers in the U.S."; W. W. Newcomb Jr., "The Indians of Texas"; Gonzalo Fernandez Oviedo y Valdez, *"Historia General y Natural de los Indios";* John Upton Terrell, "Journey Into Darkness"; Robert S. Weddle, "Spanish Sea"; Clayton Williams, "Never Again"; J. W. Williams, "Old Texas Trails."

2. *The Treasure Fleet and Massacre on Padre Island*
Carlos E. Castañeda translated the story of Agustin Padilla Dávila in "Our Catholic Heritage in Texas." Dávila wrote an account of the shipwreck in *"Historia."* Report by the Texas Antiquities Committee, "Introduction to the Dávila Account and Related Sources." Other sources include: Hodding Carter, "Doomed Road of Empire"; Vernon Smylie, "The Early History of Padre Island"; Dee Woods, "Blaze of Gold"; Writers' Round Table, "Padre Island."

3. *La Salle and the French Expedition in Texas*
Herbert E. Bolton, "Spanish Exploration in the Southwest"; Bolton, "Texas in the Middle Eighteenth Century"; Bolton, *"Athanase de Mézières* and the Louisiana-Texas Frontier"; Hodding Carter, "Doomed Road of Empire"; William C. Foster, "Spanish Expeditions into Texas"; Handbook of Texas; Henri Joutel, "Joutel's Journal of La Salle's Last Voyage," edited by Henry Reed Stiles; Fray Juan Agustin Morfi's "History of Texas, 1673-1779"; W. W. Newcomb Jr., "The Indians of Texas"; Francis Parkman, "La Salle and the Discovery of the Great West"; Robert Ricklis, "The Karankawa Indians of Texas"; Robert S. Weddle, "San Juan Bautista: Gateway to Spanish Texas"; Weddle, "Wilderness Manhunt: The Spanish Search for La Salle"; "La Salle, the Mississippi and the Gulf: Three Primary Documents," edited by Weddle; Weddle, "La Salle's Survivors," *Southwestern Historical Quarterly.*

4. *Karankawa Sunset*
Journal of Stephen F. Austin, *Southwestern Historical Quarterly;* Roy Bedichek, "Karankaway Country"; Carlos E. Castañeda, "Our Catholic Heritage in Texas"; J. H. Kuykendall, "Reminiscences of Early Texas," *Southwestern Historical Quarterly*; W. W. Newcomb Jr., "The Indians of Texas"; Kathryn Stoner O'Connor, "Presidio La Bahia"; Victor M. Rose article, "Some Historical Facts in Regard to the Settlement of Victoria"; Robert Ricklis, "The Karankawa Indians of Texas."

5. *Noah Smithwick and the Evolution of a State*
Bob Boyd, "The Texas Revolution: A Day-by-Day Account"; J. Frank Dobie, "Tales of Old-Time Texas"; T. R. Fehrenbach, "Lone Star, A History of Texas and the Texans"; Murphy Givens' columns, June 17 and 24, 2009, *Corpus Christi Caller-Times;* Stephen L. Hardin, "Texan Iliad"; W.W. Newcomb Jr., "The Indians of Texas"; Stephen B. Oates, "Rip Ford's Texas"; Noah Smithwick, "The Evolution of a State or Recollections of Old Texas Days"; Walter Prescott Webb, "The Texas Rangers."

6. *"Wildcat"Morrell and the Battle of Salado Creek*
Donaly E. Brice, "The Great Comanche Raid"; James DeShields, "Border Wars of Texas"; T. R. Fehrenbach, "Lone Star"; James Kimmins Greer, "Texas Ranger: Jack Hays in the Frontier Southwest"; Handbook of Texas; John Holland Jenkins, "Recollections of Early Texas"; Rev. Z. N. Morrell, "Flowers and Fruits in the Wilderness"; Juan N. Seguin, "Personal Memoirs"; Leonie Rummel Weyand and Houston Wade, "Early History of Fayette County"; Henderson Yoakum, "History of Texas."

7. *Bigfoot Wallace, the Battle of Mier and the Bean Drawing*
Gen. Thomas J. Green, "Journal of the Texian Expedition Against Mier"; Journal of Lewis Birdsall Harris, S*outhwestern Historical Quarterly*; Sterling Brown Hendricks, "The Somervell Expedition," *Southwestern Historical Quarterly*; Paul Horgan, "The Great River"; John Holland Jenkins, "Recollections of Early Texas"; A.J. Sowell, "The Life of Bigfoot Wallace"; George Washington Trahern, "Texan Cowboy Soldier from Mier to Buena Vista," edited by Russell Buchanan, *Southwestern Historical Quarterly*; Walter Prescott Webb, "The Texas Rangers"; Linda Wolff, "Indianola and Matagorda Island"; Henderson Yoakum, "History of Texas."

8. *Jack Hays, Ranger on the Texas Frontier*
Donaly E. Brice, "The Great Comanche Raid"; Robert J. Casey, "Texas Border"; James DeShields, "Border Wars of Texas"; Col. Richard Dodge, "Our Wild Indians"; T. R. Fehrenbach, "Lone Star"; James Kimmins Greer, "Texas Ranger: Jack Hays in the Frontier Southwest"; Journal of Lewis Birdsall Harris, S*outhwestern Historical Quarterly*; Virginia H. Taylor Houston, article, *Southwestern Historical Quarterly*; John Holland Jenkins, "Recollections of Early Texas"; Papers of Mirabeau Buonaparte Lamar; Memoirs of Mary A. Maverick; Stephen L. Moore, "Savage Frontier"; Z. N. Morrell, "Flowers and Fruits in the Wilderness"; W. W. Newcomb Jr., "The Indians of Texas"; *Telegraph & Texas Register*, July 3, 1844; Charles M. Robinson III, "Men Who Wear the Star"; A. J. Sowell, "Texas Indian Fighters"; Sowell, "The Life of Bigfoot Wallace"; Noah Smithwick, "The Evolution of a State"; Texas Indian Papers, 1844-1845; Walter Prescott Webb, "The Texas Rangers"; Walter Prescott Webb and H. Bailey Carroll, "The Handbook of Texas," 1952; Josiah Wilbarger, "Indian Depredations in Texas"; Amelia Williams and Eugene Barker, "The Writings of Sam Houston"; John Hoyt Williams, "Sam Houston."

9. *Death of an Indian Chief: Flacco the Younger*
James Kimmins Greer, "Texas Ranger: Jack Hays in the Frontier Southwest"; John Holland Jenkins, "Recollections of Early Texas"; Papers of Mirabeau Buonaparte Lamar; Memoirs of Mary A. Maverick; *Morning Star*, Houston, April 20, 1843; *Telegraph & Texas Register*, June 14, 1843; Chronicles of Fayette, The Reminiscences of Julia Lee Sinks; Julia Lee Sinks, Notes and Fragments, *Southwestern Historical Quarterly*; Noah Smithwick, "The Evolution of a State"; Amelia Williams and Eugene Barker, "The Writings of Sam Houston."

10. *Prelude to War: Zachary Taylor Lands in South Texas*
William Allen and Sue Hastings Taylor, "Aransas"; K. Jack Bauer, "Zachary Taylor"; Eugenia Reynolds Briscoe, "City by the Sea"; *Corpus Christi Caller*, Oct. 2, 1908; Samuel Chamberlain, "My Confession: Recollections of a Rogue"; Joseph Chance, "My Life in the Old Army: Abner Doubleday"; *Corpus Christi Gazette*, 1846; Napoleon

Jackson Tecumseh Dana, "Monterrey Is Ours"; Bernard Devoto, "Year of Decision: 1846"; George K. Donnelly, letter; Joseph J. Fry, "A Life of Zachary Taylor"; *Galveston News*, Feb. 16, 1883; U.S. Grant, "Personal Memoirs"; James Kimmins Greer, "Texas Ranger: Jack Hays in the Frontier Southwest"; Holman Hamilton, "Zachary Taylor, Soldier of the Republic"; W. S. Henry, "Campaign Sketches of the War with Mexico"; Ethan Allen Hitchcock, "Fifty Years in Camp and Field"; Hitchcock, unpublished diary; N.S. Jarvis, "Army Surgeon's Notes of Frontier Service — Mexican War"; William Preston Johnson, "Life of Albert Sidney Johnston"; Charles Masland, unpublished letters; Edward J. Nichols, "Zach Taylor's Little Army"; Stephen B. Oates, "Rip Ford's Texas"; John James Peck, "The Sign of the Eagle"; Geoffrey Perrett, "Ulysses S. Grant, Soldier and President"; Justin H. Smith, "The War with Mexico"; Lota M. Spell, "Pioneer Printer: Samuel Bangs in Mexico and Texas"; Frank Wagner's Research Papers; Alpha Kennedy Wood, "Texas Coastal Bend."

11. *Daniel P. Whiting, Sarah Bourjett and the Bombardment of Fort Brown*
Francis Edward Abernethy, "Legendary Ladies of Texas"; K. Jack Bauer, "Zachary Taylor"; Samuel Chamberlain, "My Confession: Recollections of a Rogue"; Joseph Chance, "The Great Western: A Giant Woman of Legend," *Flour Bluff Sun*, Dec. 25, 1998; Murphy Givens, "Amazon Called the Great Western," *Corpus Christi Caller-Times*, Dec. 30, 1998; U.S. Grant, "Personal Memoirs"; Stephen B. Oates, "Rip Ford's Texas"; Geoffrey Perrett, "Ulysses S. Grant, Soldier and President"; Justin H. Smith, "The War with Mexico"; Robert H. Thonhoff, "Taylor's Trail," *Southwestern Historical Quarterly*, July, 1966; Bill Walraven, "The Legendary Sarah Rode with Zachary," *Corpus Christi Caller*, Nov. 26, 1975; Daniel P. Whiting, "A Soldier's Life," edited by Murphy Givens.

12. *Billy Rogers, Mustang Gray and Retribution on the Rio Grande*
The American Flag, Matamoros, July 31 and Dec. 9, 1846, July 3, 1847, June 14, 1848; *Corpus Christi Caller*, Dec. 7, 1941 and June 5, 1952; Samuel Chamberlain, "My Confession: Recollections of a Rogue"; Joseph Chance, "The Mexican War Journal of Captain Franklin Smith"; Chance, "Mexico Under Fire: The Diary of Samuel Ryan Curtis"; Jeremiah Clemens, "Mustang Gray: A Romance"; Mark Crawford, "Encyclopedia of the Mexican-American War"; Mrs. Frank DeGarmo, "Pathfinders of Texas"; J. Frank Dobie, "The Mustangs"; John B. Dunn, "Perilous Trails of Texas"; Donald S. Frazier, "The United States and Mexico at War"; Murphy Givens and Jim Moloney, "Corpus Christi: A History"; Givens, "Billy Rogers Left His Mark," *Corpus Christi Caller-Times*, Jan. 25, 2011; Murphy Givens' columns, Feb. 9, Feb. 16, 2005 and Nov. 17, 2010, *Corpus Christi Caller-Times*; W. S. Henry, "Campaign Sketches of the War with Mexico"; Hobart Huson, "Refugio"; N.S. Jarvis, "Army Surgeon's Notes of Frontier Service — Mexican War"; Daniel Kilgore, "That's Billy's Mark," manuscript; Kilgore, "Notes on William L. Rogers"; John J. Linn, "Reminiscences of Fifty Years in Texas"; *The Nueces Valley*, July 29, 1871; Stephen B. Oates, "Rip Ford's Texas"; Samuel C. Reid Jr., "The Scouting Expeditions of McCulloch's Texas Rangers"; Charles M. Robinson III, "The Men Who Wear the Star"; Justin H. Smith, "The War with Mexico"; S. Compton Smith, "Chile Con Carne"; A. J. Sowell, "Rangers & Pioneers of Texas"; Charles Spurlin, "Texas Volunteers in the Mexican War"; Mary Sutherland, "The Story of Corpus Christi"; Frank Wagner's Research Papers; *The Weekly Gazette*, Corpus Christi, obituary, Dec. 17, 1877; Frederick Wilkins, "Highly Irregular Irregulars."

13. *Corpus Christi's Reef Road, Wettest Road in the World*
E. H. Caldwell, interview, biographical files, Corpus Christi Central Library; *Corpus Christi Caller-Times*, articles, Aug. 11, 1963 and May 26, 1974; *Corpus Christi Caller & Daily Herald*, Dec. 10, 1915; *Corpus Christi Press*, June 23, 1849; *Corpus Christi Star*, "The Reef," 1848; *Corpus Christi Times*, articles, Oct. 23, 1959 and Aug. 4, 1960; Murphy Givens, "Road Across the Bay Snaked Along Oyster Shell Reefs," *Caller-Times*, Oct. 13, 1998; Givens, "Comanche Warriors Vanished in Thin Air," *Caller-Times*, March 19, 2008; Keith Guthrie, "History of San Patricio County"; Handbook of Texas; N. S. Jarvis, "Army Surgeon's Notes of Frontier Service — Mexican War"; J. Williamson Moses, "Texas In Other Days"; the Nueces County Historical Society, "The History of Nueces County"; *The Taft Tribune*, Feb. 18, 1969.

14. *John Peoples and the Gold Rush*
Corpus Christi Caller-Times, article, July 25, 1927; *Caller-Times*, Jan. 18, 1959; *Corpus Christi Star*, Oct. 17, 1848. *Corpus Christi Star*, various editions from October 1848 through December 1849; *The Star*, March 24, 1849, "Letter From Mr. Peoples"; Murphy Givens, "Gone to El Dorado," *Corpus Christi Caller-Times*, Feb. 25, 1998; Givens, "California Gold Rush Revived Corpus Christi," *Caller-Times*, Dec. 28, 2005 and Jan. 2, 2006; James Kimmins Greer, "Texas Ranger: Jack Hays in the Frontier Southwest"; Brownson Malsch, "Indianola, The Mother of Western Texas"; Coleman McCampbell, "Saga of a Frontier Seaport"; Marilyn McAdams Sibley, "Lone Stars and State Gazettes"; Bill Walraven, "History of Press Here Begins With Republic," *Caller-Times*, Jan. 18, 1959.

15. *Comanches Sack Linnville, Indian Atrocities and Fort Merrill*
Paul C. Boethel, "History of Lavaca County"; Donaly E. Brice, "The Great Comanche Raid"; Caleb Coker, "The News from Brownsville"; *Corpus Christi Caller-Times*, article, Nov. 12, 1939; *Corpus Christi Caller*, Aug. 22, 1983; Col. Richard Dodge, "Our Wild Indians"; Murphy Givens' column, *Corpus Christi Caller-Times*, Aug. 15, 2007; Keith Guthrie, "History of San Patricio County"; Hobart Huson, "Refugio"; John Holland Jenkins, "Recollections of Early Texas"; J. Williamson Moses, "Texas In Other Days"; Stephen B. Oates, "Rip Ford's Texas"; *The Ranchero*, Corpus Christi, Oct. 22, Dec. 17, 1859; D. W. Roberts, *Frontier Times*; A. J. Sowell, "Texas Indian Fighters"; Frank Wagner, Research Papers, Corpus Christi Central Library; Walter Prescott Webb, "The Texas Rangers"; J.W. Willbarger, "Indian Depredations in Texas."

16. *J. Williamson Moses, Mustanger in South Texas*
J. Williamson Moses wrote columns on early Texas and his career as surveyor, Ranger and mustanger that were published in the *San Antonio Express* between 1887 and 1890. These columns were reprinted in "Texas In Other Days" edited by Murphy Givens. Other sources: Roy Bedichek, "Karankaway Country"; J. Frank Dobie, Mody Boatwright, Harry Ransom, "Mustangs and Cow Horses"; J. Frank Dobie, "Mustangs"; Thomas A. Dwyer, "From Mustangs to Mules," pamphlet; Murphy Givens, columns, Nov. 23, 2011, Jan. 12, 19, 26, 2005, and Nov. 26, 2006, *Corpus Christi Caller-Times*; U. S. Grant, "Personal Memoirs"; Keith Guthrie, "Raw Frontier"; Jack Jackson and John Wheat, "Texas by Teran"; Lloyd Lewis, "Captain Sam Grant"; Robert S. Weddle, "San Juan Batista: Gateway to Spanish Texas."

17. *Richard King, Legs Lewis and the King Ranch*
Armando C. Alonzo, "Tejano Legacy"; Victor Rodriguez Alvarado, unpublished memoirs
in author's possession; Bruce Cheeseman, "My Dear Henrietta: Hiram Chamberlain's
Letters to His Daughter"; *Corpus Christi Star,* March 26, 1849; C. L. Douglas, "Cattle
Kings of Texas"; Murphy Givens, columns, Aug. 12, 19, 1998, Aug. 22, 2001, April 2,
2003, April 13, 2005, Dec. 20, 2006, Jan. 30, 2008, June 4, 2008, Sept. 3, 2008, May 4,
11, 2011, July 20, 2011, *Corpus Christi Caller-Times*; Tom Lea, "The King Ranch"; John
Henry Brown, "Indian Wars and Pioneers of Texas"; Dick Frost, "King Ranch Papers";
Kleberg County History; Stephen B. Oates, "Rip Ford's Texas"; James Rowe, article,
Corpus Christi Caller-Times, July 12, 1953.

18. *Henry Kinney, Would-Be Emperor of the Mosquito Coast*
Elmer Baldwin, "The Past and Present of LaSalle County" (Illinois); Bruce Cheeseman,
"Maria von Blucher's Corpus Christi"; Earl W. Fornell, "Texans and Filibusters in the
1850s," *Southwestern Historical Quarterly;* Murphy Givens' columns, Feb. 10, 17, 24,
1999; Jan. 27, 2010; Aug. 3, 2011, *Corpus Christi Caller-Times;* W. R. Gore, "The Life of
Henry Lawrence Kinney," master's thesis; Gen. Thomas J. Green, "Journal of the Texian
Expedition Against Mier"; Hobart Huson, "Refugio"; *Indianola Bulletin,* March 11, 18,
25, April 8, 15, 22, 29, 30, May 6, 13, 20, 1852; Henry Kinney, Letters to Mirabeau
Lamar, Papers of Mirabeau Buonaparte Lamar; Coleman McCampbell, "Saga of a
Frontier Seaport"; Coleman McCampbell, letter to Bob McCracken, Nov. 13, 1954;
Charles G. Norton, Colonel Henry Lawrence Kinney, Founder of Corpus Christi, *Corpus
Christi Times,* May 16-31, 1938; *Nueces Valley,* March, 1852; July 17, 1858; Telegraph
and Texas Register, Houston, June 9, 1841, July 14 and 21, 1841, Aug. 4, 1841; *Texas
State Gazette,* March 6, 1852, May 8, 22, 29 1852; ; Bill Walraven, articles, Feb. 6, 1984,
May 8, 1985, Aug. 20, 1985, *Corpus Christi Caller*; Hortense Warner Ward, article, Jan.
18, 1959, *Corpus Christi Caller-Times;* Ward, "Abduction and Death of Philip Dimitt";
Ward, "The First State Fair of Texas," *Southwestern Historical Quarterly;* Amelia
Williams and Eugene Barker, "The Writings of Sam Houston."

19. *Jefferson Davis Imports Camels to South Texas*
R.C. Crane, article, October, 1925, *Frontier Times*; Chris Emmett, "Texas Camel Tales";
Murphy Givens, columns, Feb. 9, 2000, Nov. 15, 2006, March 10, 2006, *Corpus Christi
Caller-Times*; Lewis B. Leslie, "The Purchase and Importation of Camels by the United
States Government, 1855-1857," *Southwestern Historical Quarterly*; Brownson Malsch,
"Indianola, The Mother of Western Texas"; *Nueces Valley,* Jan. 28, 1858; Stephen B.
Oates, "Rip Ford's Texas"; Ed Syers, "Off The Beaten Trail"; Bill Walraven, article,
March 12, 1976, *Corpus Christi Caller*; Walter Prescott Webb, "The Great Plains"; Linda
Wolff, "Indianola and Matagorda Island."

20. *'Buffalo Hunters' and the Knights of the Golden Circle*
Hubert Howe Bancroft, "History of Texas and the North Mexican States"; C.A. Bridges,
"The Knights of the Golden Circle: A Filibustering Fantasy," *Southwestern Historical
Quarterly*; Eugenia Reynolds Briscoe, "City by the Sea"; *Corpus Christi Star,* Oct. 3, 17,
1848; *Democratic Telegraph and Texas Register,* Sept. 21, Oct. 12, 1848; Earl W. Fornell,
"Texans and Filibusters in the 1850s," *Southwestern Historical Quarterly; Galveston
News,* Oct. 10, Nov. 18, 1848; Murphy Givens, columns, June 29, 29, 2005 and Jan. 12,
2011, *Corpus Christi Caller-Times*; Hobart Huson, "Refugio"; J. Williamson Moses,
"Texas In Other Days"; Stephen B. Oates, "Rip Ford's Texas"; *The Ranchero,* Corpus

Christi, March 31, Sept. 15, Sept. 22, Sept. 29, Oct. 13, Oct. 27, Nov. 3, 1860, July 6, 1861; Paul Spellman, "Forgotten Texas Leader"; *Weekly Telegraph*, Houston, Nov. 7, 1860; Clarence R. Wharton, "Texas Under Many Flags."

21. *John Kittredge and the Bombardment of Corpus Christi*
William Adams, "The Bombardment of Corpus Christi," vertical files, Corpus Christi Central Library; W. David Allred, "The Wackiest Battle of the Civil War," *Texas Parade,* June 1961; *Army and Navy Journal,* Nov. 7, 1963; Andrew Anderson, "Do You Know the Story of Corpus Christi?" biographical files, Corpus Christi Central Library; Eugenia Reynolds Briscoe, "City by the Sea"; Bruce Cheeseman, "Maria von Blucher's Corpus Christi"; Norman C. Delaney, "The Vicksburg of Texas," *Corpus Christi Times,* Aug. 14, 15, 16, 1977; *Frontier Times,* "Corpus Christi Shelled by Gunboats," April 14, 1942; Murphy Givens, columns, Oct. 28, 1998, Jan. 19, 2000, May 2 and May 9, 2001, Dec. 31, 2003, Jan. 7 and 14, 2004, Sept. 17, 2008, *Corpus Christi Caller-Times*; Hobart Huson, "Refugio"; Allen W. Jones, "Military Events in Texas During the Civil War, 1861-1865"; Ed Kilman, article, *Corpus Christi Caller-Times,* Jan. 18, 1959; Clarence LaRoche, "Corpus Christi: The Vicksburg of Texas," *San Antonio Express,* March 7, 1965; Marjorie Maltby, "Old Stories About Corpus Christi," vertical files, Corpus Christi Central Library; Ernest Morgan, articles, *Corpus Christi Caller-Times,* Feb. 5, Feb. 19, March 5, March 12, 1961; *New York Herald,* "The Capture of Corpus Christi, Texas," Nov. 16, 1862; Official Reports, "The Bombardment of Corpus Christi, August, 1862; Navy Records and Library, Biographical Sketch of John W. Kittredge's career in the U.S. Navy, dated Jan. 25, 1939; Rosalie Bridget Hart Priour, "The Adventures of a Family of Emmigrants Who Emmigrated to Texas in 1834"; *The Ranchero,* July 13, 20, 1861, Aug. 19, 1962; Anna Moore Schwien, "When Corpus Christi Was Young," biographical files, Corpus Christi Central Library; Mary A. Sutherland, "The Story of Corpus Christi"; War of the Rebellion, Official Records of the Union and Confederate Armies: reports of H. Wilke, E. E. Hobby, A.M. Hobby; Alpha Kennedy Wood, "Texas Coastal Bend"; Ralph A. Wooster, "Texas and Texans in the Civil War."

22. *Sally Skull and the Cotton Road*
Eugenia Reynolds Briscoe, "City by the Sea"; *Corpus Christi Caller,* articles, March 4, 1937; July 6, 1963; Robert W. Delaney, "Matamoros, Port for Texas During the Civil War," *Southwestern Historical Quarterly;* J. Frank Dobie, "A School Teacher in Alpine," *Southwest Review;* John B. Dunn, "Perilous Trails of Texas"; T. R. Fehrenbach, "Lone Star"; James Arthur Lyon Fremantle, "The Fremantle Diary"; Murphy Givens, columns, Jan. 6, 1999, July 27, Aug. 3, Aug. 10, 2005, Aug. 1, 2007, June 29, 2011, *Corpus Christi Caller-Times*; The Handbook of Texas; Paul Horgan, "Great River"; John Warren Hunter, "Heel-Fly Time in Texas"; Dan Kilgore, "Two Sixshooters and a Sunbonnet: The Story of Sally Skull"; Tom Lea, "The King Ranch"; Stephen B. Oates, "Rip Ford's Texas"; Refugio County History, "The Story of Sally Skull"; Ronnie C. Tyler, "Cotton on the Border, 1861-1865," *Southwestern Historical Quarterly;* Bill Walraven, column, Feb. 26, 1982, *Corpus Christi Caller.*

23. *Nathaniel P. Banks and the Invasion of South Texas*
William Allen and Sue Hastings Taylor, "Aransas"; Capt. C. Barney, "Recollections of Field Service With the Twentieth Iowa Infantry Volunteers: What I Saw in the Army"; Eugenia Reynolds Briscoe, "City by the Sea"; Shelby Foote, "The Civil War," Vol. 1; Murphy Givens, columns, Nov. 6, 13, 20, 27, 2002, Dec. 31, 2003, Jan. 7, 14, 21, 28,

2004, April 14, 2010, *Corpus Christi Caller-Times*; The Handbook of Texas; James G. Hollandsworth, "Pretense of Glory: The Life of Nathaniel P. Banks"; Hobart Huson, "Refugio"; Edwin Lufkin, "History of the 13th Maine Regiment"; Ernest Morgan, "North Recaptures Coast Easily," *Corpus Christi Caller-Times*, May 28, 1961; Geoffrey Perrett, "Ulysses S. Grant, Soldier and President"; Maj. William C. Thompson, commander of the 20th Iowa; Thompson Letters, Corpus Christi Central Library; War of the Rebellion: N. P. Banks to Gen. H.W. Halleck, Chap. XXXVIII; War of the Rebellion: The Rio Grande Expedition, Chap. XXXVIII; War of the Rebellion, Gen. Hamilton P. Bee's report: Chap. XXXVIII; War of the Rebellion, Gen. T.E.G. Ransom's report: Chap. XXXVIII; Alpha Kennedy Wood, "Texas Coastal Bend"; Dudley G. Wooten, "A Comprehensive History of Texas: Military Events and Operations in Texas and Along the Coasts and Border, 1861-1865."

24. Benjamin F. Neal, Chipita Rodriguez and Hanging Times

Eugenia Reynolds Briscoe, "City by the Sea"; Helen Chapman diary, May 15, 1866, copy in author's possession; *Corpus Christi Caller*, April 25, 1902; *Corpus Christi Crony*, April 26, 1902; *Corpus Christi Weekly Gazette*, July 19, 1873; Jim Davis, "Bloody Hatchet Murderer of South Texas," *Real West*, January 1971; Maude T. Gilliland, "Horsebackers of the Brush Country"; Murphy Givens' columns, April 22, 1998, July 29, 1998, April 14, 1999, Aug. 9, 2000, Nov. 30, 2005, Nov. 7, 2007, Aug. 26, 2008, *Corpus Christi Caller-Times*; Keith Guthrie, "History of San Patricio County"; Guthrie, "Raw Frontier," Vol. 2; The Handbook of Texas; Hobart Huson, "District Judges of Refugio County"; Huson, "Refugio"; Eli Merriman, "Reminiscences of the Civil War," vertical file, Corpus Christi Central Library; Ernest Morgan, "North Recaptures Coast Easily," *Corpus Christi Caller-Times*, May 28, 1961; Travis Moorman, articles, Jan. 18, 1959, Nov. 13, 1959, March 24, 1963, Nov. 13, 1970, *Corpus Christi Caller-Times*; *The Ranchero*, Oct. 29, 1863; Vernon Smylie, "A Noose for Chipita"; "Pioneer Printing in Texas," *Southwestern Historical Quarterly*; Bill Walraven, article, Dec. 20, 1982, *Corpus Christi Caller;* John D. Young, J. Frank Dobie, "A Vaquero of the Brush Country."

25. Mat Nolan and the Defeat of Cecilio Balerio

Eugenia Reynolds Briscoe, "City by the Sea"; *Caller-Times,* article, Jan. 23, 1983; Murphy Givens, columns, Aug. 23, 30, Sept. 6, 2000, Feb. 27, 2008, Aug. 4, 2010, April 6, 2011, *Corpus Christi Caller-Times;* Hobart Huson, "Refugio"; Ernest Morgan, "The Century-Old Mystery: Why Was Mat Nolan Killed?" July 30, 1961, *Corpus Christi Caller-Times*; Mat Nolan's reports dated March 6 and March 15, 1864, War of the Rebellion, Vol. XXXIV, Pt. 1; Stephen B. Oates, "Rip Ford's Texas"; Oates, John S. "Rip" Ford, *Southwestern Historical Quarterly*; Frank Wagner, "The Shooting of Sheriff Mat Nolan"; Wagner, "Cecilio Balerio," Wagner Research Papers, the Corpus Christi Central Library; Bill Walraven, articles, Feb. 19, 1982, Oct. 20, 1983, Nov. 10, 1983, *Corpus Christi Caller*; Dudley G. Wooten, "A Comprehensive History of Texas: Military Events and Operations in Texas and Along the Coasts and Border, 1861-1865."

26. Thomas Noakes' Diary of Dry Weather and Hard Times

Murphy Givens, columns, May 5, May 12, 1999, Dec. 10, 2008, Oct. 14, 2009, May 5, 2010, *Corpus Christi Caller-Times;* Thomas Noakes' Diary, Four Volumes, Corpus Christi Central Library; Bill Walraven, articles, Jan. 9, 1981, April 7, 1982, Feb. 26, 1988, *Corpus Christi Caller.*

27. *Rip Ford and the Last Battle of the Civil War*
T. R. Fehrenbach, "Lone Star"; Murphy Givens, columns, Dec. 8, 1999, Dec. 12, 2007, May 14, 2008, Dec. 7, 2011, *Corpus Christi Caller-Times;* Tom Lea, "The King Ranch"; Stephen B. Oates, "Rip Ford's Texas"; Oates, John S. "Rip" Ford, *Southwestern Historical Quarterly*; Texas Handbook; Harold B. Simpson, "Rangers of Texas"; Dudley G. Wooten, "A Comprehensive History of Texas: Military Events and Operations in Texas and Along the Coasts and Border, 1861-1865."

28. *Confederates Leave for Mexico; Occupation of South Texas Begins*
Eugenia Reynolds Briscoe, "City by the Sea"; Helen Chapman diary, May 15, 1866, copy in author's possession; Bruce Cheeseman, "Maria von Blucher's Corpus Christi"; J. B. Dunn, "Perilous Trails in Texas"; Murphy Givens, columns, Jan. 28, 2004, Nov. 10, 2010, Dec. 14, 2011, Jan. 18, 2012, *Corpus Christi Caller-Times;* Hobart Huson, "Refugio"; J. Williamson Moses, "Texas In Other Days," edited by Murphy Givens; Thomas Noakes' Diary, Four Volumes, Corpus Christi Central Library; *The Ranchero,* May 27, June 4, June 17, July 5, July 6, July 13, July 15, July 23, July 28, Aug. 10, Aug. 18, Aug. 20, Aug. 22, Aug. 25, Sept. 3, Sept. 6, 1865; Edwin S. Redkey, "A Grand Army of Black Men"; William L. Richter, "It Is Best To Go In Strong-Handed: Army Occupation of Texas, 1865-1866"; Anna Moore Schwien, "When Corpus Christi Was Young," biographical files, Corpus Christi Central Library; United States Colored Troops Infantry, the Civil War Archive; *Southwestern Historical Quarterly*, volumes, LIV, LVIII, VI, XI, XL, 72, 76; Alexander Watkins Terrell, "From Texas to Mexico and the Courts of Maximilian in 1865"; Bill Walraven, articles, Oct. 14, 1982, Aug. 13, 1985, *Corpus Christi Caller;* War of the Rebellion: Louisiana and the Trans-Mississippi, Chapter LX; Dee Woods, article, Aug. 17, 1939; Ralph A. Wooster, "Lone Star Generals in Gray."

29. *Gov. Edmund Jackson Davis and Reconstruction*
Dave Allred, "Ex-Corpus Christi Law Student Was Stormy Governor," April 15, 1956, *Caller-Times;* Marie v. Blucher, "E. J. Davis House," vertical files, Corpus Christi Central Library; T.R. Fehrenbach, "Lone Star"; Murphy Givens, columns, July 9, 16, 23, 2003, Jan. 9, 2008, *Corpus Christi Caller-Times;* Garth Jones, "A Hated Texan: His Monument Towers Highest in State Cemetery," Feb. 20, 1958, *Caller-Times;* Tom Lea, "King Ranch"; E. T. Merriman, "Random Recollections of Nearly Ninety Years," Corpus Christi Central Library; *Nueces Valley*, April, 1858; Stephen B. Oates, "Rip Ford's Texas"; *Ranchero*, April 21, 1861; Anna Moore Schwien, "When Corpus Christi Was Young"; vertical files, Corpus Christi Central Library; Mary Sutherland, "The Story of Corpus Christi"; Edna May Tubbs, "E.J. Davis, Only Republican To Ever Govern Texas Came From Corpus Christi," Aug. 27, 1939, *Corpus Christi Caller;* Bill Walraven, "Texans hated first Republican governor," Nov. 9, 1978, *Corpus Christi Caller.*

30. *The Sutton-Taylor Feud*
Austin Daily State Journal, Nov. 13, 1870; C.L. Douglas, *"Famous Texas Feuds";* Roy Dunn, *"Life and Times of Albuquerque, Texas," Southwestern Historical Quarterly; The Fayette County New Era,* La Grange, Aug. 8, 1873; *Galveston News,* Sept. 14, 1869; Gonzales County History, "Creed Taylor" biography; Murphy Givens, column, Nov. 2, 2011, *Corpus Christi Caller-Times;* Keith Guthrie, "History of San Patricio County"; John Wesley Hardin, "The Life of John Wesley Hardin As Written by Himself"; Hobart Huson, "Refugio"; Brownson Malsch, "Indianola, The Mother of Western Texas"; Nellie Murphree, "DeWitt County History"; W.C. Nunn, "Texas Under the Carpetbaggers";

Chuck Parsons, "DeWitt County History"; David Pickering, "Brush Men and Vigilantes"; J. R. Polley, "The Taylor Boys," *Frontier Times*; Karon Mac Smith, "On the Watershed of Ecleto and the Clear Fork of Sandies"; C. L. Sonnichsen, "The Grassroots Historian," *Southwestern Historical Quarterly*; Sonnichsen, "I'll Die Before I Run"; Walter Prescott Webb, "Texas Rangers"; Linda Wolff, "Indianola and Matagorda Island"; John D. Young and J. Frank Dobie, "A Vaquero of the Brush Country."

31. *Trail Drives to Louisiana and Kansas*
Jesse James Benton, "Cowboy Lore"; *Corpus Christi Caller-Times, articles,* Sept. 17, 1939, Feb. 15, 1948, Oct. 2, 1952, Jan. 18, 1959; J. Frank Dobie, "The Longhorns"; Chris Emmett, "Shanghai Pierce: A Fair Likeness"; Maude Gilliland, "Rincon"; Murphy Givens, columns, Feb. 16, 23, March 1, 2000, July 11, 2001, Feb. 13, 2008, Jan. 10, 2009, May 26 and Sept. 8, 2010, Jan. 19, 2011, *Corpus Christi Caller-Times;* J. Marvin Hunter, "The Trail Drivers of Texas"; Hobart Huson, "History of Refugio"; Henry B. Jameson, "Miracle of the Chisholm Trail"; Elizabeth A.H. John, "Storms Brewed In Other Men's Worlds"; Clara M. Love, "History of the Cattle Industry in the Southwest"; Brownson Malsch, "Indianola, The Mother of Western Texas"; *San Antonio Express and News,* article, Oct. 3, 1965; Jimmy M. Skaggs, "The Cattle Trailing Industry"; T.U. Taylor, "The Chisholm Trail and Other Routes"; Robert Weddle, "Changing Tides."

32. *Killer Storms Sealed the Fate of Indianola*
James Porter Baughman, "The Maritime and Railroad Interests of Charles Morgan," dissertation, Tulane; Kent Biffle, article, Dec. 1, 1985, *Dallas Morning News;* John Henry Brown, "History of Texas"; Paul Freier, article, Dec. 20, 1978, *Port Lavaca Wave;* Murphy Givens, columns, June 14, 2000, Dec. 6, 2006, May 16, 2007, Aug. 6, 2008, March 10, 2010, Jan. 19, 2011, Nov. 2, 2011, Nov. 11, 2011, *Corpus Christi Caller-Times;* Hobart Huson, "Refugio"; Huson, "St. Mary's of Aransas"; John J. Linn, "Reminiscences of Fifty Years in Texas"; Brownson Malsch, "Indianola, The Mother of Western Texas"; Travis Moorman, article, Nov. 18, 1956, April 25, 1965, *Corpus Christi Caller-Times; Southwestern Historical Quarterly,* "Reminiscences of C.C. Cox," Vol. VI; Ed Syers, article, May 31, 1963, *Corpus Christi Times;* Bill Walraven, article, May 28, 1978, *Corpus Christi Caller;* Bert C. West, article, Sept. 15, 1957, *Corpus Christi Caller-Times; Nueces Valley,* article, Jan. 28, 1858; Linda Wolff, "Indianola and Matagorda Island"; John D. Young and J. Frank Dobie, "A Vaquero of the Brush Country."

33. *John Dunn and the Noakes Raid*
Andrew Anderson, "Do You Know the Story of Corpus Christi?" biographical files, Corpus Christi Central Library; E. H. Caldwell, memoirs, edited by Robert J. Caldwell; *Corpus Christi Weekly Gazette,* March 27, 1875; Ruth Dodson, "The Noakes Raid," *Frontier Times;* John Dunn, "Perilous Trails of Texas"; Dunn, "When Mexican Raiders Swooped Down on Corpus," April, 1920, *Corpus Christi Caller;* George Durham, Clyde Wantland, "Taming the Nueces Strip"; Lois Felder, "Nueces River Village Raided 75 Years Ago," March 28, 1950, *Corpus Christi Times;* Murphy Givens, columns, Aug. 4, Aug. 11, Aug. 18, Aug. 25, Sept. 1, Sept. 8, 2004, Nov. 26, Dec. 3, 2006, *Corpus Christi Caller-Times;* Handbook of Texas, "Nuecestown Raid of 1875"; Hobart Huson, "History of Refugio"; Tom Lea, "The King Ranch"; Leopold Morris, "The Mexican Raid of 1875 on Corpus Christi," *Texas Historical Association Quarterly*; Thomas Noakes' Diary, Four Volumes, Corpus Christi Central Library; Bill Walraven, article, Jan. 18, 1959, *Corpus Christi Caller-Times;* Dee Woods, "Stories of Noakes Raid," Aug. 24, 1939, *Corpus*

Christi Caller; Woods, "Difficulties Encountered In Finding Hanging Site," Aug. 26, 1939, *Corpus Christi Caller;* John Young and J. Frank Dobie, "A Vaquero of the Brush Country."

34. *Capt. Henry Scott, Leader of Vigilantes*
Armando G. Alonzo, "Tejano Legacy"; Eugenia Reynolds Briscoe, "City by the Sea"; L.E. Daniell, "Personnel of the Texas State Government"; "History of Goliad County"; Murphy Givens, columns, Sept. 7, 14, 2005, March 16, 2011, *Corpus Christi Caller-Times;* W.C. Holden, "Law and Lawlessness on the Texas Frontier," *Southwestern Historical Quarterly;* J. Marvin Hunter, "The Trail Drivers of Texas"; Hobart Huson, "History of Refugio"; *Huson, "St. Mary's of Aransas"; Nueces Valley, June 13, 1874;* "Refugio County History"; Abel G. Rubio, "Stolen Heritage"; *"Weekly Caller,* Feb. 28, 1891, Henry Scott's obituary; John Young and J. Frank Dobie, "A Vaquero of the Brush Country."

35. *Peeling Cattle and the Skinning War*
Robert and William Adams, memoirs, vertical files, Corpus Christi Central Library; William Allen and Sue Hastings Taylor, "Aransas: The Life of a Texas Coastal County"; Andrew Anderson, "Do You Know the Story of Corpus Christi?" biographical files, Corpus Christi Central Library; Eugenia Reynolds Briscoe, "City by the Sea"; E. H. Caldwell, memoirs, edited by Robert J. Caldwell; *Corpus Christi Advertiser,* July 26, 1872; *Corpus Christi Caller-Times,* Nov. 28, 1902; *Caller-Times'* "Centennial Journey"; J. Frank Dobie, "The Longhorns"; John Dunn, "Perilous Trails of Texas"; Murphy Givens, columns, March 11, 1998, Dec. 18, 2007, *Corpus Christi Caller-Times;* Hobart Huson, "History of Refugio"; Tom Lea, "The King Ranch"; Elmer R. Johnson, article, Nov. 22, 1936, *Corpus Christi Caller-Times*; *Nueces Valley,* editions of March, 1872; Hortense Warner Ward, "Great Slaughter Made Coast A Boneyard," Jan. 18, 1959, *Corpus Christi Caller-Times;* Ward, "Hide and Tallow Factories," manuscript; Walter Prescott Webb, "The Great Plains"; Alpha Kennedy Wood, "Texas Coastal Bend"; John Young and J. Frank Dobie, "A Vaquero of the Brush Country."

36. *Robert and William Adams and the Great Sheep Era*
Robert Adams, "Learning by Hard Licks," interview, Corpus Christi Central Library; Paul H. Carlson, "Texas Woolly Backs"; Bruce Cheeseman, "Maria von Blucher's Corpus Christi"; Diary of Oscar M. Edgerley, "Sheep Rancher, 1861," copy in the author's possession; Murphy Givens, columns, Dec. 22, 1999, June 14, 2000, June 26, 2002, Dec. 25, 2002, Jan. 1, 6, 13, 2003, Aug. 20, 27, Sept. 3, 2003, July 2, 2008, Sept. 2, 2009, Dec. 30, 2009, Jan. 6, 13, 2010, *Corpus Christi Caller-Times;* Handbook of Texas; William Headen, "Historical Sketch," published in 1883, vertical files, Corpus Christi Central Library; Val W. Lehmann, "Forgotten Legions, Sheep in the Rio Grande Plain of Texas"; Coleman McCampbell, "Era of Wool and Sheep in Nueces Valley," *Frontier Times*; *Ranchero,* April 28, 1860. Grady Stiles, "Sheepmen's Heyday Here Short-Lived," Jan. 18, 1959, *Corpus Christi Caller-Times;* Mary Sutherland, "The Story of Corpus Christi"; W. G. Sutherland, "Sandy McNubbin Tells Of Vanished Herds of Sheep in South Texas," July 19, 1925, April 13, 1930, *Corpus Christi Caller*; Frank Wagner, Research Papers, Corpus Christi Central Library; Dee Woods, article, Aug. 5, 1939, *Corpus Christi Caller.*

37. *Barbed Wire and the Fence-Cutting War*
Andrew Anderson, "Do You Know the Story of Corpus Christi?" biographical files, Corpus Christi Central Library; Ira Aten, "Fence-Cutting Days in Texas," *Frontier Times*; Paul H. Carlson, "Texas Woolly Backs"; *Corpus Christi Advertiser*, Nov. 12, 1868; *Corpus Christi Caller*, article, Oct. 11, 1885; *Corpus Christi Times*, Aug. 20, 1946, article on John Ireland; Roger C. Conger, article, *Southwestern Historical Quarterly*; *David Dary, "Cowboy Culture"*; T. R. Fehrenbach, "Lone Star"; Wayne Gard, "The Fence-Cutters," *Southwestern Historical Quarterly*; Murphy Givens, columns, April 18, 2007, July 8, 15, 2009, *Corpus Christi Caller-Times;* Don Graham, "Kings of Texas"; Tom Lea, "The King Ranch"; Mrs. S.G. Miller, "Sixty Years in the Nueces Valley"; Lewis Nordyke, "Great Roundup"; Nueces County History; *Nueces Valley*, May 1861; Ernest Staples Osgood, "The Day of the Cattlemen"; John C. Rayburn, article, Jan. 18, 1959, *Corpus Christi Caller-Times;* Diane Solether Smith and Holland McCombs, "The Armstrong Chronicle"; A. Ray Stephens, "The Taft Ranch"; Bill and Marjorie K. Walraven, "Empresarios' Children: The Welders of Texas"; Walter Prescott Webb, "The Great Plains"; Dee Woods, *"Diary Records Day When Texas Ranges Fenced," Sept. 15, 1939, Corpus Christi Caller;* John Young and J. Frank Dobie, "A Vaquero of the Brush Country."

38. *Uriah Lott, the Gringo Who Built Railroads*
J. L. Allhands, "Gringo Builder"; Allhands, articles, Feb. 17-20, 1939, *Brownsville Herald*; Allhands, articles, May, *Corpus Christi Caller*; Bruce S. Cheeseman, "Perfectly Exhausted with Pleasure: The 1881 King-Kenedy Excursion Train to Laredo," booklet; *Corpus Christi Caller-Times*, "Tex-Mex Railroad Boosted Early Development of Area," April 27, 1952; *Corpus Christi Crony*, March 8, 1902; *Corpus Christi Times*, article, May 1, 1936; Murphy Givens, columns, Dec. 1, 1999, April 16, 2008, *Corpus Christi Caller-Times;* Tom Lea, "The King Ranch"; "A Thumbnail History: Texas Mexican Railway Company," pamphlet; Texas-Mexican Railway, Symbol of International Friendship," publication, 1982. E.T. Merriman, "First Railroad to the Border Faced Many Difficulties," *Corpus Christi Caller-Times*, March 9, 1924; Merriman, "Random Recollections of Nearly Ninety Years," Corpus Christi Central Library. Bill Walraven, article, "A guy could lose his pants doing business in 1877," *Corpus Christi Caller*; Walraven, "Uriah Lott, Railroad Builder," Jan. 18, 1959, *Corpus Christi Caller-Times*.

39. *Droughts, Rain Battles and an Arctic Norther*
Andrew Anderson, "Do You Know the Story of Corpus Christi?" biographical files, Corpus Christi Central Library; Cabeza de Vaca, *"Naufrágios,"* translated by Fanny Bandelier; *Corpus Christi Caller*, Feb. 17, 1899; Centennial History, *Corpus Christi Caller-Times;* J. Frank Dobie, "I'll Tell You a Tale," "Longhorns," "Tales of Old-Time Texas"; Murphy Givens, columns, Jan. 27, 1999, July 26, 2000, March 27, 2002, March 22, 2006, Dec. 3, 2006, April 16, 2008, Dec. 23, 2009, Aug. 24, 2011, *Corpus Christi Caller-Times; King Ranch Special Edition, 1953, Corpus Christi Caller-Times; Laredo Times,* Feb. 17, 1899; Travis Moorman, article, Feb. 12, 1960, *Corpus Christi Caller;* Thomas Noakes' Diary, Jan. 24, 1864, Corpus Christi Central Library; David Pickering, article, March 21, 1971, *Corpus Christi Caller-Times*; Edward Powers, "War and the Weather"; Dr. John C. Rayburn, article, Jan. 18, 1959, *Corpus Christi Caller-Times; San Antonio Express,* Feb. 17, 1899; "Alex Sweet's Texas," edited by Virginia Eisenhour.

40. *George H. Paul and the South Texas Land Rush*
J. L. Allhands, "Gringo Builder"; Anne Chambers, article, Aug. 12, 1956, *Corpus Christi Caller-Times; Corpus Christi Caller,* articles, July, 1891, Dec. 21, 1900, Dec. 30, 1901; *Corpus Christi Caller-Times,* articles, Jan. 18, 1959, Aug. 5, 1964; *Corpus Christi Herald,* April 13, 1910; T. R. Fehrenbach, "Lone Star"; Murphy Givens, columns, March 1, 2006, Nov. 24, Dec. 1, Dec. 7, 2010, *Corpus Christi Caller-Times;* Keith Guthrie, "History of San Patricio County"; Guthrie, "Great Land Lottery of Aransas Pass," *The Journal of South Texas;* Hoyt Hager, article, Jan. 23, 1983, *Corpus Christi Caller-Times;* George H. Paul, article, Oct. 31, 1957, *Robstown Record; Robstown Record, article, Jan. 18, 1959; Robstown Record, 50th anniversary edition, Oct. 31, 1957; Robstown Record, 75th anniversary edition, Nov. 18, 1982;* A. Ray Stephens, "The Taft Ranch"; Grady Stiles, article, July 12, 1953, *Corpus Christi Caller-Times;* Dee Woods, article, July 23, 1939, *Corpus Christi Caller-Times.*

41. *Pat Dunn, the Duke of Padre Island*
Corpus Christi Caller, March 26, 1937; Bill Duncan, April 24, 1966, *Caller-Times;* Ernest G. Fischer, July 24, July 31, Aug. 7, Aug. 14, Aug. 21, 1927, *Corpus Christi Caller;* Murphy Givens, columns, Sept. 28, Oct. 5, Oct. 12, 2005, *Corpus Christi Caller-Times;* Jerry Needham, Oct. 19, 1978, *Caller-Times;* Pauline Reese, "History of Padre Island," thesis, 1938, Texas College of Arts and Industries; Grace Dunn Vetters, vertical files, Corpus Christi Central Library; Writers' Round Table, "Padre Island."

42. *Ranch Life in South Texas*
Corpus Christi Caller-Times, articles, Nov. 16, 1941, Jan. 18, 1959; J. Frank Dobie, "Coronado's Children"; Dobie, article, Jan. 18, 1959, Feb. 16, 1986, *Corpus Christi Caller-Times;* Dr. Clotilde P. Garcia, article, *Bulletin of the Nueces County Historical Commission;* Maude Gilliland, "Rincon"; Murphy Givens, columns, June 3, Nov. 11, 2009, July 6, 2011, *Corpus Christi Caller-Times;* Keith Guthrie, "Raw Frontier"; Jack Jackson and John Wheat, "Texas by Teran"; Mrs. S. G. Miller, "Sixty Years in the Nueces Valley"; Hattie Mae Hinnant New, "Lagarto"; Robert H. Thonhoff, "The First Ranch in Texas."

INDEX

330

Buena Vista, 86, 87
Buena Vista Hotel (Riviera Beach), 297
Buffalo Hunters (Sierra Madre
    Filibuster), 119, 151-152
Burks, Amanda, 234
Burleson, Edward, 116
Burnet, David G., 30, 116
Burnett, Matthew, 36

Cabeza de Vaca (see Nuñez Cabeza de
    Vaca)
Cabeza de Vaca, Doña Teresa, 1, 5
Cadiz, Spain, 1
Calallen, 102, 193
Caldwell, E. H., 97, 253, 265
Caldwell, Matthew, 37-41, 55
California (sloop), 141
Callahan, Charles, 102
Calvert, Susan, 57
Camargo, Tamaulipas, 19, 45, 92, 93,
    128, 316
Camerena, Don, 142, 143
Cameron County, 314
Cameron, Ewen, 46, 47, 48, 49
Camino Real, 17
Campbell, Joseph, 250
Camp Verde, 148, 149
Campo Borrego (Padre Island), 307
Campo Bueno (Padre Island), 307
Canadian River, 202
Cape Horn, 99, 100, 103
Carbajal, José M. J., 143, 152, 202
Carroll, William, 197
Carson Association, 101
Cart Road (and Cart War), 242, 243
Casa Blanca, 312, 315, 316
Casimir House, 244
Castillo, Dr., 5
Castillo Maldonado, Alonso del, 4, 5
Castroville, 279
Cavelier, Colin, 14
Cavelier, Abbé Jean, 13-15
Cedar Bayou, 175
Centennial House, 217
*Central American (*newspaper), 145
Cerro de las Campanas, 212
Cerro Gordo, 85
Chamberlain, Hiram, 129
Chamberlain, Samuel, 94

Champini (goat keeper), 206
Champion (steamboat), 127
Chandler, D. T., 66
Chapman, Helen, 111, 131, 213, 220
Chapman, William, 131, 271, 272
Chargres, Panama, 101, 103
Charleston, S.C., 115
Cherokee Indians, 38
Chevalier, Mike, 55
Chicago & Alton Railroad, 283
Chicago, Illinois, 231, 236, 279
Chihuahua, Mexico, 101, 102, 283
China, Mexico, 93, 94
Chisholm, Richard, 224
Chisholm Trail, 231, 233
Choate, Crockett, 224
Choate, John, 224
Chocolate Bayou, 109, 258
Cibolo Creek, 32, 243
Clark, Edward, 209
Clark, Hines, 254
Clark, Jasper, 266
Clark, William, 93
Clarksville, 218
Clemens, Jeremiah, 94
Clements, R., 143
Cleveland, Grover, 274
Clinton (steamship), 172, 226
Clinton (town), 223, 224, 226
Coahuila, 151
Coakley, F. M., 247
Cody, Judge, 160
Cojo (Karankawa chief), 23
Coke, Richard, 221-222
Cole, E. B., 297
Coleman County, 280
Coleman-Mathis-Fulton Pasture
    Company (later Taft Ranch), 264,
    277, 296, 298, 301
Collins, N. G., 285, 296
Colon, Samuel, 270
Colonel Cross (steamboat), 129
Colorado River (Texas), 17, 149
Colt firearms, 56, 57, 107, 112
Colt, Sam, 57
Comanche Indians, 26, 32, 33, 34, 37,
    54-57, 59-62, 93, 95, 105-113, 117,
    118, 119, 124, 187, 202, 203, 207,
    229, 241, 312

Dobie, J. Frank (quoted), 34, 92, 168, 229, 235, 237, 289, 290, 291, 311, 316, 317
Doddridge, Lott & Company, 273, 283
Doddridge, Perry, 274, 284
Dodge, Richard, 106, 107
Doherty, Etta, 295, 299
Doherty, Henry, 299
Doke (or Doak), 199
Dolores, 19
Donelson, Andrew Jackson, 66
Donnelly, George K., 69
Don Patricio Causeway, 310
Dorantes, Andrés, 4, 5
Dorantes, Pablo, 5
Douay, Anastase, 13-15
Doubleday, Abner, 69
Doughty, Dan, 257
Doughty, James M., 264
Dowling, Dick, 172
Doyle, James, 109
Doyle, John, 166
Driscoll Ranch, 297
Driscoll, Robert, 287-288, 297
Duhaut, Pierre, 13-15
Dull, J. J., 285
Dunlap, Flossie (Harrop), 299
Dunlap, Harvey, 299, 301
Dunman, Coon, 258
Dunn, Catherine (Hickey), 306
Dunn, Clara (Jones), 308
Dunn, John, 305
Dunn, John (Red), 92, 214, 245-254
Dunn, Lalla, 308
Dunn, Lawrence, 306
Dunn, Lelia (Nias), 254
Dunn, Matt, 214
Dunn, Matthew, 245
Dunn, Mike, 251
Dunn, Patrick F., 304-310
Dunn, Thomas Sr., 306
Durango, 313
Durst, James, 271
Duval County, 183, 266, 272
Duval, John, 108
Dwyer, John, 182
Dwyer, Thomas, 120

Eagle Pass, 15, 219

Eastland, William, 48
Edey & Kirsten Company, 273
Edgerly, Oscar, 272
Ellis, John T., 291
El Mocho (Karankawa chief), 23
El Paso, 4, 87, 103, 168, 201, 202
El Pista, 75
El Surdo (Karankawa chief), 23
Emma (ship), 145
Enchanted Rock, 53, 55
Encinal (later Webb) County, 153
Ennis, 303
Erie Canal, 138
Erskine, Andrew, 57
Escandón, Jose de, 18, 19, 120
Escobedo (or Escobar), Manuel, 92, 93
Escovar, Joseph, 24
Espíritu Santo (galleon), 7-9
Essex Mining Company, 101
Estevanico (also Estabanico), 4-6
Evans, George F., 273, 284

Fabens, Joseph, 145
Fairmont, Indiana, 299
Falfurrias, 188, 296, 301
Falls of the Brazos, 35
Fannin, James W. Jr., 36, 54
Fehrenbach, T. R. (quoted) 34, 207, 260, 297
Fence-Cutting War, 277-280
Fennessey, Edward, 259
Ferrer, Jose, 7
Filisola, Vicente, 75
First Presbyterian Church, 134
Fisher, William S., 43-46
Flintoff, Thomas, 143
Flores, Juan, 259, 260
Floresville, 16, 183, 242
Flour Bluff, 138, 160, 161, 263, 264, 296, 297, 307
Flour Bluff (vessel), 265, 277
Flournoy, George, 210
Fogg's Bar & Billiards, 284
Fogg, John, 285
Fogg's Livery Stable, 285
Ford, John S. (Rip), 57, 87, 94, 105, 108, 109, 111, 112, 128, 141, 153, 165, 187, 188
Forrest, Nathan Bedford, 311

334

336

342

344

Printed in the USA
CPSIA information can be obtained
at www.ICGtesting.com
LVHW091040151123
763629LV00002B/3/J

9 780983 256533